The Writer's Guide to
Everyday Life in the 1800s

THE WRITER'S GUIDE TO

Everyday Life

in the

1800s

by
Marc
McCutcheon

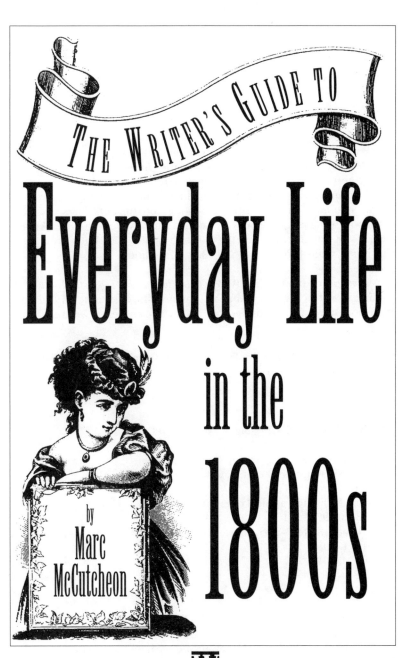

WRITER'S DIGEST BOOKS
Cincinnati, Ohio

This hardcover edition of *The Writer's Guide to Everyday Life in the 1800s* features a "self-jacket" that eliminates the need for a separate dust jacket. It provides sturdy protection for your book while it saves paper, trees and energy.

Other fine Writer's Digest Books are available from your local bookstore or direct from the publisher.

97   96   95   5   4

Library of Congress Cataloging-in-Publication Data

McCutcheon, Marc.
    The writer's guide to everyday life in the 1800s / by Marc McCutcheon.
        p.   cm.
    Includes bibliographical references.
    ISBN 0-89879-541-9
    1. United States—Social life and customs—19th century—Miscellanea.   I. Title.
    E165.M5   1993
    973.8′4—dc20   92-43336
    CIP

Chapter opening collage courtesy of: Melissa Mitchell (top four photographs); Lori Wilson (family portrait); Detroit Public Library (Surrender of Gen. Lee notice); Shelburne Museum, Shelburne, Virginia (Brougham 1980); Home Library of Useful Knowledge (phrenology diagram, 1883).

Edited by Robin Gee and Catherine M. Brohaugh
Designed by Sandy Conopeotis Kent

DEDICATION

To Kara,
the best little office assistant I ever had.
And to Dee, for restraining
the best little office assistant I ever had.

Special thanks to
Joan and Clayton Winchenbach,
who let me borrow so liberally from their
wonderful old library in the barn.

INTRODUCTION

Writers working on nineteenth-century westerns, romances, mysteries, historical dramas . . . where do they find obscure information on everyday life in the 1800s?

For example, was it proper to wear a boiled shirt with one's Sunday-go-to-meetin' clothes?

Which was worth more, two bits, a fip or a picayune? Could you trade any of these for a ninepence?

What popular fashion was as dangerous as a six-shooter: the bustle, the hoop skirt or bloomers?

If you wanted to get drunk, would you down an anti-fogmatic or baldface? Could you get as corned in a grocery as you could in a groggery? How about a dram or bucket shop?

What in tar-nation was a booby hut and why were they so popular in winter?

Which carriage would keep you dry in a downpour: a barouche or a landau? Could you order pin-striping for your piano-box buggy?

What was the difference between a burner and a cracksman? Would either of these likely be involved in a cathauling?

Unfortunately, few of those illuminating little details of the 1800s have ever been consolidated in one volume before. While there are enough books on political events and general history to fill a small wagon train, and more than enough works on the Civil War to sink a monitor and a large showboat combined, no reference on everyday life in the nineteenth century has ever been compiled.

And that's exactly what the writer of a bodice ripper or a western or a Victorian murder mystery needs to avoid spending perhaps hundreds of hours at the library winnowing minutiae: a reference book she can have at her fingertips to find out in an instant which medicines and instruments doctors used when making house calls and why one was likely to feel worse after their visits . . . what a cooper and a lamplighter did for a living . . . what the fashionable (and not so fashionable) man or woman wore in every decade of the century . . . what songs families sang in their parlors and musicians played in the streets . . . how housewives preserved meat in pork barrels . . . what street vendors cried to sell their wares in Philadelphia and New York . . . how much it cost to mail a letter . . . how young lovers got away from the watchful eyes of parents in winter . . . what devious prostitutes did to strip their customers of more than just their pantaloons . . . how cowboys stopped a stampede and then lulled those dogies to sleep.

Such particulars will add color, depth and realism to any fiction (or nonfiction) setting. But here, too, the writer must use caution; anachronisms lie in wait to ambush and strip the credibility from the amateur historian at every turn.

For example, could a fictional character pick up a phone and call the police for help in 1870? How about 1876? Or, what would one be eating for breakfast in 1841? Were cornflakes around then? How about coffee? More traps: Was Sears & Roebuck even heard of before 1890? When did Boston install gas street lighting? How about London? When did stethoscopes or anesthetics come into use?

And what about slang and everyday street language? Did nineteenth-century citizens use terms such as nerd or dude or dead meat or man alive!? The answers may surprise you . . . or trip you up.

The conscientious writer double-checks facts before an editor gets a chance to raise a question. To facilitate such research, this book is specially designed with anachronistic pitfalls in mind. To avoid them, you'll find quick-reference chronologies at the back and also in the larger, general text, in which dates are cited whenever possible.

Reference books, as a whole, tend to be rather dull affairs, so to make this one more readable and illustrative, I've included actual quotations from nineteenth-century citizens concerning or describing key words and definitions. For instance, along with a definition of the bowie knife is one man's horrified reaction to witnessing Bowie himself handle it. You'll find similar quotes about the first horse-pulled buses (their drivers were as mad as New York cabbies), about bloomers and how they initially shocked the nation, about nineteenth-century safes and how to crack one, and much more.

Use this reference for verification of facts and dates, for ideas and, most of all, for inspiration. Read it through. Feel the period come alive. Borrow from it to make your own work live.

And now if you'll excuse me, I really must take my leave or, as one generation of Americans used to say, absquatulate.

Or was that skedaddle?

Marc McCutcheon
S. Portland, Maine
February 1992

1

SURRENDER OF GEN. LEE!

"The Year of Jubilee has come! Let all the People Rejoice!"

200 GUNS WILL BE FIRED

On the Campus Martius,

AT 3 O'CLOCK TO-DAY, APRIL 10,

To Celebrate the Victories of our Armies. 1865

Every Man, Woman and Child is hereby ordered to be on hand prepared to Sing and Rejoice. The crowd are expected to join in singing Patriotic Songs.

ALL PLACES OF BUSINESS MUST BE CLOSED AT 2 O'CLOCK.

Hurrah for Grant and his noble Army.

By Order of the People.

SLANG AND EVERYDAY SPEECH

H umbug? Shecoonery? Useless truck or gum? Hornswoggling? Honey-fuggling? Not in this book, dear sir! The Americanisms in this book are the genuine article, I swan to mercy, a huckleberry above anyone's persimmon. Some pumpkins, a caution, 100 percent certified by a Philadelfy lawyer. If not, dad-blame it, I'll hang up my fiddle, and you can sass me, knock me into a cocked hat, give me jesse, fix my flint, settle my hash, ride me out on a rail and have a conniption fit, you cussed scalawag.

Now ain't that the beatingest language you ever did hear? Sure beats the Dutch! Pshaw! Do tell!

And so, dear reader, here be but a microcosm of America's nineteenth-century colloquialisms and slang, some from the upper class, some from the lower, and much from the strata in between.

Slang

absquatulate: to take leave, to disappear.

1843: A can of oysters was discovered in our office by a friend, and he absquatulated with it, and left us with our mouth watering.
Missouri Reporter, *February 2*

1862: Rumor has it that a gay bachelor, who has figured in Chicago for nearly a year, has skedaddled, absquatulated, vamosed, and cleared out. Rocky Mountain News, *Denver, May 10*

accelerator: a velocipede. (See also Bicycling in Amusements, p.191.)

acknowledge the corn: to admit the truth; to confess; to acknowledge one's own obvious lie or shortcoming.

1840: David Johnson acknowledged the corn, and said that he was drunk. Daily Pennant, *St. Louis, July 14*

1846: I hope he will give up the argument, or, to use a familiar phrase, acknowledge the corn.

Mr. Speight, Mississippi, U.S. Senate, Congressional Globe, *January 28*

1850: He has not confessed the corn, as the saying is, that he did preach disunion? *Mr. Stanly, North Carolina, House of Reps.,* Congressional Globe

across lots: to push on straight through despite obstacles.

1853: "Go to hell across lots."

Brigham Young, Journal of Discourses, *March 27*

1869: I came cross lots from Aunt Sawin's and I got caught in those pesky blackberry bushes in the graveyard.

Harriet Beecher Stowe, Old Town Folks

algerine: a pirate.

1844: They have called the law for punishing treason an Algerine law; they have denominated us the Algerine party; and they have talked a great deal about Algerine cruelties.

Mr. Potter, Rhode Island, House of Reps., Congressional Globe, *March 12*

all creation, all nature, all wrath: everything or everybody.

1819: Father and I have just returned from the balloon—all nature was there, and more too. Massachusetts Spy, *November 3*

1833: I could eat like all wrath . . . I'll be down on him like all wrath anyhow. *J.K. Paulding,* Banks of the Ohio

1839: He pulls like all creation, as the woman remarked when the horse ran away with her. Yale Literary Magazine

all-fired: hell-fired.

1835: His boss gin him a most all-fired cut with a horsewhip.

Boston Pearl, *November 28*

1852: In my opinion, Dan Baxter would make an all-fired good deacon.

Knickerbocker Magazine, *August*

1866: O Sall, did you ever see such an all-fired sight of shoes?

Seba Smith, Way Down East, *p.289*

1872: You were too all-fired lazy to get a stick of wood.

J.M. Bailey, Folks in Danbury, *p.80*

all on one stick: a conglomeration or combination.

1830: He kept a kind of hotel and grocery store, all on one stick, as we say. *N. Dana,* A Mariner's Sketches, *p.18*

all-overish: uncomfortable.

1855: I grew—all-overish—no other phrase expresses it.

Putnam's Magazine, *December*

allow: to admit; to be of the opinion.

1840: She said she would allow he was the most beautiful complected child she had ever seen. Knickerbocker Magazine

1866: Where is Hamlin? I allow that he is dead, or I would ask him too.
C.H. Smith, Bill Arp, *p.23*

all possessed, like: like someone or something possessed by the devil.
1857: He'd carry on like all possessed—dance and sing, and tell stories, jest as limber and lively as if he'd never hefted a timber.
Putnam's Magazine, *January*
1878: She dropped a pan o' hot oysters into the lap of a customer and set him to swearin' and dancin' like all possessed.
J.H. Beadle, Western Wilds, *p.184*

all to pieces: completely; absolutely.
1839: "I know him all to pieces," replied the gentleman.
Charles Briggs, Harry Franco
1847: I knew him all to pieces as soon as I caught sight of him.
Charles Briggs, Tom Pepper

almighty: huge.
1848: I felt almighty blue. Stray Subjects, *p.109*

amalgamation: the mixing of blacks and whites.
1839: The Senator further makes the broad charge that Abolitionists wish to enforce the unnatural system of amalgamation. We deny the fact. *Mr. Morris, Ohio, U.S. Senate*, Congressional Globe
1847: Amalgamation, even by marriage, is not at all dreaded [in Texas]. Parties of white and coloured persons not unfrequently come over from Louisiana. Life of Benjamin Lundy, *p.117*

anti-fogmatic: raw rum or whiskey.
1829: The takers of anti-fogmatics, juleps, or other combustibles.
Savannah Mercury, *July 1*
1852: Tom Nettles [was] mixing a couple of rosy anti-fogmatics.
As Good as a Comedy, *p.134*
1855: A thirsty throat, to which anything like delay in an anti-fogmatic is almost certain bronchitis. *W.G. Simms*, Border Beagles, *p.55*

Arkansas toothpick: a long knife. Also known as a California or Missouri toothpick.
1855: We mistrust that the author of that statement saw a Missouri toothpick, and was frightened out of his wits.
Herald of Freedom, *Lawrence, Kansas, June 9*
1869: A brace of faithful pistols in his belt, and a huge Arkansas toothpick, or bowie knife, in a leather sheath.
A.K. McClure, Rocky Mountains, *p.377*

backing and filling: Literally, the alternate movements of a steamboat. Metaphorically, changing one's mind; waffling.

1848: The steam was well up on both boats, which lay rolling, and backing and filling, from the action of the paddles, at the dock.
Stray Subjects, *p.174*

1854: Men will be sent to Congress who will not back and fill, and be on one principle for one week, one month, and one moon, and upon another principle another week, and month, and moon.
Mr. Stephens, Georgia, House of Reps., Congressional Globe, *December 11*

bad egg: a bad person; a good-for-nothing person.
1864: A bad egg—a fellow who had not proved to be as good as his promise. The Atheneum, *p.559*

balderdash: nonsense; foolishness; empty babble.

bar, barr: the popular pronunciation and spelling of bear, as used prolifically in the South.
1843: They say you've no barr nor turkey out thare in Filledelfy?
R. Carlton, The New Purchase

1847: All the marks left behind showed me that he was the bar.
T.B. Thorpe, The Big Bear of Arkansas, *p.25*

beans, don't know, don't care: anything; something; nothing.
1857: "Well, then," said the General, "I don't care beans for the railroad, not a single old red-eyed bean, not a string-bean."
Knickerbocker Magazine, *February*

beat the Dutch: to beat all or beat the devil.
1840: Of all the goings on that I ever did hear of, this beats the Dutch.
Knickerbocker Magazine, *February*

1854: Well, it does beat the Dutch, and the Dutch, you know, beat the d---l. Knickerbocker Magazine, *May*

beatingest, beatemest, beatenest: anything or anyone that beats the competition.
1874: I reckon I am the beatin'est man to ax questions in this neck of timber. *Edward Eggleston,* The Circuit Rider, *p.119*

bee: a gathering of friends, family and neighbors to carry out a specific, time-consuming job, e.g., a corn-husking or quilting bee.
1829: This collection of neighbors is called a Bee, and is the common custom to assist each other in any great piece of labor, such as building a house, logging, etc. The person who calls the bee is expected to feed them well, and to return their work day for day.
Basil Hall, Travels in North America, *pp.311-312*

b'hoy: a rowdy young man; reveler; ruffian. See also G'hal.
1847: [He] had lived too long in the wire grass region to misunderstand

the character of that peculiar class of b'hoys who dwell there.
Knickerbocker Magazine, *March*

1852: [The occupants of the sleigh] are of not-to-be-mistaken Bowery cut — veritable b'hoys. *Charles A. Bristed,* The Upper Ten Thousand, *p.29*

1853: My off-handed manner just suited the b'hoy, on whom any superfluous politeness would have been thrown away.
Knickerbocker Magazine, *July*

biddy: a hen.

1874: [The English hens] had a contented cluck, as if they never got nervous, like Yankee biddies. *Louisa May Alcott,* Little Wives

big bugs: bigwigs; important people.

1853: Who is that walking there with the big bugs in front? he eagerly asked. Why, don't you know? That is the Governor.
Daily Morning Herald, *St. Louis, May 10*

1856: Hiram was beloved by many of the big bugs at Washington.
Knickerbocker Magazine, *March*

1856: She's one of the big bugs here — that is, she's got more money than almost anybody else in town. Widow Bedott Papers, *No.25*

biggest toad in the puddle: the most important person in a group.

bodaciously: an exaggeration of "bodily."

1833: It's a mercy that the cowardly varmints hadn't used you up bodaciously. *James Hall,* Legends of the West, *p.38*

1878: I saw a man in Stockton, California, who had been bodaciously chawed up to use his own language, by a grizzly bear.
J.H. Beadle, Western Wilds, *p.118*

body: a person.

1798: This hot weather makes a body feel odd. How long would a body be going to Washington? *Davis,* Travels in America, *p.223*

boodle: a crowd of people.

1833: He declared he'd fight the whole boodle of 'em.
Seba Smith, Major Jack Downing, *p.183*

border ruffians: those living outside the civilized settlements.

1857: A great majority of the people of the West, on the borders, may be emphatically termed Border ruffians. The Eastern people call them by that name. *John Taylor at the Bowery, Salt Lake City, August 9*

1860: I only wanted to convince gentlemen . . . that Indianians made better border ruffians than we did.
Mr. Craig, Missouri, House of Reps., Congressional Globe, *January 4*

born days, in all one's: lifetime; since one was born.

1840s: Where have you been all your born days, not to know better than that? Sam Slick in England, *ch.ii*

[not] born in the woods to be scared by an owl: refers to one who is experienced and therefore unafraid.

brick in one's hat, to have: to be drunk.
1854: A seedy-looking old negro, with a brick in his old hat, and a weed 'round it. Knickerbocker Magazine, *August*

bub and sis: brother and sister, especially applied to children.
1872: Many eminently genteel persons, whose manners make them at home anywhere, are in the habit of addressing all unknown children by one of the two terms, bub and sis, which they consider endears them greatly to the young people. Poet at the Breakfast Table, *ch.i*

bucket shop: a gin mill; a distillery.
1881: A bucket-shop in New York is a low gin-mill or distillery, where small quantities of spirits are dispensed in pitchers and pails [buckets]. When the shops for dealing in one-share or five-share lots of stocks were opened, these dispensaries of smaller lots then could be got from regular dealers and were at once named bucket-shops.
New York Evening Post, *October*

buckskin: a Virginian.
1824: We suspect that Capt. Tribby Clapp doodled the Buckskins.
Franklin Herald, *April 13*

bully for you!: well done; good for you.
1861: Bully for you! alternated with benedictions, in the proportion of two bullies to one blessing. Atlantic Monthly, *June, p.745*
1864: The freckles have vanished, and bully for you.
Daily Telegraph, *November 18*

bummer: the original word for bum. A lazy hobo or drunk.
1857: The irreclaimable town bummer figured in the police court.
San Francisco Call, *April 28*
1860: Another great sham connected with our social life is that of spreeing or bumming. Yale Literary Magazine
1862: A great majority of the bummers, who so long infested this city, have either left or gone to work. Rocky Mountain News, *Denver, May 10*

bunkum: claptrap.
1827: This is an old and common saying at Washington, when a member of Congress is making one of those hum-drum and unlistened-to long talks which have lately become so fashionable. . . . This is cantly called talking to Bunkum: an honorable gentleman, long ago, having said that he was not speaking to the house, but to the people of a certain

county [Buncombe] in his district, which, in local phrase, he called Bunkum. Niles' Weekly Register, *September 27*

1843: Mr. Weller of Ohio thought the question had been sufficiently debated, for nearly all the speeches had been made for Buncombe. *Mr. Underwood, Kentucky, House of Reps.*, Congressional Globe, *December 11, p.43*

candle-lighting: dusk.

1810: From dinner to dark I give to Society; and from candle-light to early bed-time I read. *Thomas Jefferson, from Monticello, February 26*

1824: The Rev. Mr. Kidwell, a Unitarian Universalist, will preach at the courthouse at early candle light on Sunday evening. Liberty Hall and Cincinnati Gazette, *March 26*

1853: The dancing commenced at early candle-lighting, and continued until long after midnight. *Turnover*, A Tale of New Hampshire, *p.80*

1888: The meeting was appointed for early candle-lighting. American Humorist, *August*

cap the climax: to beat all; to surpass everything.

1804: Your correspondent caps the climax of Misrepresentation. Lancaster Intelligencer, *February 21*

1811: It caps the climax of French arrogance and turpitude. Massachusetts Spy, *September 18*

1821: To cap the climax of his infamy and barbarity, he severed the head from the body of the infant. Pennsylvania Intelligencer, *March 21*

1860: All that was wanting to cap the climax to this absurd [Lincoln] nomination was the selection of Hannibal Hamlin as a candidate for Vice-Presidency. Richmond Enquirer, *May 25, pp.4-5*

carryings-on: frolicking, partying, etc.

1840s: Everybody tuck Christmas, especially the niggers, and sich carry-ins-on—sich dancin' and singin'—and shootin' poppers and sky-rackets—you never did see. Major Jones's Courtship

catawamptiously chawed up: utterly defeated, badly beaten. An expression largely confined to the South and West, from at least the 1840s on.

catch a weasel asleep, to: referring to something impossible or unlikely, in regard to someone who is always alert and is seldom or never caught off guard, e.g., You can't trick old Joe any sooner than you can catch a weasel asleep.

caution, a: a warning. Also a ludicrous example, or someone or something striking.

1839: Off we hied to the prairie, and the way the feathers flew was a caution. *John Plumbe*, Sketches in Iowa, *p.56*

1840: The way Mrs. N. rolls up her eyes when the English are mentioned is certainly a caution. *Mrs. Kirkland*, A New Home, *p.259*

1851: The way he squalled, rolled, kicked, puked, snorted, and sailed into the air, was a caution to old women on three legs.
An Arkansaw Doctor, *p.151*

cavort: to frolic or prance about.

1834: Government's bought their land, and it's wrong for them to be cavorting around quiet people's houses any more.
C.F. Hoffman, A Winter in the Far West, *p.28*

1845: She better not come a cavortin' 'bout me with any of her carryins on. *W.T. Thompson,* Chronicles of Pineville, *p.178*

chance: a quantity.

1819: A considerable quantity is expressed by a smart chance; and our hostess at Madison said there was a smart chance of Yankees in that village. *David Thomas,* Travels, *p.230*

1833: "There's a smart chance of cigars there in the bar, stranger, if you'd try some of them," said one of the hooshiers.
C.F. Hoffman, A Winter in the Far West, *p.219*

1833: There was a right smart chance of sickness when she came to the settlement. *James Hall,* Legends of the West, *p.88*

chirk: cheerful. Synonyms: chirp, chirpy.

1843: She is not very chirk, but more chirkier than she had been; and all our folks appear more chirkier than they really feel, in order to chirk her up. Yale Literary Magazine, *p.26*

1857: Chirk and lively we both were. Knickerbocker Magazine, *January*

1878: I didn't feel real cherk this week, so't I didn't go to sewin' s'ciety.
Rose T. Cooke, Happy Dodd

1878: Ef there's a mortal thing I can do to help ye, or chirk ye up, I want to do it right off. *Rose T. Cooke,* Happy Dodd

circumstance: anything to speak of.

1836: [The new hotel] will be a smasher, to which the Astor House will be no circumstance. Philadelphia Public Ledger, *November 16*

1854: You'd better think of all the pretty girls you ever seed, all at once, and then it won't be a circumstance. Elvira takes the rag off everything there's about these parts. Knickerbocker Magazine, *December*

1856: To be beaten by a mere circumstance of a gal-child.
W.G. Simms, Eutaw, *p.394*

1857: I've travelled on the cars in my day, but that kind of going wasn't a circumstance to the way we tore along.
S.H. Hammond, Wild Northern Scenes, *p.62*

cocked hat: To knock someone senseless or to shock him completely. To knock into a cocked hat.

1833: I told Tom I'd knock him into a cocked hat if he said another word. *J.K. Paulding,* Banks of the Ohio, *p.217*

1840: Why pummel and beat over again that which is already beaten to a jelly, jammed into a cocked hat, and flung into the middle of next week?

Mr. Wick, Indiana, House of Reps., Congressional Globe, *July 20, p.545*

1848: It has completely knocked us into a cocked hat.

Seba Smith, Major Jack Downing, *p.306*

1852: We will knock [the groggeries] into a cocked hat.

Ezra T. Benson, at the Tabernacle, Salt Lake City, Journal of Discourses, *September 12*

Cockneyisms: speaking in a Cockney dialect or pronouncing words with a Cockney accent, a popular speech affectation in Philadelphia from the beginning of the century to 1860. Some of the Cockneyisms were influenced by the writings of Charles Dickens.

1800: [In Philadelphia, Noah Webster] will find the London Cockneyisms flourish in perfection — veal — here converted into "weal," — and wine into "vine," — the hot-water-war he will find described as a "hot vater var," etc. Aurora, *June 20*

1830: It is almost impossible to distinguish Americans from English, especially Philadelphians, who like Cockneys talk about "wery good weal and winegar." *N. Dana,* A Mariner's Sketches, *p.16*

codfish aristocracy: a contemptuous term for people who have made money in business.

1850: We should regard it as somewhat strange if we should require a codfish aristocracy to keep us in order.

Mr. Butler, South Carolina, U.S. Senate, Congressional Globe, *July 9, p.1248*

1853: D. is evidently a retainer of the codfish aristocracy, who will only go where the price will match with his dignity.

Daily Morning Herald, *St. Louis, April 22*

1860: The defender of genius against vulgar money bags, alias codfish aristocracy. Richmond Enquirer, *May 15*

cold as a wagon tire: dead.

1833: If a man was as cold as a wagon tire, provided there was any life in him, she'd bring him to. *James Hall,* Legends of the West, *p.88*

coloured person, person of color: a Negro.

1812: Christopher Macpherson is a man of color, brought up as bookkeeper by a merchant, his master, and afterwards enfranchised.

Thomas Jefferson to John Adams, April 20

conniption fit: a fit of hysteria.

1833: Ant Keziah fell down in a conniption fit.

Seba Smith, Major Jack Downing, *p.218*

1842: The Vermont papers are going into conniption fits, because their state is in debt $150,000. Philadelphia Spirit of the Times, *August 23*

1859: She went into a conniption at the sight of the poor Snap. Harper's Weekly, *November 19*

considerable: no small specimen.

1816: He is considerable of a surveyor. *Pickering,* Vocabulary

1843: Wal! You're considerable of a critur, you are, by thunder! You eternal, great, green-eyed, black-devil! Yale Literary Magazine

1852: He is really worth knowing, and considerable of a man, as we say — no fool at all. *Charles A. Bristed,* The Upper Ten Thousand, *p.142*

Continental: the money issued by Congress during the Revolutionary War. It eventually became synonymous with anything worthless.

1874: I tole him as how I didn't keer three continental derns fer his whole band. *Edward Eggleston,* The Circuit Rider, *p.120*

1888: I am not worrying about the nomination. I don't care a Continental if I don't receive it. Missouri Republican, *February 16*

coon's age: a long time.

1845: We won't hear the end of this bisness for a coon's age: you see if we do. *W.T. Thompson,* Chronicles of Pineville, *p.72*

1848: I never did like this Yanky way of married people livin' all over creation without seein' one another more'n once in a coon's age. *W.E. Burton,* Waggeries, *p.16*

1851: This child hain't had that much money in a coon's age. Adventures of Captain Simon Suggs, *p.155*

coot: an idiot; a simpleton; a ninny.

1856: He's an amazin' ignorant old coot, tew. Widow Bedott Papers, *No.9*

1857: It is a poor coot, let me tell you, that will make such excuses. *H.C. Kimball, Salt Lake City,* Journal of Discourses, *September 20, v, p.251*

corned: drunk.

1840: William McG. brought a load of corn to market, and got corned on the strength of it. Daily Pennant, *St. Louis, May 27*

cotton to: to take a liking to, a popular expression throughout the South and West from early in the century on.

cow-hide, cow-skin: a whip made of cowhide. Also used as a verb, to whip or flog.

1801: Dinah was armed with a cow-skin, while Cloe had nothing but the simple weapons of nature. Massachusetts Spy, *June 24*

1818: The enraged barrister, with a hand-whip, or cow-hide as they are called . . . actually cut his jacket to ribbons.

M. Birbeck, Letters from Illinois, *p.60*

1855: His lady had cow-hided him in the streets of his native city.

Thomas B. Gunn, New York Boarding Houses, *p.215*

cracker: a poor white of the South, named after the crackling whips used by rural Southerners.

1842: We saw many of the country people coming into town; some on horseback, some in waggons, and some on foot. . . . Single-breasted coats without collars, broad-brimmed and low-crowned hats, and gray hair floating in loose locks over their shoulders, were among their perculiarities. . . . They are called by the townspeople, Crackers, from the frequency with which they crack their whips.

J.S. Buckingham, Slave States, *p.210*

1847: I met one of the country crackers, as the backwoodsmen are called, who, having been to Wetempka with a load of shingles, was on his way home. Knickerbocker Magazine, *May*

crazy as a loon: very crazy.

1854: The old man'll run as crazy as a loon a-thinkin' 'bout his household affairs. *H.H. Riley,* Puddleford, *p.140*

critter: creature; varmint; a contemptible person.

1833: It would be ridic'lous if it should be a bar; them critters sometimes come in here, and I have nothing but my knife.

Knickerbocker Magazine, *p.90*

1836: My little critter [a mustang], who was both blood and bottom, seemed delighted. Colonel Crockett in Texas, *p.149*

1836: The old critter says he is married, and makes his wife work in the printing office. Philadelphia Public Ledger, *September 24*

1842: One of the clerks in the Baltimore Post Office, on opening a bag of letters, discovered a live garter-snake in the same. The critter bore no postmark or frank. Philadelphia Spirit of the Times, *July 28*

dang: euphemism for damn, e.g., dang it all or dang you.

dash!: euphemism for damn, e.g., dash it all.

dashing: showy, elegant or spirited, especially in dress.

dead meat: a corpse, from 1860 on.

death on: very fond of or very talented at.

1847: A long, lanky, cadaverous lawyer, who was death on a speech, powerful in chewing tobacco, and some at a whisky drinking.

Robb, Streaks of Squatter Life, *p.30*

deef: deaf.

1896: You're a-goin' to do what? I reckon I'm a-goin' a little deef.
Ella Higginson, Tales from Puget Sound, *p.68*

designs: plans; schemes; intentions. Commonly used throughout.

1846: I like gentlemen's society when I know they have no designs upon my heart and when I know any cordiality of mine will not be misinterpreted. *Mary Butterfield, letter to fiancé, October 31*

didoes: to cut up didoes was to get into mischief.

1835: Must all the world know all the didoes we cut up in the lodgeroom? *D.P. Thompson,* Adventures of Timothy Peacock, *p.170*

1838: If you keep a cutting didoes, I must talk to you like a Dutch uncle.
J.C. Neal, Charcoal Sketches, *p.201*

diggings: one's home; lodgings; community.

1838: It's about time we should go to our diggings.
J.C. Neal, Charcoal Sketches, *p.119*

1842: With whom did the idea originate? It's novel in these diggins at least. Philadelphia Spirit of the Times, *May 6*

1853: How dare you talk thus in these days, and above all in these diggings. Fun and Earnest, *p.239*

dipping: chewing snuff.

1853: This horrible practice, called in lower Virginia and North Carolina dipping, is of respectable standing.
Putnam's Magazine, *February, p.142*

1857: She was suspected of a mysterious habit denominated in Southern parlance dipping—in other words, of chewing snuff.
Thomas B. Gunn, New York Boarding Houses, *p.221*

dirk: to stab with a dirk or dagger.

1825: He had changed his mind as to the dirking. . . . [He] swore the fellow ought to be dirked, the usual phrase for the punishment of slight offences among these humane republicans.
J.K. Paulding, John Bull in America, *pp.39,146*

1830: The assassin determined to dirk him in the street on his return.
Massachusetts Spy, *June 2*

doggery: a cheap drinking establishment; in modern lingo, a dive.

1848: The drunkard, while reeling homeward from the doggery, is attracted by both sides of the street, which accounts for his diagonal movements. *Dow,* Patent Sermons, *p.99*

1850: A doggery is too contemptible for any man who has a soul more elevated than the swine to condescend to. Frontier Guardian, *March 20*

1854: And then the doggery-keepers got to sellin' licker by the drink, instead of the half-pint, and a dime a drink at that.
J.G. Baldwin, Flush Times in Alabama, *p.65*

1855: Some say that this fellow-feeling between him and the marshal results from the fact that he was a doggery-keeper in the states. Weekly Oregonian, *April 7*

doings: "fixins" for a meal.

1843: A snug breakfast of chicken fixins, eggs, ham-doins, and even slapjacks. *R. Carlton,* The New Purchase, *p.58*

1847: Flour doins an' chicken fixins, an' four uncommon fattest big goblers rosted I ever seed. Billy Warwick's Wedding, *p.104*

1859: Tell Sal to knock over a chicken or two, and get out some flour, and have some flour-doins and chicken fixins for the stranger. Knickerbocker Magazine, *March*

done gone: a pleonasm (redundancy) used frequently by Negroes of the period.

1836: He had done gone three hours ago.

"A Quarter Race in Kentucky," New York Spirit of the Times, *p.22*

do tell: phrase used to express fascination with a speaker's subject.

1842: Among the peculiar expressions in use in Maine we noticed that, when a person has communicated some intelligence in which the hearer feels an interest, he manifests it by saying: "I want to know"; and when he has concluded his narrative, the hearer will reply: "O! do tell!" *J.S. Buckingham,* Eastern and Western States, *p.177*

1853: Do tell! I want to know! Did you ever! Such a powerful right smart chance of learning as you have is enough to split your head open right smack. Daily Morning Herald, *St. Louis, April 11*

1853: At last sez I, "Jidge, did you ever have your portrait tuck?" "No," sez he, as ugly as you please. "Dew te," says I.

Knickerbocker Magazine, *September*

dram shop: a small drinking establishment, from early in century.

dude: a dandy.

1883: The new coined word dude ... has travelled over the country with a great deal of rapidity since but two months ago it grew into general use in New York. North Adams Transcript, *June 24*

1888: If the term dude had been invented [in 1866] it would have been applied to a Texas horseman.

Mrs. Elizabeth Custer, Tenting on the Plains, *p.212*

1891: Joe then went east, and married a young dudine out there.

A. Welcker, Woolly West, *p.69*

elephant, to see the: to see it all, to experience it all. Sometimes pertaining to war, to see battle.

1840: That's sufficient, as Tom Haynes said when he saw the elephant.

A.B. Longstreet, Georgia Scenes, *p.10*

1851: I think I have seen the elephant, as far as public life is concerned.
Mr. Hale, New Hampshire, U.S. Senate, Congressional Globe, *January 22, p.304*

1854: I am a miner, who wandered away from down-east, and came to sojourn in a strange land, and see the elephant.
Knickerbocker Magazine, *April*

1873: He had lost all his money, consisting of seven twenty-dollar gold pieces, and a bundle containing a valuable steam gauge. He had seen the elephant (rather too close a view, he thought), was many hundred miles from home, among strangers, and without a dollar in his pocket. *Edward Savage,* Police Records and Recollections, *p.121*

exfluncticate: to utterly destroy.
1839: The mongrel armies are prostrate—used up—exfluncticated.
Chemung *(New York)* Democrat, *November 30*

1840: . . . the Administration is bodaciously used up, tetotaciously exflunctified.
Mr. Wick, Indiana, House of Reps., Congressional Globe, *July 20, p.545*

express: the mails; a mail stage.
1851: The religious papers which have the greatest circulation are papers of a small size, and are transmitted mostly by express.
Mr. Duncan, Massachusetts, House of Reps., Congressional Globe, *January 15, p.245*

1854: There are two large express companies, Adams & Co. and Wells, Fargo & Co., which carry mail matter by Nicaragua, charging from twenty-five to fifty cents on a letter.
Mr. Latham, California, Congressional Globe, *April 7, p.872*

F.F.V.: First Families of Virginia, of which many claimed to be members to gain special treatment, but eventually used in jest.
1850: [He was] the first of his race to acknowledge that he was not an F.F.V. Odd Leaves, *p.178*

1857: Mr. Floyd, as everybody knows, as an F.F.V., and the soul of honor accordingly. Harper's Weekly, *April 11*

1861: They must do better down in Virginia than they have done, or F.F.V., instead of standing for First Families of Virginia, will get to mean the Fast Flying Virginians. Oregon Argus, *August 10*

fice, fiste, fyst: a worthless dog; a mongrel.
1843: Did you ever see a pack composed of five or six little fice dogs, barking furiously? Missouri Reporter, *St. Louis, June 29*

1863: What other Pete can I mean but your dirty little fice dog?
J.B. Jones, Wild Western Scenes, *p.15*

1874: [The barking ranged] all the way from the contemptible treble of an ill-mannered fice to the deep baying of a huge bulldog.
Edward Eggleston, The Circuit Rider, *p.72*

1890: All the dogs of the regiment were with us, apparently, from the lofty and high-born staghounds down to the little feist, or mongrel, of the trooper. *Mrs. Elizabeth Custer,* Following the Guidon, *p.78*

fist, make a: to succeed at something.

1834: A chap would make a blue fist of takin' a dead aim through double sights, with the butt end of a psalm in his guzzle.
The Kentuckian in New York, *p.25*

1838: He reckoned he should make a better fist at farming than edicating. *Caroline Gilman,* Recollections of a Southern Matron, *p.46*

1841: You made a poor fist of this business.
W.G. Simms, The Kinsmen, *p.24*

fit: popular slang for fought.

1835: Any body can get in, if only he fit big battles enough. I'd give a year's sellary in a minute, if Mr. Van Buren had ever fit a great battle so as to be called a hero. Bucks County Intelligencer, *November 4*

1839: Here's a going to be one of the peskiest battles that ever was fit.
Chemung *(New York)* Democrat, *April 17*

1845: There's a mighty chance of lawyers' lies in the papers . . . but some of it is true. I did strike the old lady, but she fit me powerfully first.
Cornelius Mathews, A Court Scene in Georgia, *p.140*

1869: He hadn't fit the Arminians and Socinians to be beat by a tom-turkey. *Harriet Beecher Stowe,* Old Town Stories

fix: a dilemma; a problem; a jam.

1833: When a man has head religion, he is in a bad fix to die—cut off his head, and away goes his body and soul to the devil.
James Hall, Legends of the West, *p.43*

1839: The Americans are never at a loss when they are in a fix.
Marryat, Diary in America, *p.106*

fixings: trimmings, accessories, etc.

1825: The veteran trapper was furnished with such other appliances, or fixens, as he would term them, as put him in plight again to take the field. New Hampshire Patriot, *Concord, May 23*

1842: Our friends who love oysters and sparkling rosy wine, and other little fixens in the eating way, will do well to drop in at the Bath House Refectory. Philadelphia Spirit of the Times, *January 22*

1842: People can't afford to purchase the rich golden and rosy beef-steaks, as formerly. They keep soul and body together with greens and onions, shad, and such like fixins.
Philadelphia Spirit of the Times, *April 16*

1845: Our ladies are sadly in want of the little fixins made by the milliners. *Letter to the* Bangor Mercury

1848: [He] makes a heap of money by selling Yankee made Ingin fixins, sich as moccasins, bead-bags, card-cases, and a heap of fancy articles,

sich as the Ingins themselves never dreamed of makin.
Major Jones's Sketches of Travel, *p.167*

fix one's flint: to settle a matter.
1837: I thought I had fixed your flint yesterday.
Knickerbocker Magazine, *April*
1843: "Take it easy, Sam," says I, "Your flint is fixed."
Sam Slick in England
1847: Stranger, if you don't shet your mouth a little closer than a Gulf clam, I'll fix your flint in short order.
J.K. Paulding, American Comedies, *p.197*

fleshy: fat.
1807: A large, fleshy, rugged, strong, active child.
Massachusetts Spy, *August 26*
1840: Mrs. Ferret is what we call a fleshy or lusty woman; she weighed two hundred and twelve, in Neal Hopper's new scale at the mill.
John P. Kennedy, Quodlibet, *p.110*

frolic: a celebration; a party; a wild time. Also, a fight.
1815: He happened to get both eyes gouged out yesterday in a frolic.
J.K. Paulding, John Bull in America, *p.218*
1833: They meant to have a reaping frolic when the corn should be ripe.
Harriet Martineau, Briery Creek, *p.18*

full chisel: at full speed; executed with everything you've got.
1832: I met an express coming on full chisel from Philadelphia.
Seba Smith, Major Jack Downing, *p.168*
1878: The only way to get that fellow to heaven would be to set out to drive him to hell; then he'd turn and run up the narrow way full chisel. *Harriet Beecher Stowe,* Poganuc People

funeral, not one's: not one's business; none of one's concern.
1875: Wanted: A nice, plump, healthy, good-natured, good-looking domestic and affectionate lady to correspond with, object—Matrimony. She must be between 22 and 35 years of age. She must be a believer in God and immortality, but no sectarian. She must not be a gadabout or given to scandal. . . . Such a lady can find a correspondent by addressing . . . Post Office Box 9, Yuma, A.T. Photographs exchanged! If anybody don't like our way of going about this . . . business, we don't care. It's none of their funeral.
Lonely hearts classified ad in the Arizona Sentinel, *July 10*
1896: It ain't any of your funeral, I guess, if I did turn [the clock] back.
Ella Higginson, Tales from Puget Sound, *p.184*

gallnipper: a large mosquito.

1842: The gallnippers of Florida are said to have aided the Seminoles in appalling our armies. *Mrs. Kirkland,* Forest Life, *p.184*

1888: Our rainwater was full of gallnippers and pollywogs . . . banks of mud all bred mosquitoes, or gallnippers, as the darkies call them. *Mrs. Elizabeth Custer,* Tenting on the Plains, *pp.76-77*

g'hal: a rowdy girl; a reveler or ruffian girl. See also B'hoy.

1848: Go it, all ye g'hals, and ye b'hoys, as much as you can, while you are young. *Dow,* Patent Sermons, *p.167*

gone coon, gone sucker: a goner.

1840: I was afeared you were a gone coon. *C.F. Hoffman,* Greyslaer, *p.221*

1845: The acquisition of Canada . . . is put down on all sides as a gone coon. *Mr. Giddings, Ohio, in Congress*

1851: I feared that I should lose my way, and then I knew I was a gone sucker. An Arkansaw Doctor, *p.109*

Gotham: New York City.

1836: An Albany or Newark dog is well worth fifty cents, if brought to Gotham's authorities, as if actually killed in Gotham's streets. . . . We understand that a dog's flesh is quite a luxury in Gotham market. Philadelphia Public Ledger, *August 5*

1840: Col. Johnson was in New York, drinking juleps at Delmonicos. He was warmly received by Gothamites. Daily Pennant, *St. Louis, July 22*

go the whole hog: to go all the way.

1830: As ladies now wear pantaloons and boots, I see no reason why they should not go the whole hog and mount the hat and swallow-tail coat likewise. *N. Dana,* A Mariner's Sketches, *p.186*

1833: T. Hamilton quotes a placard, "Jackson for ever. Go the whole hog!" The expression, I am told, is of Virginian origin. In that state, when a butcher kills a pig, it is usual to demand of each customer, whether he will go the whole hog. Men and Manners in America, *pp.17-18*

gouge: to gouge at your opponent's eyes in a fight, a widely referred to tactic throughout the century.

1820: In most cases both parties were severely bruised, bitten, and gouged, and would be weeks in recovering. *Peter Burnett,* Recollections, *p.19*

1826: . . . I saw more than one man who wanted an eye, and ascertained that I was now in the region [on the Mississippi] of gouging. *T. Flint,* Recollections, *p.98*

1830: "Gouge him! Gouge him!" exclaimed a dozen voices. *George Prentice,* Northern Watchman, *Troy, New York*

1843: Rowdy Bill was famous as a gouger, and so expert was he in his anti-optical vocation, that in a few minutes he usually bored out his adversary's eyes, or made him cry "peccavi."

R. Carlton, The New Purchase, p.158

greased lightning: anything very fast.

1833: He spoke as quick as greased lightning.

Boston Herald, *January 15*

1837: If I didn't fetch old dug-out through slicker than snakes, and faster than a greased thunderbolt. *R.M. Bird,* Nick of the Woods, *p.90*

1842: The horse went up the street like a blue streak of greased lightning. Philadelphia Spirit of the Times, *September 7*

grist: a quantity.

1833: There has been a mighty grist of rain lately up above.

J.K. Paulding, Banks of the Ohio, *p.133*

1847: He owes old Sambo a whull grist of fourpences for blackin' his boots, runnin' of ar'nds, and sich like small chores.

J.K. Paulding, American Comedies, *p.142*

1853: That old Greke that folks tell so much about never poured out sich a grist of oratory in all his born days.

Seba Smith, Major Jack Downing, *p.411*

grit: guts; courage; toughness.

1834: Mother says before I was a week old I showed that I was real grit.

Seba Smith, Major Jack Downing, *p.25*

1855: They are full of grit, and ready to swallow Cuba alive.

Seba Smith, Major Jack Downing, *p.434*

grocery: a drinking establishment. See also Doggery, Dram shop, Groggery.

1830: Wilson told the Sheriff to take the jury to a grocery, that he might treat them, and invited every body that chose to go. Some men who have held a good standing in society followed the crowd to the grocery. Jeffersonian, *June 30*

1857: Some will set up a small grocery or groggery; they go into debt to those who have a bigger groggery.

John Taylor at the Bowery, Salt Lake City, Journal of Discourses, *August 9, v, p.119*

groggery, grog shop: a low drinking establishment; a dive.

1835: Long lines of unpainted, wretched looking dwellings, occupied as groggeries. *Ingraham,* The South West, *p.190*

1843: To enlarge the Congressional districts . . . would break the power of mere shake-hands and grog-shop influence.

Mr. Underwood, Kentucky, House of Reps., Congressional Globe, *April 21*

grum: surly; gloomy; glum.

1834: The poet looked gloomily, or what is vernacularly called grum.
Robert Sands, Writings, *p.187*

1842: The sun seems extraordinarily sulky and grum.
Philadelphia Spirit of the Times, *June 18*

gum: lies; exaggerations. As a verb, to dupe someone.

1843: Now this was all gum; Sam could not read a word.
R. Carlton, The New Purchase, *p.255*

1844: He was speaking of the moon hoax, which gummed so many learned philosophers. Yale Literary Magazine, *xiv, p.189*

guttersnipe: a homeless child who roamed and slept in the streets. Hundreds roamed the larger cities throughout much of the century.

1890: Guttersnipe is the name which has been given to the more weakly street arab, the little fellow who, though scarcely more than a baby, is frequently left by brutalized parents at the mercy of any fate. This little chap generally roams around until he finds some courageous street arab, scarcely bigger than himself, perhaps, to fight his battles and put him in the way of making a living, which is generally done by selling papers. In time the guttersnipe becomes himself a full-fledged street arab . . . with two hard and ready fists, and a horde of dependent and grateful snipes. Darkness and Daylight in New York, *p.116*

hang up one's fiddle: to give up.

hankering: a strong desire, used throughout the century.

1847: I took an awful hankerin after Sofy M —, and sot in to looking for matrimony. *Robb,* Streaks of Squatter Life

hash, settle one's: to settle one's business.

1824: The parties settled the hash, and retired to comfortable quarters, to quaff cogniac. Microscope, *Albany, February 28*

1837: I've settled his hash, though. Knickerbocker Magazine, *April*

1849: I completely settled his hash. Yale Literary Magazine, *xiv, p.179*

high-falutin: highbrow; stuck up.

1854: Old Mrs. Peabody was allers a dreadful high-falutin critter, with stuck-up notions, and old P. is a soft head, driven by his wife, just as our old rooster is driven about by that cantankerous crabbed Dorking hen. *J.W. Spaulding,* Weekly Oregonian, *December 23*

1862: Educated peepul, kernel, ain't got any more wit or common sense than other folks, but they try to make you believe they have, an' will talk high falutin words just to frighten you if they kin.
Seba Smith, Major Jack Downing, *August 14*

hoe-down: a Negro dance.

1855: The revellers set to sprawling through various rude high-legged reels and hoedowns. Knickerbocker Magazine, *September*

1885: [The negroes] danced their vigorous hoe-downs.
Library Magazine, *New York, July 1*

hook, on one's own: on one's own; one's own doing.

1836: Did he make these forgeries on his own hook, or at the instigation of the big bug? Philadelphia Public Ledger, *August 24*

1837: The enthusiastic Jerseyman, who, without belonging to either side, was found at the battle of Monmouth, fighting on his own hook entirely. *R.M. Bird*, Nick of the Woods

hooter: an atom; a tiny amount.

1839: Now the Grampus stopt, and didn't buge one hooter.
"Major Jack on Board a Whaler," Havana Republican, *August 21*

1848: Politicians don't care a hooter, so long as their own selfish ends are obtained. *Dow*, Patent Sermons, *p.6*

1853: Let him be as dirty as the mortal in Missouri, who is assessed as real estate, still it makes not a hooter of difference. *Dow*, Patent Sermons

horn: a glass of liquor or ale.

1824: I went to be after taking one horn. Microscope, *Albany, April 3*

1840: I'll bet a horn of Monongahela whiskey that you have had your supper. Knickerbocker Magazine, *September*

1840: He called lustily for a horn of baldface and mollasses.
Daily Pennant, *St. Louis, April 28*

horn spoon, by the: an exclamation of surprise, shock or anger.

1853: "By the horn spoons!" repeated the skipper suddenly.
Knickerbocker Magazine, *February*

hornswoggle, honey-fuggled: to cheat; to pull the wool over one's eyes.

1856: Pardon me for using the word; but Sharp honey-fuggled around me.
Mr. Bennet, Nebraska, House of Reps., Congressional Globe, *July 22, p.965*

1860: P.F. is going to hornswoggle the Democrats. Oregon Argus, *May 12*

1862: Now we want the particulars as to how much honey fugling and wool pulling was done. Rocky Mountain News, *Denver, August 14*

1865: I ain't no giant killer. I ain't no Norwegian bar. I ain't no boar-constrikter. But I'll be hornswoggled if the talkin an the writin an the slanderin has got to be done all on one side any longer. Some of your folks have got to dry up, or turn our folks loose.
Bill Arp, Letter to Artemus Ward, *September 1*

hoss: widely used for horse.

1852: That was a long race, I tell you, hosses.
H.C. Watson, Nights in a Blockhouse, *p.29*

1853: Hello, old hoss, whar hev you been this coon's age?
Paxton, A Stray Yankee in Texas, *p.201*

huckleberry above a persimmon: a cut above. The phrase had many variations and shades of meaning.
1836: It is a huckleberry above my persimmon to cipher out how I find myself the most popular bookmaker of the day.
Colonel Crockett in Texas, *p.13*
1844: She's a great gal that! Show me another like her any whar, and I am thar directly. She's a huckleberry above most people's persimmons. Philadelphia Spirit of the Times, *August 24*
1885: I'm a huckleberry above that persimmon.
Admiral Porter, Incidents of the Civil War, *p.204*

huffed, huffy: angry; irritated; offended.
1800: The Philadelphia Gazette is huffed at our stating a fact.
Aurora, *Philadelphia, December 18*
1855: They said that some mischief was going on, and some of them were right huffy about it.
George Smith at the Mormon Tabernacle, Journal of Discourses, *March 18*

hull: frequently used for whole.
1835: Six months ago, this hull country was the most prosperous in the world. Colonel Crockett's Tour, *p.79*
1845: "I've bought out the hull grocery," sings out Jake Miller, standin' in Capn' Todd's store with a hull raft of fellers.
St. Louis Reveille, *September 1*
1849: I vow my hull share o' the spoils wouldn't come nigh a V spot.
Biglow Papers, *No.8*

hum: frequently used for home.
1819: When he talked of hum, I took him for a wag, but soon found he so pronounced home.
"An Englishman," in the Western Star, *quoted in* Massachusetts Spy, *May 12*
1848: Wen I left hum, I hed two legs, an' they worn't bad ones neither.
Biglow Papers, *No.8*
1856: There wa'nt nobody to hum but her, so I went right in ker dash, and sot down. Weekly Oregonian, *August 2*
1860: I was a little shaver, helping the bigger boys Calvin and Enoch . . . to drive the cows hum of an evening. Knickerbocker Magazine, *September*

humbug: a deception; a hoax; an imposter; the equivalent of the modern B.S.
1836: Dissection of Joice Heth — Precious Humbug Exposed. The anatomical examination of the body of Joice Heth yesterday, resulted in the exposure of one of the most precious humbugs that ever was

imposed upon a credulous community. [Ed. Note: P.T. Barnum had claimed the woman was 161 years old.] New York Sun, *February 25*

1873: Wherever these lectures were holden, it became necessary to detail a large force of police to preserve the peace, and rough times we often had of it. Indeed, it really seemed that everybody was bent on a row, and perfectly infatuated with humbug. *Edward Savage,* Police Records and Recollections, *p.114*

husking bee, husking frolic: a social event in which the community came together to husk corn and to drink; they often ended with drunken brawls.

1838: A fight came off at Maysville, Kentucky in which a Mr. Coulster was stabbed in the side, and is dead; a Mr. Gibson was well hacked with a knife; a Mr. Farr was dangerously wounded. This entertainment was the winding up of a corn husking frolic, when all doubtless were right merry with good whiskey. New York Daily Whig

1847: I must pass on to the antagonisms of the corn-husking. When the crop was drawn in, the ears were heaped into a long pile or rick, a night fixed on, and the neighbors notified, rather than invited, for it was an affair of mutual assistance. As they assembled at nightfall, the green glass quart whiskey bottle, stopped with a cob, was handed to every one, man and boy, as they arrived, to take a drink. *Dr. Drake,* Pioneer Life in Kentucky, *pp.54-56*

I snore, I swan, I swow: socially acceptable alternatives to the expression "I swear," which was considered impolite, originating with the youth of New England.

Johnny, John: a Chinaman.

1857: He knows. He's seed the Johnnies goin' into that there doorway next block. *Thomas Gunn,* New York Boarding Houses, *p.275*

1873: I passed out of the Chinese theater, with a lady and two children. We had to walk through a crowd of Johns. *Charles Nordhoff,* California, *p.85*

1878: The melancholy Johns with glazed caps and black pigtails, like a lot of half-drowned crows. *J.H. Beadle,* Western Wilds, *p.401*

Jonathan: the American people. Also known as Brother Jonathan or Uncle Sam.

1846: Jonathan was hard to provoke; but when once you did get him up, he remained at a dead white heat for a long while. *Mr. Root, Ohio, House of Reps.,* Congressional Globe, *December 24*

1848: Jonathan is declared to be in his right in supporting his diplomatic agents like private gentlemen. *Mr. Ingersoll, Pennsylvania, House of Reps.,* Congressional Globe, *June 30*

Jonathan: a downeaster; a yankee.

1827: A tall, boney, Jonathan, whose appetite was in proportion to the magnitude of his frame. Massachusetts Spy, *November 14*

1843: Occasionally you will see some honest country Jonathan, with his waggon full of yankee notions. Yale Literary Magazine, *ix, p.44*

kick: to protest or to object to something; to complain.

1842: [Members of Congress] kicked against receiving any more petitions. Philadelphia Spirit of the Times, *January*

1857: I have to live under their laws, and when they take a notion to swear away my character, I musn't kick. *J.G. Holland,* The Bay Path, *p.69*

1888: The tariff is of no good to [the colored man]. But that is not what he kicks about. New York Herald, *July 29*

knee-high to a . . . : humorous description of short stature or youth.

1824: He has lived with me ever since he was knee-high to a musquitoe. *Letter to the* Microscope, *Albany, June 12*

1833: A bit of a rogue he was, too, when he wasn't more'n knee-high to a bumblebee. *John Neal,* The Downeasters, *p.78*

1841: He has been known in the Congaree ever since I was knee high to a splinter. *W.G. Simms,* The Kinsmen, *p.63*

1853: To see little saplings, some of them scarce knee-high to a milk-stool . . . bigger b'hoys, green as unsunned pumpkins. . . . *Dow,* Patent Sermons

land sakes: socially acceptable alternative for Lord's sake, considered to be a profanity.

1846: Jedediah, for the land's sake, does my mouth blaze? Knickerbocker Magazine, *January*

1888: Land sakes! Thet poor cretur never had the spunk to kill himself. Harper's Weekly, *January 21*

lay: price; terms; salary.

1816: He bought a large drove [of cattle] at a good lay. Massachusetts Spy, *September 4*

1853: A few months saw him handling the ropes upon a whaler, at a good lay. Captain Priest, *p.49*

let her rip: let it go!

1853: [Captain Muggs's] spirited "let her rip" was an infinite improvement on the "fire" of the old Steuben manual. Life Scenes, *p.209*

1854: As it is all for the good of the party, Let her rip. Weekly Oregonian, *April 22*

1857: Presently I heard, "All set; let her rip." Knickerbocker Magazine, *November*

like a book: to speak eloquently or with a large vocabulary.

1829: You talk like a book, Mr. Bond. Massachusetts Spy, *January 28*

1833: [She] sang like a nightingale and talked like a book.
James Hall, Legends of the West, *p.11*

1833: An educated and travelled Yankee . . . talking like a book, even to the washerwoman. *John Neal,* The Downeasters, *p.26*

likely: able-bodied; attractive; serviceable.

1823: Notice. Will be sold at the mansion house of John Vivion deceased, all the personal estate of said deceased, consisting of Seven Negroes. . . . Two likely young Girls, between the ages of 20 and 25. Two likely Boys, between the ages of 16 and 20. And one likely young Girl of the age of five years. Missouri Intelligencer, *August 5*

limb: the socially acceptable or polite word for leg.

1854: [The Indian maiden] was seated on a rock, her legs (beg pardon, her limbs) stretched far asunder. Knickerbocker Magazine, *June*

liquor: to take a drink.

1836: Having liquored, we proceeded on the journey.
Colonel Crockett in Texas, *p.70*

1839: It's a bargain then . . . come, let's liquor on it.
Marryat, Diary in America, *p.239*

little end of the horn: same as short end of the stick. To come out of a situation disadvantaged.

1805: I am very much afraid I shall come out at the little end of the horn. Baltimore Evening Post, *July 5*

1817: If the farmers and the traders, instead of attending closely to their proper callings, are busy here and there, they will assuredly come out at the little end of the horn. Massachusetts Spy, *February 19*

1855: You used to hear brother Joseph tell about this people being crowded into the little end of the horn, and if they kept straight ahead they were sure to come out at the big end. *Brigham Young, April 8*

log-rolling: a community effort to roll logs and clear land for a cabin's construction.

1833: The good villagers resorted to what, in woodland phrase, is called log-rolling, which means a combined effort of many to do what is either difficult or impossible to one. *J.K. Paulding,* Banks of the Ohio

1889: In some localities more thickly settled than others, neighbors render each other mutual assistance. In this case, the trunks of very large trees were cut down, chopped into logs, rolled together, and set on fire. Hence the phrase log-rolling in the vocabulary of our political common-places. *Phelan,* History of Tennessee, *p.28*

mad as a March hare: very angry, from early in the century.

make a die: to die.

1825: I wonder [the dog] didn't go mad; or make a die of it.
John Neal, Brother Jonathan, *p.398*

1845: They said Billy was gwine to make a die of it, and had sent for 'em. *W.T. Thompson,* Chronicles of Pineville, *p.72*

1848: I'm afraid I'm going to make a die of it. I'm going to create a vacancy. Stray Subjects, *p.195*

man alive: popular exclamation expressing surprise, shock, etc.

1840: Man alive! what do you put yourself in such a plaguy passion for?
Mrs. Kirkland, A New Home, *p.168*

1845: Man alive! I never heard of sich a oudacious perceedin' in my life. This town's got a monstrous bad name for meanery and shecoonery of all sorts, but I never know'd they 'low'd pirates here before.
W.T. Thompson, Chronicles of Pineville, *p.47*

mind, have a: to have a notion; to be willing.

1803: He, having a mind to coax the dog to stay with him, took a piece of bread. Massachusetts Spy, *March 2*

1829: If they have a mind to take the trouble, let them tell fourty lies a week. Massachusetts Spy, *January 28*

1830: I s'pose a Governor has a right to flog anybody he's a mind to.
Seba Smith, Major Jack Downing, *p.87*

1878: Well, figger it as you're a mind to; maybe you'll die of somethin' else after all. *Rose T. Cooke,* Happy Dodd, *ch.xii*

mitten, to get or give the: a lady, in turning down a proposal, is said to give the gentleman the mitten.

1838: Young gentlemen who have got the mitten, and young gentlemen who think they are going to get the mitten, always sythe [sigh].
Joseph C. Neal, Petter Ploddy, *p.14*

1853: Uncle Jo's gal gin him the mitten, to the singing school.
Turnover, A Tale of New Hampshire, *p.8*

1855: He went off suddenly to California; likely enough, Kitty gave him the mitten. *D.G. Mitchell,* Fudge Doings, *p.116*

mosey: to saunter or shuffle along.

1836: You're not going to smoke me. So mosey off.
Philadelphia Public Ledger, *December 2*

1846: Lanty Oliphant! bawled Dogberry; . . . Mosey in and be sworn.
A Quarter Race in Kentucky, *p.38*

1888: A third moseyed off some distance, to sit down and lick his wounds. Chicago Inter-Ocean, *February 6*

most: used for almost.

1815: Dorothy vows she will heat some water and scald any man that comes for any further taxes. I'm most afraid to see a stranger ride up. Massachusetts Spy, *June 14*

1830: I'm plagued most to death with these ere pesky sore eyes. Massachusetts Spy, *October 13*

1840: I reckon he drank most two quarts of [catmint tea] through the night. *A.B. Longstreet*, Georgia Scenes, *p.193*

mought: used for might, especially in Philadelphia, where Cockneyisms (see entry) were popular.

1843: It was about two o'clock, he guessed it mought be more, or it mought be less. *Cornelius Mathews*, Writings, *p.14*

1848: You mought as well look for a needle in a haystack, as try to find a nigger in New York. *Major Jones*, Sketches of Travel, *p.12*

1855: The reglar Fakilty mout have save life, then agin they mout not. Knickerbocker Magazine, *March*

mudsill: the uneducated, working class.

1858: In all social systems there must be a class to do the menial duties, to perform the drudgery of life. That is, a class requiring but a low order of intellect and but little skill. . . . It constitutes the very mudsill of society and of political government. *Mr. Hammond, South Carolina, U.S. Senate*, Congressional Globe, *March 4, p.71*

1862: [The secessionists] speak of the labouring millions of the free States as the mudsills of society, as a pauper banditti, as greasy mechanics and filthy operatives. *Mr. Julian, Indiana, House of Reps.*, Congressional Globe, *January 14, p.328*

1863: It pleased certain Southern orators and writers to characterize [the North] as the abode of the mudsills and tinkers. *O.J. Victor*, History of the Southern Rebellion, *p.93*

nigger in the woodpile: a way of explaining the disappearance of fuel or any unsolved mystery.

1862: These gentlemen . . . spoke two whole hours . . . in showing—to borrow an elegant phrase, the paternity of which belongs, I think, to their side of the House—that there was a nigger in the woodpile. *Mr. Kelley, Pennsylvania, House of Reps.*, Congressional Globe, *June 3, p.2527*

no-account: worthless.

1853: Yes, Massa, dem no 'count calves done fool me again. *Paxton*, A Stray Yankee in Texas, *p.282*

1881: Mitchell of Oregon is another of the no-account men. Philadelphia Record, *February 8*

1888: Did I come way off down in this here no count country to wash white counterpanes for dogs? *Mrs. Elizabeth Custer*, Tenting on the Plains, *p.255*

nohow, no way you can fix it: not at all.

1833: They don't raise such humans in the Old Dominion, no how. *James Hall,* Harpe's Head, *p.91*

1833: This ain't no part of a priming to places that I've seed afore, no how. *James Hall,* Legends of the West, *p.190*

1836: [They] would have nothing to do with the affair, nohow they could fix it. Colonel Crockett in Texas, *p.125*

1843: I couldn't read a chapter in the Bible no how you could fix it, bless the Lord! *R. Carlton,* The New Purchase, *p.141*

1854: Here's my six-shooter, but you can't toll me up thar, nohow. Knickerbocker Magazine, *June*

not by a jugful: not at all.

1835: Did you ever follow the business of peddling? Not by a jugful, Mister; I never was one of your wooden nutmeg fellers. *D.P. Thompson,* Adventures of Timothy Peacock, *p.87*

1854: Take medicine, said I. "Not by a jugful," said Jim. *H.H. Riley,* Puddleford, *p.162*

1855: Not by a jugful, Mr. Souley; Cuba is the most valuable patch of ground we've got. *Seba Smith,* Major Jack Downing, *p.429*

notions: a wide range of miscellaneous articles for sale.

1819: This cleared up the mystery of the toys and play-things, which, with hats, bonnets, shoes and stockings of various sizes, [and] Webster's spelling-books, were part of the notions. *"An Englishman," in the* Western Star, *May 12*

1830: I thought I'd go and see about my load of turkeys and other notions. *Seba Smith,* Major Jack Downing, *p.49*

1846: She had a cargo of notions, consisting of Boston china, onions, apples, coffins in nests, cheese, potatoes, etc. *Cornelius Mathews,* Writings, *p.309*

odds, ask no: ask no favor.

1857: I ask no odds of them, no more than I do of the dirt I walk on. *H.C. Kimball at the Bowery, Salt Lake City,* Journal of Discourses, *July 12*

1857: I swore I would send them to hell across lots if they meddled with me; and I ask no more odds of all hell today. *Brigham Young,* Journal of Discourses, *July 26, p.78*

off the reel: immediately.

1833: [I had a mind] to have a fight with him off the reel, and settle the right of soil at once. *J.K. Paulding,* Banks of the Ohio, *p.78*

1856: You have got to promise right off the reel that you won't say another word. *Harriet Beecher Stowe,* Dred, *ch.xlviii*

old man, old woman: one's spouse. Also, one's father or mother.

1843: "He's your old man, mam?" Mrs. C. assented.
R. Carlton, The New Purchase, *p.62*

1855: As we were talk about the war [she] said . . . "What does your old man think about it?" I answered as well as I could, and am amused at this appellation, purely western, she has given my husband.
Sara Robinson, Kansas, *p.138*

1859: [She] feels that she has a right to spend every cent that the old man allows her. *J.G. Holland,* Titcomb's Letters, *p.195*

old orchard: whiskey.

1810: Come, ye lovers of Old Orchard, let us take a walk into the fields.
Robert Thomas, The Farmer's Almanack, *September*

1844: The old orchard went merrily around . . . tea, coffee, and old orchard served to wash down the good things. Lowell Offering

one-horse: small, limited, inferior.

1854: I'm done with one-horse bedsteads, I am.
Aneed, New York Journal of Commerce

1857: A Mormon elder says he has visited and preached in the following places in Texas: Empty-Bucket, Rake-pocket, Doughplate, Bucksnort, Possum Trot, Buzzard Roost, Hardscrabble, Nippentuck, and Lickskillet; most of which, however, he says, are merely one-horse towns. Harper's Weekly, *November 14*

1858: A country clergyman, with a one-story intellect and a one-horse vocabulary. Autocrat of the Breakfast Table, *ch.ii*

1859: Close by the little one-horse church, skirted by the belt of cedars.
Knickerbocker Magazine, *March*

opine: to be of the opinion.

1830: Not a few leeches in that city, we opine, will vote for him.
Northern Watchman, *August 17*

1842: [General Winfield Scott] had better keep his fingers to scratch his own ears with, we opine. Philadelphia Spirit of the Times, *August 27*

1854: We opine that he would have carried with him . . . prayers and good wishes. Weekly Oregonian, *October 7*

ornary: mean.

1830: You ornery fellow! do you pretend to call me to account for my language? Massachusetts Spy, *July 28*

1854: [He was] sent to Freehold court-house last term for 'busin' his wife. Awful ornary! Knickerbocker Magazine, *March*

1857: That poor ornary cuss of a red-haired, cross-eyed grocery-keeper.
Knickerbocker Magazine, *November*

painter, panter: popular pronunciation and spelling of panther.

1803: My master . . . said that I ought to live among painters and wolves,

and sold me to a Georgia man for two hundred dollars.
John Davis, Travels in the U.S.A., *p.382*

1845: It might be a painter that stirred [the dog], for he could scent that beast a great distance. *W.G. Simms*, The Wigwam and the Cabin, *p.48*

1850: The bar and painter got so sassy, that they'd cum to the tother side of the bayou, and see which could talk impudenest. "Don't you want some bar meat or painter blanket?" they'd ask; bars is monstrous fat, and painter's hide is mighty warm. Odd Leaves, *p.170*

pardner, pard: friendly variation of partner, popularly used in mining camps.

1854: Pardners keep clus arter one another.
H.H. Riley, Puddleford, *p.126*

1883: The mine is wirked by two pardners, who dig and wash by turns.
D. Pidgeon, An Engineer's Holiday, *p.132*

1893: Many an old hunter has buried his pard in the Missouri River.
Alex Major, Seventy Years on the Frontier, *p.260*

peaked: thin or sickly in appearance.

1859: He looks peakeder than ever. Professor at the Breakfast Table, *ch.9*

1860: I lived on bread-and-milk nearly six weeks, until my face grew as peaked as a crow's beak. Yale Literary Magazine, *xxv, p.169*

1871: His mother was jest about the poorest, peakedest old body over to Sherburne. *Harriet Beecher Stowe*, Miss Elderkin's Pitcher

1878: When I came here, she was as peaked as a young rat.
Rose T. Cooke, Happy Dodd, *ch.36*

peart: fresh and happy; sprightly.

1820: These little fixins make a man feel right peart.
Hall, Letters from the West, *p.304*

1833: I wish that fellow would shut the door; he must think that we were all raised in a saw-mill; and then he looks so peart whenever he comes in. *C.F. Hoffman*, A Winter in the Far West, *p.209*

1888: [The boys] from being starved, wretched, and dull, grew quite peart under [Eliza's] good care.
Mrs. Elizabeth Custer, Tenting on the Plains, *p.171*

person of color: a Negro.

1801: People of color. . . . This new fangled name for the black race, which has . . . crept into the vocabulary of the U.S., seems to have been borrowed from that fruitful source of innovations, the philosophical school of Paris. "Z," Port Folio, *p.163*

1806: At the white ball-room [in New Orleans] no lady of colour is admitted. *Thomas Ashe*, Travels in America

1815: [Died] in Grafton, Sarah, a woman of color.
Massachusetts Spy, *November 29*

1833: "Well, as I was saying, the nigger" — "I think he might call um gemman of choler," muttered blackey.

J.K. Paulding, Banks of the Ohio, *p.213*

Philadelphia lawyer: popularly credited with nearly superhuman intellect by the masses.

1803: It would puzzle a dozen Philadelphia lawyers to unriddle the conduct of the democrats. Balance, *November 15, p.363*

1824: The New England folks have a saying, that three Philadelphia lawyers are a match for the very devil himself. Salem Observer, *March 13*

1824: Politics has got into a jumble that a Philadelphy lawyer couldn't steer through them. *John P. Kennedy,* Quodlibet, *p.160*

1848: It would puzzle a Philadelphia lawyer to pint out the latitude of enything like [the United States] in all creation.

W.E. Burton, Waggeries, *p.68*

picayune: used to signify something small or frivolous. (See also Money and Coinage, p.148.)

1837: The hon. senator from Kentucky by way of ridicule calls this a picayune bill.

Mr. Young, Illinois, U.S. Senate, Congressional Globe, *December 22*

1841: Some gentlemen affected to consider it a small concern, a picayune affair.

Mr. Underwood, Kentucky, House of Reps., Congressional Globe, *February 20*

picture: one's face; one's person.

1825: Young Bob's dad — consarn his pictur — spry as a cat, swom like a fish. *John Neal,* Brother Jonathan, *iii, p.387*

1829: "Consarn his picture!" said Jeff in a low tone.

John P. Kennedy, Swallow Barn, *p.448*

1847: Wall, my sister Marth made me a bran new pair of buckskin trowsers to go in, and rile my pictur if she didn't put stirrups to 'em to keep 'em down. *Robb,* Streaks of Squatter Life, *p.61*

pile on the agony: to add insult to injury.

1852: If you have any more agony to pile on him, put it on.

Knickerbocker Magazine, *October*

1856: I haven't piled on the agony as I might have done.

Knickerbocker Magazine, *December*

1857: Three raving, lying, free-negro journals, is piling up the agony a little too steep. Oregon Weekly Times, *November 14*

plank, plank down, plank up: to pay in cash.

1824: His guardy was sent for, and he planked the cash.

Nantucket Inquirer, *April 19*

1835: His patient returned, and, planking ten dollars, took possession of her invaluable medicine.

Daniel P. Thompson, Adventures of Timothy Peacock, *p.104*

1851: He would plank down the very money he had received.

Daniel B. Woods, Sixteen Months at the Gold Diggings, *p.75*

plug-ugly: a Baltimore rowdy; any rowdy or ruffian.

1857: The city of Baltimore, from whose midst the plug uglies claim to hail. Oregon Weekly Times, *August 1*

1863: Colonel Butler is a tall, fully developed, imposing man, devoid of the slightest resemblance to an ideal Plug Ugly.

James Parton, Butler in New Orleans, *p.79*

1865: A brawny fellow, with a plug-ugly countenance, looked over my shoulder at the book. *A.D. Richardson,* The Secret Service, *p.108*

plum, plumb: entirely; completely.

1850: His breeches split plum across with the strain, and the piece of wearin' truk wot's next the skin made a monstrous putty flag.

Odd Leaves, *p.51*

1858: He wur plum crazy an' jumped over the frunt ov the pulpit.

Olympia Pioneer, *February 26*

1893: "You're plumb crazy," she remarked. Harper's Weekly, *p.1211*

plunder: personal belongings; baggage.

1815: We heard these men uniformly calling their baggage plunder.

T. Flint, Recollections, *p.6*

1817: [We carried] our plunder (as the Virginians call baggage) in a light Jersey wagon. *J.K. Paulding,* Letters from the South, *p.38*

1818: When you arrive at a house [in Kentucky], the first inquiry is, where is your plunder? as if you were a bandit; and out is sent a slave to bring in your plunder: i.e. your trunk, or valise.

Arthur Singleton, Letters from the South and West, *p.106*

1842: [In Virginia] you hear the driver say, "Here, you nigger fellow, tote this lady's plunder to her room." Upstairs is pronounced "upstarrs"; the words "bear" and "fear" are pronounced "barr" and "farr"; and one passenger was told, "The room upstarrs is quite preparred, so that your plunder may be toted . . . whenever you've a mind."

J.S. Buckingham, Slave States, *p.293*

pony up, post the pony: pay up.

1838: It was my job to pay all the bills. "Salix, pony up at the bar, and lend us a levy." *J.C. Neal,* Charcoal Sketches

poor as Job's turkey: very poor.

1840s: The professor is as poor as Job's turkey, if it wasn't for that powerful salary the trustees give him.

R. Carlton, The New Purchase, *Vol. II, p.85*

powerful: great; extreme; a large quantity.

1833: Gentlemen, good evening; this has been a powerful hot day.
James Hall, Harpe's Head, *p.86*

1835: He was powerful tired. *Washington Irving,* Tour of the Prairies, *ch.xiii*

1869: Our men has mostly gone across to Californy to see what's the chances for fodder. Folks tell us it's powerful dry over there.
J. Ross Browne, Apache Country, *p.461*

pucker: in a state of irritation or anger.

1826: My wife will be in a fine pucker when she finds this sum exhausted. Massachusetts Spy, *November 1*

1837: A terrier dog in a pucker is a good study for anger.
J.C. Neal, Charcoal Sketches, *p.124*

1847: If I am delayed, Blair and Rives will get in a pucker.
Robb, Streaks of Squatter Life, *p.15*

puke: a Missourian.

1838: The suckers of Illinoy, the pukes of Missouri, and the corncrackers of Virginia. *Haliburton,* The Clockmaker, *ii, p.289*

1852: Sundry Hoosiers, Buckeyes, Suckers, Pukes, and Wolvereens, all wide awake, and ready for business. Knickerbocker Magazine, *April*

1856: You can search the house, but as for this puke of a Missourian, he shall not come in. *Sara Robinson,* Kansas, *p.205*

pull foot: to leave in a hurry.

1825: Yah! how [the Indians] pulled foot, when they seed us comin'.
John Neal, Brother Jonathan, *p.107*

1831: Jerry pulled foot for home like a streak of lightning.
Seba Smith, Major Jack Downing, *p.142*

1837: He had pulled foot for Baltimore, and sold the rest of his tooth powder. Philadelphia Public Ledger, *March 6*

quilting bee: a social event in which women get together to make a quilt.

1832: The females have . . . meetings called quilting bees, when many assemble to work for one, in padding or quilting bed coverings or comforters. *S.G. Goodrich,* System of Universal Geography, *p.107*

1835: He informed us that his wife had got a number of her neighbors with her for a quilting frolic.
C.J. Latrobe, The Rambler in North America, *p.135*

rambunctious: rowdy, disorderly or boisterous.

1847: [An old he-bar] is as ramstugonous an animal as a log-cabin loafer in the dog-days. A Swim for a Deer, *p.120*

1851: The old lady bawled out, "There comes our ramstuginous little doctor." An Arkansaw Doctor, *p.81*

1856: You rambunctious old wool-grower!
San Francisco Call, *December 17*

reckon: to think or guess.

1819: Asking very civilly, "Can we breakfast here?" I have received a shrill "I reckon so." Massachusetts Spy, *January 8*

1855: Boys say with us, and everywhere, I reckon, "You worry my dog, and I'll worry your cat."
Dr. Ross, Tennessee, in the "New School" General Assembly, Buffalo

retiracy: retirement.

1843: I'd a powerful sight sooner go into retiracy, nor consent to that bill. *R. Carlton,* The New Purchase, *p.74*

1851: If we didn't elect him, I'd go into retiracy.
Seba Smith, Major Jack Downing, *p.341*

ride out on a rail: to be forced to leave town.

1866: Others proposed giving him a good coat of tar and feathers, and riding him out of town on a rail. *Seba Smith,* Way Down East, *p.251*

rip-roaring, rip-staver, rip-snortin': an impressive person or thing.

1833: In ten minutes he yelled enough, and swore I was a rip-stavur.
Sketches of Davy Crockett, *p.144*

1846: What a rip-snortin' red head you have got! Yale Literary Magazine

1856: "Hallo, Judge," said Major H., "that's a rip-roaring hat you've got." San Francisco Call, *December 19*

rum-hole: a small drinking establishment, especially in New York.

1872: The State of New York alone, we believe, uses the term rum-holes for its smaller grog shops. *De Vere*

Sabbaday, Sabberday: the Sabbath day.

1833: He makes poetry himself sabbadays—made more poetry 'an you could shake a stick at. *John Neal,* The Downeasters, *p.135*

1848: Capting, I sorter recking it ain't entered into your kalkilation as this here is Sabberday. *W.E. Burton,* Waggeries, *p.16*

sakes alive: the equivalent of good heavens or for God's sake.

1846: "Law sakes alive," was the reply, "I ain't no how."
Mrs. Kirkland, Western Clearings, *p.78*

Salt River: to row someone up Salt River is to beat him up or to give him hell.

1833: See if I don't row you up Salt River before you are many days older. *J.K. Paulding,* Banks of the Ohio, *p.133*

1838: When you want to be rowed up Salt River again, just tip me with the wink. *B. Drake,* Tales and Sketches, *p.36*

1843: If I don't row you up Salt Crick in less nor no time, my name's not Sam Townsend. *R. Carlton,* The New Purchase, *p.261*

Sam Hill: euphemism for the devil.

1839: What in sam hill is that feller ballin' about?
"Major Jack on a Whaler," Havana Republican, *August 21*

1868: He had bought him a little bobtailed mouse-colored mule, and was training him like Sam Hill.
Mrs. Elizabeth Custer, Following the Guidon, *p.142*

savage as a meat axe: extremely savage.

1835: A little dried up man, who was whetting his knife against the side of the fire-place, and looking as savage as a meat axe.
James Hall, Tales of the Border, *p.58*

1842: Ridin' makes one as savage as a meat axe.
Mrs. Kirkland, Forest Life, *p.126*

savagerous: savage.

1837: The strongest man in Kentucky, and the most sevagerous at a tussle. *R.M. Bird,* Nick of the Woods, *p.96*

1849: The turtle popped out its head, and rolled its eyes, while a sort of wheeze issued from its savagerous mouth. Frontier Guardian, *August 8*

school ma'am, school-marm: a woman teacher.

1840: At the age of fifteen were we qualified for the responsible station of country schoolma'ams. Lowell Offering, *p.74*

1864: Before this day of larger ideas, to be a school-ma'am was to be a stiff, conceited, formal, critical character.
J.G. Holland, Letters to the Joneses, *p.254*

1878: He up and married one o' them school-marms sent out from Boston. *J.H. Beadle,* Western Wilds, *p.188*

seed: often used for saw or seen.

1825: Yah! how [the Indians] pulled foot, when they seed us comin. *John Neal,* Brother Jonathan, *p.107*

set by, set much by: to regard; to esteem. From early in the century.

set store by, to: to set value upon; to appreciate.

1840s: He [the Ohio boatman] observed very feelingly, that he set more store to this song than to all the rest. *Hall,* Letters from the West

seven by nine: something or someone of inferior or common quality, originating from common window panes of that size.

1846: [The charge was] re-echoed by every little paltry seven by nine Locofoco print, and every brawling bar-room politician.
Mr. Root, Ohio, House of Reps., Congressional Globe, *December 24*

shakes, great: of great consequence.
1825: I'm no great shakes at braggin' — I never was.
John Neal, Brother Jonathan, *p.195*

shaw, pshaw!: an expression of contempt or incredulity.
1845: O, shaw, 'taint gwine to rain, no how, and I'm all fixed.
W.T. Thompson, Chronicles of Pineville, *p.165*
1846: She hollered fur her fiddler, but oh, shaw, he couldn't do hir a bit of good. Quarter Race, *p.89*
1850: P'shaw, gal, your wits are turned through going to school.
Knickerbocker Magazine, *September*
1857: Psha! nonsense! will nothing satisfy you?
Knickerbocker Magazine, *May*

shecoonery: a corruption of chicanery.
1845: This town's got a monstrous bad name for meanery and she-coonery of all sorts. *W.T. Thompson,* Chronicles of Pineville, *p.47*

shines, to cut: to pull practical jokes or tricks; to make funny business.
1839: We cut a few shines with the girls, and started to the tavern.
History of Virgil A. Stewart, *p.69*
1842: It is said that some females in England cut up a shine in order to go to Botany Bay, where they are sure of finding husbands.
Philadelphia Spirit of the Times, *September 15*
1851: My horse snorted, he kicked, he rared up, and cut more shines than a snapping turtle on hot iron. An Arkansaw Doctor, *p.87*

shucks: worthless people or things (from corn or pea shucks).
1847: He ain't wuth shucks, and ef you don't lick him for his onmannerly note, you ain't wuth shucks, nuther. *Robb,* Streaks of Squatter Life, *p.135*
1851: I kalkilated them curs o' hisn wasn't worth shucks in a bar fight.
Polly Peablossom's Wedding, *p.51*

shut pan: shut up; shut your mouth.
1833: Shut pan, and sing small, or I'll throw you into the drink.
J.K. Paulding, Banks of the Ohio, *p.213*
1835: I shut pan on the subject, and fell to eating my dinner.
Colonel Crockett's Tour, *p.102*
1853: Spicer raised his hand to stop the speech, but the lawyer wouldn't shut pan. *Paxton,* A Stray Yankee in Texas, *p.139*

sin to Moses, sin to Crockett: something that would shame either Moses or Davy Crockett.
1833: The way he fights is a sin to Crockett.
Sketches of Davy Crockett, *p.30*
1838: "Ay, ay, sir; it's a sin to Moses, such a trade . . . ," said the stoker.
E. Flagg, The Far West, *p.71*

1861: The way some of your city wags stuff our honest clod-hoppers is a sin to Moses. Oregon Argus, *March 23*

skedaddle: to flee.

1861: No sooner did the traitors discover their approach than they skedaddled, a phrase the Union boys up here apply to the good use the seceshers make of their legs in time of danger. Missouri Democrat, *August*

1862: Skadaddle is a newly invented word, now greatly in vogue among our brave soldiers on the Potomac. It is equivalent to the verb to absquatulate, and is like that other army verb (to vamose) which our soldiers brought from their campaign in Mexico.
Oregon Argus, *January 18*

skeery: to be afraid or cautious.

1845: I was skeery and bashful at first, in meeting with a young and beautiful creature like her. *W.G. Simms*, The Wigwam and the Cabin, *p.108*

1847: I ain't easy skeer'd, but I own up that old fellow did kind a make me skeery. *Robb*, Streaks of Squatter Life, *p.144*

1851: My! I feel so skeary-like, for I've never been aboard one of these steaming boats. *Lady E.S. Wortley*, Travels, *p.108*

slantindicular: slanting.

1832: This is sorter a slantindickelar road, stranger [said the Yankee].
Memoirs of a Nullifier, *p.37*

1833: He looked up at me slantendicular, and I looked down at him slantendicular; and he took out a chaw of turbaccur, and said he, "I don't value you that." Sketches of Davy Crockett, *p.144*

slick: to fix or dress up.

1840: Mr. F. was slicked up for the occasion.
Mrs. Kirkland, A New Home, *p.243*

1847: H. went to work, loading up his big bore, with as much care as a girl fixes herself when she slicks up. The Great Kalamazoo Hunt, *p.44*

smart, right: a large quantity.

1842: I asked whether the people made much maple-sugar when a planter answered, "Yes, they do, I reckon, right smart," meaning in great quantities. *J.S. Buckingham*, Slave States, *p.327*

1855: Thar ain't been much rain lately, but thar's right smart of snow, and its about half melted snow. *Farnham*, Travels in Prairie Land, *p.361*

1856: I sold right smart of eggs dis yer summer.
Harriet Beecher Stowe, Dred, *ch.39*

smart as a steel trap: particularly intelligent and quick.

1830: A feller with an eye like a hawk, and quick as a steel trap, for a trade. *Seba Smith*, Major Jack Downing, *p.49*

1856: [A little girl] with sparkling, intelligent eyes, thin, expressive lips, and as smart as a steel trap. Knickerbocker Magazine, *September*

smile: a drink; to take a drink.

1852: I imbibed a final smile to my own health, and left my allies alone.
Yale Literary Magazine

1870: [This gentleman] asked me to smile. I had learned by experience that this is the slang phrase for taking a drink. I smiled all the more readily, because the morning was intensely cold.
W.F. Rae, Westward by Rail, *p.337*

1888: We took a smile of old Bourbon apiece.
Chicago Inter-Ocean, *February 6*

soaplock: a rowdy. Named after a hairstyle (cut short behind and long in front and parted to fall below the ears on the sides, sometimes as far as the collar) worn by such a rowdy.

1840: In that living, moving, ranting band, the boys, negroes, loafers, and a new species of the same animal, familiarly known in the city of New York as soap-locks, took the lead.
Mr. Watterson, Tennessee, House of Reps., Congressional Globe, *April 2, p.376*

1840: The hostility between the Yankee soap locks and the Dutch musicians, in regard to Ellsler serenade, has come to a happy termination.
Daily Pennant, St. Louis, *September 12*

1848: You will behave yourselves as men, patriots, and gentlemen should; and not like soaplocks and rowdies. *Dow*, Patent Sermons, *p.164*

sockdologer: a powerful punch or blow.

1837: I hit him one polt—it was what I call a sogdolloger—that made him dance like a ducked cat. *R.M Bird*, The Hawks of Hawk-hollow, *p.105*

1848: As I aimed a sockdollager at him, he ducked his head.
Jones's Fight, *p.41*

1860: Anti rushed on, with great force, and planted a sockdologer on the bridge of Wheel-horse's smeller. Oregon Argus, *June 16*

some pumpkins: someone or something impressive.

1846: One of them thinks he's got a scrub [horse] that's some pumpkins.
A Quarter Race in Kentucky, *p.118*

1851: We went on until the third or fourth set, and I thought I was some pumpkins at dancing. An Arkansaw Doctor, *p.97*

1853: "Got a smart chunk of a pony thar." "Yes, Sir, he is some pumpkins sure; offered ten cows and calves for him; he's death on a quarter." *Paxton*, A Stray Yankee in Texas, *p.44*

sot: a corruption of set or sat.

1833: The elegantest carriage that ever mortal man sot eyes on.
James Hall, Legend of the West, *p.185*

1837: Why don't you buy a digestion of the laws, so as to know what's right and what's wrong? It's all sot down.
J.C. Neal, Charcoal Sketches, *p.189*

1857: Well, Squire, I sot right down on a stone.
J.G. Holland, The Bay Path, p.197

sour on: to get sick of someone or something; to give up something out of disgust.

1862: Guess the M.P. will sour on William C., when he has seen him for about fifteen minutes. Rocky Mountain News, *Denver, November 20*

spree: to go out on a spree is to go out and carouse; to party and get drunk.

1834: He is not quarrelsome, even when he gets caught in what they call in the West a spree. *Albert Pike, Sketches, p.32*

1846: [He had] struck him with a fire-brand, and burnt his body in several places, during a drunken spree.
Rufus Sage, Scenes in the Rocky Mountains, p.73

1864: You came into the neighborhood with a cigar in your mouth, and a reputation for spreeing. *J.G. Holland, Letters to the Joneses, p.229*

Square: sometimes used for Squire.

1850: Look o' here, Square, one o' them quarters you gin me last was a pistareen. Knickerbocker Magazine, *February*

1857: Well, Square, I don't feel in fighting trim.
J.G. Holland, The Bay Path, p.55

squatter: one who settles on land without legal title, a widespread practice in the West. (See also Cowboys and the Wild West, p.250.)

1809: This unceremonious mode of taking possession of new land was technically termed squatting, and hence is derived the appellation of squatters. *Washington Irving, History of New York, p.188*

1810: If the nation were put to action against every Squatter, for the recovery of their lands, we should only have law suits, no lands for sale. *Thomas Jefferson, "The Batture at New Orleans," Works, viii, p.588*

1821: A squatter is a person who plants himself in the wilderness upon any piece of ground which he likes, without purchasing it of the proprietor. Large tracts have been occupied in this manner.
T. Dwight, Travels, p.221

Squire: a justice of the peace or magistrate.

1817: He is not in the least danger of receiving an uncivil answer, even if he should address himself to a square. *John Bradbury, Travels, p.320*

1822: It was proposed by some of them to couple themselves, and go to a young Justice and be married. This it was thought would be fine fun, and a clever joke on the young Squire. Massachusetts Spy, *May 22*

1844: I've snaked it about these woods for a week, looking for a squire to hitch us. Yale Literary Magazine, *x, p.167*

States, the: used in the western territories to denote the organized states back east.

1845: Here we met Dr. White, a sub-Indian agent, accompanied by three others, on their way from Oregon to the States.
Joel Palmer, Journal, *p.50*

1854: President Young says he does not know of but one old bachelor in all the Territory of Utah, and he has gone to the States.
Orson Hyde, at the Mormon Tabernacle, Journal of Discourses, *October 6, ii, p.84*

1857: A man writing from Southern Oregon to the N.Y. Tribune says that some of the people are going to California, and others are talking of going back to America. New York Tribune

steady habits: the land of steady habits was New England.

1813: Troops were assembled, ready to repel any invasion of the soil of steady habits. Massachusetts Spy, *June 16*

1828: Ours is the land of steady habits. And this town is remarkable for severity of religious discipline, if not for morality.
Yankee, *Portland, Maine, April 2*

1830: A real blue-nose, fresh from the land of steady habits.
Northern Watchman, *Troy, New York, November 30*

store: the word shop was used most popularly throughout the 1700s but gradually gave way to store in the early 1800s.

1883: In America, the word shop is confined to the place where things are made or done, as barber-shop, carpenter-shop; a place where things are sold is a store. *E.A. Freeman,* Impressions of the U.S., *p.61*

streaked: frightened or annoyed.

1834: I felt streaked enough, for the balls were whistling over our heads.
Seba Smith, Major Jack Downing, *p.18*

1878: I felt orful streaked, but I knowed [my rifle] had never failed yet.
J.H. Beadle, Western Wilds, *p.416*

suspicion: to suspect.

1834: They began to suspicion, maybe, that they had got the wrong sow by the ear. The Kentuckian in New York, *p.64*

1836: I suspicion he's one of that bounding brotherhood.
Knickerbocker Magazine, *January*

1851: He didn't know I was thar. If he had er suspicioned it, he'd no more swore than he'd dar'd kiss my Sal.
Polly Peablossom's Wedding, *p.51*

1890: They kinder suspicioned from my looks that I had found good prospects. *Haskins,* Argonauts of California, *p.250*

tote: to carry.

1833: In our day, merchants were well enough satisfied to tote their plunder upon mules and pack horses. *James Hall,* Legends of the West, *p.49*

1833: I brought at four turns as much as I could tote, and put it on the bank. Sketches of Davy Crockett, *p.103*

1851: Thar goes as clever a feller as ever toted an ugly head.
Adventures of Captain Simon Suggs, *p.140*

1852: I heard it said when I was a child, that it was allowable to make the Devil tote brick to build a church.
Mr. Stanly, North Carolina, House of Reps., Congressional Globe, *June 12, p.693*

trace: a trail or path.

1829: George offered to take the trace through the woods to the bank of the Mississippi, where the physician resided.
Timothy Flint, George Mason, *p.41*

1833: On either side was the thick forest, sometimes grown up with underbrush to the margin of the trace.
James Hall, Legends of the West, *p.187*

1834: The trace had been rudely cut out by some of the earlier travellers through the Indian country, merely traced out, — and hence perhaps the name — by a blaze, or white spot, made upon the trees by hewing them from the bark. *W.G. Simms,* Guy Rivers, *p.62*

truck, spun truck: garden produce intended for market. Later, it came to mean any quantity of "stuff."

1833: [It was remarked that] it took a powerful chance of truck to feed such a heap of folks. *James Hall,* Legends of the West, *p.9*

1840: And what did they do for Lucy's cough, Mis' Barney? O dear me, they gin her a powerful chance o' truck. I reckon, first and last, she took at least a pint o' lodimy. *A.B. Longstreet,* Georgia Scenes, *p.193*

1857: Women exchanging their wool-socks, bees' wax, tow-linen, etc., for spun truck, apron check, dye-stuff, and so on.
Knickerbocker Magazine, *August*

1862: School larnin is mighty poor truck to put into a feller's head, onless he's got a good deal of brains there.
Seba Smith, Major Jack Downing, *December 6*

tuckered out: exhausted.

1853: Set us to runnin, an I could tucker him; but he would beat me to jumpin, all holler. *Turnover,* A Tale of New Hampshire, *p.59*

1857: You got all tuckered out, playin' and runnin' out doors, and would come in with your eyes lookin' as heavy as lead.
J.G. Holland, The Bay Path, *p.59*

vamose: to leave quickly.

1848: The united faces of the company would have reached a mile. They bolted, mizzled, flew, vamosed. *Stray Subjects, p.198*

1855: Our hero vamosed rather hurriedly. Oregon Weekly Times, *June 16*

1857: Another pair of jail-birds have vamosed the log jail at Jacksonville. The new institution, it is hoped, will not prove so leaky.
Oregon Weekly Times, *August 1*

varment, varmint: a wild animal or objectional person.

1827: They scent plunder; and it would be as hard to drive a hound from his game as to throw the varmints [Indians] from its trail.
James Fenimore Cooper, The Prairie, p.93

1837: The fossil remnant of some antediluvian varmint, in the shape of a molar tooth, was dug up. Baltimore Commerical Transcript, *August 25*

1842: Killed. A mad dog in Locust Street yesterday. The varmint had run into the midst of a colored temperance meeting.
Philadelphia Spirit of the Times, *June 6*

1858: For nearly a fortnight a regular live comet has been visible. Time of appearance, early in the evening. It is rumored to us that the same varmint is occasionally seen flitting athwart the sky of mornings.
Oregon Weekly Times, *October 2*

Virginia fence: a staggering drunk was said to make this (a zig-zagging fence) when he walked. Anyone or anything that meanders. Any fence constructed in this manner.

1824: You pass no stone walls [in Virginia] but hedge, or in-and-out zig-zag cedar rails, or wattled fences.
Arthur Singleton, Letters from the South and West, p.59

1826: The universal fence [in the West] is split rails, laid in a worm trail, or what is known in the North by the name of Virginia fence.
T. Flint, Recollections, p. 206

1853: His acres were enclosed with harsh stone walls, or an unpicturesque Virginia fence, with its zig-zag of rude rails.
Life Scenes, *p.99*

wake snakes: to raise a ruckus.

1848: This goin' ware glory waits ye hain't one agree'ble feetur. An ef it worn't for wakin' snakes, I'd come home again short meter.
Biglow Papers, *No.2*

1852: Wake snakes, and come to judgement—the times are big with the fate of nations.
Mr. Brown, Mississippi, House of Reps., Congressional Globe, March 30, p.359

want to know: a New England expression equivalent to today's "Really? What else happened?"

1842: Among the peculiar expressions in use in Maine we noticed that, when a person has communicated some intelligence in which the hearer feels an interest, he manifests it by saying "I want to know"; and when he has concluded his narrative, the hearer will reply "O! do tell!" *J.S. Buckingham,* Eastern and Western States, *p.177*

1853: Jedediah Homespun up and spent a quarter to see the Siamese Twins (Eng and Chang). "How long you fellows been in this 'ere hitch?" "Forty-two years," was Eng's reply. "Du tell! Gettin' kind o' used to it, I calculate, ain't you?" "We ought to," said they. "Want to know! wall, I swar you air hitched queer. Weekly Oregonian, *September 3*

whip: to defeat or beat an opponent.

1815: If the enemy attack us in our present position, we must whip five to one. Massachusetts Spy, *February 8*

1838: Three hundred Indian warriors have thought proper to whip, on our soil, two companies of militia. Jeffersonian, *Albany, June 23*

1852: I felt as though I could whip all the mobs in Missouri.
Ezra T. Benson, at the Mormon Tabernacle, Journal of Discourses, *August 28, vi, p.263*

whip one's weight in wild cats: to defeat a powerful opponent.

1829: Every man who could whip his weight in wild cats burned with desire of reaping renown by an encounter with Francisco.
Massachusetts Spy, *February 11*

1841: That confidence of a western man, which induces him to believe that he can whip his weight in wild cats, is no vain boast.
A Week in Wall Street, *p.46*

whitewash: to gloss over or hide one's faults or shortcomings.

1800: If you do not whitewash [President Adams] speedily, the Democrats, like swarms of flies, will bespatter him all over, and make you both as speckled as a dirty wall, and as black as the devil.
Aurora, *Philadelphia, July 21*

1839: I am confident every effort will be used by the committee to whitewash the black frauds and corrupt iniquities of Swartwout, and to blackwash the Administration.
Mr. Duncan, Ohio, House of Reps., Congressional Globe, *January 17, p.103*

wrathy: angry.

1834: This kinder corner'd me, and made me a little wrathy.
Seba Smith, Major Jack Downing, *p.90*

1842: Oh! you're wrothy, an't ye? Why, I didn't mean nothing but what was civil. *Mrs. Kirkland,* Forest Life, *i, p.126*

1857: On Sunday morning, if breakfast is delayed, he is apt to be wrathy.
Thomas B. Gunn, New York Boarding Houses, *p.34*

1888: Some grew hot and wrathy if laughed at, and that increased our fun. *Mrs. Elizabeth Custer,* Tenting on the Plains, *p.420*

Yankee notions: things made in New England, made widely known by traveling Yankee peddlers.

1825: The tallow, corn, cotton, hams, hides, and so forths, which we had got in exchange for a load of Yankee notions.
John Neal, Brother Jonathan, *ii, p.298*

1826: Pit-coal indigo, wooden nutmegs, straw baskets, and Yankee notions. *T. Flint,* Recollections, *p.33*

1828: People abroad have no idea of what is meant here by Yankee notions, and are liable therefore to mistake our wooden ware for intellectual ware. Yankee, *Portland, Maine, January 1*

1843: Occasionally you will see some honest country Jonathan, with his wagon full of Yankee notions. Yale Literary Magazine, *ix, p.44*

1889: The camps were full of pedlers of Yankee notions, which soldiers are supposed to stand in need of.
John D. Billings, Hard Tack and Coffee, *p.213*

Appalachian Speech

The speech of ordinary, down-home or uneducated folk of Appalachia, particularly that of the southern regions, as it evolved throughout the 1800s, with many terms or peculiar pronunciations still in use today.

a body: person, man or woman.
acrost: across.
afeared: afraid.
afore: before.
agin: against.
aim: intend.
argie: argue.
backards: backwards.
bile: boil.
brung: brought.
call: reason.
chur: chair.
didje: did you.
drank: drink.
druther: I'd rather.
exter: extra.
ezactly: exactly.
fitten: appropriate.
fixen: intending.
guvment: government.
heerd: heard.
hern: hers.
hesh up: hush up.
hisn: his.
holler: valley.

idee: idea.
jist: just.
keer: care.
lasses: molasses.
Law, Laws: euphemism for Lord.
nary: never.
nigh: near.
ourn: ours.
pizen: poison.
poke: bag.
pone: corn bread.
puny feelin': sick.
richeer: right here.
shortsweetenin': sugar.
sich: such.
spell: for a time.
study on it: think about it.
stump liquor: corn liquor.
tolable: tolerable/mediocre.
tother: the other.
uppity: snobbish.
vittles: food.
whup: whip.
widder: widow.
yaller: yellow.
yourn: yours.

Swear Words, Taboo Words, Euphemisms

Although seldom found in print, swear words or taboo words were undoubtedly uttered just as profusely in the streets as they are now. In polite or mixed company, of course, euphemisms were used, especially by women and children. Many connotations of words used today remain curiously unchanged from the nineteenth century to the twentieth. In cases where no definition appears, the reader can use his or her imagination and extrapolate from current usage. Also note that some words that seem harmless today were considered highly vulgar not so long ago.

adventuress: euphemism for a prostitute or wild woman.

ass, ass-backwards (also **bass-ackwards**), **asswipe:** used throughout the century.

balls: shortened from ballocks, used throughout the century.

bastard: used throughout the century.

bitch: in the sense of a slutty, promiscuous person (as a dog in heat) and actually applied to either sex early in the century. Its use to denote a crabby person, especially as applied to a female, came much later.

blame: euphemism for damn, used throughout the century and especially in New England.
1840s: I wasn't goin' to let Dean know; because he'd have thought himself so blam'd cunning. Mrs. Claver's Western Clearings, *p.70*

blazes: euphemism for hell or the devil.

bloody: British swear word, from mid-1700s on.

boot-licker: the equivalent of an ass-kisser.

breast: not used in mixed company. "Delicate" citizens went so far as to call a chicken breast a bosom.

bull: a taboo word due to its association with sexual potency. Polite folk spoke of a cow brute, a gentleman cow, a top cow, or a seed ox.

bull: in reference to lies or exaggerations, widely popularized by Civil War soldiers, from 1860s on.

cherry: vulgar term for a young woman, from at least mid-century on.

clap: for venereal disease, from the 1700s on.

cockchafer, cocksucker, cockteaser: all from at least mid-century on.

condom: taboo because contraceptives were illegal for most of the century.

crap: euphemism for shit, from at least mid-century.

cunt: highly vulgar, used throughout the century.

cussed: a somewhat acceptable swear word, meaning cursed, contemptible, mean, etc.
1840: Blast the cussed old imp! Knickerbocker Magazine, *xvi, p.323*
1841: Billy, Billy, you are a cussed fool! S. Lit. Messenger, *vii*
1869: I told Simpson I didn't want to go among a set of folks who were such cussed fools they couldn't speak English.
Barnum, Struggles and Triumphs, *p.250*
1880: At another time she stopped them by planting herself directly on the track, out of pure cussedness. Harper's Magazine, *April*
1892: This is the cussedest business I was ever in.
Harper's Magazine, *January, p.287*

dad: a euphemistic form of God, e.g., dad-blame it.

1834: I'll be dad shamed if it ain't all cowardice.
   Carruthers, Kentuckian I, *p.216*
1845: I'll tetch 'em together quicker'n lightnin,—if I don't, dad burn
   me! *W.T. Thompson,* Chronicles of Pineville, *p.182*

damn: a more powerful swear word in the nineteenth century than now. Acceptable euphemisms included blame, dang, darn, dern, ding, and others. Gol was sometimes used as an euphemistic prefix, e.g., the Gol-derned idiots.

devil: a more powerful expletive in the nineteenth century than now.

dickens: a euphemism for devil, e.g., What the dickens are you going on about now? Popularly used from the second half of the century.

dratted: a mild expletive, sometimes used as an euphemism for damned, throughout most of the century.
1840s: I was never so dratted mad; for the fellows were coming in in
   gangs, and beginnin' to call for me to come out and take the command. Major Jones's Courtship, *p.22*

fart: used throughout the century, e.g., I don't give a fart. Not worth a fart in a whirlwind.

French pox: euphemism for syphilis.

fuck: used throughout the century.

hell: euphemistically known as blazes, heck, Jesse, Sam Hill, thunder, and others.

hell-fired: euphemistically known as all-fired or joe-fired.

horny: sexually aroused. Used throughout the century.

inexpressibles: euphemism for pants or trousers. See Pants. (See also Clothing and Fashion, p.116.)

Jesse: hell. To give one jesse is to give one hell or to beat the hell out of him.
1845: He turned on the woman and gave her Jesse.
   Cornelius Mathews, Writings, *p.243*
1847: You've slashed the hide off er that feller in the lower town, touched
   his raw, and rumpled his feathers,—that's the way to give him jessy.
   Robb, Streaks of Squatter Life, *p.31*

Jew: to drive a hard bargain, from early in the century; used by Jew and non-Jew alike.

jo-fired: a variation of all-fired and hell-fired.

1834: It's jo-fired hard, though, I'll be hanged if it ain't.
Vermont Free Press, *July 19*

knock up: to impregnate, from as early as 1813.

leg: considered a naughty term; limb was used as a polite substitute.

lickfinger: the equivalent of a kiss-ass, used throughout.

lick-spittle: same as lickfinger.

limb: used as a polite substitute for leg, which was considered naughty.

Mary: an effeminate homosexual, from the 1890s.

Nancy, Nancy-boy: an effeminate man, from 1800 on.

necessary: euphemism for the outhouse or water closet; the bathroom. Used throughout the century.

Negro: considered taboo because it had been used as a euphemism for a slave during the eighteenth century.

oath: any swearing involving the name of God or Jesus; any swear word. 1872: O, the cold-blooded oaths that rang from those young lips!
James McCabe, Lights and Shadows of New York Life, *p.480*

pants, trousers: not spoken of aloud in polite circles, especially during the first half of the century. Acceptable alternatives: inexpressibles, un-mentionables, nether garments, and sit-down-upons.

piss, pisspot: used throughout the century.

piss proud: a term for a false erection, i.e., one produced in the morning and not necessarily by sexual arousal. Used throughout the century.

prick: used throughout the century.

puss, pussy: dual meaning. Used widely as endearing appellations for women throughout the century, but also used in the vulgar sense (female genitalia) in some circles.

quim: female genitalia, used throughout the century.

randy: wanton or lecherous, from 1847 on.

redneck: a poor, white rural Southerner, from 1830 on.

scalawag: a mean, rotten or worthless person, from at least the 1840s.

screw: euphemism for sexual intercourse, used throughout the century. Also, to drive a hard bargain, used thoughout the century.

shit: used throughout the century.

snatch: female genitalia, used throughout the century.

snore, swan, swow: Euphemisms used by New Englanders for the word swear, which was once itself considered a swear word. Used thoughout the century.
1848: "Well! I swan!" exclaimed the mamma, giving a round box on the ear to a dirty little urchin, "what made you let the little huzzy have your specs?" Mrs.Claver's Forest Life, *Vol. 1., p.29*
1848: I took a turn round Halifax, and I swan if it ain't the thunderinest, drearyist place I ever seen and the people they call blue-noses.
Letter from Hiram Bigelow in Family Companion

sodomite: homosexual, used throughout the century.

son of a bitch: a very popular epithet throughout the American West from mid-century on.

strumpet: a whore, used throughout the century.

tarnal: a Yankee swear word, from the 1700s on.
1825: I know your tarnal rigs inside and out, says I.
John Neal, Brother Jonathan, *i, p.158*
1848: The ship drifted on tew a korril reef, and rubbed a tarnal big hole in her plankin. *W.E. Burton,* Waggeries, *p.17*

tarnation, nation: euphemisms for damnation, widely used throughout the century.
1801: The Americans say, Tarnation seize me, or swamp me, if I don't do this or that. *Colonel G. Haner,* Life, *ii, p.151*
1824: General Key is a tarnation sly old fox, for one that looks so dull.
Microscope, *Albany, April 3*
1827: [The Militia system] by burning a nation sight of powder, makes way with a good deal of villainous saltpetre.
Massachusetts Spy, *October 31*
1843: You've got this child into a tarnation scrape this time.
Knickerbocker Magazine, *August*
1847: [He remarked to me that it was] all-nation hot inside the clap-boards. Knickerbocker Magazine, *July*

twat: female genitalia, used throughout the century.

whoremonger: not a pimp, but one who patronized prostitutes frequently.

SURRENDER OF GEN. LEE!

"The Year of Jubilee has come! Let all the People Rejoice!"

200 GUNS WILL BE FIRED
On the Campus Martius,
AT 3 O'CLOCK TO-DAY, APRIL 10,
To Celebrate the Victories of our Armies. 1865

Every Man, Woman and Child is hereby ordered to be on hand prepared to Sing and Rejoice. The crowd are expected to join in singing Patriotic Songs.

ALL PLACES OF BUSINESS MUST BE CLOSED AT 2 O'CLOCK.

Hurrah for Grant and his noble Army.

By Order of the People.

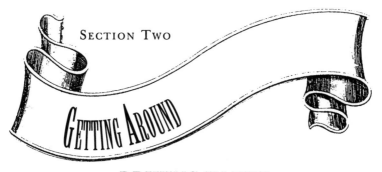

GETTING AROUND

DRIVING IN THE
NINETEENTH CENTURY

Under ideal road conditions, a coach driven by a fresh team of horses could "cut dirt" at the breakneck pace of nine miles per hour. Yet driving conditions throughout much of the century were rarely ideal. Although paving stones, cobbles and macadam smoothed major thoroughfares, rutted slurries of mud and horse dung were more the standard on secondary and rural roads. In spring, vehicles got stuck in these quagmires so often that the expression "up to the hub" became a national colloquialism to illustrate *any* intractable predicament.

Imperfect roads contributed to mishaps and unpleasantries of all kinds. Potholes broke wheels and axles, ditching some vehicles. Washboard surfaces jounced passengers out of their seats, and sometimes—if they were riding on the roof—onto the road. An English traveler in America in the 1820s wrote of being "tossed about like a few potatoes in a wheel-barrow. Our knees, elbows, and heads required too much care for their protection to allow us leisure to look out of windows."

Bad roads and driver impatience frequently combined to turn a coach over. During any long stage trip, in fact, passengers expected and were mentally prepared for at least one turnover. Such a prospect occasionally brought on a case of hysterics, as witnessed by Frances Trollope in 1829: "When we had again started upon our new wheel, the driver, to recover the time he had lost, drove rapidly over a very rough road, in consequence of which, our self-seeking old lady fell into a perfect agony of terror, and her cries of 'We shall be over! Oh, Lord! We shall be over! We must be over! We shall be over!' lasted to the end of the stage . . . which was a most fatiguing one."

One New Yorker in 1839 reported that his stage turned over nine times on a trip to Cincinnati and back. Such a high rate of accidents was more often attributed to alcohol than bad roads alone, and rightly so. Drivers throughout the period were notorious for their drunkenness.

But drink and kidney-crushing roads weren't the only shortcomings of coach and carriage travel. Although city roads were relatively smooth, traffic jams sometimes stopped vehicles for minutes at a time.

"Oftentimes the throng of vehicles is so dense that the streets are quickly 'jammed,' " wrote James McCabe of New York traffic in 1872. "Carriages, wagons, carts, omnibuses, and trucks are packed together in the most helpless confusion. . . . In a few minutes, however . . . a squad of gigantic policemen dash into the throng of vehicles. They are masters of the situation, and woe to the driver who dares disobey their sharp and decisive commands. The shouts and curses cease, the vehicles move on one at a time to the routes assigned them, and soon the street is clear again, to be 'blocked afresh' . . . in less than an hour."

Automobiles made their debut very late in the century, but few people thought much of them. They broke down a lot and couldn't surmount hills like a strong team of horses could. In 1895 there were only four cars in the entire country. In 1896 the number grew to sixteen. In 1899 there were 2,300 and by 1900, some 8,000. The cry, "Get a horse!" became a national joke reflecting popular skepticism toward the automobile at the time.

Carriages, Coaches and Wagons

Accommodation: the first horse-pulled bus, or omnibus, in America, introduced in New York in 1829; it resembled a long stagecoach and had four rows of seats, each seat carrying three passengers; the fare was a shilling for a route encompassing Broadway, Wall and Bleecker streets. Unlike most buses to follow, the Accommodation ran on rails.

barouche: an open, fair-weather, four-wheeled vehicle having only one small folding hood to protect half of its four passengers (two on a seat aligned face to face) in the event of rain. Though it was sometimes used as a parade carriage for presidents and other dignitaries, its popularity was eclipsed by the landau (see entry), which had two hoods. The barouche originated in the 1860s but it was more often called a brett or caleche after 1880.

bob-sleigh: a large sleigh mounted on two sleds instead of runners.

booby hut: an enclosed coach mounted on runners or sleds for winter use. The booby hut was used throughout the century and was noted for its ungainly appearance. Also known as a Boston booby.
1846: Some of the ladies of the wealthy classes are seen in the very cold weather driving about in a covered conveyance, enclosed partly with glass; it is a monstrously grotesque-looking affair, and its name is

worthy of its appearance; it is called a Booby-hut.
Eliot Warburton, Hochelaga

1888: They collided with Crowley's booby hack, knocking the horse down. Boston Globe

boot: a leather cargo trunk on a Concord (see entry); any cargo box.

box: the driver's seat on a coach.

brougham: originating in England in 1837, an elegant, boxlike coach enclosing two passengers (a four-passenger model, the double-brougham, or clarence, was also available) and pulled by one or two horses. Coachman-driven from the outside, the brougham was used as a cab in both the United States and England. It was one of the most desired vehicles for private driving, although few in the middle class could afford one or its upkeep.

buckboard: an open, four-wheeled carriage having one or more seats mounted on one or more pliable boards running lengthwise from the front to the rear axle. The buckboard originated in the United States around 1813 and became a favorite among settlers in the West.

1880: The mail [in the Southwest] is carried in buckboards drawn by one or two ponies or mules. Congressional Record, *February 26*

buggy: a generic term denoting a wide variety of vehicles. Originally, a runabout (see entry) with a top.

business buggy: a four-wheeled buggy with collapsible top and rear storage area for sample cases and parcels. The body was sometimes constructed with cane or rattan side panels, a decorative trend of the 1890s.

cab: short for cabriolet, one type of vehicle commonly used as a public hack or vehicle for hire. Eventually, cab came to denote any vehicle for hire.

cabriolet: originally, a two-wheeled vehicle resembling a nautilus shell. Later, American versions had four wheels and a folding top over the rear seat and a box for the driver out front. A popular vehicle for hire, also called a panel-boot Victoria.

calash, caleche: a small, two-wheeled open carriage holding two passengers under a folding top and a driver out in the open in front. Also, a four-wheeled vehicle resembling a barouche. Also, the hood itself.

carriage trade: the post-Civil War rich, upper class.

carriageway: any road suitable for carriage traffic.

carriole: an open sleigh, popular in Canada.

CARRIAGE COLORS

Popular colors for carriages and coaches included black (the most popular), brown, plum, purple, wine, claret, primrose, olive green, sea green, emerald green, maroon, canary, cobalt blue, blue and red. Many vehicles were multicolored. The wheels, axles, springs and shafts were of either the same or a different color than the body; often these were green, carmine, black or striped. Striping (a gold stripe on a black body was all the rage in the 1860s and 1870s) was popular, as was decorative scrollwork. Mountings were available in brass, ivory, silver or gold. See also Upholstery.

---

carryall: popular slang for any practical rather than handsome carriage, of various sizes.

1814: It is an unfair sight, to see women guiding their carryalls to pamper the city with their luscious melons, without a man.

Arthur Singleton, Letters from the South and West, *p.27*

1837: We mounted our carryall, a carriage which holds four.

Harriet Martineau, Society of America, *p.276*

1853: Taking his wife in the old fashioned but strong carryall, he journeyed some fourty miles. Daily Morning Herald, *St. Louis, March 11*

celerity wagon: a lighter, cheaper and faster model of Concord (see entry) coach, used on mail runs with few passengers.

chaise: popular in the first half of the century, a one-horse, two-wheeled open carriage carrying two passengers and usually equipped with a folding hood. Americans called it a shay.

clarence: a large coupe (see entry) or a double-brougham.

Cleveland Bay: one of the most widely used carriage horses in England and America; a large draft horse of even temperament.

coach: any large, enclosed carriage having four wheels. Also called a town coach.

coachman: the driver of a coach. However, this term was rarely used with stagecoach drivers in the United States. A stage driver was more often called the driver, whip, Charlie or Jehu.

coal-box buggy: extremely popular in the United States from 1862 on, a tall and narrow, four-wheeled open buggy resembling a grocer's coal box.

cock horse: a supplementary horse stationed at the bottom of a steep hill along a driving route. It was cared for by a postilion and hitched to any team that needed help in surmounting the hill. See also Postilion.

Concord: the most popular stagecoach of the century, built by the Abbot, Downing Co. of Concord, New Hampshire, and exported around the world. Although pre-1827 coaches were distinctly egg-shaped, the Concord was flattened on top to allow freight and, later, passengers to ride on the roof. On some Concords, the roof could hold up to twelve people while the interior—with its three padded leather seats—had room for nine. Other than passenger and luggage space, the Concord boasted a long list of desirable features, among them a nearly indestructible set of wooden wheels and a powerful brake system. Its fit and finish, too, were renowned, with its outstanding joinery, and multicoat paint and varnished sheen. Delicate scrollwork often decorated its side panels while doors were individually painted with a variety of landscapes. Its suspension system consisted of leather straps, or thoroughbraces, on which the vehicle rocked fore and aft—like a rocking chair—whenever a bump or chuckhole was encountered. This made for a less jarring, more humane ride for both passengers and horses. Around midcentury, a light Concord (a heavier, Wells Fargo model was sold for driving out west) could be purchased for about twelve hundred dollars; cheaper, stripped-down models (celerities and mud wagons) could be bought for about five hundred dollars. Light, eastern Concords were driven by four horses, while the heavier western versions required six and sometimes more. See Celerity, Mud wagon, Stage, Swift wagon.

Conestoga: a large, lumbering covered wagon used widely from the mid-eighteenth century to the latter part of the nineteenth century, originally designed in the Conestoga Valley of Lancaster County, Pennsylvania.

Conestogas were popular freight vehicles and, in addition to supplying the army in the War of 1812, were used most effectively in the migration to the American Midwest, sometimes parading in caravans of one hundred or more.

The body of a Conestoga was characteristically boat-shaped. That is, its fore and aft were slanted to prevent cargo (up to ten tons, according to some estimates) from slipping out on steep inclines. This was an important design consideration because many Conestogas were driven over mountainous terrain. Specifically, its underbody—painted blue—was fourteen feet long while its upperbody—painted red—stretched to nineteen feet.

Of course, the most famous feature on a Conestoga was its white canvas or cloth cover, which stretched over a skeleton of wooden bows. This cover was typically suspended higher at the ends than in the middle, the whole waterproofed with linseed oil. For privacy—because families literally lived in these wagons—the front and rear openings could easily be drawn shut with ropes.

The tires of a Conestoga were made of wrought iron and were sometimes nearly as broad as twelve inches. The wooden wheels—the front smaller than the rear—could all be removed quickly for repairs or to float a wagon over a deep river. A tool box at the side of the wagon contained everything from wrenches to hammers for wheel repairs. A grease bucket also hung from the rear axle for wheel lubrication.

The Conestoga was usually pulled by six horses, although as many as ten were employed for heavy loads. Any draft animal could pull one of these wagons, but one beast was actually bred for the job: the powerful, sixteen-hands-high Conestoga horse of Lancaster County, Pennsylvania. Bay or dapple-gray in color, these horses were frequently rigged with elaborate or ornate gear, for example, a heavy harness system trimmed with brass, a hoop of five to six tinkling bells, and a stiff brush called a Russian cockade standing up from the forehead. Together, the huge, trundling wagon and team of decorated, snorting horses made for a spectacular sight on American roads.

The driver of the Conestoga rarely rode in the wagon itself, preferring instead to walk alongside or to sit on the left-hand wheel horse. At high speeds, the driver often rode on a precarious seat known as the lazy board, a kind of footboard that pulled out from the left side of a wagon.

Although a few Conestogas made it to California, it was more often a simple, covered farm wagon that made the passage from the plains to the West. The farm wagon was notably lighter, smaller and boxier. More often than not, it plied the plains with either mules or oxen, which were cheaper to buy and maintain. In any event, all covered wagons that traveled to the West were affectionately known as prairie schooners.

1888: Everything was transported in the great army wagons called prairie schooners. These were well named, as the two ends of the wagon inclined upward, like the bow and stern of a fore-and-after.
Mrs. Elizabeth Custer, Tenting on the Plains, *pp.351-352*

1890: Heavily loaded schooners, drawn in some instances by twelve large mules, could often be seen stringing along the road for miles, laden with household goods, hardware, groceries and provisions.
Haskins, Argonauts of California, *p.205*

corduroy road: an early primitive road comprised of logs and saplings laid side by side, a source of numerous leg injuries to horses.

coupe: an enclosed half-coach, similar to a brougham.

curricle: a two-wheeled open carriage, heavier than the chaise or the gig and pulled by two horses; used largely in the first half of the century.

cutter: also known as the country cutter, the most popular sleigh in

America before the Civil War. It resembled the early tin bathtub and was sometimes referred to as the bathtub sleigh.

dashboard: a board of leather screen located at the front of a carriage to prevent mud from splashing back from the horses' hooves onto the passengers.

Dearborn: a light, covered four-wheeler furnished with curtains on the sides, from at least the 1820s on. The Dearborn was light enough to be pulled by one horse.

1820: I don't live extravagantly—I keep a little Dearborn wagon, and now and then take a side box at the theater. Massachusetts Spy, *March 15*

1836: A horse on Friday last ran away with a dearborn, in which was four persons. Philadelphia Public Ledger, *June 13*

1846: The well-known vehicle, called a dearborn, with its four light wheels and mere shell of a box is in such general use as to have superseded almost every other species of conveyance.
James Fenimore Cooper, Redskins

dickey: the front driver's seat or the exterior rear seat for servants on upscale vehicles.

doctor's cutter: a sleigh with a large top to protect a doctor from the elements when making house calls in winter.

dog cart: used from midcentury on, a small, open, two-wheeled vehicle with two transverse, back-to-back seats, originally designed to carry dogs in a ventilated boot to sporting events but later used as an all-purpose vehicle.

donkey cart: a small, open, two-wheeled cart pulled by a donkey or pony and used by children throughout the century.

Dougherty wagon: a passenger wagon of American design. It hung on steel springs and was used widely in the West, particularly by the army.

drag: a large, handsomely styled, Concord-like coach having seats inside as well as on the roof, front and back. The drag was used for private upscale or sport coaching and for taking people out on picnics (a boxlike component on the roof opened up to form a table); the owners and guests typically rode outside on the roof while footmen or grooms sat inside; popular in the United States from the 1870s on, especially in New York.

1876: Fifth Avenue and Central Park and the great driving avenues were crowded with vehicles of every kind, and two of the four-in-hands were among the throng. These were the old Dorking coach . . . driven by Col. Jay, and the drag of Mr. James Gordon Bennett, driven by himself. The coaches were crowded, many ladies being seated among the gentlemen on the top. The servants and grooms were inside, according to the custom. *New York Times, February 20, p.6*

1877: Last but by no means least . . . came Col. Delancey Kane with his familiar primrose drag, the Tally-Ho. *New York Times, May 27, p.12*

dray: a heavy cart or wagon used for hauling. Also, a draft horse.

drummer's wagon: a merchandise wagon used by drummers serving storekeepers. (See also Occupations, p.132.) These wagons were noted for the colorful painted scenes and gilt scrollwork decorating their side panels.

dugway: popular slang for a simple, dug-out road.

fanning: the English coachman's euphemism for whipping the horses.

fingerboard: a sign board with a pointing finger indicating the direction to a place, especially located at a crossroads, used throughout the century.

1827: He'll need no finger board to tell him which way his road lies.
James Fenimore Cooper, Prairie, xvii

1845: At their . . . forks there were no finger boards . . . to point the true way. *Dr. Drake, Pioneer Life in Kentucky, ix, p.235*

footman: a servant who was sometimes provided with a kind of rumble seat (dickey) at the rear exterior of a wealthy family's coach.

four-in-hand: popular term for the driving of four harnessed horses.

freight wagon: a huge wagon having six-foot wheels with inch-thick tires, noted for making permanent ruts in roads all over the country.

George IV phaeton: an elegant, slipper-shaped carriage with folding hood, pulled by two horses. This vehicle was very popular with women because it was graceful and was open to allow the passengers' fashions to be seen and admired from the street; from second half of the century.

gig: a one-horse, two-wheeled carriage, similar to a chaise. Like all two-wheeled vehicles, the gig had a higher accident rate than the more stable four-wheeled varieties. An old saying that "half the coachmen were killed out of gigs" may be at least partially due to their high numbers on the road. Used throughout the century.

governess cart: an open, basketwork cart for pulling children for fun.

groom's seat: a small seat or rumble seat where a groom or footman rode at the back of a coach or carriage.

guard's bag: a small bag with strap, used by coachmen to hold coach keys, way-bill, and a watch for time-keeping.

gurney: a two-wheeled, four-passenger, rear-entry cab made of sheet iron and having glass windows, popularly used in New York. The driver sat in front, as distinguished from the driver of a hansom cab (see entry).

hackney: not necessarily any one type of carriage, but one for public hire; a cab.

hansom cab: the classic cab, based on an 1836 design. It was noted for having its driver's seat located high in the back of the vehicle instead of at the front. The driver communicated to his passengers through a trap door in the roof. Although difficult to climb onto—the first step being about eighteen inches off the ground—the interior offered snug, romantic seating for two people and blinds for privacy. Hansoms were popular in England from early on but were not successfully introduced in America until late in the century.

hearse: a somber black and silver-trimmed vehicle having an elliptical or oval window at the sides to show the coffin inside. The roof was often decorated with trimmed-feather plumes.

hitching post: a post for hitching horses.

horn: a three- to five-foot copper or brass horn sometimes blown by a driver to clear the road ahead or to announce arrival. Some horns could play up to six notes.

horse-car: a tram car pulled by a horse.

Jenny Lind: an early, four-wheeled buggy with a fixed roof and curtains for privacy, named after the famous singer.

jumpseat wagon: a tall, box-shaped, open-sided wagon with a front seat that folded down and back and a rear seat that "jumped" forward, to make a single-seater. It was equipped with side curtains for privacy.

knight of the ribbons: nickname for a stage driver.

lamps: for night driving, a candle- or oil-burning set of lamps with reflectors. Most coaches were equipped with at least two lamps; some had as many as five.

landau: a German-designed, four-wheeled carriage having two face-to-face passenger seats and a roof made in two sections, either of which could be folded down; used throughout the century.

landaulette: a coupe with a collapsible top at the rear.

leaders: the lead horses in a team. See also Swing team, Wheel team. 1890: Mr. Prescott Lawrence was the second in line with a yellow and rose bodied coach, drawn by gray and roan leaders and chesnut and brown wheelers. New York Times, *May 25, p.2*

macadam: a gravel-paved road; its invention helped usher in the carriage age; from the beginning of the century on.

mud wagon: a rugged but cheaper model of Concord coach specifically designed for rough or muddy roads.

near: term used to designate the left side of a carriage, coach or team of horses, e.g., the near swing horse. See also Off.

off: term used to designate the right side of a carriage, coach or team of horses, e.g., the off swing horse. See also Near.

omnibus: the first bus, pulled by horses. By 1835 there were about one hundred omnibuses trundling about New York City. In the early days, fares were collected by a young boy waiting at the door but eventually a fare box—lowered from the ceiling—was adopted. Since the driver sat above and outside the bus, change-making was an annoying process. Even worse was the passenger's signal for a stop: tugging on a rope attached to the driver's leg!

Drivers of omnibuses had a notorious reputation for recklessness, as many cabdrivers do today.

1835: . . . the character of the omnibus driver has become brutal and dangerous in the highest degree. They race up and down Broadway with the utmost fury, committing scenes of outrage, in which the lives of citizens riding in light vehicles are put in imminent hazard. Not content with running upon everything which comes in their way, they turn out of their course to break down other carriages. Yesterday, a gentleman driving down Broadway, and keeping near the west side, was run down by an omnibus going up, the street being perfectly clear at the time. A ferocious spirit appears to have taken possession of the drivers, which defies law and delights in destruction. It is indispensable that a decisive police action should be held on those men, or the consequences of their conduct will result in acts which will someday shock the whole city. New York Journal of Commerce, *May 6*

Owensboro: a popular manufacturer of farm and freight wagons.

phaeton: a name denoting a wide variety of four-wheeled carriages with folding tops. It was driven not by a coachman but by the owner and was a favorite among physicians and women.

piano-box buggy: another name for a runabout (see entry), which had a body shaped like a piano box.

pod: a small, one-horse sleigh. It usually carried farmers' goods but could be used in an emergency to carry passengers.

pointing: English coachman's euphemism for cracking the wheel horse with the tip of the whip.

Portland cutter: the most popular sleigh following the Civil War. It was noted for its ample leg room and low center of gravity, which helped to prevent overturning.

postilion: one who provided one horse or a pair of horses to a traveling team to help in pulling a carriage, coach or wagon over a steep hill. The supplemental animal was unhitched once the peak was surmounted.

prairie schooner: any covered wagon that plied the plains to the West. See also Conestoga.

pung: a small sled-wagon.
1836: There has been a flitter of snow this week, and the pungs, the crates, the sleds, sledges, sleighs, and substitutes would much amuse you to look upon. . . . The driver of a pung had a negro boy by his side. Boston Pearl, *March 12*
1850: Pungs of butter, oats, mutton defiled along.
   Sylvester Judd, Richard Edney, *p.116*
1851: These were sledges or pungs coarsely framed of split saplings, and surmounted with a large crockery-crate. *Sylvester Judd*, Margaret, *p.74*

reinsman: a title applied to a master coachman.

rig: slang for any carriage or coach.

road coach: an English traveling and sport coach similar to a drag (see entry).

rockaway: an American-designed, multipassenger carriage built for the middle class. Although different styles were available, one universal feature was a roof that extended over the driver to protect him from the elements. It was also noted for its window, through which driver and passengers could converse.
1852: The long-tailed bays were left harnessed to the Rockaway, a sort of light omnibus, open at the sides, and very much like a char-a-banc, except that the seats run cross-wise, and capable of accommodating six to nine persons. *Charles A. Bristed*, The Upper Ten Thousand, *p.81*

rumble seat: a rear, exterior seat, reserved for a footman or groom on upscale vehicles.

runabout: an open, four-wheeled, one-seat vehicle with optional folding top and a body resembling a piano box; its overall shape greatly resembled the Model T automobile. Introduced in the mid-1850s, it quickly established itself as the most popular carriage in America. Sears offered runabouts in the last decade of the century for as low as $24.95, although upscale versions were priced as high as $425. With a top, the runabout was popularly known as a buggy.

runner: a steel or wooden runner or blade on a sleigh.
1857: I left in a hackney carriage, the wheels whereof had turned into runners. *George H. Derby,* The Squibob Papers

sharpshooter: a farmer who used his team of horses to drive freight in the off-season (winter) or when hauling rates were high.

shay: see Chaise.

shell drive: a roadway made of oyster shells.
1873: From the depot the omnibus rolled along the shell road [at Galveston] as smoothly as if upon glass. *J.H. Beadle,* The Undeveloped West, *p.798*
1888: To the General, the best part of all our detention was the shell drive along the ocean. *Mrs. Elizabeth Custer,* Tenting on the Plains, *p.273*

six-horse whip: a twenty-two-foot-long whip, long enough to reach the leaders in a six-horse team.

skid: a brake shoe that was suspended under a wheel by a long chain whenever a stop was desired.

sleigh: an open or enclosed vehicle mounted on runners for winter driving. More people owned sleighs than coaches or carriages in the North. Sleighs were cheaper to buy and maintain.

sociable: a rear-entry bus introduced in New York in 1829, the same year as the Accommodation (see entry). It had long side seats that carried about ten passengers each; its Wall Street to Bleecker route cost one shilling.

span: a pair of horses driven together.
1851: I saw two dandies in a light wagon coming up, driving a span of horses most furiously. *Joel Ross,* What I Saw in New York, *p.168*
1857: How I longed for an American cutter, with a span of fast horses! *Bayard Taylor,* Northern Travel, *p.155*

spider phaeton: a four-wheeled vehicle resembling a nautilus shell. It had an exterior footman's seat in the rear and was widely popular with young businessmen in the second half of the century.

spike team: two wheelers and a single leader. Also known as a unicorn team.
1849: Mr. Root of Ohio thought a spike team would drive just as well. *House of Reps.,* Congressional Globe, *December 6*

stagecoach: See Stage Lines, p.68.

state coach: an ornate, four-wheeled, enclosed coach used by aristocrats of England. A state coach seated four people face to face. Its exterior panels were usually dressed with heraldic paintings and family crests. Also known as a town coach. Any state-class vehicle.

sulky: a simple, one-passenger vehicle noted for its open, skeleton frame, used mainly on the racetrack, from 1830s on. Sulkies designed for road use were called road carts.

surrey: a large, boxy, open family vehicle having two long seats facing forward and frequently, a fringed, canopy top. It was extremely popular during the 1880s and 1890s, with an estimated one million vehicles sold between 1885 and 1900.

swift wagon: the Indian name for the Concord stagecoach.

swing team: the middle pair of horses in a six-horse team. See also Leaders, Wheel team.

Tally-Ho: originally, the nickname of a noted New Yorker's sport coach; the name was eventually adopted to denote any large, upscale sporting coach, especially a drag.

tandem driving: driving one horse in front of the other, single-file. In tandem driving, the wheel horse (closest to the vehicle) does all the actual pulling to save the strength of the leader for some later duty, such as a race or some other purpose.

teamster: one hired to care for and/or drive a team of horses. (See also Occupations, p.138.)

thoroughbraces: thick leather straps on which the body of some coaches, such as the Concord, were suspended, allowing for a less jarring ride.

tiger: English term for "a boy or a man of almost midget size" that assisted as a footman and stood on a footman's seat at the rear of upscale coaches.

towelling: English coachman's euphemism for flogging the horses.

trap: a four-wheeled, open vehicle characterized by a front seat that divided to allow passage to the back seat, which was capable of folding down. Traps sometimes had canopy tops. Popular from the second half of the century.

Troy: a coach similar to a Concord, built in Troy, New York.

turnout: collective term for horses, carriage and accompanying equippage.
1877: Mr. Theodore A. Havermeyer appeared with one of the most

attractive turnouts in the line. The horses were all about 15.3, the wheelers dark brown and the leaders a pair of dark brown Hungarian thoroughbreds, all driven in silver-mounted harness. The coach, built by Brewster and Co., of Broome Street, was dark blue, with blue and black undercarriage. New York Times, *May 27, p.12*

upholstery: popular choices in carriages and coaches: leather, corduroy, broadcloth, satin and Morocco (a soft, fine goat leather) in various colors.

Victoria: an elegant, four-wheeled vehicle resembling a giant slipper. It had plush upholstery and a collapsible top and was used by the upper classes for park riding from the 1830s on. Also known as a Milord.

vis-a-vis: any four-wheeled vehicle having face-to-face seats, used throughout the century. Also known as a sociable.

waggonette: introduced by Prince Albert in the mid-1840s, a four-wheeled, enclosed vehicle seating six people on two facing seats along the sides.

wagoner: one who drove freight, as a truck driver does today.

water wagon: an oversized barrel on wheels, used to sprinkle water on dirt roads to keep the dust down, and often followed by children in the summer. Hitched behind freight wagons, it was also used in the West as a storage container for watering the horses.

wheel team: in a two-, four- or six-horse team, the pair of horses closest to the coach or wagon. Also called wheelers.

whip: a stage-driver's whip was often a five-foot hickory stick with a twelve-foot buckskin lash. Also, the nickname of any coach driver. See also Six-horse whip.

Stage Lines

Butterfield Overland Mail Route: used by John Butterfield's stage line from 1858 on, an express route starting from St. Louis and Memphis and stretching west through Fort Belknap and El Paso, to Tucson and Fort Yuma and on to Los Angeles and San Francisco. Also known as the Oxbow Route.

celerity wagon: a lighter, cheaper and faster model of Concord coach, used on mail runs with few passengers.

Central Overland and Pony Express Route: a route used by stages and freight wagons from roughly the 1840s on and by the Pony Express in 1860 and 1861. It started from points in St. Joseph, Missouri, and Atchison, Kansas, and swept west to Fort Laramie, Wyoming, Salt Lake City, Carson City and Sacramento.

Concord: See Carriages, Coaches and Wagons, p.57.

conductor: an employee of a stage line (usually a senior driver) who traveled with a stagecoach and looked after passengers and freight on long runs.

deadhead: slang for a nonpaying passenger.

division: a stage route comprised of several drives, totaling 150 to 450 miles.

drive: a section of a stage route, usually no more than sixty miles, comprised of several stages at the end of which both driver and vehicle were changed.

Eastern Stage Co.: a large and prosperous stagecoach syndicate of New England from 1818-1838.

express: mail or a mail delivery service by stagecoach.
1851: The religious papers which have the greatest circulation are papers of a small size, and are transmitted mostly by express.
   Mr. Duncan, Massachusetts, House of Reps., Congressional Globe, *January 15*
1861-1862: In going overland, a stage-coach left Atchison, the eastern starting point, every morning at eight o'clock, shortly after the arrival of the mail by train on the St. Joseph & Atchison railroad from the East. The mail came over the Missouri River on the steam ferry-boat "Ida" and was taken direct to the post office, where it remained until loaded on the stage, and was then carried across the plains to California, six times a week. No mail arrived from the East on Monday morning, the coach that left Atchison that morning was in charge of a messenger, and was called a "messenger coach."
   The messenger coach was loaded with express packages of various kinds, besides a strong box that two persons could handle, containing the treasure and the most valuable of the smaller packages. On the regular Concords the safe was carried in the front boot, under the driver's box. Whenever there happened to be an extra-big run of express packages (enough to comfortably fill the stage), no passengers were taken on that trip; but it was a very rare occurrence if the express coach left Atchison without at least one or more, and often it carried as many as half a dozen passengers, either for Denver, Salt Lake, or on through to the western terminus.
   The charges on express matter other than gold dust, coin, or currency, between Atchison and Denver, were at the uniform rate of one dollar per pound. More express matter was carried to Denver,

Central City and Black Hawk in 1863 than to all other points combined on the main stage line.

The number of mail pouches carried west on the stage-coach six times a week ran about as follows: San Francisco, two; Sacramento, one to two; Virginia City and Carson, Nev., one each; Salt Lake, one to two; Denver, two. *Frank Root,* The Overland Stage to California

expressman: an express stage driver.

mustangs: wild horses used to drive stagecoaches when trained horses were in short supply; they were frequently involved in accidents.

outriders: escorts or guards who sometimes rode alongside a stage, especially through hostile Indian country.

road agent: a criminal who robbed stagecoaches; a highway robber. (See also Crime, p.217.)

shotgun rider: one who sat next to a stage driver and carried a shotgun to protect passengers and freight from Indians and road agents. Also known as riding shotgun.

shouldering: the dishonest pocketing of the full fare from a passenger who failed to register at the booking office and who boarded from outside the station. Drivers kept these fares secret to supplement their incomes.

stage: the section of road between relays of animals, usually from ten to twelve miles.

stagecoach: any coach used in transporting people or freight in stages or relays. The most popular model of coach was the Concord.

1865: The conditions of one man's running stages to make money, while another seeks to ride in them for pleasure, are not in harmony to produce comfort. Coaches will be overloaded, it will rain, the dust will drive, baggage will be left to the storm, passengers will get sick, a gentleman of gallantry will hold the baby, children will cry, nature demands sleep, passengers will get angry, the drivers will swear, the sensitive will shrink, rations will give out, potatoes become worth a gold dollar each, and not to be had at that, the water brackish, the whiskey abominable, and the dirt almost unendurable. I have just finished six days and nights of this thing; and I am free to say, until I forget a great many things now very visible to me, I shall not undertake it again. Stop over nights? No you wouldn't. To sleep on the sand floor of a one-story sod or adobe hut, without a chance to wash, with miserable food, uncongenial companionship, loss of seat in a coach until one comes empty, etc., won't work. A through-ticket and

STAGECOACH ETIQUETTE

1877: The best seat inside a stagecoach is the one next to the driver. You will have to ride with back to the horses, which with some people, produces an illness not unlike sea sickness, but in a long journey this will wear off, and you will get more rest, with less than half the bumps and jars than on any other seat. [When anyone] . . . who traveled thousands of miles on coaches offers, through sympathy, to exchange his back or middle seat with you, don't do it. . . . Bathe your feet before starting in cold weather, and wear loose overshoes and gloves two or three sizes too large. When the driver asks you to get off and walk, do it without grumbling. He will not request it unless absolutely necessary. If a team runs away, sit still and take your chances; if you jump, nine times out of ten you will be hurt. In very cold weather abstain entirely from liquor while on the road; a man will freeze twice as quick while under its influence. Don't growl at food at stations; stage companies generally provide the best they can get. Don't keep the stage waiting; many a virtuous man has lost his character by so doing. Don't smoke a strong pipe inside especially early in the morning; spit on the leeward side of the coach. If you have anything to take in a bottle, pass it around; a man who drinks by himself in such a case is lost to all human feeling. Provide stimulants before starting; ranch whiskey is not always nectar. Be sure and take two heavy blankets with you; you will need them. Don't swear, nor lop over on your neighbor when sleeping. Don't ask how far it is to the next station until you get there. Take small change to pay expenses. Never attempt to fire a gun or pistol while on the road; it may frighten the team and the careless handling and cocking of the weapon makes nervous people nervous. Don't discuss politics or religion, nor point out places on the road where horrible murders have been committed, if delicate women are among the passengers. Don't linger too long at the pewter wash basin at the station. Don't grease your hair before starting or dust will stick there in sufficient quantities to make a respectable "tater" patch. Tie a silk handkerchief around your neck to keep out dust and prevent sunburns. . . . Don't imagine for a moment you are going on a picnic; expect annoyance, discomfort and some hardships. If you are disappointed, thank heaven.

Omaha Herald

fifteen inches of seat, with a fat man on one side, a poor widow on the other, a baby in your lap, a bandbox over your head, and three or four persons immediately in front, leaning against your knees, makes the picture, as well as your sleeping place, for the trip.

Demas Barnes, The Far Western Frontier, *p.8*

star route: a mail route contracted to an individual or firm by the government.

1854: A star bid is where a party agrees to carry the whole mail on a certain route for a certain sum of money.

Mr. Jones, Louisiana, House of Reps., Congressional Globe, *April 20*

station: the home of a station master, stage driver or other line employee, where passengers were fed meals and fresh teams of horses or mules were supplied. On long runs, passengers had to sleep overnight sprawled together, often on a cold, dirt floor. Stations were spaced approximately ten to fifteen miles apart, but not all of them had accommodations for passengers. See also Swing station.

1865: From Kearney the houses are principally of sod or adobe, one story high, and generally without floors—stations from ten to fifteen miles apart, horses good, four to a coach, eating stations about two per day, meals as good as could be expected.

Demas Barnes, The Far Western Frontier, *p.25*

1872: Gila City consists of one adobe house in which reside two men who keep the stage station, wash gold from a gulch close by and sell lightning whiskey to anyone who can drink it.

Letter in Los Angeles Star

swing station: the home of a stock tender, where fresh relays of horses or mules were provided but no meals were available for passengers.

Wells Fargo: the largest express and express banking company in the West, from 1852.

RAILROAD

The early nineteenth-century citizen was as electrified by the sight of a train rumbling down a track as we might be by the shuttle soaring off into space. "I saw today for the first time a Rail Way Car," wrote Christopher Baldwin in 1835. "What an object of wonder! How marvelous it is in every particular. It appears like a thing of life. . . . I cannot describe the strange sensation produced on seeing the train of cars come up. And when I started in them . . . it seemed like a dream."

Despite the wonder of it all, early trains subjected passengers to sundry discomforts. Along with a pervasive unease over potential derailments and boiler explosions, passengers complained about the racket the cars made over the tracks and of the ashes and cinders that constantly rained on them from the locomotives' smokestacks. One woman found thirteen holes burned in her gown from the engine's relentless belching of sparks. Others registered horror over the number of livestock being run down and at the potential for pedestrian accidents at railway crossings.

Still, there was no stopping the forward progress of the railroad. Even before midcentury, trains rattled along at speeds of twenty miles per hour—twice as fast as the stagecoach, four times as fast as the canal boat. To the entrepreneur that meant one thing: profit.

The profit-minded Americans wasted no time in laying down track. In 1835 but 700 miles of rail stretched across the country. That grew to 9,000 miles by 1850 and to over 30,000 by 1860. In 1890, America was cross-stitched with more than 200,000 miles of track. By then, transcontinental train travel had already shed its novelty image and had, in fact, become as natural as a stroll down the lane.

baggage smashers: common nickname from midcentury on for baggage handlers who, according to passenger reports, "treated each piece of baggage as if they owed it a personal grudge."

Baltimore and Ohio Railroad: America's first practical railroad. Passenger service was begun on a mile-and-a-half track between Mount Clare and the Carrollton Viaduct, outside of Baltimore, in 1830. The five open cars were initially pulled by a single horse. Riders paid nine cents for a round-trip excursion, which proved to be wildly popular.

1830: Notwithstanding the great heat of the weather for the last three weeks, the amount of weekly travel on the railroad has not diminished, the average receipts being above one thousand dollars per week. In the hottest time of the hottest days the quick motion of the cars causes a current of air which renders the ride at all times agreeable. In many instances strangers passing through Baltimore, or visiting it, postpone their departure for a day and sometimes longer, to enjoy the pleasure of an additional ride on the railroad. We only repeat the general sentiment when we say, it is the most delightful of all kinds of traveling. Baltimore Gazette, *July*

Best Friend of Charleston: running out of Charleston, South Carolina, the first regularly scheduled passenger train pulled by a steam locomotive. It ran for about six months and in June 1831 exploded, killing the fireman and injuring the engineer. The locomotive was rebuilt and rechristened *Phoenix*. To restore passenger confidence, a flatcar piled high with protective cotton bales was placed between the locomotive and its passenger cars.

brigades of cars: the original name given to a train. On August 27, 1830, the Baltimore and Ohio used the term "train of cars" in an advertisement, and the name stuck.

butch: also known as a train butch or a news butch. Peddlers, usually young men, who sold newspapers, magazines, dime novels, peanuts, cigars, sandwiches, and so forth, on the Transcontinental Railway. Horatio Alger featured train butches in some of his novels.

1880s: First he offers you yesterday's newspapers. Next time he walks

through the carriage he drops two or three handbooks, guides, maps or magazines beside each traveler; the next trip he forces the choice of apples or pears, then oranges, California grapes, dried figs, maple sugar; last he brings his basket of peanuts, and throwing two or three into everyone's lap, he has completed the round, not for the day but for the nonce; he will begin again at the beginning, for sure, after dinner. This itinerant trader certainly should be supressed; his prices are extravagant and his office unnecessary.
Major William Shepherd, Prairie Experiences

Central Pacific Railroad: built the western portion of the Transcontinental Railway. See also Union Pacific Railroad.

conductor: the director, guard and ticket-taker on a passenger train.
1853: "But where's my bundle?" asked the fat man. "Conductor! where's my bundle?" The conductor knew nothing about it. Life Scenes, *p.129*
1854: "Tickets! Tickets, gentlemen!" cried the conductor as he passed our friends. Yale Literary Magazine, *xx, p.16*

cow-catcher/cow-plough: a framework or fender constructed on the nose of a locomotive to catch or shovel off cattle, hogs or other obstructions on a track, from 1838 on.
1842: The engine came suddenly in contact with a small wagon, loaded with fish, relieved the horses, threw aside the driver, and absolutely brought the fish safely into Camden on the cow-catcher.
Philadelphia Spirit of the Times, *June 25*
1866: Within two yards of my window I saw a dark object disappear under the cow-catcher. *A.D. Richardson,* The Secret Service, *p.107*
1874: The cow-catcher turned into a deer-catcher for the moment.
B.F. Taylor, World on Wheels, *p.42*

deadhead: a nonpaying passenger. As a verb, to let someone ride for free.

depot: a railway station. The term was used throughout the railroad era.
1836: I arrived at the depot of the Boston and Providence Railroad.
Boston Pearl, *January 23*

derail: describing a train slipping off a track. The term was used from at least midcentury on.

dining car: introduced in 1863 on the Philadelphia, Wilmington and Baltimore lines, a restaurant car comprised an eating bar and a simple steambox in which precooked food was kept warm. The more lavish Pullman Dining Car was introduced in 1868 on the Alton and Chicago line. See also Refreshment saloons.

dining station: see Refreshment saloons.

fireman: one who threw wood or shoveled coal into the firebox of a locomotive. Early trains burned forty to two hundred pounds of coal per mile, and a good fireman could move more than two tons of coal in less than thirty minutes.

full chisel: term sometimes used to describe the speed of a locomotive, specifically full tilt.

Great Race: the race between the Central Pacific and Union Pacific Railroads to complete the Transcontinental Railway. The two joined tracks at Promontory Point, Utah, on May 10, 1869.

heating: most of the early trains were heated by woodstoves at the end or in the middle of each car. Passengers often complained of being too hot or too cold, depending on where they sat in relation to the stove.

hell on wheels: an expression that grew out of the construction of the Union Pacific Railway in 1867. As the track progressed westward, the saloons, gambling halls and prostitutes of one town were transported on flat cars to the new depot, thus literally moving "hell on wheels."
1867: . . . these settlements were of the most perishable materials — canvas tents, plain board shanties, and turf-hovels — pulled down and sent forward for a new career, or deserted as worthless, at every grand movement of the Railroad company. . . . Restaurant and saloon keepers, gamblers, desperadoes of every grade, the vilest of men and women made up this Hell on Wheels, as it was most aptly termed.
Samuel Bowles, Our New West

horse railroad: a train or bus pulled by a horse or horses.
1858: Busy Cambridge Street with its iron river of the horse railroad.
Autocrat of the Breakfast Table, *ch.8*
1859: These gentlemen ask the power to run a horse-railroad along Pennsylvania Avenue for two or three miles.
Mr. Wilson, Massachusetts, U.S. Senate, Congressional Globe, *January 29*

hotel car: a Pullman dining and/or sleeping car.
1869: The hotel car is divided into sections forming staterooms wherein parties of four can be accommodated. Between these rooms are seats arranged in the usual way. At the rear is a kitchen, which, though small, contains every appliance necessary for cooking purposes. . . . A wine cellar contains the liquors which are likely to be in demand. . . . At stated intervals the conductor walks around taking passengers' orders, who make their selections from a bill-of-fare . . . five different kinds of bread, four sorts of cold meat, six hot dishes, to say nothing of eggs cooked in seven different ways and all the seasonable

vegetables and fruits. . . . The meal is served on a table temporarily fixed to the side of the car and removed when no longer required.
W.F. Rae, Westward by Rail

1871: Two of us chartered [from Niagara to Chicago] a compartment like the cabin of a ship with a comfortable sofa above which a board was fixed at night, so as to form a second sleeping berth. The beds were regularly made, boots put outside the door for cleaning, and hot water brought in the morning by an active black boy. Meals were served on a table carried into the cabin. The bill-of-fare . . . for lamb chop or mutton chop and tomato sauce the price was seventy-five cents; fresh mackeral, fifty cents; omelet with ham, fifty cents. . . . A cup of French coffee, tea or chocolate was fifteen cents. The kitchen, clean and commodious, had every appliance for cooking.
James Macaulay, Across the Ferry, *pp.137-138*

iron horse: popular appellation for a locomotive.

1846: The iron horse with the wings of the wind, his nostrils distended with flame, salamander-like vomiting fire and smoke.
Mr. Cathcart, Indiana, House of Reps., Congressional Globe, *February 6*

1854: The same progress has transferred our persons and our commerce from the horse and the slow and dull creaking wagon to the iron horse of the railroad.
Mr. Elliot, Kentucky, House of Reps., Congressional Globe, *May 10*

Jim Crow car: any rail car in which Negroes were segregated from white passengers, originally a practice of the Eastern Railroad in Massachusetts from 1838-1843. The cars came back into use when racial segregation was enforced in the South after 1877. (See also Slavery and Black Plantation Culture, p.217.)

ladies' cars: cars in which women could ride in comfort and escape the smoking, spitting and flirting of the male passengers. Male companions could also ride in these cars. Primarily employed in the South.

1856: Ladies cars are barbarisms. There is no more seclusion, nor safety against tobacco indecencies, where a lady journeys with married gentlemen or gallants, than where she may chance to have the company of bachelors or stray benedicts. Holly's Railroad Advocate, *September 20*

lightning express: any very fast train.

1860: The scenery of a long tragic drama flashed through his mind as the lightning express train whishes by a station.
Professor at the Breakfast Table, *ch.6*

1861: There is now a lightning train between the cities of Washington and New York.
Mr. Colfax, Indiana, House of Reps., Congressional Globe, *March 2*

parlor car: an upscale car furnished with comfortable chairs, sofas, etc., designed by George Pullman, from 1875 on.
1882: In the parlor car we occupied today a Negro presided over a pantry which was at one end of it and dealt out for consumption fruit, strawberries and cream, tea, coffee, milk, lemonade, gin, sherry cobblers . . . mint juleps. *W.G. Marshall,* Through America

porter: employed in Pullman cars and almost exclusively Negro, sometimes nicknamed George, after George Pullman. Porters made up beds, stowed luggage, awakened passengers, etc., and were generally tipped by the passengers.

Promontory Point, Utah: where the Central Pacific and Union Pacific Railroads met and joined to form the Transcontinental Railway.

Pullman Cars: plush, upscale passenger cars, including dining cars, hotel cars, parlor cars and sleepers, designed by George Pullman and employed in the second half of the century.

refreshment saloons: dining stations located along the towns on a railway line. They were established by the railroads and widely used before the advent of the dining car. The stops at these stations were sometimes as brief as fifteen minutes, requiring passengers to bolt their food and run.
1857: If there is any good word in the English language more shamefully misused than another, it is the word refreshment, as applied to the hurry scurry of eating and drinking at railroad stations. The dreary places in which the painful and unhealthy performances take place are called Refreshment Saloons, but there could not be a more inappropriate designation for such abominations of desolation. . . . The traveler who has been riding all night in a dusty and crowded car, unable to sleep, and half suffocated with smoke and foul air, will be suddenly roused . . . by hearing the scream of the steam whistle, which tells of the near approach to a station; but before the train stops, the door of the car opens, and the conductor shouts at the top of his voice, "Pogramville—fifteen minutes for breakfast!"
New York Times, *June 10*

refrigerated car: the first was developed in 1868.

roundhouse: a circular building used for housing and switching locomotives.
1870: Engineers and firemen often . . . have to spend considerable time around the roundhouse. Railroad Gazette

sleeping car: a few crude sleeping cars were in use by the 1840s, but the definitive models were designed by the Wagner Palace Car Company and by George Pullman in the 1860s.

1860: There was no longer an aisle of double seats but the cabin of a small steamer with curtained berths and closed portholes. The bottom berths were wide and comfortable with room to roll and turn. There were two high berths to choose from; both wicker trays, ledged in, cushioned and rugged. The one was about a foot and a half higher than the other and I chose the top one as being nearer the zinc ventilator. I clambered to my perch and found it was like lying on one's back on a narrow plank. If I turned my back to the car wall the motion of the train bumped me off my bed altogether and if I turned my face to the wall I felt a horrible sensation of being likely to roll backward into the aisle.

Description of a Wagner Sleeping Car, from Walter Thornbury, Criss-Cross Journeys

smoking car: a separate car in which men could go to smoke.

1860: The smoking car is small, with seats running all around, and there is a table in the middle on which the newsboy generally spreads his store of intellectual sophistry. *Walter Thornbury,* Criss-Cross Journeys

speed of trains: throughout most of the century, trains traveled at twenty to thirty miles per hour; the fastest went forty.

spitting/spittoons: men frequently spat wherever they pleased on trains, so the railroad strategically placed spittoons throughout their cars.

1846: Both in New England and in New York tobacco-chewing is a habit by far too prevalent, but this plague in American life only begins to show itself in its detestable universality after he has crossed the Hudson on his way South. A New York railway car is a clean affair as compared to one on the line between Philadelphia and Baltimore. . . . It frequently happens that the seats, the sides of the car, the window hangings, where there are any, and sometimes the windows themselves are stained with the pestiferous decoction.

The Western World, Travels in the United States in 1846-47

1853: The moment the cars start a string of filthy lads stream in offering for sale sweetmeats, apples, books and other important wares, and they are succeeded by travelers who, if they find no other accommodations, stand up in the middle of the cars and spit away.

Alfred Bunn, Old England and New England

spotter: in the second half of the century, a railway detective who observed conductors to prevent them from selling tickets directly to passengers and pocketing the fares, a common practice of the 1880s and 1890s.

telegrapher: on the transcontinental railway and other long distance, western runs, a vital member of the train crew. He carried a device called a box relay, which could be attached to the telegraph line that ran along the tracks to call for help in the event of derailments, breakdowns, robberies, etc. Telegraphers usually had little to do during a trip and so they often doubled as baggage handlers.

Tom Thumb: the first locomotive built in America. It was pitted against a horse-pulled train in a celebrated race over a nine-mile course from Riley's Tavern to Baltimore on September 18, 1830. It lost the race due to mechanical failure.

transcontinental railroad: the first transcontinental railroad in America was completed on May 10, 1869, at Promontory Point, Utah, with the linkup of the Central Pacific and Union Pacific Railroads. By the end of the century, five major transcontinental railroads were linking the east with the Pacific Ocean: the Union Pacific-Central Pacific, the Northern Pacific, Southern Pacific, Santa Fe, and Great Northern. A sixth, the Canadian Pacific, ran across Canada.

Union Pacific Railroad: built the eastern portion of the first transcontinental railway. See also Central Pacific Railroad.

1866: The men who go ahead (surveyors and locators) are the advance guard, and following them is the second line (graders) cutting through the gorges, grading the road and building the bridges. Then comes the main body of the army, placing the ties, laying the track, spiking down the rails, perfecting the alignment, ballasting and dressing up and completing the road for immediate use. Along the line of the completed road are construction trains pushing "to the front" with supplies. The advance limit of the rails is occupied by a train of long box-cars with bunks built within them, in which the men sleep at night and take their meals. Close behind this train come train loads of ties, rails, spikes, etc., which are thrown off to the side. A light car drawn by a single horse gallops up, is loaded with this material and then is off again to the front. Two men grasp the forward end of the rail and start ahead with it, the rest of the gang taking hold two by two, until it is clear of the car. At the word of command it is dropped into place, right side up—thirty seconds to the rail for each gang, four rails to the minute. As soon as a car is unloaded, it is tipped over to permit another to pass it to the front and then it is righted again and hustled back for another load. . . . Quick work, you say—but the fellows of the Union Pacific are tremendously in earnest.

Newspaper correspondent's account of laying the first transcontinental railway, May

vestibule: introduced on Pullman cars in 1886, an elastic diaphragm that enclosed each of the open spaces between cars. Vestibules shut out the cold and the rain and made it safer to move from one car to another.

Zulu cars: railroad passenger cars with hardback seating and unupholstered sleeping facilities for carrying immigrants to the West in the last quarter of the century.

WATER TRAVEL

The steamboat became a wildly popular form of travel from about 1810 on. At the height of their popularity, steamboats from the upper and lower Mississippi, the Ohio and the Missouri were logging in at St. Louis over 2,000 times a year. One year recorded some 2,897 steamboat arrivals. Passengers loved the amenities offered on a steamboat. Indeed some boats were fitted out like floating palaces. But despite captains' boasts that their beloved low-draft vessels could go anywhere, even on a "heavy dew," the steamboat's safety record was, in fact, atrocious. Between 1811 and 1850 some 166 steamboats burned, 209 blew up, and 576 struck obstructions and sank.

With so many steamboat disasters and so little love for the kidney-crushing ride offered by the stagecoach, Americans welcomed canal travel, as it blossomed in the 1830s. "You push along so slick," one traveler observed, "there's no chance of getting one's neck broke as there is aboard those stages on the rough turnpikes; if the boat sinks, one's only up to one's knees in water." Still canal boats were small and they couldn't offer the luxuries that a steamboat could. Because of the explosive growth of the railroad, construction of new canals all but ceased in 1840, leaving the country with 3,326 miles of canalways.

Ships, Boats and Canals

ark: another name for a common flat boat, also known as a broadhorn, scow, Kentucky boat; specifically, a raftlike vessel with a shelter in its center for carrying cargo and passengers. They frequently had no sails and were thus at the mercy of a river's currents. Used widely throughout the century, especially on the Ohio and Mississippi Rivers.
1810: Wheat and other grain can be brought down the [Susquehanna] river in boats or arks, and landed at the mill-door, from whence flour can be transported in boats or arks to Have-de-grace and Baltimore. *Advertisement,* Lancaster *(Pennsylvania)* Journal, *March 3*
1817: Arks, of which hundreds are on the [Ohio] river. *M. Birkbeck,* Journey to America, *p.50*
1817: The usualy price is $75, for each, which will accommodate three or four families, as they carry from 25 to 30 tons; and it frequently happens that the ark can be sold for nearly what it cost, six or eight hundred miles lower down. *John Bradbury,* Travels, *p.317*

aye: a sailor's traditional acknowledgement of an order, often "aye, aye, sir."

barbarising: swabbing a deck with sand and cleanser.

bark, barque: a sailing vessel having three to five masts, all square-rigged except the after-mast, which was fore-and-aft rigged. These vessels grew progressively larger from midcentury on.

1849: On the 1st of February, 1849, we embarked, at the foot of Arch Street, Philadelphia, on board the barque *Thomas Walters*, under command of Captain Marshman, for Tampico, thence intending to cross Mexico, and, re-embarking at Mazatlan, to proceed up the Pacific Coast to San Francisco. . . . After the usual amount of adventures, sea-sickness and home-sickness, we arrived at Tampico on the 21st of February, where we were most happy to exchange the monotony, the junk and other salt provisions . . . for the delicious fruits and vegetables . . . of a tropical climate.

Daniel B. Woods, Sixteen Months at the Gold Diggings, *p.21*

bilboes: iron bars on the decks of some warships, to which prisoners were sometimes shackled.

blood money: money paid to innkeepers or a boardinghouse for finding men to fill vacancies on a ship's crew. See also Shanghai.

brig: a ship having two square-rigged masts. Also, a larger version, known as a brigantine. Also, a ship's prison.

brought up to the mast: being brought before the captain to answer charges of misconduct.

burgoo: a ration of oatmeal or mush sometimes served to nineteenth-century sailors.

caboose: the galley on a merchant ship. Also, a chimney-housing in the galley of a merchant ship.

1821: [They searched] every hole and corner of the vessel but the right one, and nothing was left unexamined but the caboose.

Massachusetts Spy, *August 1*

1834: [He has] set fire to the boarding of the small galley — the caboose they calls it in merchantmen. Blackwood's Magazine

canal boat: any boat specifically designed to be used in a canal and often towed by a horse, mule or a team of such. Such boats sometimes had a stable for the animals below deck, along with a compartment for hay. Some canal boats had quarters for a family and for passengers, and a large multiple-hatch area for cargo.

1825: The [Erie] canal is no more than four feet deep, so that only ships and barges expressly built for it can navigate it. The vessel that brought us to Albany today was 70 feet long, 14 wide, and drew 2 feet of water. It was covered, included a roomy salon and a kitchen, and was very neatly maintained. On account of the numerous locks on the way, progress was very slow; our ship did only three miles an hour, since passage through each lock took four minutes. The craft was drawn by a three-horse team which plodded along a narrow path parallel to the canal, even under the frequent bridges. These bridges, about 300 between Albany and Utica, are made of wood and are very coarsely built; generally they belong to farmers, and serve to connect the fields on either side. *Bernhard Karl,* This Was America, *p.155*

canallers/canawalers: commonly used name for the men who lived and worked on or along the canals. They were famous throughout the country for their hard-drinking, hard-fighting lifestyles.

canal walker: one who walked along a towpath each day to inspect a canal for any leaks in its locks or for any impending breaks in its channel banks.

Clermont: the famous steamboat. Its maiden voyage was on the Hudson River in 1807.

clipper ship: evolving from schooners around 1845, a very fast sailing ship characterized by a raking stem and an overhanging stern along with heavy sparring that carried a greater area of sail than the typical ship of the day. Serving as merchant vessels, clippers traveled from New York to San Francisco around Cape Horn during the California gold rush. On the return leg they often carried tea and spices from China. Clippers also brought tea to England from 1849 on. The use of clippers largely declined after the construction of the Suez Canal in 1869 because freight shipments were more often handled by steamers.

cobbing: in the British Navy, a disciplinary action in which a sailor was tied to the deck and spanked with a board.

cuddy: on a large ship, the carpenter's cabin. On a small vessel, any small cabin.

dart: whaler's term for a harpoon.

deadhead: a nonpaying passenger on a steamboat. As a verb, to let someone ride without paying.

doctor: nickname for a ship's cook.
1821: The cook, at sea, is generally called doctor.
Massachusetts Spy, *August 1*
1830: The cook is in fact called the doctor in all [American] merchant ships. *N. Dana,* A Mariner's Sketches, *p.33*

dog watch: a half watch on deck lasting two hours and commencing from 4 to 6 P.M. or from 6 to 8 P.M.

dugout: a canoe dug out from a log. See also Pirogue.

1819: At Wheeling . . . we purchased a small canoe, called here a dugout, or man-drowner. *Claiborne,* Life, *p.42*

1836: They flogged him to death, added the tar and feathers and placed him aboard a dug-out . . . at twelve at night.
Colonel Crockett in Texas, *p.103*

1846: We labored industriously the entire day making dugouts. Two large cotton-wood trees were felled, about three and a half feet in diameter. From these, canoes were hollowed out, twenty-five feet in length. *Edwin Bryant,* What I Saw in California, *p.47*

Erie Canal: 360-mile-long canal between Buffalo on Lake Erie and Albany, New York, completed in 1825. For description, see Canal boat.

flat boat: same as an ark.

1801: Went down the Mississippi, Jan 1 to June 30, 1801, 440 flat boats, 26 keel boats, and 7 large canoes. Massachusetts Spy, *November 25*

1829: The captain had housed his all in an ark, called in our Western language, a flat boat. Life of S.S. Prentiss, *p.31*

flogging: a form of punishment practiced by the American and British navies, meted out to sailors who were derelict in their duties or disrespectful to an officer.

frigate: a swift, medium-sized warship having three masts and one gun deck.

graveyard watch: a deck watch from midnight to 4 A.M.

half horse, half alligator: an appellation river boatmen gave to describe themselves in boast. The name came to be widely used whenever discussing river men and their tough lifestyles.

1812: "Half horse half alligator" has hitherto been the boast of our up-country boatmen when quarreling. The present season however has made a complete change. A few days ago two of them quarreled in a boat at Natchez, when one of them jumping ashore declared with a horrid oath that he was a steamboat. His opponent immediately followed him, swearing he was an earthquake and would shake him to pieces. Salem Gazette, *June 12*

1820: Eight or ten of these half horse and half alligator gentry, commonly called Ohio boatmen. *Hall,* Letters from the South, *p.89*

1847: The half horse and half alligator species of men, who are peculiar to "Old Mississippi," and who appear to gain a livelihood simply by going up and down the river. *T.B. Thorpe,* The Big Bear of Arkansas, *p.14*

hard tack: a ration of hard bread or biscuit, served on long sea voyages.

hoggees: boys, aged twelve to seventeen, who drove the horses or mules along a canal's towpath. More than one thousand hoggees were working the canals in 1850. They were paid eight to ten dollars per month, were often mistreated, and were sometimes even whipped by a boat's owners. Most hoggees put in long hours and dreamed of one day becoming steersmen.

hurricane deck: the upper deck on a steamboat.
1838: It was delightful to remove from the noise, and heat, and confusion below, to the lofty hurricane deck. *E. Flagg,* The Far West, *p. 29*

irons: handcuffs and leg manacles, used to restrain prisoners on a navy warship.

jolly boat: a small boat used for excursions to shore from a larger vessel. It was usually kept at the stern.

Jolly Roger: a black flag with skull and crossbones, the emblem of a pirate ship.

junk, salt junk: salted beef or pork, a staple provision on long sea voyages. See also citation under Bark.

keel boat: a forty- to seventy-five-foot river boat having a steering oar, mast and sails, and a heavy timber keel that extended beyond the bow to protect the hull from collisions with submerged logs. It usually had a long shed amidships for cargo and cabin. Unlike flat boats, keel boats could be poled or sometimes sailed upriver.
1820: The river [Ohio] is navigated by Steam Boats, Barges, Keel Boats, Flat Boats . . . Skiffs, Pirogues, Rafts. Western Review, *January*

keel hauling: originating in the Dutch navy, a disciplinary action in which a man was pulled underneath the keel of a ship by ropes from one side to another, a practice abandoned in the nineteenth century.

Kentucky boat: another name for an ark or flat boat.
1817: In the course of the day we passed no fewer than thirteen arks, or Kentucky boats, going with produce to New Orleans. *John Bradbury,* Travels, *p.198*
1824: Those boats called Kentucky boats, a sort of huge, square, clumsy wooden box. *John Randolph in Congress, April 15*

ketch: a two-masted, fore-and-aft-rigged vessel, with the mizzen mast stepped forward of the steering gear. Used throughout the century for cargo and for fishing.

lazarette: a ship compartment used as a quarantine for persons with contagious diseases. Also used as a holding room for troublemakers or as a storeroom on some vessels.

lock: a gated enclosure in a canal in which water is let in or out to raise or lower water levels and advance a vessel to another lock.

locktender/lockmaster: one who tended a canal's locks.

magazine: on a man-of-war, a storeroom for gunpowder and other ordnance.

man-of-war: any warship.

marry the gunner's daughter: to be flogged on a Royal Navy vessel.

missionaries: often assigned to canals to counter the rampant vice — drinking, gambling, prostitution — found in taverns along the banks.

mule drink: on a towpath, a low area where canal water sometimes flowed over, forming a pool where mules stopped to drink.

mustering: calling a crew together for a drill or inspection.

Nantucket sleigh ride: referring to the wild ride experienced by a whaling boat being towed by a whale it had harpooned.

packet: any fast sailing ship that carried passengers, freight and mail on a regular schedule. Steamships eventually replaced them after midcentury.

packet, canal: a canal boat that carried freight, passengers and mail on a regular route and schedule.
> 1842: It resembles a small Noah's Ark — a houseboat whose only deck is the roof of the cabin. In the bow, carefully cut off from the rest of the boat, is a tiny cuddy for the crew. Next back of this is the ladies' dressing room and cabin, sometimes a separate room, sometimes cut off from the main cabin only by a red curtain. Next is the main cabin, 36 to 45 feet long, which was saloon and dining room by day and men's dormitory by night. Back of this is the bar, and finally, at the very stern, is the kitchen, almost always presided over by a negro cook, who is usually the bartender also. The other members of the crew are the captain, two drivers, two steersmen, one each for the night and day shifts.
> *Charles Dickens, describing the Pennsylvania Main Line packet boat*

paddle wheel: the huge, steam-powered paddles at the rear or sides of a steamboat. A steamship (paddle-wheeler) distinguished by the use of a paddle wheel instead of a screw. See also Steamboat.

patron: the captain or steersman of a river boat. Also spelled patroon.
> 1817: Our patron, or steersman, who conducted the first boat, and directed our motions. *John Bradbury,* Travels, *p.176*
> 1826: [We went down the Mississippi] in a very large keelboat, with an ignorant patron. The whole way was one scene of disasters.
> *T. Flint,* Recollections, *p.81*

THE COST OF MAILING A LETTER IN 1815

From 1811-1812 the Congress ordered a survey of the post road from Passamaquoddy in the District of Maine to Sunbury, Georgia, to establish accurate distances between towns for calculating post rates. The rates that resulted in 1815 were as follows:

Single letter, conveyed by land for any distance not exceeding 10 miles, 6 cents.

Over 10 but not exceeding 60 miles: 8 cents
Over 60 but not exceeding 100 miles: 10 cents
Over 100 but not exceeding 150 miles: 12 cents
Over 150 but not exceeding 200 miles: 15 cents
Over 200 but not exceeding 250 miles: 17 cents
Over 250 but not exceeding 350 miles: 20 cents
Over 350 but not exceeding 450 miles: 22 cents
Over 450 miles . . . 25 cents

(Double letters charged double.)

In 1865 free delivery of mail was provided in cities with populations of over fifty thousand. In 1873, delivery was free in cities of twenty thousand or more; and in 1887, of ten thousand or more. In 1896, rural free delivery was begun.

---

pirogue, perogue: a large, dug-out canoe, frequently found in Louisiana.
1801: Having purchased a pirogue, or other large canoe, he put Jack and the other negroes he had purchased on board.
Massachusetts Spy, *September 30*
1826: In another place are pirogues of from two to four tons burthen, hollowed sometimes from one prodigious tree, or from the trunks of two trees united, and a plank rim fitted to the upper part.
T. Flint, Recollections, *p.14*

ram bow: on a man-of-war, a bow equipped with an iron or bronze projection used for ramming enemy vessels.

relay barn: along a canal, a barn where tired mules were exchanged for fresh ones.

roundhouse: on a large vessel, a deckhouse aft of the mainmast.

sail room: a compartment where sails were stored.

saloon: on a merchant ship, the officer's mess. Also, a main passenger accommodation.

salt horse: beef or pork pickled in brine, a staple during long voyages.

schooner: a ship having two or more masts, each fore-and-aft rigged, the mainmast being aft of and taller than the foremast. Used for cargo, fishing, etc., with many variations in construction according to the ship's purpose, throughout the century.

1849: After some delay . . . we embarked at San Blas on the 12th of April, in the *San Blasina*, a schooner of twenty-three tons—being thirty-six feet long and twelve wide—for San Francisco. In this miserable, unseaworthy craft, thirty-eight of us took passage. . . . We were so cramped for room on deck, the hold being filled with bananas, that three of us slept in a canoe hewed from a log, which was made secure on deck. *Daniel B. Woods,* Sixteen Months at the Gold Diggings, *p.39*

shanghai: to kidnap a sailor from one vessel to enlist him to duty on another vessel; a practice of boardinghouse landlords who were paid (see also Blood money) to fill out a ship's crew with either willing or unwilling sailors in order to prevent the captain from being short-handed, widely practiced throughout the nineteenth century.

1872: The various methods of forcing a sailor to sea are called Shanghai-ing. The practice is resorted to by landlords, to enable them to complete the crews which they have contracted to furnish to vessels. The owners and masters of these vessels are fully aware of the infamous manner in which men are procured for them, but say they must either connive at it, or let their vessels go to sea shorthanded. Usually, Shanghaiing is practiced upon drunken sailors. . . . They are made drunk . . . and are kept so until an opportunity presents itself for sending them to sea. Thus they are gotten rid of, care being taken to ship them only on voyages of two or three years duration. The land-lords receive a premium on the men furnished by them. . . . When the wretches who carry on this business are very much pressed for men, they do not hesitate to waylay sailors, knock them senseless, and convey them on board vessels in this condition. . . . They sometimes abduct men who have never trod the deck of a ship before. *James McCabe,* Lights and Shadows of New York Life, *p.784*

shanty: a song sung by the crew of a vessel to keep work in unison, especially when heaving ropes.

sloop: a small vessel having a single mast, fore-and-aft rigged, with one or two head sails. The Bermuda Sloop was a favorite of pirates and privateers early in the century, due to its speed. The Hudson River Sloop, sometimes up to ninety feet in length, carried passengers and cargo on the Hudson before the introduction of steam vessels. A Sloop-of-War was a small navy vessel having fewer than eighteen guns.

slop room: a compartment for storing extra clothes for the crew.

slops: extra clothing kept on board merchant vessels for sailors too poor to have their own change of clothes.

snag: trees and driftwood that collected in shallows or channels and menaced river navigation, especially that of steamboats. Snags were regularly removed by crews on snag boats.

snubbing post: along a canal, any post to which mules could be tied.

steamboat: the most popular form of river boat, from 1807 until the end of the century. They were powered by burning cordwood to produce steam, which turned huge paddle wheels located along the sides or at the rear. Seagoing steamboats were more and more frequently equipped with screw propellers instead of paddles after midcentury. However, riverboats continued to use paddles throughout the century due to their superior reverse power.

Early steamboat models were notorious for running afoul on snags and sinking in ice floes. Their crude boilers frequently exploded, causing spectacular fires. As their safety record gradually improved, the vessels became increasingly more lavish. Some were even called floating palaces. Showboats featuring traveling theater groups began plying the Ohio and Mississippi as early as 1836; productions included everything from Shakespeare to minstrel shows. Floating circuses, with all the attractions of land-based shows, made stops up and down the major rivers from the 1850s on.

> 1853: The word boat gives a very imperfect idea of this floating palace, which accommodates . . . from five to six hundred American citizens and others, of all classes, in a style of splendor that Cleopatra herself might envy. . . . I followed a crowd of five hundred up a handsome staircase, through spendidly furnished saloons covered with carpet of velvet pile, to the upper deck. Tea being served, we all adjourned to the gentlemen's cabin. . . . At the entrance we were met by tall, swarthy figures, clothed in white linen of unspotted purity, who conducted us to our seats. There were three tables, the entire length of the room covered with everything that was beautiful.
> *Description of the steamboat* Empire State *in* Hunt's Magazine

steersman: one who steered a canal boat.

tow path: a wide path along a canal, where a horse, mule or team of such walked at the end of a long line, towing a canal boat. Travel this way was so slow that passengers could jump onto the tow path to stretch their legs and walk a bit while the boat continued on beside them.

wait house: also known as a shanty or dog house, a small building next to a lock, in which a lock tender waited for boats to lock through.

wood up: to reload a steamboat with cordwood fuel.

Crew of a Large Nineteenth-Century Sailing Vessel

able seaman: a senior deck hand responsible for rigging, manning guns and occasionally taking the helm.

boatswain: warrant officer responsible for supervising crew and the ship's maintenance. He would beat the crew to get them to work harder; he also served as an executioner. Also spelled bosun or bos'n.

boatswain's mate: a petty officer who assisted the boatswain.

cabin boy: one who waited on and served as a "gopher" for officers.

callboy: carried the pipes and whistles of the boatswain and sometimes relayed whistled commands to other parts of the ship.

carpenter: ship's carpenter; a petty officer responsible for the upkeep of all woodwork on board.

cockswain: the helmsman of a ship's auxiliary boat; the head of this boat's crew.

conder: a lookout who gives directions to the helmsman; one who cons or directs a ship from a lookout position.

deck hand: in the merchant navy, a rank below chief officer and boatswain.

deck officer: in the merchant navy, an officer who keeps watch on the bridge.

efficient deck hand: a deck hand over the age of eighteen who has passed a competency test and who has served for at least one year.

first mate: chief officer ranking just below master on a merchant navy vessel.

foretopman: a seaman whose station is the fore topmast.

helmsman: the seaman who steers the vessel. Also known as the quarter-master, wheelman, steersman.

lady of the gunroom: Royal Navy slang for seaman responsible for the gunner's stores.

lamp trimmer: a seaman responsible for maintaining all oil lamps on a vessel.

lee helmsman: the assistant to the helmsman who stands at the lee side of the wheel.

master: the commander of a merchant navy vessel. Short for master mariner.

master at arms: officer in charge of maintaining law and order on board.

mate: first rank below the master. The mate is responsible for organization and navigation. Same as first mate.

midshipman: the lowest ranking commissioned officer.

ordinary seaman: seaman who has not yet qualified for able seaman status.

petty officer: a noncommissioned naval officer.

quartermaster: in the merchant navy, the helmsman. In the Royal Navy, a supervisor of the helmsman.

sailmaker: a crew member who constructs and repairs sails and other items made of canvas.

steward: crew member in charge of catering, provisioning and maintaining the living quarters.

storekeeper: crew member in charge of stores and their issuance to crew.

supercargo: short for superintendent of cargo; the owner or representative of the owner of a ship's cargo who travels on board a merchant vessel.

warrant officer: in the Royal Navy, a senior ranking, noncommissioned officer.

yeoman: in the Royal Navy, an assistant to the navigator. Also, an assistant to a storekeeper.

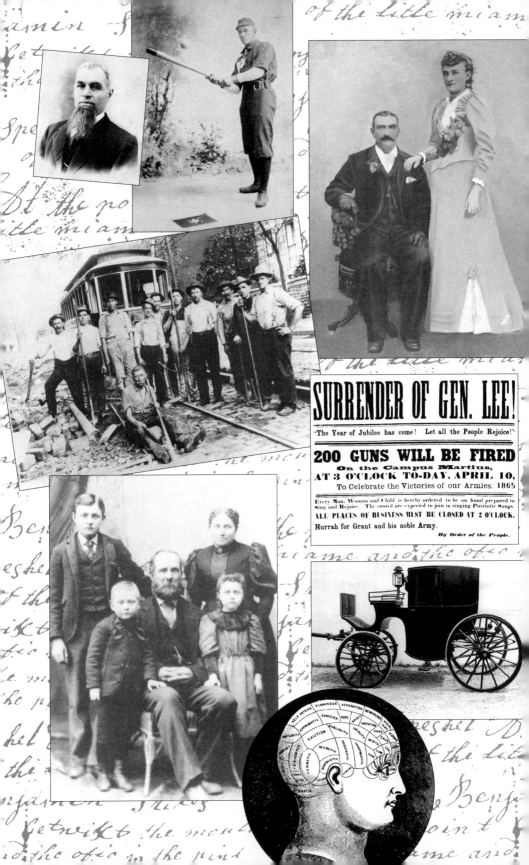

SURRENDER OF GEN. LEE!

"The Year of Jubilee has come! Let all the People Rejoice!"

200 GUNS WILL BE FIRED

On the Campus Martius,

AT 3 O'CLOCK TO-DAY, APRIL 10,

To Celebrate the Victories of our Armies. 1865

Every Man, Woman and Child is hereby ordered to be on hand prepared to Sing and Rejoice. The crowd are expected to join in singing Patriotic Songs.

ALL PLACES OF BUSINESS MUST BE CLOSED AT 2 O'CLOCK.

Hurrah for Grant and his noble Army.

By Order of the People.

AROUND THE HOUSE

A one-room log cabin with dirt or puncheon floor, simple fireplace, sawbuck table and straw mattress in which an entire family might sleep — that was as far as luxury went on the frontier and in newly settled regions of the country. Long-settled communities enjoyed roomier abodes, of course, and as the wealth of a region and of the nation grew, houses became larger, more elaborate and better equipped. Still, many city dwellers couldn't afford their own homes and lived instead in boardinghouses and dingy tenement buildings. And throughout much of the century, citizens knew little of the conveniences that spoil homeowners today.

Electricity arrived late in the century. So did the telephone. There was no television, radio or stereo, no microwave, food processor, or flick-of-the-switch lighting. Lighting came from candles or from oil or gas lamps. Refrigeration was unknown until the invention of the simple icebox. Until then, housewives preserved foods by drying, salting and smoking. Flick-of-the-dial thermostat heating would have been seen as miraculous compared with the fireplace or wood stove fire that had to be stoked relentlessly and that invariably extinguished itself during the wee — and coldest — hours of the night. The kitchen in summer must have been sweltering. Too, with water needing to be heated over the stove, little wonder that irregular bathing was the norm.

The nineteenth-century home was a woman's domain or, more accurately, her confines. Here, without electricity, without modern appliances, she did all of her chores by hand. The wash. The preserving. The cooking. The cleaning. The sewing. The tending to her average flock of at least five children. Truly, in the nineteenth-century home, a woman's work was *never* done. Imagine making all of your family's clothes by hand, as housewives did early in the century, and you begin to get an idea of just how labor-intensive the career of domestic manager was in those days.

American Empire: a style of furniture characterized by turned legs carved with acanthus leaf or horn-of-plenty motif; heavily scrolled or flattened ball feet; and brass rosette or glass knob handles. Made from mahogany, cherry or maple, furniture in this style dominated in well-to-do households from 1820-1840.

balloon-framing: a house-framing method employing two-by-fours or other small members, as distinguished from the heavy timber framing used prior to the 1840s.

bathtubs: the first was installed in a Boston hotel in 1829. More than fifteen hundred could be found in hotels and wealthy households throughout Philadelphia by 1836. However, the typical family didn't own a built-in tub until well into the second half of the century. Previously, a round, wooden or tin tub was hauled out onto the kitchen floor or into a bedroom and filled with hot water from the fireplace or stove.

beds/bedrooms: the wealthy slept in amply stuffed feather beds; the poor made do with straw mattresses. Due to the small size of the houses that predominated among the poor and middle class in the first half of the century, the parents of a family typically enjoyed the only private room — assuming there was even that. Small children and adolescents frequently slept together, two, three and four to a bed. The boys shared their beds with apprentices or other male houseguests as well. (Even travelers barely acquainted with one another slept together at roadside inns early in the century.) As the country grew wealthier, however, houses expanded, and many adolescents were provided with a room and a bed of their own. During the 1840s, 1850s and 1860s, multiple-bedroom homes became more common as families grew wealthy enough to leave their pioneer ways behind.

bell pull: a door bell. In better houses, it consisted of a round brass knob attached by wire through the front doorjamb to a bell in the front hallway. The bell was rung by pulling the knob.

Belter furniture: ornately carved rosewood furniture with rich upholstery, a favorite among the wealthy from 1844-1865.

boardinghouse: a large portion of the population lived in boarding-houses, especially in cities, throughout the century.
1840s: When we penetrate a little deeper into the domestic arrangements of the natives, we find that the most prominent feature of their private lives is its publicity. The vast majority of the town inhabitants of the United States live in boarding houses or hotels; and it would be difficult indeed to calculate the small proportion of those who live alone. *T.C. Grattan,* Civilized America

1868: . . . it has been remarked that New York is a vast boarding house. If any one doubts this, he has only to turn to the columns of the Herald, and see the long rows of advertisements on the subject. . . . All boarding houses begin to fill up for the winter about the first of October. Few of the proprietors have any trouble filling their establishments, as there is generally a rush of strangers to the City during the winter season. A few of the best houses retain their guests for years, but the occupants of the majority change their quarters every fall. *Edward Martin,* Secrets of the Great City, *pp.211,214*

1868: [The potential boarder] will have interviews with landladies of various appearances, ages and characteristics—landladies dubious and dingy, landladies severe and suspicious, landladies calm and confiding—the majority being widows. He will survey inumerable rooms—generally under that peculiarly cheerful aspect attendant on unmade beds and unemptied wash basins. . . . How a three-feet-by-sixteen-inches strip of threadbare carpet, a twelve-and-a-half-cents-Chatham-square mirror, and a disjointed chair may, in the lively imagination of boarding house proprietresses, be considered "furniture." How double, triple and even quintuple beds in single rooms . . . are esteemed highly eligible accommodations for a single gentleman. How partitions . . . may in no wise prevent the occupants of adjoining rooms from holding conversations with one another, becoming cognizant of neighboring snores, or turnings in bed. He will observe that lavatory arrangements are . . . a frail and rickety washing stand . . . a ewer and basin of limited capacity . . . and a weblike towel.
Edward Winslow Martin, Secrets of the Great City, *p.213*

1872: One is struck with the great number of handsome young widows who are to be found in these establishments. Sometimes they do not assume the character of a widow, but claim to be the wives of men absent in the distant Territories, or in Europe, and pretend to receive letters and remittances from them. The majority of these women are adventuresses, and they make their living in a way they do not care to have known. They conduct themselves with the utmost outward propriety in the house, and disarm even the suspicious landlady by their ladylike deportment. They are ripe for an intrigue with any man in the house, and as their object is simply to make money, they care little for exposure if that object is attained.
James McCabe, Lights and Shadows of New York Life, *p.507*

Boston rocker: a spindle-backed rocking chair with cyma-curved arms and seat. It was stenciled with gilt and colored designs, and was commonly found from 1820 on.

candles: used throughout the first half of the century and somewhat after for household lighting.

1845: ... candles supply the most convenient and the most general mode of obtaining artificial light for domestic purposes. Until lately, two substances only, wax and tallow, were known as material for candles; spermaceti was next introduced, and at present various substances such as stearine, etc., are added.

Thomas Webster, Encyclopedia of Domestic Economy

Cape Cod: a rectangular, one-and-a-half-story house with a pitched roof, originating in Cape Cod, Massachusetts, in the Colonial period.

carpenter gothic: Victorian house ornamentation comprised of fretworks of scrolled wood. Also known as gingerbread, bargeboard scroll and steamboat gothic.

carpeting: carpets were extremely rare at the beginning of the century. However, by 1830 nearly one out of four households had at least one carpet.

catslide house: nickname for a saltbox, named for its long, sloping rear roof and short front roof.

chamber set: a basin and large-mouthed pitcher for washing, a cup for brushing the teeth, and a chamber pot for relieving oneself at night. Such sets were provided in hotel rooms from the 1830s on and could be found in many home bedrooms from the 1840s on.

Chippendale: furniture inspired by the work of Thomas Chippendale, master furniture designer. Reigning in wealthy homes from 1750-1775, the furniture was most often made of mahogany and was characterized by curved, cabriole legs terminating in claw-and-ball feet. Decorative touches included carved foliage, scroll and shell designs.

circular sofa: a cylindrical, Victorian sofa, measuring four to seven feet in diameter and having a central column rising from its center to serve as a backrest, designed for small talk. Also known as a causeuse. Popular from 1850-1880.

clocks: inexpensive clocks became available from about 1806 on. Most families owned at least one cheap shelf clock by the 1830s.

corner chair: a wooden chair specifically designed to fit snugly in a corner, characterized by one front leg and three rear legs, popular in wealthy homes from 1775-1825.

Currier and Ives prints: prints of American scenes or of history, used to decorate the walls of some homes from the 1840s on.

daguerreotypes: the earliest photographs, the process invented in 1839. Portraits of family members were taken by this and later methods of photography and displayed on tables, shelves and walls. Previously, portraits of family members had been painted at great expense by a local artist.

deacon's bench: also known as a settee or settle; a wooden spindle-backed bench capable of seating three or four people. They were used by church elders during services, but they were also widely found in homes, on porches and in front of public buildings, including stores, throughout the century.

Dutch Colonial: originating in the Dutch-settled areas of New York and the Hudson Valley in the 1700s, a house characterized by a gambrel roof (two pitches on each side) and overhanging eaves.

early Victorian furniture: large, ponderous furniture made of mahogany, rosewood or black walnut from 1840-1850. Notable characteristics: saber legs; marble table tops; turned bedposts; mushroom-turned wooden knobs for handles; ornamentation in the form of carved medallions featuring flowers, fruits and foliage.

electricity: the first power station was constructed on Pearl Street in New York. In 1882 several miles of streets were dug up to install electric cables from the station to surrounding homes, which began receiving electric current on September 4. Electric lighting gradually replaced gas lights for the remainder of the century. Electrical appliances followed, with an electric range being exhibited at the Chicago World's Fair of 1893.

envelopes: first manufactured in 1839 in New York. Previously, letters were simply folded over and mailed.

Federal Style house: a classic revival house style in vogue from 1790-1830. Its most notable features were its round or oval rooms, brass and iron hardware, elaborate fan doorways (some with porticoes), twin front stairways and two to four chimneys flanking either end of the roof.

gas lighting/appliances: a few wealthy families had piped-in gas from central factories as early as 1821 in Baltimore, and by the 1830s in Philadelphia, New York and Boston. Philadelphia's gaslight system boasted seven hundred customers by 1836. By 1875, most large towns and all citizens enjoyed the luxuries of piped-in gas. Cooking with gas began in the 1880s.

Gothic Victorian: mahogany, rosewood or black walnut furniture commonly found in mansions, country estates and churches from 1840-1865. Notable features included pierced and carved arabesque chair backs; deeply cut, spiral-turned legs; white marble or wooden tabletops.

HOUSEHOLD TIPS

Look frequently to the pails, to see that nothing is thrown to the pigs which should have been in the grease-pot.

See that the beef and pork are always under brine; and that the brine is sweet and clean.

An ox's gall will set any color—silk, cotton, or woollen. I have seen the colors of calico, which faded at one washing, fixed by it. Where one lives near a slaughterhouse . . . the gall can be bought for a few cents. . . .

Eggs will keep almost any length of time in lime-water properly prepared. One pint of coarse salt, and one pint of unslacked lime, to a pailful of water. If there be too much lime, it will eat the shells from the eggs; and if there be a single egg cracked, it will spoil the whole. They should be kept covered with lime-water, and in a cold place . . . I have seen eggs, thus kept, perfectly sweet and fresh at the end of three years. . . .

If feather-beds smell badly, or become heavy, from want of proper preservation of the feathers, or from old age, empty them, and wash the feathers thoroughly in a tub of suds; spread them in your garret to dry, and they will be as light and as good as new.

New England rum, constantly used to wash the hair, keeps it very clean, and free from disease, and promotes its growth a great deal more than Macassar oil.

Barley straw is the best for beds; dry corn husks, slit into shreds, are far better than straw.

In winter, always set the handle of your pump as high as possible, before you go to bed. Except in very frigid weather this keeps the handle from freezing. When there is reason to apprehend extreme cold, do not forget to throw a rug or horse-blanket over your pump; a frozen pump is a comfortless preparation for a winter's breakfast.

Very hard and durable candles are made in the following manner: Melt together ten ounces of mutton tallow, a quarter of an ounce of camphor, four ounces of beeswax, and two ounces of alum. Candles made of these materials burn with a very clear light.

Honey mixed with pure pulverized charcoal is said to be excellent to cleanse the teeth, and make them white. Limewater with a little Peruvian bark is very good to be occasionally used by those who have defective teeth, or an offensive breath.

1836, in The American Frugal Housewife, by Mrs. Child

Ornamentation included pierced or incised trefoils, quatrefoils and spandrels.

Greek Revival: an early nineteenth-century house style reminiscent of classic Greek and Roman forms, characterized by Corinthian, Doric or Ionic wood-columned porticoes creating the famous "temple" look.

Door surrounds and eaves were carefully carved in Greek foliate or geometric motifs to complete the look.

Hepplewhite: furniture inspired by the designs of London cabinetmaker, George Hepplewhite, from 1785-1800. The furniture was frequently made of mahogany with a satinwood veneer. Notable features included shield-shaped, entwined heart or oval chair backs; slender, tapering legs, sometimes terminating in spade feet. Ornamentation included carved feathers, drapery festoons, eagle medallions and oval brass drawer handles.

Hitchcock chair: a wooden chair having a rush or cane seat and turned front legs ending in tiny ball feet. Painted brownish-black to simulate rosewood, it was usually stenciled with gilt and colored designs. Many Hitchcock chairs were manufactured from 1822-1843.

Italianate Victorian: popular in the United States and England throughout the mid-1800s, a classic Victorian house characterized by slightly pitched roof, square towers and round-arched windows. Today the Italianate is often seen as the classic haunted house of Hollywood.

keeping room: the common sitting room. In New England, the parlor.
1830: The chamber over the keeping room is that in which the murder
   was committed. Massachusetts Spy, *August 25*
1857: Carpets were then only known in a few families, and were confined
   to the keeping-room and parlor. *S.G. Goodrich,* Recollections, *p.74*

kerosene lamps: used widely to light homes from about 1865-1900. The whale-oil lamps previously in use were simply discarded or retrofitted with kerosene burners. Kerosene was noted for producing a smoky, torchlike light.

lard-oil lamps: used widely from about 1840 on. Lard oil was somewhat cheaper than whale oil. Noah Webster used a pair of lard-oil lamps when compiling his dictionary, published in 1836.

log houses: commonly seen inland in rural areas of the East and in any frontier land where trees were available. Such houses commonly had dirt or puncheon floors.

Louis XV, French Victorian: black walnut, rosewood and mahogany furniture popular from 1845-1870. Notable features included slender, cabriole legs with simple or whorl feet; balloon-shaped chair backs; cartouche-shaped tabletops made of marble; bedstead beds; drop-front or slant-front desks. Ornamentation included carved rose or grape motifs with leaves and tendrils, scroll carving on table legs, and handles carved in fruit and leaf motifs. The best-known of all Victorian furniture.

medallion-back sofa: a serpentine-backed sofa with a large, upholstered oval or cartouche-shaped medallion comprising the center backrest, found in homes from 1855-1870.

oven/stove: food was cooked over an open fire with heavy kettles and awkward fireplace appliances, such as a pivoting crane, until the 1820s, when cast-iron cookstoves were introduced—largely to the rich. The cast-iron stoves covered the outmoded fireplaces and burned one-third less wood. They simplified cooking because their stovetops were at waist level, which saved housewives from constantly stooping. In the 1830s, the middle class bricked up their fireplaces and purchased the new stoves in droves. By the 1850s, only rural families and poor Southerners continued with the old ways.

1830s: . . . the fireplace was the main thing in the kitchen. Of course there was a crane to hang kettles on. The brass kettles, of various sizes, was kind of dress-up kettles; the iron kettles were the everyday ones. They had legs, so they would either set on the hearth next to the fire, or hang by a pothook on the crane. . . . There wasn't too much stuff fried. . . . Things were mostly either cooked on a spit or in a pot. *Excerpt in* The Kitchen in History

1836: Economical people heat ovens with pine wood, fagots, brush, and such. . . . If you have none but hardwood, you must remember that it makes very hot coals, and therefore less of it will answer. A smart fire for an hour and a half is a general rule for common sized family ovens, provided brown bread and beans are to be baked. An hour is long enough to heat an oven for flour bread.
Mrs. Child, The American Frugal Housewife, *p.79*

parlor: a room having all the best furniture, set apart for entertaining guests or conducting special functions, such as wedding receptions, wakes, and so on. Until the 1820s, the parlor frequently played a dual role, serving as a couple's bedroom as well.

peg lamp: also known as a socket lamp; an oil lamp that could be carried from room to room and placed in a candle socket wherever light was needed.

pigs: kept as pets and as future food sources in yards, towns and cities all over America. Thousands of them ran freely on New York City streets during the first half of the century.

1804: Hogs are the most numerous of the domestic animals; they are kept by all the inhabitants [of Kentucky]. These animals never leave the woods, where they always find sufficient food . . . Every inhabitant recognizes his own by the particular manner in which the ears are cut. The pigs stray . . . and do not make their appearance again for several months. Their owners accustom them, however, to return every now and then . . . by throwing them Indian corn once or twice a week. *Francois Andre Michaux,* This Was America

1847: I cannot refrain from saying a few kind words on behalf of the favored pet of the Americans, the swine. I have not yet found any city, county or town where I have not seen these lovable animals wandering about peacefully in huge herds . . . the swine have shown certain good traits which are of real practical value; in the country they greedily devour all kinds of snakes and the like, and in the towns they are very helpful in keeping the streets "cleaner than man can do" by eating up all kinds of refuse. *O.M. Raeder, excerpted in* This Was America

puncheon floor: a plank floor, commonly used in log cabins or other frontier houses.

1838: The floor is constructed of short, thick planks, technically termed puncheons, which are confined by wooden pins.
E. Flagg, The Far West, *i, p.189*

1840: The house was constructed of logs, and the floor was of puncheons; a term, which in Georgia, means split logs, with their faces a little smoothed with the axe or hatchet.
A.B. Longstreet, Georgia Scenes, *p.12*

Queen Anne: a house style popular in the 1870s and 1880s in England and America, actually based on a combination of Elizabethan, Tudor, Gothic and English Renaissance forms. Notable features included polygonal or cylindrical towers, bay windows, balconies, and ornate woodwork.

Renaissance Victorian: furniture made of black walnut with burl-veneered panels or ash with black walnut trim, in vogue from 1860-1875.

Romanesque: an early Victorian house style in vogue from 1840-1860, characterized by tall towers, arched windows and decorative arcading beneath the eaves.

sawbuck table: a simple, homemade kitchen table, often made of pine boards with X-shaped trestle legs, common throughout the first half of the century, especially among the poor.

Second Empire: a midcentury house style originally developed in France, characterized by mansard roofs, tall arched windows and doors, iron roof pinnacles and rich ornamentation.

serpentine-back sofa: a Victorian mahogany sofa having a serpentine-arched top rail and half-lyre-shaped armrests, from 1840-1855.

shanty: a roughly built shack or small house, common in rural or poor America.

1820: [These people] lived in what is here called a shanty. This is a hovel of about 10 feet by 8, made somewhat in the form of an ordinary cow-house. *Zerah Hawley*, Tour, *p.21*

1839: The contractors upon the Brunswick and Alatamaha Canal are desirous to hire a number of Prime Negro Men until the 1st January 1840. . . . These negroes will be employed in the excavation of the canal. They will be provided with 3½ pounds of pork or bacon per week, and lodged in comfortable shantees.
J.S. Buckingham, Slave States, *p.137*

Sheraton: furniture inspired by the designs of Thomas Sheraton of London, from 1800-1820. Made of mahogany with satinwood veneer, or cherry with maple veneer, its characteristic features included turned and reeded legs; tripod and lyre-shaped chair backs; and vase and lyre-shaped table pedestals. Ornamentation included carved drapery festoons, bowknotted wheat ears, and various sprays, foliage, etc. Drawer handles were either brass rosette knobs or lions' heads with pendant rings.

sitting room: a living room or parlor.

1852: Looking from the sitting-room windows, Cassy and Emmeline could see the troops. *Harriet Beecher Stowe*, Uncle Tom's Cabin

slat-backed rocker: a simple, plain, straight-backed rocker with a rush or woven tape seat, of Shaker design from 1800-1860s.

Sleepy Hollow armchair: an upholstered, semicircular or wraparound chair with cabriole front legs, so-named because it was a favorite of author Washington Irving. Found in well-to-do homes from 1850-1870.

smoke room: A small room on the second floor or in the attic, next to a central chimney, where meats were sometimes smoked over hickory shavings; found mostly in farmhouses early in the century.

spool-turned Victorian: black walnut, maple and birch furniture noted for its spool-turned legs, bedposts, spindles, etc., from 1850-1870.

spring room: part of the kitchen or a small room just off the kitchen of a farmhouse, where spring water flowed and was captured in a large barrel.

student lamp: a commonly used kerosene lamp for reading. It was comprised of two sections, the lamp itself, and a separate oil reservoir from which oil flowed down a tube into the burner, from about 1865 on.

telephone: the first intercity lines were erected for demonstration between Salem and Boston in 1877. *Scientific American* featured a front-page story on the telephone in October of the same year. The first central switchboard, without which calls could not be made, was set up in New Haven, Connecticut, in 1878. By 1900, 1.4 million telephones were in use nationwide.

tenement house: constructed in cities from about 1840 on, mainly to house the poor.

1876: . . . half a million men, women, and children are living in the tenement houses of New York today, many of them in a manner that would almost disgrace heathendom itself. No brush could paint and no pencil describe with all the vividness of truth itself the utter wretchedness and misery, the vice and crime, that may be found within a stone's throw of our City Hall, and even within an arm's length of many of our churches. . . . From the nearly 20,000 tenement houses come 93 percent of the deaths and 90 percent of the crimes of our population. Harper's Weekly

Turkish Victorian: oversized, overstuffed furniture with coil spring seats. The upholstery was made of plush, velour, brocatelle or brocade and decorated with tassels and fringe. In fashion from 1870-1880.

Victorian house colors: fashionable Victorian house colors varied from region to region. Some popular colors included olive yellow, terra cotta, Indian red, red-brown, olive, buff, bronze green, Chinese red, lavender, pink and lime green.

wallpaper: panoramic landscapes and historical scenes were available on wallpapers from 1800-1850. Only the wealthy could afford them, however. Cheap, decorative wallpaper for the middle class became available from about midcentury on.

wash room: a laundry room in a shed off the kitchen.

water: most householders had to haul or pump water from a cistern or well until the 1830s, 1840s and 1850s, when municipal water systems began piping water into city homes for the first time. (The Croton Water Works supplied piped-in water to New York residents from 1842 on.) Rural families continued to haul and pump throughout the century. A few country homes had a windmill pump water to the attic, so that it could be dispersed through pipes by gravity to wherever it was needed in the house.

water closet: early name for the indoor bathroom. Also known as the necessary.

whale-oil lamps: tin, pewter or brass lamps that burned whale oil, used from 1800-1880s.

whatnot: a corner or side-wall arrangement of shelves for bric-a-brac, trifles and curios, for example, coral, conch shells, peacock feathers, figurines, etc., very popular in Victorian parlors from 1850-1875.

Windsor chair: the classic kitchen, tavern or everyday wooden chair. It had a plank seat, a spindled back and canted legs, and it was manufactured with numerous variations throughout the century.

wing chair: an upholstered armchair with projecting wings on either side of the headrest, made in various styles throughout the period.

wood stove/furnace: families who could afford them often had more than one. However, the poor and middle class often relied solely on the kitchen stove or a central fireplace to heat their homes. Coal furnaces — placed in the cellar — were widely used to heat homes in the second half of the century.

1846: The method of heating many of the best houses is a terrible grievance to persons not accustomed to it, and a fatal misfortune to those who are. Casual visitors are nearly suffocated, and constant occupiers killed. An enormous furnace in the cellar sends up, days and night, streams of hot air, through apertures and pipes, to every room of the house. . . . It meets you the moment the street door is opened to let you in, and rushes after you when you emerge again, half-stewed and parboiled, into the wholesome air. The self-victimized citizens who have a preposterous affection for this atmosphere, undoubtedly shorten their lives by it. Several elderly gentlemen . . . suddenly cut off . . . would assuredly have had a verdict of "died of a furnace" pronounced on their cases, had a coroner been called.

T.C. Grattan, Civilized America

SURRENDER OF GEN. LEE!

"The Year of Jubilee has come! Let all the People Rejoice!"

200 GUNS WILL BE FIRED

On the Campus Martius,

AT 3 O'CLOCK TO-DAY, APRIL 10,

To Celebrate the Victories of our Armies. 1865

Every Man, Woman and Child is hereby ordered to be on hand prepared to Sing and Rejoice. The crowd are expected to join in singing Patriotic Songs.

ALL PLACES OF BUSINESS MUST BE CLOSED AT 2 O'CLOCK.

Hurrah for Grant and his noble Army.

By Order of the People.

SECTION FOUR

CLOTHING AND FASHION

Mention nineteenth-century fashion and most people think of hoop skirts, bustles, bloomers and bonnets. Few would think of blue jeans, yet riveted Levi's were indeed part of the fashion scene from about midcentury. One might not think of turbans, either, but the fashionable nineteenth-century woman adored them, donning a wide variety from early in the period on.

American fashions were influenced by European designers, but at the beginning of the century 75 percent of all clothing in the country was homemade. Observers said they could detect the potato-sack-like cut of a homemade garment a mile away, especially next to a tailor-made piece or, later in the century, a store-bought or factory-made garment. Indeed, until the 1840s, when clothing became more readily available in stores, most Americans wore clothing sewn by themselves or their own mothers, sisters or daughters. Thus, quality varied according to a woman's skill.

Later in the century, as the nation's wealth grew, rich society women made careers of wearing the latest and best fashions to show off around town. "The elite do not wear the same dress twice," noted one New Yorker in 1872. "[The society woman] must have one or two velvet dresses which cannot cost less than $500 each; she must possess thousands of dollars' worth of laces, in the shape of flounces, to loop up over the skirts of dresses, as occasion shall require. Walking dresses cost from $50 to $300; ball-dresses are frequently imported from Paris at a cost from $500 to $1000; while wedding dresses may cost $1000 to $5000. Nice white Llama jackets can be had for $60; *robes princesse*, or overskirts of lace, are worth from $60 to $200. Then there are travelling dresses in black silk, in pongee, velour, in piqué, which range in price from $75 to $175. Then there are evening robes in Swiss muslin, robes in linen for the garden and croquet-playing, dresses for horse-races and for yacht races . . . dresses for breakfast and for dinner, dresses for receptions and for parties. . . . A lady going to the Springs takes from twenty to sixty dresses, and fills an enormous number of Saratoga trunks. . . ."

James McCabe, Lights and Shadows of New York Life, *1872*

105

Popular Fashion

adelaide boots: women's fur-topped boots, popular from 1836 to 1837.

albert: a short chain connecting a watch to a buttonhole, popular from 1849 on.

albert overcoat: a man's calf-length overcoat having breast and hip pockets and a half-circle cape resting on the shoulders, fashionable in the 1840s. Also known as a box coat or a driving coat.

alberts: side-lacing half boots with cloth tops and faux mother of pearl buttons on the front.

ankle jacks: half boots laced up with ten holes, worn by men from the 1840s.

Anne Boleyn mob: a popular dress cap or bonnet for women in 1807.

Armenian toque: woman's small turban made of tulle and satin and decorated with feathers and silver, introduced in 1817.

balmoral petticoat: a wool underskirt, frequently red with black stripes, worn under a long skirt, from 1860.

balmorals: front-lacing shoes, introduced by Queen Victoria at Balmoral, Scotland. They were worn by both sexes, from 1860.

bang-up: an overcoat.
1842: A gentleman dressed in a dark colored fashionable bang-up, with tight-bodied coat, neck-cloth, breast pin, hair and whiskers to match.
Philadelphia Spirit of the Times, *January 13*
1842: "That gentlemanly looking man in the snuff-colored bang-up, that's Mayor Scott; he's the very man." "How so?" cried a tall-strapping fellow in a white bang-up.
Philadelphia Spirit of the Times, *January 28*

banyan: a long, informal coat or overcoat with flared skirts, worn around the house by men in the morning, introduced in the 1700s but worn throughout the 1800s.
1833: In the summer, men very often wore calico morning gowns at all times of the day. A damask banyan was much the same thing by another name. *Watson,* Historical Tales of Philadelphia, *p.117*

batswing: a variation of the bowtie having a very small knot, fashionable in the 1890s.

bavolet: a frill attached to the back of a bonnet to protect a woman's neck from the sun.

beehive bonnet: a beehive-shaped bonnet, tied under the chin, made of plaited straw and trimmed with ribbon, from 1806.

Benjamin: a loose topcoat worn by men when traveling, from the 1820s.

Benoiton chains: long beads of black wood or filigreed gold or silver that hung from each side of a woman's head and draped across the bosom, popular from 1865-1870.

beret: a woman's crepe or silk evening cap, usually decorated with ribbons, flowers or feathers.

Bertha: a frilled and ribboned border covering the sleeves and falling over the top of a woman's bodice, from the 1840s.

biled shirt: see Boiled shirt.

bloomers: frilled trousers gathered about the ankles and worn under a short skirt, from midcentury on.

1851: The Turkish Dress. On Saturday afternoon, says the *Times* [Boston], a young lady of 18, daughter of a well-known West End citizen, made her appearance on Cambridge Street, accompanied with her father, dressed in a round hat, short dress, fitting tightly, and pink satin trousers. . . . The same young lady was out yesterday afternoon, for a walk around the Common and upon the Neck. . . . The "Bee" says the daughter of Dr. Hanson, of this city, appeared in the Bloomer suit at a convention at South Reading last week.
Transcript, *May 26*

1851: The New Costume. The first Bloomer made its appearance in our city yesterday. Worcester Spy, *May 29*

1853: A Bloomer was seen in Cleveland the other day. Her skirts were unusually short. Daily Morning Herald, *St. Louis, April 12*

blouse: a loose bodice or shirt worn by women and children from 1820 on.

Bluchers: popular half-boot, heavier but shorter than Wellingtons, having an open front tied over a tongue, worn for riding by men from 1814-1850; named after the Prussian general.

boas: worn by women throughout the century, a scarf of feathers or fur, e.g., swansdown, silver or black bear, stone martin, Bohemian sable, chinchilla, lynx, squirrel, fox, minx, fitch and tinged hare, possum, skunk, beaver, etc.

bodice: the corsetlike, fitted portion of a dress from the waist to the upper chest, sometimes fastened up the back with hooks and eyes and boned in front, often heavily padded at the bosom, which could be either low- or high-cut. A wide variety of styles came in and out of fashion throughout the century. For example, a bodice with a pointed-style waist was sometimes worn beginning in the 1830s. A jacket bodice became popular in 1850. An open V-neck with revers worn with a high-necked habit shirt was fashionable in 1887, and so on.

boiled shirt: popular slang for a clean shirt. Also written or pronounced as biled.
1869: In order to attend the Governor's reception, I borrowed a boiled shirt. *A.K. McClure,* Rocky Mountains, *p.412*

bolero: a woman's short jacket joined only at the breast or not at all, worn from 1890s.

bollinger: an English hat with a wide brim topped by a dome crown or hemisphere, worn in the mid-1850s. Also known as a hemisphere hat.

Bonaparte hat: a woman's helmet-shaped hat trimmed with a laurel wreath, sometimes worn cocked to one side, from 1802-1806.

bonnets: widely popular form of headwear for women for the first half of the century. See individual entries.
1802: . . . a bonnet of black velvet trimmed with a deep black lace round the front. . . . A close bonnet of purple, or other coloured silk, trimmed with ribbon of the same colour and ornamented with a flower in front. . . . A bonnet of black velvet, turned up in front, and lined and trimmed with scarlet, a scarlet feather in front. . . . A bonnet of pink silk, trimmed with black ribbon and a black feather; black lace round the front.
Descriptions of fashionable bonnets, Ladies Monthly Museum, *Philadelphia*

boot hooks: aids to help pull on the long, heavy boots worn from 1800-1870.

bowler: a man's formal hat made of stiff felt and characterized by a narrow brim and a round, black or brown crown, introduced in the 1860s.

breeches: high-waisted pants extending and narrowing to the knee or just below, sometimes fastened by three or four buttons or ties from the knee to the midcalf. Breeches were still much in use at the turn of the century but the longer pantaloons were gradually taking their place in popularity, especially for street wear. To many, breeches were the only socially correct clothes, and thus pantaloons were often banned or at least looked-down upon at formal functions during the first quarter of the century. Thereafter, breeches—otherwise known as knee breeches or small clothes—were reserved largely for sport. See also Pantaloons.

1800: When Dr. J.C. Warren returned from Europe about the year 1800, to begin practice in Boston, he found gentlemen still dressed in colored coats and figured waistcoats, short breeches buttoning to the knee, long boots with white tops, ruffled shirts and wristbands, a white cravat filled with what was called a pudding and for the elderly, cocked hats, and wigs which once ever week were sent to the barber's to be dressed, so that every Saturday night the barber's boys were seen carrying home piles of wig-boxes in readiness for Sunday church. At evening parties gentlemen appeared in white small-clothes, silk stockings and pumps, with a colored or white waistcoat. *Henry Adams, The United States in 1800, pp.64-65*

brogans: heavy, ankle-high work shoes, available ready-made and mass-produced from the 1830s on. Slave brogans were purchased by the barrelful by Southern plantations.

1860s: Experience soon demonstrated that boots were not agreeable on a long march. They were heavy and irksome . . . good, strong brogues or brogans, with broad bottoms and big, flat heels, succeeded the boots, and were found much more comfortable and agreeable, easier put on and off, and altogether the more sensible. *Carlton McCarthy, Detailed Minutiae of Soldier Life, p.20*

burnouse: a woman's small cape or shawl with attached hood, from 1830-1870s.

bustle: a crescent-shaped, wool-stuffed pad or a tier of stiff frills, worn in the back of a dress to plump out the rump, from as early as the 1830s, but finding wide popularity in the 1870s and 1880s.

1834: The diameter of the fashionable ladies at present is about three yards; their bustles (false bottoms) are the size of an ordinary sheep's fleece. The very servant girls wear bustles; Eliza told me of a maid of theirs went on Sunday with three kitchen dusters pinned on as a substitute. *Jane Welsh Carlyle, Letters and Memorials*

1840s: Some of the ladies had bustles on that would have literally throwed the whiskers, and the thing that wore them, entirely in the shade. I never knowed what a bustle was before. Would you believe it, Mr. Thompson, that I saw bustles up to Athens, that, if they'd been made out of real flesh and blood, would broke the back of any gall in Georgia to carry 'em? It's a fact. Why, some of them looked jist as much out of proportion as a bundle of fodder does tied to the handle of a pitchfork. If anything would make me sue for divorce, it would be to see my wife toting about sich a monstrous pack on her back as some of them I saw up to Athens. *Major Jones's Courtship, p.168*

butternut: the white walnut. A brownish dye was extracted from it and used to color clothing. The Confederate troops, for example, wore clothes dyed with butternut.

1810: Two pair home-made pantaloons, the one dark-colored, the other light butternut. Massachusetts Spy, *February 21*

1830: His were the coarse butternut colored, snug-setting trowsers, reaching only to the calf of his leg. Massachusetts Spy, *February 24*

1856: Home-spun cloth, dyed a brownish yellow with a decoction of the bitter barked butternut. *Derby,* Phoenixiana, *p.129*

1865: From the extreme front you catch an occasional glimpse of the Rebels, Butternuts, as they are termed in camp, from their cinnamon-hued homespun, dyed with butternut extract.

A.D. Richardson, The Secret Service, *p.256*

caba: a small handbag.

1885: The origin of the word caba applying to the small hand-bag or satchel. . . . The French cabas a frail basket, hand basket, etc., was used upon ladies' work-boxes imported thirty years ago.

Boston Journal, *September 7*

1886: The Philadelphian to the manner born knows that caba is only another name for a hand-bag, but the average New Yorker never heard it used, and would probably take the word to mean some new kind of infernal machine. (And a correspondent says it is in use throughout Pennsylvania, and is quite common in Baltimore and Washington.) New York Evening Post, *September 5*

cabriolet bonnet: a large bonnet with flaring brim, named after the carriage. Also known as a coal scuttle bonnet.

calash: a hood that folded over the head by means of cane hoops and resembled the folding hood of a carriage, early 1800s.

Caledonian cap: a small, close-fitting hat dressed with black feathers, popular in 1817.

calico: any printed cotton having two or more colors. Cowboys nicknamed women calicos after the popular dress material, from early in the century.

capot: a cardinal silk evening hood from 1816.

capote: a puff bonnet with stiff projecting brim around the face, from 1800 on.

capuchin: a cape with hood, from 1807 on.

chapeau bras: a woman's crush bonnet, from 1814.

chemise: a very long shirt, worn with knee-length stockings, under dresses and petticoats. Also commonly worn as a nightshirt throughout the century.

chemisette: white edging around the top of a low-necked bodice. Also known as a tucker.

chesterfield: a large overcoat or topcoat with a velvet collar and several pockets; widely popular men's fashion from 1840s on.

claw-hammer: slang for any evening dress coat having swallowtails.
1869: [He was] arrayed in the pride of his heart, his beautiful claw-hammer coat. *Mark Twain,* New Pilgrim's Progress
1879: The tails of his claw-hammer coat drag on the ground.
   Kingston, Australian Abroad, *p.7*

cloak: a long and voluminous overcoat without sleeves and fastened around the body like a cape. In the second half of the century cloaks had sleeves and many had detachable capes.

coal-scuttle bonnet: same as cabriolet bonnet.

coatee: a short coat, from 1802 on. Also a term denoting any coat.
1800: Ran-away, a Negro man named Isaac. He had on and took with him a home-made lincy coatee, a calico roundabout jacket, two vest-coats, etc. Lancaster *(Pennsylvania)* Journal, *September 20*
1801: Ran away, an apprentice. Had on and took with him a claret coloured cloth coat, made in the Menonist fashion, a yellow nankeen coatee, etc. Lancaster *(Pennsylvania)* Journal, *August 29*
1821: $20 Reward for a runaway apprentice, who took with him a blue coatee and pantaloons.
   Harrisburg *(Pennsylvania)* Intelligencer, *January 5*

Coburg bonnet: a soft-crowned bonnet tied under the chin, from 1816.

cocked hat: three-cornered hat with upturned brim, worn in the 1700s, early 1800s.

coiffure a l' indisposition: a lace and muslin dress cap, from 1812 on.

cornette: generic term for any bonnet tied under the chin. Also, a net or lace bonnet completely covering the hair and ears and tied under the chin.

cossack hat: a hat having a helmetlike crown and feathers at one side; the front was turned back and dressed with pearls; from 1812.

cossacks: loose, voluminous trousers having leg bottoms drawn shut by ribbons, popular from about 1817 to the 1830s.

cottage cloak: a cloak having a hood or cape tied under the chin, popular throughout the century.

crinoline: a dome, funnel or pyramidal-shaped understructure made of whalebone or spring hoops used to distend or widen skirts to as large as 18 feet in circumference. Also, the skirt itself, which was often hitched up to show a scarlet petticoat beneath. Also, a stiff horsehair fabric used to stiffen or line skirts. The crinoline, also known as the hoop skirt, was widely popular from midcentury on but gradually shrank in size until it faded from fashion in the 1870s. Many people despised the hoop skirt because it took up so much room in already crowded stagecoaches and omnibuses. Likewise, it required a wide berth at the dinner table, and it was the contributing cause of numerous accidents, some of them fatal, as witnessed below.

1865: A Young Lady Dragged Two Miles by Runaway Horses. About 11 o'clock on Thursday night a shocking accident occurred at Rahway, resulting in the death of a highly respected young lady, Miss Kate Degraw. . . . Miss Degraw, together with her two sisters, had attended a picnic a few miles out of town, in company with a young gentleman named Ennis. Upon their return the carriage drew up to the door, and the two sisters had alighted, and as the deceased was being assisted from the carriage, the horses took a sudden fright and dashed off at furious speed. The young lady's crinoline became entangled in the steps of the carriage, and with her head and shoulders dragging upon the ground, the horses made the circuit of the village twice before the citizens could stop them. When they did so the young lady was found to be lifeless, and her remains presented a mutilated and ghastly appearance. New York Times, *June 17, p.8*

1860s: . . . that monstrosity the crinoline, which once came near costing me my life. . . . I was showing a lady an engraving of Mr. Cobden which he had just given me and which hung over the fireplace. Somehow or other my volumnious skirt caught fire and in an instant I was in a blaze, but I kept my presence of mind, and rolling myself in the hearth rug by some means or other eventually put out the flames. None of the ladies present could of course come to assist me for their enormous crinolines rendered them almost completely impotent to deal with fire. Reminiscences of Lady Dorothy Neville

cummerbund: a wide silk sash worn around the waist with a dress suit; popular with fashionable gentlemen from 1890s.

dandy: any man who wore the most elegant fashions and who groomed himself meticulously. He was sometimes effeminate.

1818: They explained it by saying that a dandy was a new term for a buck or a blood; with the difference, that the Dandy aimed rather more at being effeminate, and instead of being a dashing, high-spirited fellow, which bloods generally are, that they only wished to be thought delicate and fine and pretty; that they spent all their money upon hats of a peculiar shape, and great coats (called by them surtouts) of a particular cut, with Wellington boots up to the knees, and trousers just below the calves of the legs. *Ackermann,* Repository of Arts

1845: Today Count d'Orsay walked in. I had not seen him for four or five years. Last time he was as gay in his colours as a hummingbird — blue satin cravat, blue velvet waistcoat, cream-colored coat, lined with velvet of the same hue, trousers also of a bright colour ... white French gloves, two glorious breast pins attached by a chain, and length enough of gold watch-guard to have hanged himself in — today, in compliment to his five more years, he was all in black and brown — a black satin cravat, a brown velvet waistcoat, a brown coat lined with velvet of its own shade, and almost black trousers, one breast-pin — a large pear-shaped pearl set into a little cup of diamonds — and only one fold of gold chain round his neck, tucked together right on the centre of his spacious breast with one magnificent turquoise. Well! That man understood his trade; if it be that of a dandy, nobody can deny that he is a perfect master at it, that he dresses himself with consummate skill!

Jane Welsh Carlyle, Letters and Memorials

demi-turban: a soft, muslin gauze worn around the head and tied in a bow on the right side, popular from 1800-1812.

doctors' fashions: during the first quarter of the century, physicians could be recognized on the streets by their long, black coats, gold-headed canes, and wigs.

There are Brightonians yet alive who talk to me of my uncle, Dr. Yates, remembering him with his white hair, snowy shirt frill, Hessian boots, or black gaiters, long black coat and gold-headed cane; a man of importance in the town, physician to the Sussex County Hospital.

Edmund Yates, Reminiscences

dresses and skirts: most dresses and skirts hung straight down from the body in neoclassical or Greek/Roman fashion during the first quarter of the century; they gradually widened into bell shapes in the 1820s, 1830s and 1840s and widened still further with crinolines in the 1850s and 1860s. In the 1870s and 1880s, only the rear (bustle) tended to be puffed out, while in the 1890s the shirtwaist and wasp-waist and the leg-of-mutton sleeves came into vogue. Girls' dresses throughout the century were frequently covered with aprons to help keep them clean. See individual entries.

dry goods: slang for clothing, cloth materials, etc.

1872: She is a goodly-sized lady . . . and she has the happy faculty of piling more dry goods upon her person than any other lady in the city. *James McCabe,* Lights and Shadows of New York Life, *p.143*

Eton jacket: a short coat worn by women, from 1862 on.

ferronniere: a gold chain, silk cord or velvet ribbon worn around the head with pearls, rubies or other jewels suspended from its center over the forehead; popular with wealthy women in the 1820s.

flat: a woman's low-crowned straw hat with a very wide brim. Also worn by little girls.

1821: An entire flat of Leghorn [straw] is extended over a small body like the shade of a spreading oak over a mushroom.
Massachusetts Spy, *October 17*

1855: A good-looking young squaw, who wore a large flat, to save her complexion. Knickerbocker Magazine, *xlv, p.566*

French hat: a high-crowned hat or bonnet with a small, flaring brim, often decorated with ostrich plumes, popular in 1815.

frock coat: a knee-length, military-style overcoat, worn by men from 1816 to the end of the century. The police of New York wore such a coat from the second half of the century on.

1872: Mr. Greeley's usual dress is a black frock coat, a white vest, and a pair of black pantaloons which come down to the ankle.
James McCabe, Lights and Shadows of New York Life, *p.227*

gaiters: leather and cloth leggings extending from the knee and buttoning down to the instep, worn mainly by men throughout the century. Ankle-length gaiters or spats were also worn.

gallowses: suspenders, worn throughout the century.

1824: Many of us wore gallowses, sat behind the singers, and had the choice to wear shoes or go barefoot. Microscope, *March 6*

1848: Ef I could only come across that ere Vermonter, which I was took in by, if I wouldn't spile his picter, bust my boots and gallowses.
Stray Subjects, *p.168*

Garibaldi blouse: a black-buttoned, red merino shirt worn with a belt and a black or colored skirt, popular throughout the 1860s. Boys sometimes wore these blouses with long pantaloons.

Gibson girl: the fashionable woman of the 1890s, as drawn in sketches by Charles Gibson. She was portrayed in a tailored shirtwaist with leg-of-mutton sleeves and a long skirt.

gibus: a top hat capable of being squashed flat and carried under the arm, from the 1840s.

gigot sleeves: see Leg-of-mutton sleeves.

gipsy hat: a plain straw hat tied under the chin by a ribbon that passed over the crown, from early in the century to 1820.

Godey's Lady's Book: a popular women's magazine begun in 1830 that featured color fashion plates as well as serial stories, verses, etc.

gossamer satin: a soft, thin evening-gown satin used from 1813 on.

go-to-meeting clothes: Also, Sunday go-to-meeting clothes. One's best or fanciest clothes.
1825: His go-to-meeting coat, as they call that, in America, which every farmer wears on training days and Sabbath days.
   John Neal, Brother Jonathan, *i, p.148*
1848: Thar's a sort of starchy Sunday-go-to-meetin' look about this part of [Boston] that I don't like. Major Jones's Sketches of Travel, *p.129*
1851: I pulled off my ole Sunday-go-to-meetin' coat, an slammed it down on er stump. Polly Peablossom's Wedding, *p.151*

great coat: see Overcoat.

Grecian bend: a stooped posture, considered fashionable among women from 1815 to 1819 and again in 1868. The stoop was created by a bustle worn high on the back of a skirt.

headwear: vital fashion accessory throughout the nineteenth century. Men and especially women were considered only partially dressed if they left their homes without a hat or bonnet.

Hessians: men's boots rising to just below the knee and decorated with tassels, worn most frequently with pantaloons. They were popular from the beginning of the century but fell out of fashion around 1850.
1801: All our young men of fashion wear frocks of dark blue, dark green, or dark brown cloth, with convex metal buttons, round hats with broad brims, short breeches and white stockings, or pantaloons with Hessian boots. Port Folio

high-lows: ankle boots buckled or strapped in front, from 1810 on for men and later for girls.

homespun: homemade clothing, worn widely throughout the first half of the century.
1800: Such is the desire for foreign articles, that we would rather go naked than wear a Home-spun shirt, jacket, or breechclout.
   Lancaster *(Pennsylvania)* Intelligencer, *May 7*
1809: Mr. Bacon left Pittsfield in a suit of Home-spun.
   Massachusetts Spy, *December 6*
1820: I could name several of our most distinguished public characters,

who make it a rule to wear no cloth which is not manufactured in their own families. *Hall*, Letters from the West, *p.68*

1880: Our clothing was homespun, made by our mothers and sisters — jeans and linsey for the males, and linsey and striped cotton for the females. *Peter Burnett*, Recollections, *p.11*

hoop skirt: see Crinoline.

Huntley bonnet: a black velvet cap with silk plumes, popular in 1813.

inexpressibles: prudish name given to trousers or pants to avoid being vulgar in speech, from first half of the century. Also known as sit-down-upons, unmentionables and unwhisperables.

1801: The size of a Turk's inexpressibles is very convenient, and much admired by the fair sex. Port Folio, *i, p.340*

1836: The managers have resolved to insist upon their wearing stockings and unmentionables. Philadelphia Public Ledger, *April 5*

1837: How could he see about procuring a pair of unwhisperables? Knickerbocker Magazine, *March*

1842: The child was wrapped in white linen, and then crammed into a bag made of the leg of a pair of inexpressibles. Philadelphia Spirit of the Times, *April 20*

Inverness: a great coat having a deep cape, a popular fashion among men from 1859 to the end of the century.

jacket bodice: a full-sleeved, form-fitting jacket spreading out over the waist, popular with women from about 1847 on.

jeans: blue jeans, or blue jean material, worn by rural men throughout the century. Also known as Kentucky jeans.

1848: Picture to yourself a lean, raw boned specimen of humanity, some six feet 7 or 8, without his shoes, loosely surrounded by a well-worn suit of Kentucky jeans. Yale Literary Magazine, *xiii, p.231*

1856: An elderly gentleman, clad with a suit of jeans, arose and came forward. Knickerbocker Magazine, *July*

1861: His wife, a round-faced damsel, black as the ace of spades, in a full dress of blue jeans, came up. Knickerbocker Magazine, *June*

jocket hat: a round-crowned hat with a small, curved brim, decorated with a rooster feather, popular with women throughout the 1860s.

knickerbockers: loose breeches ending at the knee, worn by boys and men of sport (golf, riding, boating, etc.) from 1860 on.

leg-of-mutton sleeves: sleeves puffed out at the shoulders; also known as gigot sleeves, popular on women's dresses from the 1820s on.

Levi's: denim blue jeans with rivets, widely popular among cowboys and westerners from midcentury on.

limerick gloves: kid gloves, worn from 1807 on.

mantle: a sleeveless coat or cape worn over the clothes, popular in various forms for women throughout the century.

marabout feathers: feathers from the marabout stork, used as decorative trimming from 1800 and after.

Minerva bonnet: a helmet-shaped bonnet with an ostrich feather across the front, fashionable in 1812.

mob cap: a bonnetlike cap with puffed crown and frill and ribbon trim, worn by women outdoors and in the kitchen, from early in the century.

moccasins: Indian shoes made of buckskin.

overcoat: any large coat, known as a great coat throughout the 1700s and up to about 1840.

pagoda: a popular parasol in 1818.

palatine: a wadded, black satin cape lined with blue-, rose- or apricot-colored satin and trimmed with black lace; it had a hood and was usually of knee-length.

paletot: in the 1830s, a short overcoat for men. In the 1860s, a full jacket for women, widening at the bottom to spread over a crinoline or hoop skirt.

pantalets, pantalettes: loose frills or false drawers worn below the knees by women and especially girls, from about 1820. They were later lengthened to become long underdrawers, from around midcentury.

1820: They are the ugliest things I ever saw; I will never put them on again. I dragged my dress in the dirt for fear someone would spy them. . . . My finest dimity pair, with real Swiss lace, is quite useless to me, for I lost off one leg, and did not deem it proper to pick it up, so walked off, leaving it on the street behind me, and the lace was six shillings a yard. . . . I hope there will be a short wear of these horrid pantalets; they are too trying. Of course, I must wear them for now, for I cannot hold up my dress and show my stockings; no one does. My help says she won't stay if she has to wash more than seven pair for Myrtilla, and I feel real low-spirited about it. Her legs are so thin she can't keep her pantalets up.
Letter in Two Centuries of American Costume

1854: The girls wore ruffles on their pantalettes, frizzled down over their shoes, nearly concealing the whole foot. *H.H. Riley,* Puddleford, *p.94*

1855: When but a little puss in pantalettes, of no more than thirteen
years old, she was a mistress of her father's house.
Putnam's Magazine, *March*

pantaloons: men's tight trousers extending to the ankles and sometimes
held on by foot straps. Later, any long trousers, baggy or tight, were
called pantaloons or pants. Early in the century, pantaloons were considered inappropriate dress in some churches and universities and at many
upper-class social functions, where knee breeches were the only accepted mode of fashion. Still, they were widely popular as street clothes
and they eventually replaced breeches for everything but sport.
1804: He was dressed in the American style; in a blue suit, with round
hat and pantaloons. *Brown*, Volney's View of the U.S.
1809: Fashions for gentlemen. Stocking pantaloons and half-boots. Nankeen trousers and gaiters, or Kerseymere pantaloons and gaiters in
one. Lancaster (*Pennsylvania*) Journal, *October 24*
1843: A young gentleman chastely apparelled in white jean pants of a
favorable cut, an elegant blue coat, and bushy whiskers.
Cornelius Mathews, Writings, *p.236*

pea jacket: a short, heavy seaman's jacket. Also worn by boys from
1850 on.

pelisse: an ankle-length, figure-fitting silk overcoat-dress with a turned-
down collar and sometimes a cape. It was worn over a lighter dress, and
usually open in the front, for house or street wear from 1800-1870.

poke bonnet: another name for a capote.

Princess dress: a dress having a tuniclike bodice extending down to
serve as an overskirt, popular in the 1870s.

Princess Polonaise dress: a very popular dress having an overskirt
attached to the bodice and draped up at the rump. It was sometimes left
unbuttoned from the waist down to reveal a pretty underskirt, in vogue
in the 1870s. Also known as the Dolly Varden dress.

quizzing glass: a rectangular glass measuring about $2\frac{1}{2} \times 1$ inches
attached to a six-inch handle, held in an affected manner by fashionable
men to observe something close up, from the 1820s and 1830s. A mon-
ocle was sometimes worn thereafter.

rationals: women's bicycle bloomers, from the 1890s.

redingote: a woman's floor-length, unlined coatdress left open in the
front to show an underdress and sometimes topped by several short
capes, from early in the century.

Regency ball dress: a velvet or satin frock trimmed around the bottom and along the front sides with a fold of satin or velvet edged with fringe. Satin and fringe epaulets were worn on the shoulders. From 1813-1819.

Regency hat: a velvet, high-crowned hat worn by women, and trimmed with sealskin and having an ostrich feather fastened at the right side and pulled over the crown to droop over the left ear, new in 1813.

Regency jacket: a long-sleeved, epaulet-shouldered, cloth jacket edged with sealskin, worn with the Regency hat, from 1813.

reticule: a small circular or lozenge-shaped handbag made of silk, satin or velvet and closed by a drawstring. Items carried in a reticule included handkerchiefs, fans, essence bottles and money; popular from 1800-1850 and widely referred to as ridicules. Also known as an indispensable.

Roman sandals: heelless slippers worn with ribbons laced across the instep and tied around the ankle, fashionable in 1817 and after.

roram: a popular hatter's cloth.
1804: One had on a new roram hat, the other a half-worn roram hat with a buckle and ribband.
   WANTED ad for two runaway apprentices, Lancaster (Pennsylvania) Journal, January 14

roundabout: a short, close-fitting jacket, also known as a monkey-jacket.
1819: He had, when he escaped, a dark cloth roundabout coat and purple or brown pantaloons. *Missouri Gazette, St. Louis, February 17*
1839: I was dressed in a white roundabout, and trowsers of the same.
   Chemung Democrat, October 2
1850: His red shirt, and snuff-colored monkey-jacket, and striped mittens. *S. Judd, Richard Edney, p.117*

sack suit: a long, loose-fitting, boxy coat worn with loose pants and waistcoat. The waistcoat could be striped satin, flowered brocade, paisley or plain and matching. From 1859 on.
1884: As a rule the men who steal the pocket-books and purses of ladies, wear a sack coat. *Allan Pinkerton, Thirty Years a Detective, p.50*

saratoga: a huge trunk, used by wealthy women to carry their clothes when traveling.
1869: This chute [in the pyramid] was not more than twice as wide and high as a Saratoga trunk. *Mark Twain, New Pilgrim's Progress, ch.27*
1894: He said he had strained [his wrist] in handling a lady's *Saratoga*.
   Howell, Traveller from Altruria, p.95

scoop bonnet: a long, narrow bonnet, popular in the 1840s.

shadbelly: a Quaker coat.

1842: "What do you ask for this?" said a gentleman in a shadbelly coat.
Philadelphia Spirit of the Times, *March 18*
1854: He had doffed the cassock, or rather the shadbelly, for the gown.
J.G. Baldwin, Flush Times in Alabama, *p.67*
1874: His coat is straight-breasted — shad-bellied, as the profane call it.
Edward Eggleston, The Circuit Rider, *p.146*

shawls: widely popular forms included Indian, paisley, embroidered, etc., of silk, wool, cotton, lace or chiffon. Worn throughout the century.

shirts: mens' shirts, often white and ruffled at the front, were almost always handmade by mothers, daughters and sisters in the first half of the century. See also Store clothes.

shirtwaist: a mannish-styled, tailored shirt, popular with women seeking the Gibson-girl look in the 1890s.

shoes: men generally wore Hessian boots, brogans, ankle boots and, for evening, pumps or thin shoes. Oxfords came into vogue in the late 1880s. White shoes made their appearance in the 1890s, as did patent leather shoes with kid or cloth tops. Women wore sandals with ribbon straps on the leg (to match their Greek/Roman dresses) or thin, flat slippers in the first years of the century. Kid house slippers and soft ankle boots were worn during the 1820s; boots with slight heels in the 1840s; and shoes with spool heels in the 1850s and 1860s. Slippers continued to be worn indoors throughout this period. Oxfords were introduced in the 1880s, while in the 1890s shoes and slippers with long, pointed toes were fashionable. An astonishing number of people apparently walked about shoeless in the first half of the century, especially in the South. Slave children frequently went without shoes all year long, while the poor throughout the country either constructed makeshift shoes or went without.
1872: I had not loitered long at the entrance . . . when from up the street, and from down the street . . . came little squads of dirty, ragged urchins — the true gamin of New York. . . . Shoes and boots (and remember it's a December night) are rather scarce — and those by which these savoyards could have sworn by grinned fearfully with sets of naked toes. One young sport . . . rejoiced in a pair of odd-mated rubber over-shoes, about the dimension of snow shoes. They saluted him as 'Gums.' *James McCabe,* Lights and Shadows of New York Life, *p.479*

skeleton suit: a young boy's suit consisting of high-waisted trousers buttoned up over a fitted jacket with a broad, white collar, from 1800-1834.

spats: see Gaiters.

spencer: a short jacket pulled in at the waist, in a variety of fabrics and designs, and usually worn over a dress for outdoor wear, from 1800-1830s, and later in altered forms.

1803: Spencers are worn both for walking and carriage dress. Levantines, spotted silks, and striped lute strings are the favorite materials. The trimming is always satin. The Augusta spencer is one of the prettiest dress spencers. The waist is finished with tab cuts in the form of leaves. In velvet spencers, black, purple and bottle green are favorite colors. The velvet is cut byas. Percale dresses are worn with these. Two Centuries of Costume in America

spun truck: slang for knitting work or yarn.

1851: Jim Bell had visited town for the purpose of buying two bunches of No. 8 spun truck. *Widow Rugby's Husband, p.72*

1857: Women exchanging their wool sock, bees' wax, tow-linen, etc., for spuntruck, apron check, dye-stuff, and so on.
Knickerbocker Magazine, *November*

stockings: common materials included cotton, lisle and, for dressy affairs, silk. Men wore black, gray or white; an occasional striped pair was also worn. Women stuck with white or light-colored stockings until the 1870s and 1880s, when red, purple and striped stockings were worn to match colorful petticoats.

store clothes: any clothes purchased at a store, as distinguished from those made at home. At the turn of the century, about 75 percent of clothing was made at home, while the rest was constructed by tailors from materials purchased at dry goods stores or other outlets. Ready-made, store clothing generally wasn't available until the 1840s. Nor was there much variety in ready-mades until the Civil War and after. See also Homespun.

1864: There ensued a contest between a pair of No. 7 boots and a few store clothes to reach the college first.
Yale Literary Magazine, *xxix, p.270*

1890: After his return, he came to our tent dressed in what the officers call cits clothes, which he termed store clothes.
Mrs. Elizabeth Custer, Following the Guidon, *p.27*

stove-pipe hat: a man's tall silk hat with a crown shaped like stovepipe, popular throughout the century. Also known as a top hat.

1855: Farmers! did you get up Know-nothingism? No. It was got up amongst stove-pipe hats and patent leather shoes. Oregon Times, *June*

1863: Those glistening silk stove-pipe arrangements are poor things for a very cold day, especially round the ears.
Rocky Mountain News, *Denver, February 19*

> Before 1860 the price for a shave was five cents; for a haircut, ten cents; and higher for shampooing and curling.

suit, matching: the fashion of wearing matching coat, vest (waistcoat) and pants didn't catch on with men until the 1850s. Previously, the separate pieces were usually of contrasting colors.

suspenders: another name for gallowses, worn from the beginning of the century on.

1834: Jest then the Gineral got in a way he has of twitchin' with his suspender buttons behind; and to rights he broke one off.
   Seba Smith, Major Jack Downing, *p.149*

top hat: same as a stove-pipe hat, sometimes known as an opera hat.

Trafalgar dress: a white satin evening gown trimmed with silver, popular after the battle of Trafalgar in 1806.

turbans: widely popular form of headwear for women throughout the first half of the century; they were usually highly ornamented and were available in a variety of styles. See also Demi-turban.

1802: Turban of white satin, with a band of muslin round the front, fastened on the left side with a gold loop; gold flower in front.
   Popular fashion described in the Port Folio

1806: A full-dress lace turban, ornamented with gold-spangled net, an aigrette in front, with a large bow of muslin confining the whole, and a row of gold, intermixed with spangled net, hanging tastefully on one side of the forehead. Two Centuries of Costume in America

1823: The materials for turbans this autumn are of the most effective kind, and well adapted for evening wear. Some are of white gossamer gauze with green and gold stripes, with the white spaces between slightly clouded with gold; others are of a rainbow striped gauze, on a green ground powdered with gold; the stripes are crimson, royal blue, green and yellow. Two Centuries of Costume in America

waistcoat: a popular mens' fashion accessory throughout the century. In 1820 two vests of two different colors or materials were sometimes worn together.

Zouave jacket: a woman's bolero-like jacket with three-quarter-length sleeves; it was characterized by its military braiding. Fashionable from the 1860s through the 1870s.

Hairstyles

a la Concierge: a woman's style in which long hair was pulled to the top of the head and pinned in a knot, popular in the late 1890s.

a la giraffe: a style in which hair was dressed very high on the back of the head, in vogue from 1830-1836.

Apollo knot: false hair coiled, looped or plaited and wired to stand up on the head, from 1826 and after.

barley-sugar curls: long drop curls worn by children throughout the century. Also worn by women with ringlets and a coiled chignon on the back of the head in 1843.

bay rum: a hair tonic widely believed to stimulate hair growth, introduced in New York early in the century. Used by men.

bear grease: used by backwoodsmen to slick down unruly hair.

beaver tail: a broad, flat loop of hair hung over the nape of the neck, from 1865. Also known as a banging chignon.

blinkers: hair brought down on either side of the face, modeled after horse blinkers, in 1857.

chignon: a knot or roll of hair worn at the back of the head and sometimes ornamented with lace, ribbons or flowers or taken up in a gold or silver net, very popular throughout the 1860s, but worn throughout the century.

earlock: a curled lock in front of the ear, worn by men and women early in the century.
1806: Both men and women cut their hair in the forehead. . . . They have long earlocks cut square at the end.
   Meriwether Lewis, Lewis and Clark Expedition, *iv*
1832: Our ear locks . . . my ears tingle and my countenance is distorted at the recollection of the tortures inflicted on them by the heated curling tongs and crimping irons. New England Magazine, *iii, p.238*

false hair: worn in various periods throughout the century. In the 1860s it was sometimes worn in spangled or chenille-dotted nets.

half-shingle: a style in which hair was allowed to grow long around the head, then cut short on top, and finally curled all around the head. Both men and women wore this style in the 1840s.

long, over the shoulder: an American style worn by rural women and Western women throughout the century.

CHRONOLOGY OF HAIRSTYLES

Men

1800-1815: sometimes worn with a small tail in back, as a holdover from the 1700s. Some professionals continued to wear wigs with small tails, although this fashion was also dying out. A prominent style throughout this period was that modeled after the busts of Roman emperors: clipped in back, with hair set in ringlets or in loose confusion on top, with locks sometimes allowed to fall over the forehead.

1815-1840: the Roman emperor look continued, along with various other styles. Luxuriant, full hair was often brushed forward or parted slightly to one side. Small moustaches and small sideburns appeared, but many men were clean-shaven.

1840-1865: full, curly hair worn in a crest. Hair brushed back or brushed forward to form a curving front lock or cowlick. Side and middle parts common. Unruly hair was oiled down and made to shine with perfumed macassar oil. Rural or backwoodsmen often used bear grease to keep their hair from sticking up. Sideburns became progressively longer and bushier from the 1840s through the 1860s. Full beards and clipped chin beards (like Lincoln's) sans moustache were in vogue, as were spade beards and Imperials with or without moustaches.

1865-1890: side and middle parts with shorter hair than in the previous period. The parts extended all the way from the front of the head to the nape of the neck during the 1870s, to the crown only during the 1880s. Pompadours were worn by some men. Muttonchops and beards under the chin were in vogue. Moustaches were frequently worn with beards during the 1880s, but a long, drooping moustache sans beard was also popular at this time. Clean-shaven faces started a comeback in 1889.

1890-1900: middle parts fashionable or parts slightly left of center. The clean-shaven look was in vogue, as were little moustaches that were waxed and turned up at the ends. Older men wore huge, drooping "walrus" moustaches. Some sideburns, muttonchops and pointed chin beards.

Marcel wave: waves arranged around the head with a curling iron, a style popular among women in the 1890s.

Marion bandelette: a waved front of hair, with pincurls on either side of the head, in vogue in the early 1880s.

pompadour: a style in which the hair was swept up high from the fore-

CHRONOLOGY OF HAIRSTYLES

Women

1800-1815: short curls waved on the forehead, back hair in simple knot. Some top knots worn. Hair was often ornamented with combs, fillets, tiaras, coronets, etc.

1815-1840: hair smooth over the forehead, frequently parted in the middle, with ringlets, puffs or loops at the sides fashionable from about 1815-1820. From the early 1820s to the early 1830s, hair was piled progressively higher in the back, culminating in a style dubbed a la giraffe. Masses of sausage curls sometimes worn from about 1828-1832. Curls and ringlets popular throughout this period.

1840-1865: topknots made smaller and moved to the back of the head. Large coils of hair at the nape of the neck and sometimes held by black or colored silk nets popular from the 1850s on. This chignon was often arranged in loops and braids in the 1860s. Front of hair was often parted in the middle, pulled smooth over temples, while puffs, ringlets or coils were worn over ears. Curls and ringlets were worn throughout period. Hair was frequently ornamented with jeweled bands, combs, flowers, foliage, and strings of pearls.

1865-1890: bun or chignon moved up on head, front hair carried back without parts. In the 1870s, hair in back was allowed to cascade down long and full, sometimes in ringlets, sometimes in huge loops. Pompadours were worn at the end of the 1880s. Hair ornaments were used throughout the period.

1890-1900: most prominent style was the psyche knot: hair pulled back from the forehead and knotted on top. Small coiffures, pompadours and French twists were worn. Hair ornaments were also worn.

head, worn at various times throughout the century by both men and women.

sausage curls: tubelike curls worn by girls. Women wore them in tumbling masses over the eyes from 1828-1832.

soaplocks: a man's style in which hair was cut short on the back of the head up to the crown, left long in front of the ears, and allowed to hang down on each side of the face. Some grew this side hair so long it could actually be tied together under the chin. Popular in the 1840s, especially among young roughs.

titus: a woman's style in which hair was cut very short around the head and curled, from the 1880s.

topknot: hair knotted on top of the head; women constructed these progressively higher from 1815-1830.

whiskers: came into fashion among soldiers and spread to civilians during the War of 1812 and again during the Civil War. Long, hanging sideburns, called Dundrearys or Icadilly Weepers, were popular in the 1860s and after, as were muttonchops. Clipped beards (like Lincoln's) sans moustache, along with the spade beard and the Imperial, also came into vogue at this time. Moustaches were worn during the War of 1812 and in the late 1820s as well as the 1850s, 1860s, 1870s and after. The clean-shaven look began to return in the 1890s.

wigs: a few men, mostly physicians and Federalists, continued to wear powdered wigs until the 1820s.

SURRENDER OF GEN. LEE!

"The Year of Jubilee has come! Let all the People Rejoice!"

200 GUNS WILL BE FIRED

On the Campus Martius,

AT 3 O'CLOCK TO-DAY, APRIL 10,

To Celebrate the Victories of our Armies. 1865

Every Man, Woman and Child is hereby ordered to be on hand prepared to Sing and Rejoice. The crowd are expected to join in singing Patriotic Songs.

ALL PLACES OF BUSINESS MUST BE CLOSED AT 2 O'CLOCK.

Hurrah for Grant and his noble Army.

By Order of the People.

OCCUPATIONS

I n 1800, four-fifths of all Americans worked on farms. During the second half of the century, many abandoned farm life to work in the city, in shops and in "manufactories." Some of these people found a better way of life. Others became disillusioned.

A growing number of the new working class were women. About forty thousand women were working full-time jobs in New York around 1870. Most sewed garments — at home or in a factory. Some toiled as shop girls, clerks, governesses and teachers. But all had one thing in common: They were paid a fraction of what the men received. "The wrongs inflicted upon the working women are many," wrote one observer in 1872. "There are hoop-skirt manufactories where, in the incessant din of machinery, girls stand upon weary feet all day long for fifty cents."

If the abuses of the working woman were bad, those of children were even worse. Despite child labor laws, tens of thousands of children could be found working in shops and factories throughout the United States, sometimes for ten and twelve hours per day, for negligible pay. They worked around dangerous machinery, with caustic substances, for employers who had little regard for their health and welfare. "Cigar-making in the tenement houses goes on, though the fact is often denied," wrote another observer in the late 1880s. "In cellars and basements boys ten and twelve brine, sweeten, and prepare the tobacco preliminary to stemming. Others of the same age keep the knives of the cutting machines clean by means of sponges dipped in rum. . . . In another workshop children from eight to ten cut the feathers from cocktails for ten hours daily they bend over their work. . . . Eight thousand children make envelopes at three and a half cents a thousand. They gum, separate and sort. . . . In [another] factory two hundred children under fifteen are employed spinning, winding and twisting flax; [many] are lacking fingers. . . ."

The black man often suffered a different kind of abuse; he could find no work at all outside of hard labor and servants' jobs because no employer would hire him.

All in all, the nineteenth century was a miserable period for workers, and especially the unskilled; the hours were long, the pay was miserly, and regard for employee health and safety was often nonexistent. There was also little protection from discrimination and sexual harassment. No health insurance, no profit sharing, and so forth. Needless to say the good old days, at least when it came to work in the 1800s, definitely weren't.

apprentice: one who worked and lived with a master craftsman or other professional to learn a skill. In many arrangements, apprentices were legally bound to obey their masters as they would their own fathers. Even during leisure time, the apprentice was subjected to the master's rule. In exchange for labor, the apprentice was fed, clothed and taught valuable skills, from which he could progress to journeyman craftsman and then finally to master with his own shop. The apprentice system largely vanished from the workplace by midcentury, when young, unskilled workers simply became independent employees.

1828: [It is] required of the youngest apprentice that he shall open the shop in the morning, build and keep fires during the day, wait on Journeymen and do all chores and go of all errands which are necessary for this shop. . . . It is my wish that my apprentices may worship on the Sabbath with me . . . further that they become a member of one of the Bible classes. . . . Such evenings as it is not customary to work I do not allow them to go anywhere they please—it is my wish that they stay at the shop.

Purley Torrey, cabinetmaker, Worcester, Massachusetts, in a letter to a prospective apprentice's father

barber: the majority of barbers in the United States throughout the century were black.

1884: In the United States the business of barbering is almost exclusively in the hands of the colored population.

Chamber's Encyclopedia of New York

barkeep: one who kept a bar, served drinks; a bartender.

1889: Drinks . . . were deftly compounded by the white-aproned barkeeps. *K. Munroe, Golden Days, vii, p.74*

barmaid: a woman who served food and drinks in a tavern, hotel or bar.

blacksmith: one who forged and shaped iron products, e.g., shoes and nails for horses, tools, utensils, pots, pans, plowshares, brands, etc.

bootblack: one who blackened and polished shoes and boots.

1817: At the house where we stopped they had a bootblack and a barber. *Essex Inst. Coll., viii, p.246*

1869: The bootblacks and baths and barbers are of European standards. *S. Bowles,* Our New West, *p.279*

borer: in Pennsylvania, a traveling salesman or peddler. Known elsewhere as a drummer.

1836: Our hotels are thronged, we may say infested, with a set of young men, clerks in mercantile houses, whose special business is to catch customers among the country merchants. In New York they are called drummers, their business being to drum up recruits to their corps of customers. In more quiet Philadelphia they are called borers, probably from some resemblance in qualities to a worm that infests fruit trees. Philadelphia Public Ledger, *August 23*

chandler: a candlemaker; he enjoyed a steady business until the advent of gas and electric lights.

child labor: long hours of labor were put in on father's farm from an early age. In 1870, child workers in factories, mills and mines numbered about 700,000; they worked twelve- to sixteen-hour days and earned around $2.50 per week, exceedingly cheap labor for greedy employers who ignored what few labor laws were in place at the time. Such abuses continued until the end of the century.

chimney sweep: widely employed throughout the century due to frequent use of fireplaces and wood stoves and the fires they caused. Chimney sweeps often employed small boys to climb inside chimneys to knock down soot with brooms and other tools.

1817: He is a brawny chimneysweep, and parades the streets in a big cap, a long stick, and a train of boys at his heels, to the great annoyance of people. *Edward Savage,* Police Records and Recollections

circuit rider: a preacher who traveled from church to church in a given district, usually serving very small populations. Also, a traveling judge serving small populations.

1838: A little, portly, red-faced man, in linsey-woolsey and a broadbrimmed hat, saluted me, and announced himself a Baptist circuitrider. *E. Flagg,* The Far West, *ii, p.60*

1850: I have to do as all other preachers, especially Methodist circuitriders—eat chickens. . . . These same circuit-riders undergo more toil and privation for less pay than the ministers of any other denomination. *James Weir,* Lonz Powers

1853: Judicial circuits, a court house and jail, Methodist circuits and circuit-riders, and meeting-houses, were established. Knickerbocker Magazine, *December*

coachman: a coach driver. Also known as a "whip."

cobbler: one who repaired shoes and boots.

constable: an officer of the peace; a policeman, especially during the first half of the century.
1819: One o'clock, night. South Watch doing good duty, but the two constables are asleep. At North Watch, constables awake. . . . The Inspector recommends that the doorman be required to wake the constable when necessary. Constable Reed arrested several persons for keeping gambling houses. One was fined $150, for keeping a new French game called Quino. *Edward Savage,* Police Records and Recollections

cooper: one who made or repaired wooden vessels, especially barrels and tubs.
1809: Pittsburgh [has] five coopers, thirteen weavers.
F. Cuming, Western Tour, *p.223*
1839: Extensive preparations had been made to prosecute the salmon fishery, and the coopers have been engaged the whole winter in making barrels to accommodate them. *J.K. Townsend,* Narrative, *p.318*
1894: He had been a well-to-do man . . . with a big cooper shop.
Frederic, Copperhead, *p.55*

cordwainer: one who made shoes.

drummer: a traveling salesman.

expressman: one who delivered mail, packages and parcels; a mailman.
1883: The expressman drove up and unloaded a queer-looking crate.
Wheelman, *ii*

farmer: in 1800, four-fifths of all Americans worked on farms. A large portion of the American population continued to work on farms as late as the Civil War.

farrier: a blacksmith who specialized in shoeing horses.

footman: employed by the wealthy, one who rode outside on the back of a coach (on the dickey seat) and who opened doors for passengers, loaded and unloaded luggage, etc.

hackman/hack driver: one who drove a carriage or coach for hire, the equivalent of the modern cabdriver.
1806: Died, in this town, Mr. Daniel Henry, hackman.
Repertory, *Boston, October 3*
1848: The hackman ax'd me what hotel I wanted to go to.
Major Jones, Sketches of Travel, *p.110*
1850: Simon rose to the post of hack-driver.
Sylvester Judd, Richard Edney, *p. 462*

hawker: a peddler who called out his wares on the street to attract customers. Also known as a huckster. See also Peddler, Street vendors.

hog reeve: one appointed to round up troublesome or stray hogs from city streets. Even as late as the 1860s, well-mannered pigs were allowed to roam city streets and parks to eat the garbage left there. They sometimes numbered in the thousands, and even New York's Broadway was frequented by them. However, the city's poor often killed these free-wheeling dinners and ate them.
1877: If I had continued in active political life, I might have risen to be a vote distributor, or fence-viewer, or selectman, or hog-reeve, or something of the kind. *J.L. Motley,* Harper's Magazine, *p.613*

hostler: a horse groom employed at a roadside inn.

hours: working hours on farms were always long. In factories and mills, twelve hours a day or more, or from sunrise to sunset, were typical throughout the century.

ice cutter: one who cut blocks of ice from ponds and lakes in winter and insulated it with layers of sawdust to preserve it for sale in warmer months.

knacker: one who purchased old or dead livestock and sold the meat or hides.

lamplighter: one appointed to light streetlamps at dusk and extinguish them at dawn. There were a variety of lamps used throughout the century, including candles, whale oil, kerosene and gas. The lamplighter often doubled as a night watchman or policeman. Also known as a gasman.
1850: The lamplighter . . . hooked his ladder on the lamp-irons, ran up and lit the lamp. *S. Warner,* Wide, Wide World
1854: Just then, the gas-man came quickly up the street, lit, as by an electric touch, the bright burners. *Cummins,* Lamplighter, *p.520*
1863: The narrow and gloomy passage slightly illuminated by one or two jets of gas, which Tom the Gasman . . . had a few moments before lighted. *Massett,* Drifting About, *p.50*
1885: A well-known colored citizen, for three years employed as a lamplighter for the City Gas Co., was . . . severely beaten.
Weekly New Mexican Review, *January 15*

liveryman: one who boarded and cared for horses for a fee.

matchgirl: a girl who sold matches in the street, from around 1840-1860s.
1844: Six for a fip! Six for a fip! Matches! Matches!
Grahams Magazine, *March*

1852: She does not allow match-girls . . . to be begging about the basement windows. Knickerbocker Magazine, *xxix, p.165*

1863: You gave this match-girl no money, I hope?
M. Harland, Husks, *p.28*

midwife: most children were born at home during the first half of the century. Only wealthy, urban women had access to a physician. Most midwives had no formal training but learned by experience.

miller: one who operated a grain-grinding mill.

monger: generic term for a dealer of any type of item, e.g., fishmonger, cheesemonger, etc.

peddler: a traveling peddler who carried a wide array of goods on a wagon and typically frequented farms and rural homes. Those from New England traveled extensively and were known throughout the country.

1809: If peradventure some straggling merchant of the east should stop at the door, with his cart load of tin ware or wooden bowls, the fiery Peter would issue forth like a giant from his castle, and make such a furious clattering among his pots and kettles, that the vendor of notions was fain to betake himself to instant flight.
Washington Irving, History of New York, *p.120*

1840s: "Can I suit you today, ma'am?" said a peddler from New England, when offering his wares for sale in Michigan. "I've all sorts of notions. Here's fashionable calicoes; French work collars and capes; elegant milk pans, and Harrison skimmers, and ne plus ultry dippers! patent pills—cure anything you like; ague bitters; Shaker yarbs; essences, wintergreen, lobely; tapes, pins, needles, hooks and eyes; broaches and bracelets; smelling bottles; castor ile; corn-plaster; mustard; garding seeds; silver spoons; pocket combs; tea-pots; green tea; saleratus; tracts; song-books; thimbles; baby's whistles; slates; playin' cards; puddin' sticks; baskets; wooden bowls; powder and shot. I shan't offer you lucifers, for ladies with such eyes never buy matches—but you can't ask me for anything I haven't got, I guess.
Mrs. Claver's Forest Life, *ii, p.113*

peripatetic artist/barber/butcher/dentist/sign painter/silhouette cutter: one who walked from town to town or from farm to farm offering his special services. Traveling artists sometimes made an excellent income painting portraits or panoramas on walls of homes and taverns. Some portrait painters charged as high as twenty-five dollars per head, although three to five dollars was more typical. Silhouette cutters produced one's likeness for less, usually fifty cents. Demand for these artists' work plummeted after the development of photography in the 1840s and 1850s, however. Demand for the wandering dentist (tooth-puller was the more apt term) also declined during this period, when more and more "professionally trained" dentists opened shop. The wandering butcher continued to find work throughout the century, as many farmers found this work appalling.

Correct Profile Likenesses, taken from 8 o'clock in the morning until 9 in the evening. M Chapman respectfully informs the Ladies and Gentlemen . . . that he takes correct Profiles, reduced to any size, two of one person for 25 cents, neatly cut on a beautiful paper. He also paints and shades them , if required, for 75 cents; specimens of which may be seen at his room. Of those persons who are not satisfied with their Profiles, previous to leaving the room, no pay shall be required. He makes use of a machine universally allowed by the best judges to be more correct than any ever before invented.

Ad for an itinerant silhouette cutter before the advent of photography

runner: one who solicited business for a hotel, boardinghouse, steamship, etc.; employed throughout the century.

1835: [At Oswego] a struggle began between the runners of the two boats. Life on the Lakes, *p.31*

1857: We shall assume that the landlord's jackals (or runners) have succeeded in inveigling a house-full of newly-arrived seamen into his den. *Thomas B. Gunn,* New York Boarding Houses, *p.278*

1866: The night being bleak and chilly, it was sweet to hear the cry of the hotel-runner (a tout is here called a runner). *W.H. Dixon,* New America, *ch.1*

sawyer: one who sawed trees or wood by hand at a lumber mill or at a lumbering operation.

sexton: one who maintained a church and sometimes rang the church bells in addition to supervising churchyard burials. Also, a churchyard gravedigger.

1868: Undertakers at fashionable funerals are generally the sexton of some fashionable church. . . . This individual prescribes the manner in which the ceremony shall be carried out, and advises certain styles of family mourning. . . . A certain fashionable sexton always refuses to allow female members of the family to follow their dead to the grave . . . as "it's horribly vulgar to see a lot of women crying about a corpse, and they're always in the way." *Edward Martin,* Secrets of the Great City, *p.85*

sharpener: one who carried a portable grindstone on his back or on a wagon and solicited customers for knife, scissor and tool sharpening.

snow warden: in the northern states, one who was appointed to keep snow flattened and evenly distributed over roads to facilitate travel by

STREET VENDOR CRIES

blade sharpening: this vendor set up a portable grinder on the street and cried, "Scissors to grind!" or "Razors, Scissors, Penknives to Grind!" while tinkling a little bell.

charcoal: sold for thirty-five cents a barrel in Philadelphia in 1850. The charcoal was used to start fires and was loudly hawked on the streets, with the cry of "Charcoal by the bushel, Charcoal by the peck, Charcoal by the frying pan, Or any way you lek!" In Philadelphia, the charcoal man blew a loud horn until 1835; a bell was then used to satisfy a city ordinance concerning noise.

fish: fishmongers with carts shouted various poems: "Fresh fish fit for the pan," or "Shad! Buy any shad?" or "Here comes the fishman! Bring out your dishpan, Porgies at five cents a pound!" The hawking was sometimes interjected by the blowing of a tin horn, which came to be known as a fish horn.

fruits and berries: in all the major cities, when in season, fruits and berries were hawked with the cry "Raaaaaaaspberrrrrrrries! Blaaaaaaaaaaaackberrrrrrries! Apples! Fresh apples!" or "Peaches here!"

hot corn: often sold by women and girls. One popular cry was, "Hot corn! Hot corn! 'Ere's yer lily-white hot corn!" Another went, "Here's your nice hot corn! Smoking hot! Piping hot! O what beauties I have got!"

milk: sold early in the morning on city streets, with cries of "Milk! Fresh milk!"

newspapers: hawked by boys with loud announcements, such as these heard in New York around 1868: " 'Ere's your 'Erald!" "Mornin' Times!" "Buy a Tribune!" "Mail!" "Express!" "Telegram!" "Post!" Along with: " 'Nuther murder!" "Tremendous sensation!" "Orful shootin' scrape!" " 'Orrible accident!" and so on.

pepperpot: Negro women hawked kettles of this stew from carts in Philadelphia, with shouts of, "Pepperpot, righthot!" or "All hot! All hot! Makee back strong! Makee live long! Come buy my pepper pot!"

sweet potatoes: the call of one Philadelphia vendor in the first half of the century went: "My hoss is blind and he's got no tail, When he's put in prison I'll go his bail. Yeddy go, sweet potatoes, oh! Fif-en-ny bit a half peck!"

wood: sold in the fall with cries of, "Wud! Wud! Wud! Wud!"

sleighs and sleds in winter. The warden used a horse-drawn plow to clear deep drifts of snow and a huge, wooden roller (also drawn by horses) to pack down snow.

street vendors: in most of the larger cities, street vendors hawked a wide variety of goods and services. Among them: oysters (hugely popular), milk, bottled water (the quality of city water was highly suspect before

THE PRICE OF TAILORING

1818

October 28	To making pantelloons .... $	.32
	To footing stockings	.25
1819		
January 14	To making vest	.42
	To silk and twill for vest	.12
April 30	To cloth pantelloons and making the same	2.50
June 8	To four yards of cotton shirting	1.32
	To making two cotton shirts	.60
	To one yard and a half of stripped linen and making the same	.75
November 10	To two yards of woollen cloth, one dollar and thirty-three cents per yard	2.66
	To trimmings and making pantelloons	.33
1820		
January 12	To one pair of woollen stockings	.50
May 5	To two yards and a quarter of woollen cloth ..	3.95
	To making coat	1.50
	To 14 gilt buttons	.50
	To silk twist and thread for coat	.20
	To cloth for pantelloons and making	1.50
June 8	To two yards and half of linen cloth, thread, and making same	1.00
	To four yards of cotton cloth, thread and making	1.75
	To trimming and making vest	.33

the advent of municipal water works), hot corn, muffins, pies, peanuts, cider, cheese, chestnuts, chickens, fish, honeycombs, pocketbooks, suspenders, socks, gloves, newspapers, boot-blacking, blade-sharpening, etc.

1872: Little girls are numerous among the street venders. They sell matches, tooth-picks, cigars, newspapers, songs and flowers. The flower girls are hideous little creatures, but their wares are beautiful and command a ready sale. These are made into hand bouquets, and buttonhole bouquets, and command from ten cents to several dollars each. *James McCabe,* Lights and Shadows of New York Life, *pp.833-834*

tailor/seamstress: both were indispensable during the first half of the century because ready-made clothing didn't become available until the 1840s. Nor was there much variety in ready-mades until after the Civil War. In the first half of the century rural folk generally spun their own cloth and sewed their own clothes, but urbanites with more money to spend often picked out materials at a dry goods store and took them to a tailor or seamstress to be made into pants, shirts or dresses, etc. The bills of one itinerant tailor working in Connecticut from 1818-1820 provide a clue as to how much tailors made on specific jobs. (See sidebar.)

teamster: one who drove a horse, mule or ox-drawn freight wagon, the equivalent of the modern-day truck driver. Also known as a wagoner.

tinker: one who repaired or made tinware.

town crier: one who read or announced news on the streets of New England, a practice largely abandoned with the advent of newspapers.

wheelwright: one who made or repaired wagon, coach or carriage wheels.

wright: any skilled workman or craftsman.

SURRENDER OF GEN. LEE!

"The Year of Jubilee has come! Let all the People Rejoice!"

200 GUNS WILL BE FIRED

On the Campus Martius,
AT 3 O'CLOCK TO-DAY, APRIL 10,
To Celebrate the Victories of our Armies. 1865

Every Man, Woman and Child is hereby ordered to be on hand prepared to Sing and Rejoice. The crowd are expected to join in singing Patriotic Songs.
ALL PLACES OF BUSINESS MUST BE CLOSED AT 2 O'CLOCK.
Hurrah for Grant and his noble Army.

By Order of the People.

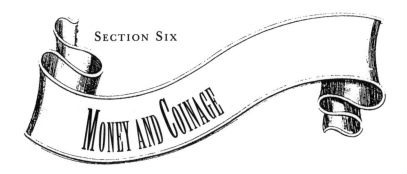

MONEY AND COINAGE

Making change in the first half of the nineteenth century must have been a formidable task. The coins in circulation throughout America included Russian kopecks, Dutch rix-dollars, various French and English specie and, most common of all, the silver dollars, halves, quarters, eighths and sixteenths minted in Mexico and South America. To confuse matters further, some coins went by different names in different parts of the country. The Spanish reale, worth 12½ cents, was a "bit" in the West, a "ninepence" in New England, a "shilling" in New York and a "levy" in Pennsylvania. Even more befuddling, many rural Americans and shopkeepers — at least up to the 1820s — persisted in reckoning their wares and wages by the outmoded English system of pence, shillings and pounds. The confusion finally ended in 1857 when the government banned all foreign coins and reckoning from the marketplace.

The rural American had a different problem; in the first years of the century the farmer rarely used money at all. Some outlying farmers lived their entire lives without even *seeing* a silver dollar. In such instances, barter or trade was the sole means of making purchases.

"The words 'buy' and 'sell' are nearly unknown [in Erie, Pennsylvania]," wrote Thomas Ashe in 1806. "In business nothing is heard but the word 'trade'. . . . But you must anticipate all this from the absence of money."

The situation was little changed in 1830, according to Frances Trollope, who wrote that "the difficulty of obtaining *money* in payment, excepting for mere retail articles, is very great in all American transactions. 'I can pay in produce,' is the offer which I was assured is constantly made on all occasions, and if rejected, 'Then I guess we can't deal,' is the usual rejoinder. This statement does not, of course, include the great merchants of great cities, but refers to the mass of people scattered over the country."

During the 1840s, the barter and trade system largely declined as more and more people left farming to take up jobs in the cities and as a wider variety of goods became available to buy.

bit: one-eighth of a dollar. Originally, this was the nickname for the Spanish reale, especially in the West and Southwest. However, in New England it was called a ninepence; in New York a shilling; and in Pennsylvania a levy or elevenpence piece. Two bits was thus widely used to denote a quarter of a dollar from the 1700s through the 1800s. See also levy, pence, piece of eight, reale, shilling.

1850: Two bits for a cup of coffee; two bits for a piece of pie; or, if hunger and economy were to be considered, two doughnuts for a quarter of a dollar. Hardly anyone said "two bits" or a "quarter" in those days. It was dos reales! cuatro reales! un peso!
Barry and Patten, Men and Memories of San Francisco, *p.132*

1856: I declare, cousin Ellis, you haven't changed a bit. Changed a bit! Course I haven't, here in Philadelphia—if I had, I should have got two fips for it. Knickerbocker Magazine, *November*

1860: The price of liquor at Salem, till recently, was two bits a drink. Now it is a bit. Take off the license, and liquor could be as well afforded for a picayune, or at least three drinks for a quarter.
Letter to Oregon Argus, *July 21*

bungtown coppers: worthless copper coins.

1840: [He took] a five cent piece and two bungtown coppers out of the till. Knickerbocker Magazine, *May*

1853: "Beware of crossed sixpences, smooth shillings, and what are called Bungtown coppers," said Cheatum.
Daily Morning Herald, *St. Louis, March 10*

1853: What is the currency of the U.S.?—Coppers, bogus, Bungtown cents, pennies, fips, fourpence, 'a' pennies, levies, ninepences, Spanish quarters, pistareens, and shinplasters. Oregonian, *August 13*

Civil War tokens: see Hard times tokens.

Confederate money: about two billion dollars in paper money and fractional currency issued by the South from 1861-1865 to finance the war with the North. It was subject to spiraling inflation and became virtually worthless after the war. Confederate money was produced with various designs, depending on the year and the bank note company doing the issuing. Many Confederate bills featured portraits of George Washington or Jefferson Davis, among others. Popular scenes included those involving mythological gods or slaves laboring in the fields; others featured trains, ships or animals. A one-hundred-dollar Confederate bill of 1862 features a picture of a steamship, a train and a Negress with a basket of cotton. The bill states, "Six months after the ratification of a treaty of peace between the Confederate States and the United States, the Confederate States of America will pay One Hundred Dollars to bearer, with interest at two cents per day." A twenty-dollar bill showed a symbol of industry seated between Cupid and a beehive. A ten-dollar issue showed Jefferson Davis and a picture of artillery. A five-dollar issue showed the Capitol at Richmond, and so on.

1864: The prices which obtained were almost fabulous, and singularly enough there seemed to be no sort of ratio existing between the values of different articles. I bought coffee at fourty dollars and tea at thirty dollars a pound on the same day. . . .

My dinner at a hotel cost me twenty dollars, while five dollars gained me a seat in the dress circle of the theatre. I paid one dollar the next morning for a copy of the Examiner, but I might have got the Whig, Dispatch, Enquirer, or Sentinel, for half that sum. For some wretched tallow candles I paid ten dollars a pound. The utter absence of proportion between these several prices is apparent. . . . A facetious friend said, "Before the war . . . I went to market with the money in my pocket, and brought back my purchases in a basket; now I take the money in the basket, and bring the things home in my pocket." . . . Towards the last . . . bartering, or "payment in kind," as it was called, became common. . . . To fix a price for the future in Confederate money when it was daily becoming more and more exaggeratedly worthless, would have been sheer folly.

A Southern journalist cited in American History Told by Contemporaries

Continental money: the paper money issued by Congress during the Revolutionary War. It was issued in numerous denominations and increased in five-dollar increments up to eighty dollars. (Some states issued money stated in pounds, shillings and pence.) By 1778 this money had depreciated to 33½ percent of its face value; by 1779, when it was scheduled to be redeemed, it had plummeted to 2½ percent of its face value. It eventually became virtually worthless. Thus, even throughout the 1800s, the term continental became synonymous with anything completely lacking in value.

1837: The Congress of the U.S. caused to be emitted that paper, always since known by the name continental money, and which no man living, if he has any recollection of it, desires ever to see restored.

Mr. Sergeant, Pennsylvania, House of Reps., Congressional Globe, *September 29, p.198*

1841: I wouldn't give a continental copper for the safety of your skin.

W.G. Simms, The Kinsmen, *p.98*

coppers: slang for cents.

dime: from 1798-1807, this silver coin featured a Liberty head (a woman with flowing hair) on one side and a heraldic eagle on the other. From 1809-1837 the Liberty head wore a Liberty cap. From 1837-1891, Liberty (now a woman in full view seated) could be found on the obverse and the words One Dime, surrounded by a wreath, on the reverse. From

1892-1916, the Liberty head returned, with the words One Dime, surrounded by a wreath, on the reverse.

double eagle: a twenty-dollar gold piece issued from 1849-1907; it featured a Liberty head with coronet on its obverse and a heraldic eagle on its reverse.

1888: Albert carried in a sack, tucked in his hip pocket, 890 dols., mostly in double eagles. Troy Daily Times, *January 31*

eagle: a ten-dollar gold piece. From 1797-1804 it featured a capped bust on one side and a large heraldic eagle on the other. No eagles were struck from 1805 to 1837. From 1838-1907, it featured the Liberty head with coronet on the obverse and heraldic eagle on the reverse.

1803: A vast river of golden eagles ready coined, which at a trifling expense in cutting canals and constructing locks may easily be turned into the treasury of the U.S.

Gazette of the U.S., *Philadelphia, November 30*

1842: His passage was $4, and he was given a gold eagle and $5 silver in change, one dollar being retained for discount on the note.

Philadelphia Spirit of the Times, *December 6*

elevenpence: 12½ cents, given in English reckoning; the equivalent of the Spanish reale. This term and levy were used to denote a reale or 12½ cents in Pennsylvania. In New York this amount was called a shilling and in New England a ninepence.

1802: [There was] a slight fracas between Ned Whiffle and Dick Slang, occasioned by the former refusing to lend the latter eleven pence, to get a glass of gin twist. Port Folio, *p.220*

1826: There were many poor people that would have made the shirts for three elevenpenny bits apiece. New Harmony Gazette, *May 3, p.256*

1835: [We] were bid farewell with the gentle charge of three elevenpenny bits each for supper and lodging. Letters on the Virginia Springs, *p.76*

fip: a five-pence or fi'penny bit; the Spanish half-reale (or medio), worth 6¼ cents. A fip is what the Pennsylvanians called a half-reale or medio, but some Southerners—especially those around Louisiana—called it a picayune.

1822: A dispute now commenced between two persons respecting some cents and a fip, which had fallen from his pocket as he rolled in the straw; one asserting that there were two fips, and the other that there was but one. Philadelphia Freeman's Journal, *September 5*

1824: We have whiskey at three fips per gallon.

Letter from Cincinnati, Massachusetts Yeoman, *March 3*

1824: In Philadelphia, every article goes by fips; so many fips a piece, or dozen. *Arthur Singleton,* Letters from the South and West, *p.28*

foreign coins: many foreign coins were in circulation and accepted as legal tender in the United States until they were banned in 1857. Most of these coins were Spanish. In fact, some 40 percent of all coins in circulation as of 1830 were of Spanish or Mexican origin. Of these, the double reale, reale and half-reale (medio) were widely used for making change. Indeed, in stores throughout the country in the first half of the century, merchandise was as likely to be priced by medios (6¼ cents) or reales (12½ cents) as by American rates. (Even as late as 1858, Horace Greeley's *Whig Almanac* was still priced at 12½ cents.) Some shopkeepers priced items by the English reckoning of shillings and pence—a throwback to Colonial days—until foreign coins and all forms of foreign reckoning were eliminated in 1857.

fractional currency: from 1863 to 1876, small notes of three, five, ten, twenty-five and fifty cents were issued by the government to help alleviate the coin shortage and to be used in lieu of postal currency (see entry). These featured the busts of Washington, Lincoln, Liberty and Columbia, and the Secretaries of the Treasury, Fessenden, Spinner, Walker and Crawford.

1865: The little notes were stuffed into the trouser pockets of the soldiers, with jacknife, the cartridge, the plug of tobacco, and other handy articles, and soon became unfit for circulation. They wore out rapidly and became ragged and filthy, and were frequently returned for redemption. *J.J. Knox,* United States Notes

gold dollar: a very small gold coin that came widely into use in the 1850s. From 1849-1854 it featured a Liberty head with a headband on its obverse and the numeral 1 on its reverse, surrounded by a wreath. From 1854-1856 it featured an Indian head wearing a feather headdress on its obverse and the numeral 1 on its reverse, surrounded by a wreath. From 1856-1889 it again featured the Indian head but with a slightly larger design. The reverse was the same.

greenbacks: see United States Notes.

half cent: issued from 1793-1857 (none were struck in 1837), it featured the bust of a woman with flowing hair on the obverse and a wreath on the reverse. This copper coin was unpopular with the public because it was widely associated with poverty and people were ashamed to use it.

half dime: a small, silver coin that was notoriously easy to lose. From 1800-1805 it featured a draped bust on the obverse and a heraldic eagle on the reverse. From 1829-1837 the bust was featured wearing a cap. From 1837-1873, it featured a seated Liberty on the obverse and the words "Half Dime" surrounded by a wreath on the reverse.

half dollar: a large silver coin featuring a Liberty bust and heraldic eagle from 1801-1807; a capped Liberty bust and heraldic eagle from 1808-1836; a full-figure, seated Liberty and heraldic eagle from 1838-1891; and a Liberty head wearing a wreath from 1892-1915.

half eagle: a five-dollar gold piece featuring a capped Liberty head and heraldic eagle from 1795-1807; a left-facing, capped Liberty head from 1807-1812; a larger diameter coin with the same design from 1813-1829; a reduced diameter coin with the same design from 1829-1834; a classic or Grecian head and heraldic eagle from 1834-1838; a classic head with coronet from 1839-1866; and a classic head and heraldic eagle again from 1866-1908.

1841: It was an open declaration of war upon the half eagles, the gold currency. . . . This gold, in half eagles, was too good for us, and must therefore be driven out of the country.

Mr. Walker, Mississippi, U.S. Senate, Congressional Globe, *p.269*

hard times tokens: a broad category that includes Civil War tokens (copperheads), Jackson cents, merchants' tokens or storecards, etc., issued from around 1830-1845 and again during the Civil War, from 1860-1865, by private individuals and businesses to help make up for the severe coin shortage due to hoarding. Most tokens were about the size of a large cent and made of copper; they largely served as cents, although legally they could not be so called. (Some clever merchants got around this by stamping their coins with One Cent and a tiny "not" just above.) They frequently featured some form of advertising ("Good for 5¢ trade at Smith's"; "Good for One Cigar at Bentley's," etc.). Even brothels ("Emporium of Joy, 729 Howard St., S.F.") were forced to use tokens as change. Other tokens featured political or social messages, for example, antislavery sentiments or mottoes such as "Union Forever" or "The Federal Government Must and Shall be Preserved." The Jackson cents or Jackson tokens of the late 1830s dealt with Andrew Jackson's campaign for Presidency and other Jackson-related matters. Civil War tokens, frequently called copperheads, were the size of small cents and featured the busts of Washington, Lincoln, Franklin and famous generals. The Confederacy alone circulated some five thousand varieties of tokens.

1837: . . . there are great quantities of copper pieces in the market which circulate as cents, but which are not so. They are too light; but the worst part . . . is the bad metal. . . . Worst of all, they are a vile debasement of the current coin, by which individuals very improperly make a large profit at the public expense, their spurious coins being generally sold by the bushel, at 50 to 62½ cents the hundred.

Globe, *Washington, November 23*

Jackson cents: see Hard times tokens.

Joe, Johannes: a gold Portuguese coin worth about eight dollars, largely used in the 1700s but sometimes referred to in the 1800s.

1825: She is coming this way; joes to coppers, that she speaks to me.

John Neal, Brother Jonathan, *p.337*

1827:Two young men found in the earth a number of gold coins, consisting of joes, half joes, etc, such as were in circulation among the French soldiers during the Revolutionary War.

Correspondence from Lynchburg, Virginia, Massachusetts Spy, *May 23*

large cent: an oversized, copper cent struck from 1793-1857, with no issue in 1815 due to a copper shortage. It featured the bust of a woman with flowing or braided hair on the obverse and a wreath on the reverse, with slight variations throughout the years. A smaller cent replaced it in 1857. Ironically, the large cent became popular for a number of uses other than spending. Housewives tossed them in their pickling crocks to give their pickles a rich green color which, it was eventually learned, poisoned people, even killing some eaters. The large cents were also tacked to the ridgepoles of new houses in New England to insure good luck. The eyes of corpses were also kept shut by these coins. Some people made necklaces of the cents as a cure for arthritis.

levy: nickname for elevenpence.

1832: He drew out rather more dollars, half dollars, levies, and fips, than his dirty little hand could well hold.

Mrs. Trollope, Manners of the Americans, *p.171*

1836: The N.Y. Transcript says that the Boston Post says that the bootblacks have struck for a levy instead of a fip, which in New York parlance is a shilling instead of a sixpence.

Philadelphia Public Ledger, *December 15*

1842: A lady entered the store, and called for a mackeral, tendering a levy in payment. Philadelphia Spirit of the Times, *March 17*

medio: the Spanish half reale, the equivalent of 6¼ cents. Variously known as a fip, picayune or six-pence, depending on location. The medio was used widely for change until it was banned from circulation in 1857.

National Bank Notes: notes issued by national banks in 1863 to replace those issued by state banks. A one-dollar National Bank note issued from 1863-1875 featured a picture of maidens at the altar on the front and the landing of the pilgrims on the back. A two-dollar note of 1875 showed a large numeral 2 lying face down in the upper-right corner and a picture of a full-figure Liberty with flag on the left; its reverse featured Sir Walter Raleigh and others smoking tobacco. A five-dollar note issued from 1863-1875 showed Christopher Columbus sighting land on the left and Christopher Columbus with an Indian princess on the right; its reverse showed Christopher Columbus landing at San Salvador in 1492.

nickel five-cent piece: noted for being one of the ugliest coins ever issued, its design from 1866-1883 comprised a shield on its obverse and the numeral 5 surrounded by a circle of stars on its reverse. From 1883-1913, it featured a Liberty head surrounded by stars on the obverse and the Roman numeral V surrounded by a wreath on the reverse.

ninepence: 12½ cents. A name denoting the Spanish reale, as used in New England. Also known as an elevenpence in Pennsylvania. Its half was a fourpence-halfpenny piece, otherwise known as a medio.

1828: A ninepence in New England, Virginia, and some other parts of the confederacy, for aught I know, is a shilling in New York and a levenpenny bit in Pennsylvania; and a half pistareen is about a sixth part less everywhere. This is the fag end of our provincial currency. Yankee, *May 14*

1836: We have heard in Marblehead the cry to strangers, peculiar to that town, Give me a ninepence, and I won't stone ye. Philadelphia Public Ledger, *August 30*

1839: Scarcely an individual [in Rye, New Hampshire] is willing to part with a fourpence ha'penny without assurance that it will bring back a ninepence. Farmer's Monthly Visitor, *p.33*

1844: She stated that she had lost a ninepence given her by her mother to purchase a pound of butter. Philadelphia Spirit of the Times, *July 24*

paper money: see Confederate money, National Bank Notes, Shinplasters, State Bank Notes, United States Notes.

pence: plural of penny. This is English reckoning for a value ranging from slightly over a cent to two cents, depending on year and location.

picayune: 6¼ cents. This is another name given the Spanish medio or half reale. This term was used largely around Louisiana and Florida. Later on, a picayune was used to denote an American half-dime or five-cent piece.

1819: Upon these the children canter, by paying a half-bit, here [in New Orleans] called a pecune. *Arthur Singleton,* Letters from the South and West, *p.127*

1835: Piccaiune, properly picaillon. Called in New England a fourpence halfpenny, in New York a sixpence, and in Philadelphia a fip. *Ingraham,* The South West, *p.205*

1835: The name Picayune is the Creole bastard Spanish for what we call a fip, the Gothamites a sixpence, and the Bostonians a fourpence halfpenny. Philadelphia Public Ledger, *February 7*

1842: He said he had still a picayune in his pocket, a small silver coin worth about 3d., and though it was the last he had he must lay it out in drink. *J.S. Buckingham,* Eastern and Western States, *p.75*

piece of eight: the Spanish silver dollar, otherwise known as the Spanish Milled Dollar or peso which, valued at eight reales, was the equivalent of an American dollar. It was used widely throughout the United States and the world. Those minted in Mexico featured a royal portrait and crowned Spanish arms on its obverse (along with the words, *Hispaniarum et Ind Rex,* i.e., King of the Spains and the Indies) and two pillars (Pillars of Hercules) decorated with banners on its reverse. Like all foreign coins, it was removed from U.S. circulation and prohibited from use as legal tender in 1857.

pistareen, pistoreen: a Spanish silver coin, minted in Spain, and valued at about one-fifth of a dollar in the 1700s and slightly less in the early 1800s.

1829: [The Bank] receives and pays out Pistareens, which formerly passed for 20 cents, at 17 cents each. Massachusetts Spy, *July 8*

1829: Pistareens are worth 18 and ¾ cents in New York.
Massachusetts Spy, *July 8*

1829: Their current value in Connecticut is 18 cents, in New York 18 and ¾ cents, and in some towns in Massachusetts only 17 cents. Their real value varies from 16 to 20 cents, and probably averages about 18 cents; the head pistareens are worth 20 cents. Massachusetts Spy, *July 29*

pocket full of rocks: slang for having plenty of money.

1850: A pocket full of rocks 'twould take to build a house of free-stone.
J.R. Lowell, Unhappy Lot of Mr. Knott

1851: Thar's a feller here named Andy Smith, with a pocket full of rocks. He has just sold a tract of land, and pocketed the dimes.
Polly Peablossom's Wedding, *p.45*

postal currency: in July 1862 the government allowed the use of postage stamps to help alleviate a massive coin shortage. Although it sounded like a viable solution at the time, the stamps quickly proved unsatisfactory due to soiling and tearing. In August a special case with a thin mica face was introduced to hold and protect each stamp, which worked well. However, a dispute between the Post Office and the Treasury soon followed, and stamps intended for use as money grew too scarce to meet demand. The shortage was eventually solved by the issuing of postage currency, special stamps measuring 2¾ × 3⅜ inches printed on heavy paper, to be used exclusively as currency. They were issued in denominations of five, ten, twenty-five and fifty cents and featured the same presidential portraits as those found on regular postage stamps. They were legal tender for amounts up to one dollar. The issuing of fractional currency followed postage currency in March 1863.

quarter: a silver coin that featured a bust of Liberty on the obverse and a heraldic eagle on the reverse from 1804-1807; a bust of Liberty wearing a cap and a heraldic eagle from 1815-1838; a full-figure, seated Liberty and a heraldic eagle from 1838-1891; and a Liberty bust wearing a wreath on the obverse and a heraldic eagle on the reverse from 1892-1916.

quarter eagle: a $2.50 gold piece featuring a capped Liberty bust and heraldic eagle from 1796-1807; a capped Liberty bust facing left (opposite of above) in 1808; a capped Liberty bust and heraldic eagle from 1821-1834; a Liberty head with a ribbon in her hair from 1834-1839; and a Liberty head with coronet from 1840-1907.

reale: Spanish coin worth one-eighth of a dollar or 12½ cents; one bit. It was in circulation throughout the first half of the century and removed in 1857. The reale (also real) and its equivalent value had several names throughout the United States including shilling in New York, ninepence in New England and Virginia, and elevenpence or levy in Pennsylvania. The half reale, valued at 6¼ cents, was called a medio. In the first half of the century merchandise was as likely to be marked by the rate of reales and half reales as American cents.

shilling: 12½ cents. The English term used to express this value; the equivalent of a bit, levy, ninepence, reale. In the first half of the century merchandise was as likely to be marked in shillings as in cents. See also York shilling.

shiners: gold coins.
1824: The Dutchmen in Albany are not so weak and illiterate as to throw away their shiners for the trash of a Cockney. Microscope, *May 22*
1827: The New Yorkers were much puzzled the other day at one of our little country banks paying out $13,000 in shiners.
Massachusetts Spy, *October 3*

shinplasters: paper currency issued in denominations as low as five cents by businesses and individuals in the 1830s and again in the 1860s to help offset severe shortages of coins. This currency was greatly disliked by the public.
1837: The shinplasters which are now so current throughout the country have received the appropriate name of hickory leaves.
Pennsylvania Republican, *June*
1837: Mr. Calhoun asked what sort of currency we had now. Was not the whole country flooded with currencies of all kinds; the shinplasters of all sorts, sizes and shapes?
U.S. Senate, Congressional Globe, *September 22, p.54*
1861: The idea of keeping up our credit by the issue of shinplasters is

all gammon.
Mr. Cutler, Ohio, House of Reps., Congressional Globe, *July 26, p.238*

1862: The currency of New Orleans was in a condition deplorably cha-
otic. Omnibus tickets, car tickets, shinplasters, and Confederate
notes, the last named depreciated 70 percent by the fall of the city,
were the chief mediums of exchange.
James Parton, Butler in New Orleans, *p.413*

1867: Though not acknowledging any superiority, at that time, of the
value of greenbacks over their shinplaster currency, [the Confeder-
ates] much preferred the former in payment to their own.
W.L. Goss, A Soldier's Story, *p.36*

short bit: ten cents; one dime; not quite a bit (12½ cents).

silver dollar: from 1798-1804 this large silver coin featured a bust of
Liberty on the obverse and a heraldic eagle on the reverse. Silver dollar
coinage was then suspended until 1831 but didn't resume until 1836.
From 1836-1839 it featured a full-figure, seated Liberty and a flying
eagle; from 1840-1873 a full-figure, seated Liberty and heraldic eagle,
with the first "In God We Trust" motto added in 1872. From 1873-
1885, the silver dollar was known as the trade dollar and was used
largely in the Orient to meet export demands; it featured a seated Liberty and heraldic eagle. From 1878-1921, it featured a Liberty head and
flying eagle.

slug: a fifty-dollar gold piece. Also known as a quintuple eagle or five-
eagle piece. This octagonal piece featured a heraldic eagle on its obverse
and a plain pattern of rays or braids on its reverse. It was legal tender
in the United States but was used most widely in California. It was struck
in 1851 and 1852.

1853: The slugs have completely annihilated the small gold in this vicinity, and silver is entirely out of the question — more scarce than slugs.
Olympia Courier, *January 1*

1853: We hope our farmers and stockraisers will have their eyes open,
and their slugs ready, to enter into a successful competition with the
speculators of California. Olympia Courier, *July 16*

1858: It is immaterial what the idol is, whether it is what the Californians
call a slug, or whether it is a twenty-dollar gold piece.
Brigham Young, Journal of Discourses, *February 7*

1862: Many a not unseemly octagonal slug had been offered me.
Theodore Winthrop, John Brent, *p.37*

small cents: made from copper and nickel and actually called nickels by
the public from 1859-1864. From 1856-1858, the design featured a flying eagle on one side and a wreath on the other. (According to the
Washington Star in 1895, "The flying eagle on the nickel cent was re-

151

moved because people insisted that it was a buzzard.") From 1859-1909, the design depicted an Indian princess wearing a feather headdress on the coin's obverse and a wreath on its reverse.

spondulicks: slang for money.
1863: Those ordering job work should come down with the spondulicks as soon as the work is done or delivered.
Rocky Mountain News, *January 29*
1876: Now let's have the spondulicks, and see how sweet and pretty I can smile upon you. Harper's Magazine, *April, p.790*
1902: The one with the spondoolix wonders harder than the one who has none. *W.N. Harben,* Abner Daniel, *p.58*

State Bank Notes: prior to 1861, all paper money was issued by private or State Banks, often with little or no financial backing (as by coins or other securities deposited in the bank). The notes could always be redeemed for coin at the above-board banks, but notes issued by some banks were worth little or nothing at all. Dishonest banks (called Wildcat banks) even went so far as to locate themselves in remote areas so their notes could not be redeemed. The State Bank notes were too numerous to detail here. See also Wildcat money.

three-cent piece: a very small and easy-to-lose silver coin that, from 1851-1873, featured a six-pointed star on its obverse and an olive sprig surrounding the Roman numeral III on its reverse. This coin was hugely popular when first issued.

three-dollar gold piece: from 1854-1889 this unpopular gold coin featured the head of an Indian princess on the obverse and the words "3 Dollars," surrounded by a wreath, on its reverse.

twenty-cent piece: another unpopular coin, roughly the size of a quarter and often confused for such. From 1875-1878 it featured a seated Liberty on the obverse and an eagle with arrows in its talons on the reverse.
1878: "It is understood by all, I think, that the coinage of the twenty-cent piece was originally a mistake." *Congressman Morrill*

two-cent piece: a bronze coin issued from 1864-1873. It featured the first appearance of the motto, "In God We Trust." Its design was comprised of a shield on the obverse and a wreath on the reverse.

United States Notes: the legal tender notes or greenbacks issued by the government in 1862. They were the dominant form of money used by the North in the Civil War and were thus affected by the war's uncertainties, depreciating to thirty-five cents per dollar in 1864 and rising to seventy-five cents as the North began to win the war. Actual face value per dollar was finally achieved fourteen years after the war. Some of the designs are described below.

One dollar, issued in 1862: portrait of Salmon Chase, Secretary of Treasury in upper left-hand corner. The reverse featured a large circle in the center of which the legal tender obligation was stated.

One dollar, issued in 1869: portrait of Washington in the center, with a large red seal to the right and a scene of Columbus sighting land to the left. Its reverse featured the legal tender obligation printed in a round space to the right. This was known as the Rainbow note due to its use of various colors: green, blue, red and black.

One dollar, issued from 1874-1917: a front design similar to that of 1869 but without the blue or green shading. Its back featured a large X in the center containing the words, United States of America.

Two dollars, issued in 1862: portrait of Alexander Hamilton on the face and a large center circle in which the legal tender obligation was printed on the back.

Vs and Xs: five- and ten-dollar bills. The fives were also called V-spots. See also State Bank Notes.

1837: My wallet [was] distended with Vs and Xs to its utmost capacity.
Knickerbocker Magazine, *January*

1837: I'll bet you a V we don't see anything of the kind.
Baltimore Commercial Transcript, *May 19*

1843: The thimble-rigger, while he pocketed the V or X of some greenhorn, did not cease to expatiate on the favorite horse.
Philadelphia Spirit of the Times, *May 27*

1849: I vow my hull sheer o' the spoils wouldn't come nigh to a V spot.
Biglow Papers, *No.8*

wildcat money: money issued by insolvent banks or banks that located in remote areas to prevent their notes from being redeemed. See also State Bank Notes.

1838: About four hundred Irishmen working on the Canal took offence at being paid in Wild-Cat money, instead of Illinois.
Jeffersonian, *Albany, April 14*

1840: [Many of the new banks] were without a local habitation, though they might boast the name, it may be, of some part of the deep woods, where the wild cat had hitherto been the most formidable foe. Hence the celebrated name Wild Cat justified fully by the course of these bloodsuckers. Mrs. Kirkland, A New Home, *p.220*

1842: We took our pay in wild-cat money.
Mrs. Kirkland, Forest Life, *i, p.111*

1853: It will be remembered that in 1837-8 Michigan was overrun with wild-cat banks, the notes of which were sent all over the west to be circulated. Daily Morning Herald, *St. Louis, February 14*

1858: We are over-run with a wild-cat currency from all God's creation, and every day we notice batches of new issues scattered amongst us. Baltimore Sun, *July 8*

York shilling: same as a shilling; 12½ cents.

1824: The bill amounted to the enormous sum of one York shilling for each gentleman. Microscope, *Albany, March 27*

1854: Apples are offered in our streets for three York shillings apiece. Weekly Oregonian, *August 5*

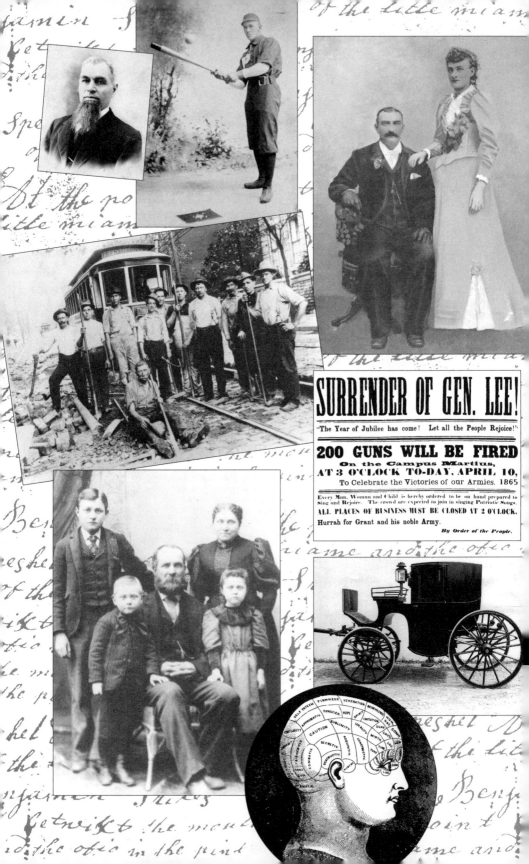

SECTION SEVEN

HEALTH, MEDICINE AND HYGIENE

B y 1800, most medical students were learning the doctoring "trade" through the apprentice system. That is, young men fifteen years of age or older were moving in and living with established physicians and trading their labor for an education. The arrangement lasted anywhere from two to six years, with some students then continuing on to a formal medical school (five were in operation by 1810) for at least two to four more years of education and a degree. However, the majority of physicians at the beginning of the century opened their practices without benefit of a degree.

Although state licensing of physicians was carried out off and on throughout the century, medical practices were rarely inspected. Quacks and charlatans practiced virtually unchecked everywhere. However, in the early days it was exceedingly difficult to judge what was quack and what was genuinely useful because treatments were generally based on ignorant notions and hunches to begin with. In fact, so-called legitimate medicine often did more harm than good, for example, bloodletting, purging, puking, and so on. Little wonder that distrust of physicians ran high and that many who were ill tried desperately to find their own cures through folk medicine before resorting to a "professional."

⚜

abortion: According to one estimate, one in every twenty-five pregnancies from 1800-1825 was ended by abortive means. By the 1860s, the number skyrocketed to one in sixth births or higher in some areas, a result of the greater availability and acceptance of abortifacients. By the Civil War, in fact, some twenty-five different chemical abortifacients—aloes, iron, various cathartic powders—were being sold through newspaper ads, circulars and pharmacies. They were advertised under such euphemistic names as "infallible French female pills" and a "cure for interrupted menstruation."

In 1861, a woman could get a surgical abortion for between ten to one hundred dollars. Women who couldn't afford the fee sometimes attempted to perform an abortion on themselves, sometimes with tragic results.

In the first half of the century, abortion was largely accepted by society as long as it was performed in the early months of pregnancy. Still, it was a source of great shame and few women talked of it openly. Between 1860 and 1890, forty states enacted antiabortion statutes, making it much more difficult to end a pregnancy and leaving the crucial decision largely to the physician. Still, most illegal abortion cases were dealt with leniently by the courts. Many cases were simply impossible to convict due to lack of evidence.

ague: a frequently used name for malarial fever or chills. See also Malaria.
1831: The new resident is subject to billious complaints, to remitting fevers, and especially to fever and ague, the general scourge of the valley. *Peck, Guide, p.40*

anesthetics: prior to the 1840s, patients sang hymns, bit a bullet, got drunk or took opium to distract themselves from the horrific pain of surgery. It's no wonder that amputations were performed in as little as forty seconds; even the thickest-skinned surgeons were repulsed by the agony involved. Ironically, nitrous oxide or "laughing gas" was first used as a form of entertainment at parties and on the stage before it found favor in dentistry around 1844. Ether was introduced — with religious protests — in 1846 and chloroform, the anesthetic of choice among European and Civil War surgeons, followed in 1848.
1839: The abolishment of pain in surgery is a chimera. It is absurd to go on seeking it. . . . Knife and pain are two words in surgery that must forever be associated in the consciousness of the patient.
Dr. Alfred Velpeau, Professor, Paris Faculty of Medicine
1844: A grand exhibition of the effects produced by inhaling Nitrous Oxide, Exhilerating, or Laughing Gas! will be given at Union Hall this evening, December 10, 1844.

Forty gallons of gas will be prepared and administered to all in the audience who desire to inhale it.

Twelve Young Men have volunteered to inhale the gas to commence the entertainment.

Eight strong men are engaged to occupy the front seats to protect those under the influence of the gas from injuring themselves or others. This course is adopted that no apprehension of danger may be entertained. Probably no one will attempt to fight. . . .

The gas will be administered only to gentlemen of the first respectability. The object is to make the entertainment in every respect a genteel affair. *Advertisements for a Laughing Gas Entertainment*, Hartford Courant

bathing: due to a lack of indoor plumbing and the time involved in heating water over a fireplace, few Americans in the first half of the century bathed with any regularity. Too, there was a belief that baths — at least in winter — caused colds and other illnesses. Consequently, some soaked themselves as seldom as once per year. When plumbing improved and bathtubs were routinely installed in homes (Philadelphia boasted having more than fifteen hundred bathtubs by 1836), bathing gradually increased to once per week. The Grahamites (see entry) went so far as to bathe three times per week, a practice many thought unnatural or wicked.

bleeding, bloodletting: draining a patient's blood, either by lancing the flesh or by applying live leeches, a widely used therapy in the physician's disease-fighting arsenal for the first half of the century. Diehards clung to the technique as late as the 1870s. Bleeding, as advocated by then medical guru Benjamin Rush (see entry), was believed to relieve tension on constricted arteries and to allow poisons to drain from the body, therefore curing any underlying disease. Rush recommended bleeding patients as much as one pint or more per day. The therapy lowered blood pressure, weakened patients, and did nothing to remedy illness of any kind, yet thousands of physicians practiced it faithfully, so powerful was the persuasiveness of Rush at the time. See also Blistering, Puking, Purging, Sweating.

1822: We have had a rather sick family lately . . . and I am on Dr. Watkins' list. He has bled me twice, and prescribed a course of calomel which I am getting safely through . . . and I expect soon to be perfectly restored. You must not expect . . . that my health is worse than it frequently is, in summer, but Dr. Watkins wishes to make a permanent cure at once of all my complaints. . . . I have no doubt that his advice is most judicious.

Virginia Randolph, granddaughter of Thomas Jefferson, in a letter to fiancé, July 26

blistering: blistering the skin to discharge disease-causing poisons from the body, an ineffective treatment for infections advocated by Benjamin Rush (see entry) and used for at least the first half of the century.

calomel: the most widely prescribed drug throughout the first half of the century. It was used in purgative therapy, as advocated by Benjamin Rush (see entry), often along with bleeding, to help relax the interior of the body and to expel disease-causing poisons. Highly toxic, large doses of the drug destroyed patients' teeth and gums and did nothing to cure disease. See also Bleeding, 1822 citation.

1829: A bilious complaint, attended by a frightful degree of fever, seized him, and for some days we feared for his life. The treatment he received was, I have no doubt, judicious, but the quantity of calomel prescribed was enormous. I asked one day how many grains I shoud prepare, and was told to give half a teaspoonful. The difference of climate must, I imagine, make a difference in the effect of this drug, or the practice of the old and new world could hardly differ so widely as it does in the use of it.

Frances Trollope, Domestic Manners of the Americans, *p.116*

carbolic spray: an antiseptic spray strongly recommended by Lister to disinfect operating rooms of germs but used only by a handful of surgeons even as late as the 1870s. Physicians were ignorant of the importance of cleanliness for most of the century. Antiseptic practices were not widely adopted until the 1880s and consequently cases of septicemia were common.

1876: Little if any faith is placed by any enlightened surgeon on this side of the Atlantic in the so-called carbolic acid treatment of Professor Lister. *Samuel Gross, Professor of Surgery, Philadelphia, in a medical review*

catarrh: frequently used name for any inflammation of the mucuous membranes, especially in the nose and throat.

cholera: epidemics of cholera due to unsanitary conditions broke out in various locations throughout the country in 1832, 1849, 1866 and 1873, with numerous smaller outbreaks throughout the century. The disease caused diarrhea and dehydration, sometimes killing its victims within hours.

1854: In the summer of 1854, the city of Boston was visited by that dreadful scourge the Asiatic cholera; and although our northern climate is not so congenial to the fearful malady as more Southern cities, yet its ravages here were amply sufficient to carry terror and dismay to every household. . . . In some instances, where life had departed but a few hours, the corpse would be so swollen, that the largest coffin would not contain it; in others the flesh would actually fall to pieces, a putrefied mass, before it could be properly laid out, the stench arising from being almost suffocating. . . . The weather again became sultry, and cholera began again to appear. A woman died at No. 18 North Bennett Street—sick sixteen hours—she was buried by friends. A woman was removed from Jefferson's block to the hospital. A member of our own Police Station died at his residence . . . after a most distressing illness of twelve hours; his body turned black immediately after death, and it was necessary to bury him without delay.

Edward Savage, Police Records and Recollections, Boston, *August 2*

consumption: the commonly used name for the lung-destroying disease of tuberculosis, one of the most frequent causes of death throughout the century. Entire families sometimes succumbed to it after unknowingly passing the disease among themselves. Benjamin Rush (see entry) thought the disease could be caused, among other things, by tobacco-smoking and cured by vigorous horseback riding, opium, or a meat diet, along with his bleeding and purging remedies. The true nature of the disease was unknown until Robert Koch discovered the tubercle bacillus in 1882.

1862: The management of this disease twenty-five years ago was certainly not in accordance with the principle of conservatism. The measures employed, medicinal and hygienic were . . . bloodletting, cathartics . . . confinement within doors.

Dr. Austin Flint, leading tuberculosis expert in 1862

1872: Bare arms and necks and short skirts are the rule, even in the bleakest weather, for children's parties . . . and so the tender frames of the little ones are subjected to an exposure that often sows the seeds of consumption and other disease.

James McCabe, Lights and Shadows of New York Life, *p.156*

contraception: In 1800, a married couple had an average of slightly over 7 children. By 1850, the number had dropped to 5.42. By 1880, it plummeted once more to 4.24.

As these numbers testify, precious few contraceptive choices existed during the first quarter of the century. Condoms made from pig and sheep intestines were available as early as the 1700s, but they reportedly cost as much as one dollar each and were washed out for repeated use. They were primarily used in Europe. Cheaper rubber condoms, costing six to twelve cents, didn't become widely available until the last quarter of the century.

One female contraceptive method used was douching. From the 1830s on, newspapers carried ads for "female syringes" for the purpose. The syringes were typically sold with such chemicals as alum or sulphates of zinc or iron, to kill sperm.

A contraceptive sponge with attached thread for easy removal was recommended by at least one publication, also from the 1830s.

Another female device was the pessary, informally known as a pisser. It was sold in over a hundred different varieties (wood, cotton or sponge) in drugstores for the purpose of correcting a prolapsed uterus. However, most women knew its real intent, as evidenced by this letter of helpful advice from Rose Williams to her newlywed friend Allettie Mosher in 1885: "Well now the thing we [use] (when I say we I mean us girls) is a thing: but it hasn't always been *sure* as you know but that was our own carelessness. . . . I do not know whether you can get them out there. They are called Pessairre or female preventive if you don't want to ask for a pisser just ask for a female preventive. They cost one dollar. . . . The Directions are with it."

According to one physician writing in 1867, New England brides whose marriages were announced in the newspaper invariably received circulars on contraceptive "instrumentalities." Those who did not, or those who remained ignorant, afraid or repulsed by "preventives" practiced the simplest and most morally acceptable birth control method of all: coitus interruptus. Physicians warned, however, that "withdrawal" was detrimental to men's health.

dental health: a large sector of the American population had rotten teeth and the chronic pain and bad breath that inevitably went with them, especially during the first half of the century. Some lost a number of teeth even before their teen years were ended. Toothbrushes were available in country stores as early as 1820, but not everyone used them or recognized their importance. Consequently, physicians (dentistry didn't become a separate profession until the establishment of the Baltimore College of Dental Surgery in 1840) and amateur dental surgeons alike did a brisk business extracting teeth. Toothless, partially toothless or cavity-filled mouths are probably why so many faces in nineteenth century photographs are unsmiling.

False teeth had been around before even George Washington's day (George wore false teeth made of carved ivory and was absolutely miserable with them), but they were ill-fitting and usually had to be removed if one wanted to eat. Transplanting teeth from the dead to the living was practiced as early as the 1700s. The poor even sold their own teeth to dentists, but the transplants often caused infections and fell out. A few lucky individuals enjoyed transplants that lasted as long as five years. Most simply had replacement teeth (teeth made of carved gold, silver or porcelain were also available throughout the century) tied or braced to existing teeth to hide embarrassing gaps. Full sets of dentures became cheaper and somewhat better-fitting after the invention of rubber around midcentury.

1784: Wanted Front Teeth, for which Two Guineas a piece will be given, by J. Browne, Surgeon and Dentist, No. 6, Nathan-Street, New York
September 29

1798: American girls are pretty, and their eyes are alive with expression; but their complexions are wan, bad teeth spoil the appearance of their mouths.
Mederic Louis Elie Moreau de Saint-Mery, Voyage aux Etats-Unis de l'Amerique, 1793-1798

1838: A young fellow, twenty or thereabouts, pained with a toothache. A doctor, passing on horseback, with his black saddlebags behind him, a thin, frosty-haired man. Being asked to operate, he looks at

MEDICAL FEES		
	Urban Philadelphia	Rural New York
advice given in office	$1-10	50¢
written advice	$5-20	?
house call	$1-2	50¢
	(Often charged less if doctor's horse was fed)	
house call per mile	$1	50¢
night house call	$5-10	75¢
vaccination	$5	$1
labor and delivery	$10-30	$4
reductions of fractures	$5-10	$2-10
hernia, reduction by operation	$25-100	$20

the tooth, lances the gum, and the fellow being content to be dealt with on the spot, he seats himself in a chair on the stoup with great heroism. The doctor produces a rusty pair of iron forceps, a man holds the patient's head. . . . A turn of the doctor's hand, and the tooth is out. The patient gets up, half-amazed, pays the doctor ninepence, pockets the tooth, and the spectators are in glee and admiration.

Nathaniel Hawthorne, Passages from the American Notebooks

1859-1862: They love sweets and delicacies to a degree that there are nowhere in the world so many dentists as here, and all make a good living. They are indispensable because the unbounded taste for sweets rots the teeth, so that artificial ones must take the place of the natural. What is more, many ladies allow whole rows of teeth to be extracted, as I myself saw, in order to replace them with prettier ones.

I.J. Benjamin, Drei Jahre In Amerika 1859-1862

doctor fees: typical fees charged by physicians, according to guidelines set by the College of Physicians of Philadelphia (1843) and the Medical Society of Washington County, New York (1837), depending on rural or urban location. (See sidebar.) These fees were slightly lower twenty years earlier and slightly higher twenty years later.

doctor's remedies: a typical horse and buggy doctor carried castor oil, calomel, jalap, peruvian bark or cinchona (for malarial fevers), nux vomica, splints, forceps and stethoscope (after 1819) in his bag. He might also carry any number of patent medicines, to be used when no other recourse was available to him.

1850: They not only attended an entire family for twenty-five dollars a year, but furnished the medicines themselves. . . . Castor oil was the principal beverage. The dose was half a dipperful, with a dipperful of New Orleans molasses added to help it down and make it taste good, which it never did. The next standby was calomel; the next,

rhubarb; and the next, jalap. Then they bled the patient and put mustard plasters on him. It was a dreadful system.
Mark Twain, recalling physicians' remedies in his autobiography

dyspepsia: indigestion.

Grahamites: followers of a major health movement in the 1830s and 1840s, begun by Sylvester Graham (of Graham cracker fame), who advocated vegetarianism and the consumption of whole wheat products; frequent bathing (as much as three times per week); regular exercise; and avoidance of many of the popularly prescribed drugs of the day, particularly calomel.

heroin: sold as a cough medicine by the Bayer company in 1898.

infant and child mortality: infants and children suffered a high death rate through much of the century. Those who did not die from a traumatic delivery faced the possibility of succumbing to infections of the lungs and intestinal tract or to diphtheria, whooping cough and scarlet fever. Children also suffered from measles, mumps and chicken pox.

jalap: a powder used as a cathartic.

malaria: spread by mosquitoes and causing debilitating fevers, chills and weakness, outbreaks were common throughout the South and West. Victims suffered from the condition throughout their lives but were vulnerable to a host of other potentially deadly diseases. Malaria was commonly referred to as the ague (see entry).
1832: To have the ague is in some places so common that the patient can hardly claim the privilege of sickness.
Jack Larkin, The Reshaping of Everyday Life, *p.79*

mental illness: families often hid away or shunned their mentally ill relatives out of shame. Through much of the century, the mentally ill were thought to be utterly incurable, being possessed by evil and/or punished by God. They were confined in asylums and usually left to languish for life. Often they were beaten, ill-fed and neglected. In the 1870s, the *North American Review* wrote that these institutions "would disgrace Turkey with their filth, vermin, contagious disease and food hardly less fatal than starvation."

miasma: the bad air or poisonous effluvium thought to be responsible for many diseases, throughout much of the century.

morphine: first used extensively during the Civil War to control the pain of the wounded. Morphine was also found in Winslow's Baby Syrup and Kopp's Baby Friend, medicines used to lull a child to sleep, with addictive side effects that sometimes lasted a lifetime.

nurses: not professionally trained until the establishment of Bellevue Nursing School in 1873. Nurse's caps and striped blouses were introduced at Bellevue in 1876.

opium: used to help control mild pain through much of the century. It was abused as a recreational drug from as early as 1840. In 1868, it was estimated that at least 100,000 people from all stations of life were addicted to the drug, which was openly sold in drugstores in pill form or as laudanum.

1871: Walk along the streets any day and you will meet opium slaves by the score. . . . They are slaves, abject slaves suffering exquisite torture. Once in the fetters of opium and morphine they are, with few exceptions, fettered for life. *Lafcadio Hearn, describing the drug problem in Cincinnati*

patent medicines: nonprescription, quack remedies, frequently laced with alcohol, purporting to cure everything from consumption to old age. Contrary to their high-sounding title, such nostrums were not patented; only their trade names were, for example, Prof. Low's Liniment and Worm Syrup, Dr. Flint's Quaker Bitters, Dr. Townsend's Sarsaparilla, and so on. Early in the century, patent medicines were sold by peddlers and hucksters. By the 1860s, some fifteen hundred different nostrums were vying for advertising space in newspapers, testifying to their popularity with an ill and gullible public.

1817: The good people of the United States suffer great impositions . . . from patent medicines. *Ann. 14th Congress, 2 Sess., p.469*

1849: It is quite customary to laugh at the patent medicine men.
Foster, New York in Slices, p.107

1872: Bitters . . . and such liquors . . . either ruin the tone of the stomach, or produce habits of intemperance. The "washes," "lotions," "toilet fluids," etc., are generally apt to produce skin diseases. . . . The "tooth washes," "powders," and dentrifices are hurtful. They crack or wear away the enamel of the teeth. . . . The principal constituent of these dentrifices is a powerful acid. The "hair dyes" advertised . . . contain such poisons as nitrate of silver, oxide of lead, acetate of lead, and sulphate of copper. The "ointment" and "unguents" for promoting growth of whiskers and moustaches, are either perfumed and colored lard, or poisonous compounds, which contain quick lime, or corrosive sublimate.
James McCabe, Lights and Shadows of New York Life, p.808

1863: Hostetter's Celebrated Stomach Bitters. A Pure and powerful tonic, corrective and alternative of wonderful efficacy in disease of the stomach, liver and bowels. . . . Prevents fever and ague and bilious remittent fever: Fortifies the system against miasmas and the evil effects of unwholesome water. Invigorates the organs of digestion and the bowels: Steadies the nerves, and tends to prolong life. Cures dys-

MEDICAL TREATMENTS

Acute Tonsilitis — Quinsy: The removal of a tonsil is but the work of a moment on the part of the surgeon. . . . During an acute case of tonsilitis, or quinsy, the patient should remain in bed; poultices, or flannels wrung out of hot water, may be applied to the throat; steam may be inhaled, and a gargle of a saturated solution of chlorate of potassium in water may be used. In addition, the following prescription will be found of great use: Quinine — 24 grains; Morphine — 1 grain. Make six powders. Take one every four hours.

Dyspepsia: commonly called a bilious attack, or fit of indigestion. The regurgitation of fluid from the stomach, waterbrash, and the heartburn, may be relieved by moderate doses of subnitrate of bismuth.

Diarrhea: If in the beginning of a diarrhea the bowels are freely evacuated by some mild cathartic, nothing further is generally required. For this purpose a small dose of salts, or what is better, castor oil, may be taken. If the diarrhea continues, twenty-five drops of laudanum may be taken every three to six hours. Or instead, five-grain doses of Dover's powder, or a sixth of a grain of morphine.

Constipation: Attention should first be directed to a cure of the bad habit of irregularity. The patient should go regularly every morning after breakfast, and take plenty of time to complete the act. Every house should have a comfortable closet, free from bad smells. If in the country, where there are no sewers . . . the privy should be well built, the outside well boarded up and battened and the inside lathed and plastered, so as to keep out the wind. . . . The diet should be, in good part, articles which leave a large residue of undigested matter to be carried out of the body . . . vegetables, salads, cabbage, greens . . . corn bread, oat meal, cracked wheat, etc. A glass of cold water taken . . . before breakfast is often very useful. . . . A small pill of aloes, or of aloes and strychnine, which may be had at drug stores, will be found very effective. One pill should be taken every night. . . .

Cholera: There is a premonitory diarrhea, and if this be effectually treated there is little danger of the full development of the disease. . . . If more than eight years old, full doses of laudanum should be given, together with acetate of lead and bismuth. For an adult, twenty-five to forty drops of laudanum, or instead, one-sixth to one-quarter grain of morphine after every movement of the bowels. Small doses of red pepper, in addition to the opiates, are useful. . . .

Catarrh: Quinine in two-grain doses, three times a day; laudanum in small doses and iodide of potassium in five-grain doses three times a day . . . powders and solutions snuffed up the nose usually do harm. . . . The most effective treatment for a chronic case . . . a change of climate. The writer has known some excellent cures to result from a residence in Northern Wisconsin, or in the region of Lake Superior.

Phthiriasis — Lousiness: In the case of phthiriasis from head lice, the hair of the head should first be thoroughly soaked in common kerosene oil, two or three times a day, and wrapped up in cloth for the first twenty-four hours. This will kill both the lice and their nits. At the end of the twenty-four hours the hair should be thoroughly washed. . . .

Rheumatism: Notwithstanding the popularity of salicylic acid, or the salicylate of soda . . . during the last few years, we believe that as much or more may be accomplished by the use of what has been known as the alkaline treatment. The alkali, either bicarbonate of potassa or soda, should be given in full doses, every three to four hours. Lemon juice may be added to the dose. . . . Tincture of aconite applied to the swollen joints often affords relief. Chloroform liniment or soap is also used for this purpose. The salicylate of soda is much employed, perhaps at this time more than any other remedy.

1883, in The Home Library of Useful Knowledge, *by R.S. Peale, "assisted by eminent specialists in each department"*

pepsia, liver complaint, sick and nervous headache, general debility, nervousness, depression of the spirits, constipation, colic, intermittent fevers, seasickness, cramps and spasms, and all complaints of either sex. *Advertisement in* New York Times, *March 2, p.5*

1863: The Vigor of Youth Is Restored by Dr. Powers' Essence of Life or Invigorating Elixer, and Dr. Powers' Radical Pills. . . . Young man! Are you subject to that soul and body destroying disease resulting from secret habits? Dr. Powers' Invigorating Essence and Radical Pills briefly cure the very worst cases, while innocent of anything deleterious. . . . Prepared and sold by Dr. Powers, No. 12 Laight St., Ny. Afflicted, try them! *Advertisement in* New York Times, *March*

1863: Pure Iodine in pure Water. A cure for Scrofula, Consumption, Rheumatism, Syphilis, Mercurial Disease, etc. Dr. H. Anders & Co., No. 428 Broadway. *Advertisement in* New York Times, *March*

phrenology: a popular "science" of the 1830s and 1840s that held that a person's intellect and personality could be "read" in the shape and bumps of the skull. Many people of the period paid a phrenologist to "read" their skulls. Amateur phrenology was popular at parties. Although it was largely discredited after the 1840s, many people maintained their belief in it throughout the century.

1836: Although I am no Phrenologist, yet, if there is a word of truth in the doctrine, I have the bumps of a roving disposition.

Campaigns Rocky Mts., *p.14*

1870: Slim, spare, with a head that would defy phrenology and Lavater to read, he has had uniform success.

M.H. Smith, Twenty Years Wall Street, *p.295*

1876: A phrenologist and a mesmerizer came — and went again and left the village duller and drearier than ever.

Mark Twain, Tom Sawyer, *p.178*

premature burial: nineteenth-century Americans and Europeans suffered a bizarre but exceedingly common fear of being interred alive. The fear arose out of the reputations of physicians who, lacking modern medical knowledge (and often a medical degree, especially in the first half of the century), occasionally pronounced comatose or unconscious patients dead prematurely. The deceased would sometimes miraculously revive during funeral services, much to the dismay of friends and family. These incidents were always widely publicized in the local papers.

To the Victorians, the fear of premature burial became all-consuming, and many bizarre measures were taken to prevent it. Thanks to the Society for the Prevention of People Being Buried Alive and other concerned citizens, death was handled more tentatively than ever before. For example, the deceased were left lying in their caskets for days or weeks on end before being deemed sufficiently dead to bury. When the Duke of Wellington died in 1852, this macabre postponement ritual reached an extreme: The Duke was not buried until two months after his death.

A simpler method of allaying premature-burial anxiety was to place crowbars and shovels in the deceased's caskets; if they revived, they could dig their way out. Also in use was a pipe that went through the ground and into the casket, to be used for emergency communications. Wealthy families even hired servants to wait by the pipes and listen for calls for help. Wealthy families who wanted their dead to stay that way had yet another option: coffins fitted with special nails that, when driven, punctured capsules of poison gas.

The most popular device by far, however, was the Bateson Revival Device, advertised as "a most economical, ingenious, and trustworthy mechanism, superior to any other method, and promoting peace of mind amongst the bereaved at all stations of life. A device of proven efficacy, in countless instances in this country and abroad." The device, patented by George Bateson, came to be known as Bateson's Belfry. It consisted of an iron bell mounted on the lid of the casket just above the deceased's head. The bell was connected to a cord through the coffin that was placed in the dead person's hand, "such that the least tremor shall directly sound the alarm." Although there is no record of this device actually saving someone's neck, it did, nevertheless, enjoy brisk sales for many years and made Bateson a rich man.

Ironically, Bateson himself feared premature interment so powerfully that it is thought he was driven mad by his preoccupation. In 1886 he committed suicide by dousing himself with linseed oil and setting himself on fire.

puking: dosing a patient with emetics to produce vomiting, a practice advocated by Benjamin Rush (see entry) and used by thousands of doc-

168

tors to relieve tension on arteries and expel poisons from the body to cure any underlying disease. Like many of Rush's treatments, puking did nothing to cure anyone's illness.

purging: dosing a patient with powerful laxatives to relax the interior of the body and expel poisons, a common treatment for a wide range of illnesses throughout the first half of the century. Some doctors continued the practice as late as the 1870s, despite evidence that it was ineffective.

Rush, Benjamin: hugely influential Professor of the Institutes of Medicine at the University of Pennsylvania, beginning in 1791, and physician to the Pennsylvania Hospital from 1783-1813. Known as the Hippocrates of American Medicine by devoted followers, Rush lectured to and persuaded thousands of students and physicians to subscribe to his ideas about medicine and the human body. Among these ideas were that Negroes were black due to a form of leprosy; tobacco caused madness and tuberculosis (consumption); yellow fever outbreaks were produced by "noxious miasmas." Although ahead of his time in advocating humane treatment of the mentally ill, Rush's ideas about disease treatment were questioned by some of his peers. At the center of the controversy were his bloodletting, blistering, puking, purging and sweating treatments to relieve nervous constriction of blood vessels caused by an accumulation of poisons from the disease state. Some of Rush's adversaries clearly thought such therapies were ineffectual at best and harmful to the patient at worst. Nevertheless, Rush's ideas held fast throughout the first half of the century, with some older and rural physicians clinging to his bleeding and purging therapies through the 1870s. Today Rush is remembered as the man responsible for more blood loss than any general in U.S. history.

sex education: because the printing and dissemination of "pornography" was prohibited through much of the century, the U.S. population—including physicians—was largely ignorant of the mechanics of sexual and reproductive function. See also Contraception.

1812: Onanism produces seminal weakness, impotence, dysury, tabes dorsalis, pulmonary consumption, dyspepsia, dimness of sight, vertigo, epilepsy, hypochondriasis, loss of memory, manalgia, fatuity, and death. *Dr. Benjamin Rush*

1821: [The] more remote any individual state or society was placed from moral and political habits, and the various causes which are capable of interfering with the actions of nature, the less frequent would be the occurence of the menstrual phenomenon, and . . . in some instances, it might be wholly unknown or nearly so. *John Power, M.D.*, Essays on Female Economy

1870: Do a pregnant mother's experiences affect the offspring? Indeed they do. The eminent Dr. Napheys reports the case of a pregnant lady who saw some grapes, longed intensely for them, and constantly thought of them. During the period of her gestation she was attacked and much alarmed by a turkey-cock. In due time she gave birth to a child having a large cluster of globular tumours growing from the tongue and exactly resembling our common grapes. And on the child's chest there grew a red excresence exactly resembling a turkey's wattles. *Professor Oswald Fowler, lecturer of health and education,* Sexual Science

1874: Everything which inflames one appetite is likely to arouse the other also. Pepper, mustard, ketchup and Worcestershire sauce—shun them all. And even salt, in any but the smallest quantity, is objectionable; it is such a goad toward carnalism [promiscuity] that the ancient fable depicted Venus as born of the salt sea-wave.
Dio Lewis, M.D., Chastity, or Our Secret Sins

1870s: We distinctly warn that it [masturbation] leads to insanity, not rarely, but frequently. . . . We have taken pains to examine with care the latest reports of a large number of insane asylums in the United States, to ascertain precisely how many of their inmates have been driven there by this vice. The average we have found to be nearly nine per cent of all males in whom the causes were assigned; and in one prominent institution in Ohio, fourteen per cent.
George Napheys, M.D., The Transmission of Life, Counsels on the Nature and Hygiene of the Masculine Function, *pp.74-75*

1880: I personally know of a young man sent to the insane asylum as a result of continuous masturbation practices. . . . At the request of his mother . . . the son was castrated. . . . Two years later she reported that he was earning a salary of $1800 a year and had married an unsexed girl. Can anyone deny the great benefit castration was to this young man and his mother?
Bethenia Ownes-Adair, M.D., Professor at the University of Michigan, author of Oregon's Human Sterilization Bill

1891: Every man who has sexual relations with two women at the same time risks syphilis, even if the two women are faithful to him, for all libertine behavior spontaneously incites this disease.
Alexandre Weill, The Laws and Mysteries of Love

stethoscope: the first model was a simple wooden tube, in use from 1819 on.

surgery: surgery was performed without anesthesia before the 1840s and without antiseptics before the 1880s. Surgeons typically wore their street clothes and frock coats while operating up until the 1880s.

sweating: making patients sweat out the poisons causing their disease was a common practice, as advocated originally by Benjamin Rush.

Thomsonians: followers of Samuel Thomson, who advocated the use of herbal medicines instead of traditional therapies. The herbal medicine movement grew from 1800-1860.

tuberculosis: see Consumption.

women doctors: the first training school for women physicians was the Women's Medical College of Pennsylvania, founded in 1850.

yellow fever: also known as the black vomit, the disease was spread by mosquitoes and destroyed the liver and kidneys; a telltale symptom was skin that had turned yellow or jaundiced. An outbreak of the disease practically decimated Philadelphia in 1793. An 1853 epidemic in New Orleans left nearly eight thousand dead. An 1878 epidemic in Memphis killed five thousand and frightened twenty thousand of its thirty-eight thousand citizens into fleeing the city. The disease wasn't eliminated until 1900.

SURRENDER OF GEN. LEE!

"The Year of Jubilee has come! Let all the People Rejoice!"

200 GUNS WILL BE FIRED
On the Campus Martius,
AT 3 O'CLOCK TO-DAY, APRIL 10,
To Celebrate the Victories of our Armies. 1865

Every Man, Woman and Child is hereby ordered to be on hand prepared to Sing and Rejoice. The crowd are expected to join in singing Patriotic Songs.
ALL PLACES OF BUSINESS MUST BE CLOSED AT 2 O'CLOCK.
Hurrah for Grant and his noble Army.
By Order of the People.

SECTION EIGHT

FOOD, DRINK AND TOBACCO

uropean travelers griped vociferously about the awful food they found almost uniformly throughout America. "I will venture to say," declared Volney, "that if a prize were proposed for the scheme of a regimen most calculated to injure the stomach, the teeth, and the health in general, no better could be invented than that of the Americans. In the morning at breakfast they deluge their stomach with a quart of hot water, impregnated with tea, or so slightly with coffee that it is mere colored water; and they swallow, almost without chewing, hot bread, half baked, toast soaked in butter, cheese of the fattest kind, slices of salt or hung beef, ham, etc., all which are nearly insoluble. At dinner they have boiled pastes under the names of puddings and the fattest are esteemed the most delicious; all their sauces, even for roast beef, are melted butter; their potatoes and turnips swim in hog's lard, butter or fat; under the name of pie or pumpkin, their pastry is nothing but a greasy paste, never sufficiently baked. To digest these various substances they take tea almost instantly after dinner, making it so strong that it is absolutely bitter to the taste, in which state it affects the nerves so powerfully that even the English find it brings on a more obstinate restlessness than coffee. Supper again introduces salt meats or oysters. As Chastellux says, the whole day passes in heaping indigestions on one another; and to give tone to the poor, relaxed and wearied stomach, they drink Madeira, rum, French brandy, gin or malt spirits, which complete the ruin of the nervous system." (In *The United States in 1800*, by Henry Adams.)

If there was one thing European travelers complained about more than food, however, it was America's love affair with chewing tobacco and spitting. They were disgusted to find evidence of it everywhere: in statehouses, in courtrooms, in theaters, trains and churches. "Men came into the lower tier of boxes without their coats," Frances Trollope observed in a theater in 1830, "the spitting was incessant, and the mixed smell of onions and whiskey was [beyond disgust]." In describing a traveling preacher, she wrote: "He stepped solemnly into the middle of the room and took a chair that stood there, but not to sit upon it; he turned

173

the back towards him, on which he placed his hands, and stoutly uttering a sound between a hem and a cough, he deposited freely on either side of him a considerable portion of masticated tobacco." Another observer at a dance in Washington wrote that "one night as I was walking upstairs to valse, my partner began clearing his throat. This I thought ominous. However, I said to myself, 'surely he will turn his head to the other side.' The gentleman, however, had no such thought but deliberately shot across me. I had not courage enough to examine whether the result landed in the flounce of my dress."

With all the hemming, hawking and tobacco dribbles, is it any wonder the Europeans found American food so unappetizing?

ale cocktail: a mixed drink comprised of ale, ginger and pepper, from at least 1838 on.

apple brandy: a liquor distilled from apple cider, enjoyed throughout the century. Also known as apple jack.
1865: At the store or tavern of every village . . . apple brandy is always for sale by the glass. Nation, *i*

apple butter: spiced apple juice and pulp, cooked to a buttery consistency, used throughout the century.
1862: The woman fed us on pies, apple and quince butter — she said she had no cow butter — and coffee. *Gray*, War Letters, *p.15*

apple dumpling: a pocket of dough filled with baked apples, a favorite pastry eaten throughout the century.

apple jack: same as apple brandy.
1890: I had had some experience with Kentucky apple-jack, which it was popularly believed among the boys would dissolve a piece of the fattest pork thrown into it. Congressional Record, *April 21*

ash-pone: a coarse corn bread baked in ashes.
1824: What slaves I have seen, have fared coursely upon their hoe-cakes and ash-pone. *Arthur Singleton*, Letters from the South and West, *p.78*
1832: Hoe-cake . . . and ash-pone, a course cake baked under the ashes, are in common use, as bread.
S.G. Goodrich, System of Universal Geography, *p.260*

bacon and collard greens: very popular meal components, served in the South throughout the century.

baking powder: sold commercially from the late 1860s on. Previously, housewives leavened their cakes and biscuits with sour milk and molasses or pearl ash or saleratus (potassium bicarbonate) with less-than-perfect results. Saleratus, for example, often gave food an alkaline taste.

baldface: slang for old brown whiskey; whiskey.

bannock: cakes of Indian meal fried in lard, eaten throughout the century.

batter cake: another name for a griddle cake, waffle or pancake, eaten throughout the century.

beans: eaten throughout the century, especially in New England. Beans in tomato sauce were first successfully canned and sold commercially by Van Camp in 1861.

beaten biscuits: eaten in the South for breakfast prior to the Civil War. The name was derived from the dough, which had to be repeatedly pounded with a hammer or mallet to knead it.

beef dodger: a corncake filled with minced beef, eaten throughout the century.

bimbo: an alcoholic drink comprised of brandy and sugar flavored with lemon.
1837: The U.S. Gazette asks what is a bimbo? Not toddy, we hope. The Boston Transcript answers that it is much worse. Bimbo is a rascally compound of brandy and sugar, flavored with lemon peel. An invention of the devil to make drunkards.
Baltimore Commercial Transcript, *September 5*

blackstrap: slang for any cheap alcohol, named after the thick molasses used in the processing of industrial alcohol.
1821: What champagne is to homely blackstrap. Blackwood, *x, p.105*
1833: He was taking mighty pulls at a huge tankard of blackstrap which stood beside him. *W.J. Snelling*, Expose of Gaming, *p.10*

Boston baked beans: navy beans cooked with pork and molasses, eaten throughout the century.

Boston brown bread: bread made of corn meal, rye or wheat steamed in molasses and other ingredients, eaten throughout the century.

brandy sour: a drink comprised of brandy, lime or lemon juice, bitters and carbonated water, from at least the 1860s.

brandy toddy: brandy mixed with hot water and sugar.

breakfast: the typical American breakfast in the 1800s was sometimes as simple as oatmeal or as elaborate as eggs served with meat or sausages, potatoes, cheese, bread and butter, buckwheat pancakes with Vermont maple syrup and coffee or tea. Cold cereals generally weren't available until the end of the century.

1837: We breakfasted at half-past seven on excellent bread, potatoes, hung beef, eggs and strong tea.

Harriet Martineau, Society in America, *p.195*

brown betty: a pudding of apples and bread crumbs, from at least mid-century on.

buckwheat cakes: griddlecakes made of buckwheat flour, eaten throughout the century.

bullock's heart: a delicacy, roasted and sometimes stuffed.

1836: A bullock's heart is very profitable to use as a steak broiled just like beef. There are usually five pounds in a heart, and it can be bought for twenty-five cents. Some people stuff and roast it.

Mrs. Child, The Frugal Housewife, *p.45*

calf's head: a hearty dish, boiled.

1836: Calf's head should be cleansed with very great care; particularly the lights. The head, the heart, and the lights should boil full two hours; the liver should be boiled only one hour. It is better to leave the wind-pipe on, for if it hangs out of the pot while the head is cooking, all the froth will escape through it. The brains, after being thoroughly washed, should be put in a little bag, with one pounded cracker, or as much crumbled bread, seasoned with sifted sage, and tied up and boiled one hour. After the brains are boiled, they should be well broken up with a knife, and peppered, salted, and buttered.

Mrs. Child, The Frugal Housewife, *p.48*

candy: peanut brittle, taffy, fudge, pralines and honey popcorn balls were a few of the candies made throughout much of the nineteenth century. After the 1840s, gumdrops, lozenges and jujube paste became available in general stores. An impressive variety of penny candy came later.

canned goods: some commercially canned foods were available as early as the 1820s, but variety was limited until the 1860s and 1870s.

champagne: used throughout the century.

cheese: made by farmers' wives and sold to general stores from early in the century on.

cheesecake: eaten throughout the century.

cherry pie: eaten throughout the century.

chewing gum: chewed throughout the century, especially spruce gum.

1836: The down east girls have a droll way of amusing themselves, viz., by chewing spruce gum, mingled as it frequently is with dirt, mosquitoes, and swamp flies. Philadelphia Public Ledger, *May 21*

chewing tobacco: used widely throughout the century, with frequent spitting in streets, saloons, stores, government buildings and elsewhere. Although spittoons were frequently put out, chewers often disregarded them or missed, so that floors everywhere were frequently awash or stained with tobacco juice, much to the distaste and complaint of non-chewers and foreign visitors to the United States. Even lower-class or rural women either chewed tobacco or dipped snuff until about 1820 or so.

1827: [The floor of the Virginia House of Burgesses was] actually flooded with their horrible spitting
Margaret Hall, The Aristocratic Journey

chicken: eaten fried, or in stews, pies, etc., throughout the century.

chicken fixins: chicken with dressings, or any fancy chicken dish.

1845: Our traveler forgot his surprise at the diminutive area of the Texas capital, over a good supper of corn-dodgers and chicken-fixins. *Cornelius Mathews,* Writings, *p.164*

1859: Tell Sal to knock over a chicken or two, and get out some flour, and have some flour doins and chicken-fixins for the stranger.
Knickerbocker Magazine, *March*

chipped beef: very thin slices of smoked meat, eaten throughout the period.

chitlings, chitlins, chitterlings: the small intestines of hogs, prepared like tripe, a Southern specialty.

1880: Hot corn-pone, with chitlings, southern style.
Mark Twain, Tramp Aboard, *p.575*

chocolate: available throughout the century. Milk chocolate for candy bars was invented late in the century.

chowder: fish, clam and corn chowder, New England favorites throughout the century.

cider: apple cider, a favorite beverage throughout the century.

cigar: introduced in the 1790s from the Caribbean. Cigar smoking was taken up widely by rich men from early in the century.

cigarette, cigarita, cigarrito: cigarette smoking was known as early as the 1830s, but it didn't catch on until the second half of the century. The earliest commercial cigarettes were manufactured in London and New York after the Crimean War. Brand names included Opera Puffs, Bon

Ton, Fragrant Vanity Fair, Turkish Orientals, Three Kings, Old Rip, Old Judge and Canvas Back. Production of cigarettes increased dramatically with the invention of the automatic cigarette-making machine, with one billion cigarettes manufactured in 1885. These machine-made cigarettes were called by various names, including Cameo, Cross Cut, Duke's Best, Pedro, Cyclone and Velvet Mouthpiece, all sold with the label, "These cigarettes are manufactured on the Bonsack Cigarette machine." As popular as cigarettes became, chewing and pipe tobacco were even more popular throughout the century.

cobbler: a drink consisting of wine, sugar, fruit juices and crushed ice, from around midcentury. Also, a fruit pie from midcentury.

cocktail: any mixed alcoholic drink, from at least 1806.

cocoa: also known as hot chocolate, a favorite beverage often drunk at breakfast, throughout the century.

coffee: drunk throughout the century. However, tea was the more popular beverage until after the Civil War. Coffee was lightened with Borden condensed milk as early as the 1860s. Chase and Sanborn coffee was sold in sealed cans as early as 1878. Maxwell House canned coffee followed a few years later.
1860s: How often, after being completely jaded by a night march . . .
   have I had a wash, if there was water to be had, made and drunk my
   pint or so of coffee, and felt as fresh and invigorated as if just arisen
   from a night's sound sleep. *John D. Billings,* Hard Tack and Coffee

coleslaw: eaten throughout the century, but often referred to as cold slaw.

collard greens: kale leaves, a favorite Southern vegetable often served with bacon.

cookie: a name for a flattened cake, throughout the century.

corn juice: another name for corn liquor, throughout the century.

corn pone: a loaf of bread made of Indian corn meal, milk and eggs, a Southern specialty throughout the century.
1886: A Southern society has been formed in New York, and its members
   are confident in being as happy over the corn-pone and the hog-jowl
   as the New Englanders over doughnuts and hard cider.
   Boston Journal, *December 8*

crackers: eaten throughout the century.

cracklin' bread: corn bread mixed with the residue of fried hog fat, a Southern favorite.

1853: Scarcely eating anything . . . a light condiment of cracklin' bread, and a half-pint of hog brains. *J.G. Baldwin,* Flush Times in Alabama, *p.160*

1887: Half dozen pones of cracklin' bread, made from Georgia-raised hogs. Boston Journal, *December 31*

dodger: a small loaf of corn bread.

1842: While the dodgers were baking, the bear meat was frying, and what he called coffee was also making. American Pioneer, *i, p.75*

doughnut: eaten throughout the century.

1809: The table . . . was always sure to boast an enormous dish of balls of sweetened dough, fried in hog's fat, and called dough nuts, or oly koeks. *Washington Irving,* Knickerbocker's History of New York, *iii, p.iii*

dutch oven: a large cast iron kettle with a close-fitting lid, for baking or roasting. Also, a tin container covering the top half of meat while the bottom half cooks over a fire.

egg-nog: enjoyed throughout the period.

fixins: another word for dressings, trimmings, etc.

1842: Our friends who love oysters and sparkling rosy wine, and other little fixins in the eating way, will do well to drop in at the Bath House Refectory. Philadelphia Spirit of the Times, *January 22*

flapjacks: pancakes, eaten throughout the century.

flip: a drink comprised of beer, rum and sugar, a favorite throughout the century.

1801: Punch and politics, flip and religion, tod and ministers, make one general compound, and share largely in their malevolent jargon. Massachusetts Spy, *September 30*

1878: Polly she nursed him up with a mug of flip and a lot o' 'lection cake till he was as pleasant as a young rooster. *Rose T. Cooke, "Cal Caulver and the Devil,"* Harper's Magazine

general store: foods available in general stores from the beginning of the century on: salt, spices, sugar, molasses, raisins, fruits, vegetables, cheese, eggs, butter, fresh baked goods, salted meats and fish, tea, coffee, wine and chocolate. Beer, whiskey, molasses and vinegar were dispensed through spigots from barrels. Pickles and crackers were also sold from barrels. Customers could stock up on dried legumes from bushel baskets on the floor or, from at least the 1860s, purchase a can of Van Camps beans in tomato sauce. Canned goods weren't widely available until the Civil War and after. See individual food entries.

ginger beer: enjoyed throughout the century.

gingerbread/gingersnaps: throughout the century.

gin-sling: a drink comprised of gin, lemon and other ingredients, popular throughout the century.

1802: The men of New England pass their evenings by their own firesides. Their breakfasts are not of whiskey julep, nor of gin-sling, but tea and coffee. Massachusetts Spy, *August 4*

grog: rum and water, or gin and water.

gumbo: a rich soup originating in Louisiana, eaten throughout the century.

1819: The dish of dishes in New Orleans is a French dish, called gumbo. It is a kind of save-all, salmagundi soup, made of the ends of every variety of flesh, mingled with rice, and seasoned with chopped sassafras, or with okra, a vegetable esculent.

Arthur Singleton, Letters from the South and West, *p.130*

hoecake: a cornmeal cake similar to corn pone and ash cake, formerly baked on a hoe over coals. A Southern specialty.

1803: 'Tis mayhap some negur-man that has run away, and is now come out of the woods to beg a hoe-cake or a bit of hominy.

John Davis, Travels in the U.S.A., *p.129*

1857: Dem common niggers is only good to hoe de corn and fry de hoecake. Knickerbocker Magazine, *December*

hog and hominy: pork and boiled corn, staples of the poor in the South, particularly slaves. Some Southerners lived on little else.

1816: [If a man] can be content with hog and hommany, he can live easier in Ohio. Massachusetts Spy, *January 10*

1847: I can give you plenty to eat; for beside hog and hominy you can have bar-ham and bar sausages, and a mattrass of bar-skins to sleep on. *T.B. Thorpe,* The Big Bear of Arkansas, *p.21*

1848: My niggers has got plenty of hog and hommony to eat.

Major Jones, Sketches of Travel, *p.105*

1861: [The inn at Georgetown, South Carolina, supplied] hog and hominy, and corn-cake, for breakfast; waffles, hog and hominy for dinner; and hog, hominy, and corn-cake for supper.

Knickerbocker Magazine, *October*

1869: The transition from the luxurious tables of the East to the "square meals" of the West is fortunately gradual, and by the time the traveler reaches Omaha, he is prepared for hog and hominy, or whatever may be presented. *A.K. McClure,* Rocky Mountains, *p.30*

hot dog: introduced in St. Louis in the 1880s.

ice box: patented in 1803, a wooden chest with a tin container to hold ice on top and a pan underneath to catch meltwater, used to keep foods fresh. By the 1830s, ice was readily available to everyone.

ice cream: a favorite throughout the century. A portable, hand-cranked ice cream churn for homemakers was invented in 1846. Ice cream was vended in the streets of New York as early as 1828.

1800: Bosse, French cook, at the New Caveau Hotel, Phila., supplies Ice Cream and other refreshments. Aurora, *March 7*

1837: They halted at a confectioner's, and called for ice-creams.
Knickerbocker Magazine, *March*

Indian pudding: a pudding made from cornmeal, milk, sugar, molasses and spices, throughout the century.

Johnnycake: originally thought to be known as Shawnee cake or journey cake, a simple cake made of corn meal, water and sugar.

ketchup: a favorite condiment from the beginning of the century, but time-consuming for the housewife to make. Heinz ketchup was sold in a bottle for the first time in 1876.

1801: Get them quite ripe on a dry day, squeeze them with your hands till reduced to pulp, then put half a pound of fine salt to one hundred tomatoes, and boil them for two hours. Stir them to prevent burning. While hot press them through a fine sieve, with a silver spoon till nought but the skin remains, then add a little mace, 3 nutmegs, allspice, cloves, cinnamon, ginger and pepper to taste. Boil over a slow fire till quite thick, stir all the time. Bottle when cold. One hundred tomatoes will make four or five bottles and keep good for two or three years.
Mrs. Samuel Whitehorne, Sugar House Book, *from the Newport Historical Society*

kinnikinnic: a mixture of tobacco and sumac leaves or other ingredients, smoked in a pipe by the Indians.

1817: I observed that they did not make use of tobacco, but the bark of Cornus Sanguinea, or red dog wood, mixed with the leaves of Rhus glabra, or smooth sumach. This mixture they call kinnickineck.
John Bradbury, Travels in America, *p.91*

1823: The Kinnecanick, or, as the Omawhaws call it, Ninnegahe, mixed or made tobacco, is composed partly of tobacco, and partly of the leaves of the sumach. *E. James,* Rocky Mountain Expedition, *p.331*

1839: [The Indian Chief] smokes the article called kanikanik, a mixture of tobacco and the dried leaves of the poke plant.
J.K. Townsend, Narrative, *p.31*

1890: Kinnikinnic is a mixture of willow bark, sumach leaves, sageleaf, and tobacco, and this is thoroughly mingled with marrow from buffalo bones. *Mrs. Elizabeth Custer,* Following the Guidon, *p.101*

Log Cabin syrup: Towle's Log Cabin maple syrup was sold in a tin shaped like a log cabin from 1887 on.

long nine: nickname for a cheap, nine-inch cigar.

1830: No more discomposed ... than a Providence lady is at passing the fourfold row of long-nine-smoking beaux, that are regularly drawn up on Sunday forenoon in Market Square.
N. Dana, A Mariner's Sketches, pp.213-214

1844: The segars were long nines, such as are made and sold in Massachusetts for a penny a grab. Philadelphia Spirit of the Times, November 5

1847: The long dank American cigar, nine inches long, and nine for a cent. Knickerbocker Magazine, December

1857: They were garnered by stable-boys smoking long-nines.
Autocrat of the Breakfast Table, ch.ii

long sauce: another name for large vegetables.

1850: There were cabbages ... parsnips, turnips ... carrots; in short, long and short saase of every description.
Knickerbocker Magazine, October

macaroni: eaten throughout the century.

1802: Dined at the President's—[on] a pie called macaroni, which appeared to be a rich crust filled with the strillions of onions or shallots. ... Mr. Lewis told me ... it was an Italian dish, and what appeared like onions was made of flour and butter.
Cutler, Life and Corr., ii, p.71

martini: a drink comprised of gin and vermouth, invented between 1860-1862 and briefly known as a Martinez.

mint julep: a favorite alcoholic beverage, originating in the South early in the century and drunk especially in hot weather.

mock oysters: imitation oysters made from a mixture of corn, eggs, butter and flour fried in oil, concocted in the South during the Civil War to replace real oysters, which were, along with many other foods, in short supply.

Monongahela: whiskey distilled on the river of that name. Any American-made whiskey.

1834: [He] cleared his throat with the contents of a tumbler of Monongahela, which seemed to stand permanently full by his side.
W.G. Simms, Guy Rivers, i, p.68

1837: There is the independent loafer—the one who sleeps in the market, drinks old Monongahela, and dines on a crust.
Baltimore Commercial Transcript, September 2

1857: We proceeded to make a banquet worthy of the gods, washing it down with that species of nectar known as Monongahela.
Knickerbocker Magazine, September

New England fare: favorites throughout the century: boiled dinner comprised of corned beef, carrots, potatoes, turnip, cabbage and squash; baked beans with brown bread; all types of seafood, including lobster, clams, oysters and fish chowders; fresh vegetables in summer; cellar vegetables, such as potatoes, turnips and squash, in winter; desserts including apple pie, pumpkin pie, plum pudding, bread pudding, etc.

oysters: hugely popular nationwide from 1810-1870. They were sold in streets, in "oyster rooms," in saloons with drinks; they were broiled, boiled, deviled, curried, fricaseed, fried, scalloped, steamed, stewed, made into sauces, tossed into omelettes and so on. Oysters were the center attraction of many parties.

pan-dowdy: apples, sugar and spices baked in a deep dish crust.
1846: Such glowing encomiums on pandowdy and pumpkin pie!
 Yale Literary Magazine, xi, p.235

pastries: popular throughout the century, in shops, in restaurants and at home.
1844: In pastry stores . . . peppermint cakes and mince-pies . . . give a relish for seasoning and palate-tickling food.
 Uncle Sam, Peculiarities II, *p.256*

pemmican: dried or smoked buffalo meat or venison, eaten by frontier folk and Indians throughout the century.
1804: [The Indians] then put before us the dog which they had been cooking, and Pemitigan and ground potatoe and several platters.
 George Rogers Clark, Lewis and Clark Expedition, *p.168*
1824: Pemmican is the meat of the buffalo . . . cut into thin slices, which are jerked in the sun or smoke . . . it is then dried before the fire until it becomes crisp, after which it is [pounded]. *Keat*, Narrative, *p.447*

pepper: used throughout the century.

pepperpot: a stew comprised of tripe and doughballs, very popular in Philadelphia.
1800: Daniel Dunn of the Leopard Tavern in Laetitia Court, advertises Pepperpot of a superior quality at 6 o'clock every evening.
 Aurora, *Philadelphia, June 19*
1803: An old negro-woman [in Philadelphia] was passing . . . with some pepperpot on her head. *John Davis*, Travels in the U.S.A., *p.45*
1814: [In Philadelphia] the ear is regaled with cries of "pepperpot, right hot," etc. *Arthur Singleton*, Letters from the South and West, *p.27*

pork barrel: a barrel filled with brine, used to preserve pork in one's cellar. See also Preserving food.

1845: I hold a family to be in a desperate way, when the mother can see the bottom of the pork barrel. *James Fenimore Cooper,* Chainbearer, *viii*

1886: When the pork barrel was empty they shot a hog.
Century Magazine, *September*

potato chips: see Saratoga chips.

preserving food: before the advent of refrigeration and home-canning, housewives employed a number of methods to preserve foods. Fruits and vegetables, for example, were sliced thin, threaded on strings, and hung up to dry in a cool place. By cooking in water, these foods could be brought back to a moist consistency again. Some vegetables, such as squash and potatoes, kept well for months in the family root cellar. Other foods, such as butter, might be preserved simply by submerging them in well or spring water. In the Southwest, thin strips of meat could be dried under the sun. In the more humid East, salting or smoking or both were necessary. One widely used technique was to pack pieces of meat in a barrel filled with a brine solution. The brine had to be strong enough to float an egg. To this, molasses, brown sugar or even ale was sometimes added for flavoring. The barrel was then kept in a cool place, usually the cellar. Although meat could be kept for great lengths of time in this way, exhaustive rinsing, scrubbing and soaking were necessary to make the meat even remotely palatable. Corning meat was sometimes simpler, as observed in the *American Frugal Housewife*, a cookbook published in 1836: "When you merely want to corn meat you have nothing to do but rub in salt plentifully, and let it set in the cellar a day or two. If you have provided more meat than you can use while it is good, it is well to corn it in season and save it. In summer, it will not keep well more than a day and a half; if you are compelled to keep it longer, be sure to rub in more salt, and keep it carefully covered from cellar flies." By the 1830s many city dwellers had ice boxes and could keep their foods fresh for short periods with cut ice. Rural and poor families who could not afford a steady supply of ice continued the traditional preserving methods for much of the century.

pretzels: throughout the century.

pumpkin pie: throughout the century.

root cellar: a storage space under the house or dug out of a hill, where turnips, cabbages, carrots, potatoes, squash and onions could be kept relatively fresh throughout the winter.

saloon: the better establishments across the nation boasted of serving as many as 150 different mixed drinks. To help attract customers, they often served free lunches and snacks, provided drinks were purchased.

1840s: (Choice of drinks at a fashionable bar-room, from an advertisement)

Plain mint julep	I.O.U.	Milk punch
Fancy do	Tippe na Pecco	Cherry do
Mixed do	Moral suasion	Peach do
Peach do	Vox populi	Jewett's fancy
Pineapple do	Ne plus ultra	Deacon
Claret do	Shambro	Exchange
Capped do	Virginia fancy	Stone Wall
Strawberry do	Knickerbocker	Sifter
Arrack do	Smasher	Soda punch
Racehorse do	Floater	Slingflip
Sherry cobbler	Pig and whistle	Cocktail
Rochelle do	Citronella Jam	Apple-jack
Tip and Ty	Egg Nog	Chain-lightning
Fiscal agent	Poor man's punch	Phlegm-cutter
Veto	Iced do	Tog

Saratoga chips: invented in 1853 at Saratoga Springs, New York, the original potato chips.

snuff: powdered tobacco, inhaled through the nostrils. Many rural and lower-class urban women dipped snuff up until the 1820s. Thereafter the practice was largely confined to poor Southern or Western women.
1815: Pray put your snuff box aside when you are working over your butter. Farmer's Almanack
1837: Among the country people [of North Carolina], the proffer of the snuff-box, and its passing from hand to hand is the usual civility. *Remark of a traveling Englishwoman*

sorghum: sorghum syrup and sugar served as a substitute for cane sugar in the South throughout the Civil War.

sour crout: eaten throughout the century.
1818: A jolly Dutchman from the Hague, grumbling because there was no sour crout on the table. Massachusetts Spy, *August 26*
1829: It is said the Dutchman get cloyed with her name, so dissonant with his beloved sour-kraout and buttermilk. Massachusetts Spy, *November 4*

sourdough: sour fermented dough used as a starter or as leaven for making a new batch of bread. A starter of sourdough was always kept on hand by cooks on the cattle range and by goldminers who, in Alaska, were nicknamed sourdoughs.

spider: a three-legged frying pan used for cooking over a kitchen fire or hearth.

store tea: tea purchased in a store, as distinguished from homemade.

1843: Tisn't none of your spice-wood or yarb-stuff, but the rale gineine store tea. *R. Carlton,* The New Purchase, *i, p.64*

1856: A country fellow at a Georgia hotel was asked what kind of tea he would take: "Why, store tea of course; I don't want any of your sassafras stuff." San Francisco Call, *December 27*

1859: Instead of store-tea, they had only saxifax tea-doin's without milk. Knickerbocker Magazine, *March*

1874: A little store tea—so called in contradistinction to the sage, sassafras, and crop-vine teas in general use. *Edward Eggleston,* The Circuit Rider, *p.57*

succotash: corn and beans boiled together, eaten throughout the century.

1869: The Indian dish denominated succotash, to wit, a soup of corn and beans, with a generous allowance of salt pork. *Harriet Beecher Stowe,* Oldtown Folks, *ch.15*

suppawn: cornmeal mush and milk, largely from the first half of the century.

1833: I helped myself with an iron spoon from a dish of suppawn and fishing up a cup from the bottom of a huge pan of milk I poured the snowy liquid over the boiled meal, which rivaled it in whiteness. *C.F. Hoffman,* A Winter in the Far West, *p.141*

sweet potato pie: a pie made of sweet potatoes, brown sugar, eggs, cinnamon and butter, a Southern specialty.

syllabub: a drink similar to eggnog, but made with white wine, brandy, sugar, and whipped cream, traditionally served at Christmas early in the century, especially in Charleston.

tea: widely drunk throughout the period. The first Atlantic & Pacific Tea Company, or A&P, opened in 1859 on Vesey Street in New York. Its rows of tea bins contained teas from around the world. By 1880, there were ninety-five A&P stores from Boston to Milwaukee. See also Store tea.

tea cake: a cake made from three cups of sugar, three eggs, one cup of butter, one cup of milk, a spoonful of dissolved pearlash, and four cups of flour, well beaten. A favorite throughout the period.

Thanksgiving feast: Thanksgiving fare was very similar whether one was dining in New England or in the South. Depending on the wealth of the family, a dinner might include any or all of the following: stuffed (herb or chestnut stuffing) turkey, roast suckling pig, oysters on the half-shell, hot rolls, celery, radishes, olives, cranberry sauce, fried or mashed potatoes, squash, turnip, onions in cream, giblet gravy, mincemeat pie, pumpkin pie, vanilla ice cream, coffee, etc.

tomatoes: widely believed to be poisonous and generally not eaten until the early 1880s.

turkey: eaten throughout the century.

1890: The turkey should be cooped up and fed some time before Christmas. Three days before it is slaughtered, it should have an English walnut forced down its throat three times a day, and a glass of sherry once a day. The meat will be deliciously tender, and have a fine nutty flavor. *Mrs. Stephen J. Field,* Statesman's Dishes and How to Cook Them

vinegar: used throughout the century, especially for making pickles. In the general store, it was kept in two-hundred-pound barrels and dispensed through spigots to the customer.

waffles: made in a waffle iron and eaten throughout the century.

1824: If their course ash-pones irritate the palate as they descend, their soft waffles, with their hollow cheeks floating in honey, soothe all again. In fine, the rich Kentuckians live like lords.

Arthur Singleton, Letters from the South and West, *p.96*

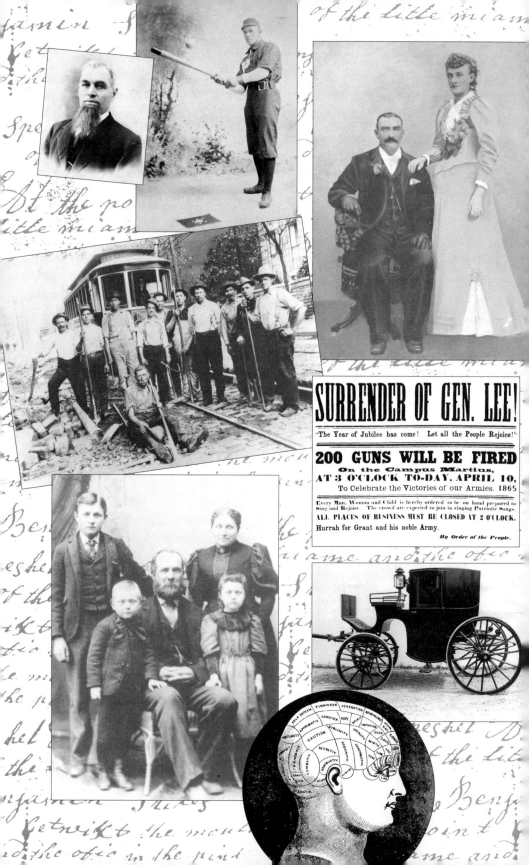

SURRENDER OF GEN. LEE!

"The Year of Jubilee has come!   Let all the People Rejoice!"

200 GUNS WILL BE FIRED
On the Campus Martius,
AT 3 O'CLOCK TO-DAY, APRIL 10,
To Celebrate the Victories of our Armies. 1865

Every Man, Woman and Child is hereby ordered to be on hand prepared to Sing and Rejoice.   The crowd are expected to join in singing Patriotic Songs.
ALL PLACES OF BUSINESS MUST BE CLOSED AT 2 O'CLOCK.
Hurrah for Grant and his noble Army.

By Order of the People.

Americans were divided on how best to spend weekend leisure time. How the Sabbath was observed, for example, varied from family to family and from community to community. The pious allayed all forms of recreation, attended church services twice on Sunday, and restricted laughter and play in their households. An observer traveling in 1830 noted that some cities, including Philadelphia, chained off their streets to prevent horses from passing.

But not everyone felt so strongly about keeping the Sabbath somber. Many families socialized and played together after church services. New Orleans citizens marked the Sabbath by drinking, dueling, partying and presenting slave dances to African drums in the public squares.

More women respected the Sabbath than men, probably because church was almost always at the center of the nineteenth-century woman's social life. Surely "there is no other country in the world where religion makes so large a part of the amusement and occupation of the ladies," Frances Trollope wrote in 1830. Throughout the period, women flocked to prayer meetings and revivals; they sang hymns together and took part in various church-related endeavors.

Men also attended church, but not in the same numbers. Many men spent the Sabbath puttering about the house, or fishing, hunting, playing cards, gambling, drinking and so forth.

The first forty years of the century are notable for the role that alcohol played in men's lives. Many observers of the period were struck by the fact that more men could be found with liquor on their breath than not. Ministers imbibed before sermons; doctors before surgery. Lawyers took drams before trying cases; farmers before plowing fields. The tavern for men was what church was for women: the center of social life and a home away from home.

Temperance societies burgeoned from the 1840s on and aided thousands of men in geting off the "demon drink." Although per capita consumption fell after peaking in the 1820s, alcohol remained a prevalent part of male amusement throughout the century. Women also drank on occasion, but usually in more reasonable quantities. Through-out the period a double standard existed; it was acceptable for a man to appear drunk but never a woman.

balloons: hot-air balloons were still a novelty in the beginning of the century. Wherever one was set up a mob soon gathered. Many purchased tickets simply to watch the balloon owner make an ascension. Others paid premium rates for rides in tethered balloons, with some balloon-owners making as much as one hundred dollars per day in the larger cities.

1801: Having obtained a deed of the exclusive right for the county of Hartford of the Archimideal Phaeton, Vertical Aerial Coach or Patent Foederal Balloon begs to inform the Public that the Machine erected near Mr. John Lee's is now strengthened and supported in all its parts—rendered perfectly safe and secure, and elegantly painted and redecorated—system and regularity established, so that voyagers may be treated with slow and steady or more rapid movements as they may order; so that persons of a timid cast will enter with assurance and be much delighted; others may progress 500 yards per minute. Attendance daily from 3 o'clock till dark. Parties of 2, 4, 8 or more will be waited on at their call at any hour of the day. *Advertisement in* Connecticut Courant, *June 9*

1819: Father and I have just returned from the balloon—all nature was there and more too. Massachusetts Spy, *November 3*

baseball: evolving from the British game of rounders and played in the United States as early as 1834, when the rules were similar to today's except baserunning was clockwise and a baserunner could be thrown out simply by hurling the ball at him. The game gained national recognition with the first formally organized match between the Knickerbockers and the New Yorks at Elysian Fields on June 19, 1846. First uniforms worn: 1851. First pay for players: 1864. Gloves introduced: 1875. First electrically lit game: 1883.

basketball: introduced in 1891 and originally played with a soccer ball and two peach baskets.

bear-/bull-baiting: a barbaric form of entertainment in which dogs were set loose on a tethered bear or bull, usually in an enclosure behind a tavern, with the fighting allowed to continue until the participants were either torn to shreds or thoroughly gored. The sport and the gambling that went with it were banned but matches were conducted illegally undercover or publicly in districts where ordinances were rarely enforced or nonexistent, for example, the early South and West, until the 1830s.

bicycling: the forerunner of the bicycle, the velocipede, was ridden — with difficulty — from about 1840 on. Its wheels were made of wood and it had to be walked along because early models had no pedals or chain propulsion. The later addition of pedals to the front wheels of these bicycles, sometimes called boneshakers, made them much more acceptable among the horse-weary population. In 1878, the United States began manufacturing bicycles with huge front tires, which few women rode due to their difficulty in mounting and riding. Finally, in 1885 the British introduced a bike with equally sized tires, called the safety, which allowed women and children to take up riding in droves. Women also rode huge tricycles during this period. Twenty thousand people owned bikes in 1882. That number expanded to over one million in 1893 as the entire nation fell in love with the sport.

1877: The silence of the bicycle . . . constitutes its chief danger to pedestrians. Scientific American, *July*

1883: We donned our knickerbockers . . . and bicycled to the wharf. Wheelman

1896: The alarmingly pessimistic view of the bicycle question is not justified by the facts. It is doubtless true that many young women ride to excess. It is also doubtless true that to the woman of impure life the wheel may offer a convenient means for facilitating the execution of immoral designs, but that the pastime itself has a tendency to degrade or demoralize is a proposition too absurd for a moment's consideration. A woman who will violate the decencies and proprieties of life while wheeling will violate them on other occasions. Where one woman rides to destruction on the wheel a thousand maintain all the decorum, modesty, and circumspection that characterize the well-bred, self-respecting women from the ideal American homes. Chicago Times-Herald

billiards: a favorite tavern pastime, and often bet on, throughout the century. The first national championship match was held in 1859.

bowling: played throughout the century. The game of Nine Pins was eventually banned and discredited due to its association with gambling.

1815: Bowling greens have become of late mightily fashionable, to the ruin of many unfortunate young men. Scarcely a day passes without the rattle of pins in front of landlord Toddy Stick's house. Every boy is distracted to get away from his work in order to take his game. At sun two hours high, the day is finished, and away goes men and boys to the bowling alley. Haying, hoeing, ploughing, sewing, all must give way to sport and toddy. Old Farmer's Almanac

1839: An act was passed to prohibit playing at nine pins; as soon as the law was put in force, it was notified everywhere, Ten Pins played here.
Marryat, Diary in America

1842: [At Virginia Springs] there is a ten-pin alley under a shed, at which ladies exercise themselves as well as men.
J.S. Buckingham, Slave States, *ii, p.324*

boxing: bare-fisted boxing, popular throughout the century, held a special attraction to Southern plantation owners, who pitted their best slaves against one another and bet on them.

burlesque: heralded in by the Broadway production of *The Black Crook,* which featured fifty skimpily-clad dancing girls in 1866. The show ran for 474 performances and was followed by *British Blondes,* which played around the country for twenty years.

checkers: played throughout the century.

chess: played throughout the century.

chuck-a-luck: a game in which players bet on which numbers would come up on three thrown dice.

1836: I thought I'd make a rise on a chuck-a-luck, but you never saw such a run of luck. A Quarter Race in Kentucky, *p.24*

circus: the circus began around 1830, when acrobatic troupes joined forces with menageries and horse shows. There were thirty circuses traveling about the country by 1836. In 1871, P.T. Barnum opened "The Greatest Show on Earth" in Brooklyn. His show became the Barnum and Bailey Circus ten years later.

1870: In the autumn of 1870 . . . I began to prepare a great show enterprise, comprising a Museum, Menagerie, Caravan, Hippodrome and Circus, of such proportions as to require five hundred men and horses to transport it through the country. On April 10, 1871, the vast tents, covering nearly three acres of ground, were opened in Brooklyn, and filled with ten thousand delighted spectators, thousands more being unable to obtain entrance. The success which marked the inauguration of this, my greatest show, attended it the whole season, during which time it visited the Eastern, Middle and Western States from Maine to Kansas. . . . At the close of a brilliant season, I recalled the show to New York, secured the Empire Rink, and opened . . . on 13 November. . . . The exhibitions were continued daily . . . until the close of the holidays, when necessary preparations for the spring campaign compelled me to close. *P.T. Barnum*

coaching: a favorite sport of the rich. Carriages and coaches paraded throughout the major parks and carriageways every weekend throughout spring and summer.

cockfighting: conducted undercover in the North and publicly in the South, the laws against this bloodsport were so feebly enforced that matches were regularly advertised in newspapers. A cockfight could be set up anywhere, but they were most frequently found on plantations. The roosters, eagerly bet on, were equipped with pointed steel gaffs on their feet to help assure that a match would reach a deadly conclusion, much to the satisfied horror of wagering spectators.

1812: Let there be a horse race, or a cockfight and . . . notice the multitudes who attend. American Rev. Hist., *October*

cotillion/cotillon: an elaborate, four-couple dance, characterized by frequent changes of partners, the forerunner of the square dance, from 1800 on. Also known as the quadrille.

1807: As I never dance cotillons, holding them to be monstrous distorters of the human frame. *Washington Irving*, Salmagundi

1832: They call their dances cotillons instead of quadrilles, and the figures are called from the orchestra in English.

Frances Trollope, Domestic Manners of the Americans, *p.215*

craps: a gambling dice game originating as "crabs" at the beginning of the century in New Orleans.

1843: The game of Craps . . . is a game lately introduced into New Orleans, and is fully equal to faro in its . . . ruinous effects.

J.H. Green, Expose of Gambling, *p.88*

croquet: introduced to the United States from England in 1860 and gaining wide popularity among men and women after the Civil War.

dances: especially popular among young men and women in their courtship years, at parties, weddings, barn raisings, husking bees, appleparings, sleighing frolics, etc. Music was most often supplied by a fiddler. See also Cotillion, Double shuffle, Fandango, Juba (in section 11), Two-step, Waltz.

dime novels: cheap, sensational novels, costing a dime. The first dime novel, published in 1860, was *Malaeska; the Indian Wife of the White Hunter*, by Mrs. Anna Sophia Stephens. It sold 300,000 copies in its first year alone. This was followed in the same year by *Seth Jones, or Captives of the Wild Frontier*, by Edward Ellis, which sold 450,000 copies. Published in orange covers, the novels featured such characters as Calamity Jane, Deadwood Dick and Kit Carson among others, involving tales of Indians, gunfighters, pioneers, hunters and so on. They were widely read by Civil War soldiers and adolescents. (See also Chronologies of Noted Books and Novels, p.290, and Selected Magazines, p.293.)

1873: A Danbury boy whose imagination had become diseased by too close devotion to dime novels, started off yesterday to seek fame. *J.M. Bailey,* Folks in Danbury, *p.280*

dogfights: two dogs pitted against one another, often in the cellar of a tavern, and bet on.

double shuffle: a heel and toe dance, popular among blacks from at least 1835 on.

draw poker: played from at least 1845 on.

1857: Draw-poker, and other gambling games were played every night and on every Sunday. *Gihon,* Geary and Kansas, *p.221*

drinking: widely indulged in at home when entertaining, at frolics, at huskings, taverns, dances and weddings. Hard cider was the favorite drink of the North for the first half of the century, while corn liquor and other forms of alcohol reigned in the South. Although both sexes indulged, drunkenness was considered shameful for a woman but not for a man. Consequently, the taverns and saloons were always dominated by men. Temperance movements managed to reduce consumption of alcohol somewhat at various periods throughout the century. See also Saloons, taverns, grog shops.

fandango: a dance social, throughout the century, especially in the Southwest.

1844: Respecting fandangos . . . this term, as it is used in New Mexico, is never applied to any particular dance, but is the usual designation for those ordinary assemblies where dancing and frolicking are carried on. *Gregg,* Commerce of Prairies

faro: a very popular card game in which a player bet against the banker as to what card would be chosen from a dealer's box, throughout the century.

1844: Sharpers keep a public gaming table, that is open day and night, where faro, roulette, rouge et noir, and other desperate games are played. *Featherston-Haugh,* Slave States, *p.28*

1861: In one corner Larrap had unrolled a greasy Faro cloth and was dealing. *Theodore Winthrop,* John Brent, *xv, p.170*

1886: The northern sidewalk of Pennsylvania Ave., between the Indian Queen Hotel and Capitol gate, was lined with faro banks. *Poore,* Reminiscences, *p.61*

football: developed in the 1870s and 1880s from rugby.

gambling halls: hugely popular in cities and towns throughout America.

1876: There are a great variety of games; roulette, faro, poker, and keno are most popular. There are extravagantly decorated salons furnished with every luxury, and low filthy dives. The former make a pleasant impression — nothing unsavory on the surface that might frighten away the high-strung pleasure-seekers. There are rooms furnished with every comfort; thick carpets, marble tables, alabaster figurines, gilded mirrors, soft chairs, and velvet drapes . . . embellish the first-class playing rooms. The buffet is amply equipped; a drink of brandy or claret costs as little as the food — at most a tip to the Negro waiters on leaving. . . . Some of these places are not public, but charge an admission fee for which food and liquor are supplied. In most of the better-class establishments there is a secret device for opening the door, but it is not to difficult to gain an entree. . . . In New York City some 30,000 people earn a living from gambling and from similar branches of industry.

E.O. Hopp, excerpted in This Was America, *p.327*

gander-pulling: the cruel sport of hanging a duck or goose upside down by its feet, while a man on horseback rode under it and tried to twist its head off, a rural pastime practiced throughout the century.

golf: popular from the 1880s on.

horse racing: popular throughout the century.

keno, kino: a game similar to bingo. Hugely popular among the middle and lower classes, it was played throughout much of the century.

1876: In the busiest districts of New York, in the vicinity of the theaters and other pleasure spots, are scores of keno houses, open and accessible to all, often separated from a bar only by a swinging door.

Entering one of these larger establishments . . . you see a brilliantly lighted hall, in which there are a great number of little round tables on which lie keno cards and buttons. Around each table are five or six chairs, and by eight in the evening all will generally be occupied. . . . The leaders of it all . . . stand on an elevated platform. One of them sells the tickets, little ivory chips about as big as a silver dollar with a black half-moon in the middle; the other watches the urn. The keno urn is naturally ornate and elegant, the cover comes off so that the ivory keno balls, each with a number on it, can be put in; a revolving mechanism makes it possible to shake up the balls; and revolt at the very bottom is a little opening through which a single ball is released when a spring is pressed. On the wall behind the man who manipulates the balls in the urn is a large board with countless holes under each of which is a number.

To play, you must first of all select one or more cards, which lie on the tables. Keno is a game of chance yet there are frequently exciting scenes in the choice of a card, since many people through superstition attach a particular significance to certain numbers. . . . Before the game begins boys pass about gathering the money or tokens, each of which stand for twenty-five cents. The boys call out the number of the card and the man at the urn puts a little peg into the hole on the big board corresponding to that number. As soon as all the numbers are entered on the board and all the cards are paid for a Negro puts the Keno balls into the urn. On the balls are numbers which correspond to the little figures on the cards. . . . The balls in the urn are set in motion and can be heard clicking against each other . . . a ball appears, its number read aloud; and every fortunate one who finds that number on his card puts on it one pile of black buttons lying on the table. The first to fill a row of five numbers is the winner and receives the purse after a deduction of ten percent as the fee of the house. . . . When a player successfully fills his row, he calls out, "Keno!" *E.O. Hopp, excerpted in* This Was America, *pp.328-329*

lyceum: an organization that arranged lectures by a wide range of speakers. Also the lecture hall itself. Subjects included everything from alcoholism to phrenology to slavery; widely attended in halls across America from 1826 on.

monte: a card game in which players bet on a bottom and top layer of two cards each, from 1836 on.

mumble-the-peg, mumble-peg, mumblety-peg: a boy's game in which a knife was thrown from various positions in order to make the blade stick in the ground. An unsuccessful player was originally penalized by having to pull a peg out of the ground with his teeth. From 1845.

music: singing in church, in taverns, and around the fireplace at home was a popular pastime throughout the century. Some three hundred songs were printed in Boston from 1810-1814 alone, testifying to the volume of music available at the time. Many of these songs, selling for a penny or two per sheet, were traditional British folk ballads, such as "Barbara Allen," "Chevy Chase," and "The Children in the Wood."

Negro minstrel music became a big hit from the 1840s on. From 1840-1860s singing families, such as the Alleghanies, the Bakers, the Hutchinsons and the Moravians, sang their own ballads in concert halls, churches and barns throughout the East, always to popular reception.

The biggest hits of the century were probably those of composer Stephen Foster. In the 1850s, "Old Folks at Home," "Oh! Susanna," "My Old Kentucky Home," and "Camptown Races" were on the lips of anyone who could carry a tune. No other songs came close to their popularity until the Civil War period, when "Dixie," "Battle Hymn of the Republic," "Tenting on the Old Camp Ground" and "Tramp, Tramp, Tramp" were sung by an enthusiastic though fractured nation.

Musical tastes grew somewhat wilder toward the end of the century.

In the 1890s, Scott Joplin's ragtime music became all the rage. A big hit of the 1890s: "There'll be a Hot Time in the Old Town Tonight."

1849: I have heard "Susannah" sung at least forty times today, and now it's bedtime and Tommy Plunkett is picking out the tune on his banjo and singing it loud enough to keep most of us awake. Don't he ever get tired ot it? I used to like that song, but enough is enough, and I believe it will drive me crazy before we get to California.

Andy Gordon, 49er, diary entry, June 10

1852: "Old Folks at Home," the last negro melody, is on everybody's tongue, and consequently in everybody's mouth. Pianos and guitars groan with it, night and day; sentimental young ladies sing it; sentimental young gentlemen warble it in midnight serenades; volatile young bucks hum it in the midst of their business and their pleasures; boatmen roar it out stentorially at all times; all the bands play it . . . the street organs grind it out at every hour . . . the "singing stars" carol it on the theatrical boards, and at concerts. Albany State Register

musical instruments: of all musical instruments, the fiddle or violin was most frequently at hand at dances and taverns. The harmonica and banjo were also widely heard. The piano was owned by few in the middle class. However, young women of wealthy families were taught how to play the instrument from 1800 on. Singing ballads with the piano thus became a central part of parlor entertainment for the rest of the century.

Classical music performances by philharmonic groups could be heard throughout much of the century in the larger cities. Brass bands were on hand at a variety of functions, while street musicians — especially organ grinders and fiddlers — could be heard at any hour, nearly every day for penny donations.

1829: You hear the violin or piano fort, of an evening, almost in every house. *Royall*, Pennsylvania, i, p.103

1872: The vast majority of the strolling harpers and violinists are . . . generally boys below the age of sixteen. They are chiefly Italian [and are] commonly to be found in the street in pairs; but sometimes three work together. . . . There are several hundreds of these children on the streets . . . dirty, wan monkey-like little creatures. . . . All day long, and late into the night, they must ply their dreary trade.

James McCabe, Lights and Shadows of New York Life, *p.327*

Negro minstrel show: a show in which white entertainers blackened their faces with cork in order to impersonate Negroes. These shows, playing to packed houses from the 1840s through much of the remainder of the century, featured singing and dancing and gradually evolved to include jokes and skits, performed by such troupes as the Virginia Minstrels, the Christy Minstrels, the Ethiopian Serenaders, and the Kentucky Rattlers, to name a few.

TRAVELING EXHIBITIONS AND AMUSEMENTS

1795: Balloon ascension.
Exhibition of an African lion.
1796: Magic show by a magician named Signor Blitz.
1797: Exhibition of an elephant and a bison.
1802: Ventriloquism act.
1805: A great tunny fish, found stranded.
1807: Exhibition of phantasmagoria apparatus.
1808: 60-foot dead whale towed to Salem for exhibition, then on to Boston for same.
1809: Exhibition of fencing.
Exhibition of a woman born without hands, who "embroidered flowers and cut watch papers and other fancy pieces," presumably with her toes.
1816: Exhibition of an elephant.
Exhibition of a tiger.
1817: "The Temple of Industry," a panorama [a large, illuminated box with scenes that pass by on rollers] of thirty-six workers engaged at their occupations.
1818: Exhibition of a kaleidoscope.
An albino woman with "silky white hair and pink eyes."
1820: A buffalo.
A caravan comprised of a lion, a llama and an ocelot.
An exhibition of two camels.
1821: An exhibition of glass blowing.
1824: A mermaid "the lower part of a codskin stuffed and neatly connected with the breast and head of a baboon."
A mummy from Thebes.
1831: Siamese twins.
An Ourang Outang and a Unicorn.
1834: Circus.
1836: Master S.K.G. Nellis, "born without arms, was exceedingly skillful with his toes—he cut paper likenesses and executed fancy pieces in writing, drawing, shooting with the bow and arrow and in playing the violoncello."
1838: Balloon ascension.
1839: Exhibition of a giraffe and an ibex.
1840: M. Bihin, a giant from Belgium.
1843: Tom Thumb, Jr., standing just twenty-five inches in height.
A seven-year-old girl weighing 240 pounds.

1845, Annals of Salem (Massachusetts), by Joseph Felt

1843: First Night of the novel, grotesque, original and surprisingly melodious Ethiopian band, entitled the Virginia Minstrels, being an exclusively musical entertainment combining the banjo, violin, bone castanets, and tambourine, and entirely exempt from the vulgarities and other objectionable features which have hitherto characterized negro extravaganzas. New York Herald, *February 6*

1853: Ethiopian Minstrelsy is on the increase. We now have, in New York, six companies of Minstrels in full blast. Musical World, *October 8*

1854: The only places of Amusement where the entertainments are indigenous are the African Opera Houses, where native American vocalists, with blackened faces, sing national songs, and utter none but native witticisms. These native theatricals . . . are among the best frequented and most profitable places of amusement in New York. Putnam's Monthly, *February*

oyster parties: any party at which oysters, wildly popular through much of the century, were the central food.

1861: You'll have enough to do . . . when I give my oyster parties. Vanity Fair, *February 9*

plays: see Theater.

ratting: a blood sport in which live rats were placed in a ring (often in the cellar of a tavern) and allowed to be attacked and killed by a dog or weasel, with bets running on how long it would take for so many rats to be killed. (See also Crime, p.278.)

roller skating: in the 1880s, nearly every city and large town had a roller-skating rink. The sport was enjoyed by both men and women.

running: foot races were popular from the 1830s on. The runners were called pedestrians or peds.

saloons, taverns, grog shops: widely attended, especially by men, for drinking, gambling, socializing, etc. Early in the century Rochester, New York, had a population of only eight thousand yet it boasted having an astonishing one hundred drinking establishments. See also Drinking.

sex: premarital sex, although taboo, was widely practiced from early in the century on. Records show, in fact, that one third of New England brides in the 1790s were already with child when they married—this despite New England's civil statutes against fornication. (Prenuptial pregnancy rates fell from the 1840s on, due to a stronger community focus on chastity and more widespread knowledge of birth control.)

1798: The choice of a lover is unexceptional, it is public, and the parents hardly take notice because such are the customs of the country. The chosen man comes into the house whenever he pleases. He takes the object of his affections for a walk whenever he likes. He often comes for her on Sunday in a cabriolet and brings her back in the evening without being questioned as to their doings. *Moreau de Saint-Mery, excerpted in* This Was America, *p.97*

sleighing: wildly popular throughout the North in winter, especially among lovers. Because sleighs were relatively inexpensive, more middle-class families were likely to own one than a carriage.

1807: He recollects perfectly the time when young ladies used to go sleigh riding . . . without their Mammas. *Washington Irving,* Salmagundi

1842: Those who have sweethearts take them out on sleighing frolics. *Uncle Sam,* Peculiarities, *p.44*

1895: [On] . . . sleighing parties . . . we pile into a double pung, ride in the moonlight. *Coffin,* Daughters of Revolution, *p.87*

socializing: formal and informal forms of socializing were the most common amusements throughout the period. Then as now, folks liked to visit one another, usually after supper and on weekends. The middle class gathered in their parlors, talked, sang, played games, and so on. The upper class might hold more formal get-togethers, as this one described by Frances Trollope around 1829: "Where the mansion is of sufficient dignity to have two drawing rooms, the piano, the little ladies, and the slender gentlemen are left to themselves, and on such occasions the sound of laughter is often heard to issue from them. But the fate of the more dignified personages, who are left in the other room, is extremely dismal. The gentlemen spit, talk of elections and the price of produce, and spit again. The ladies look at each other's dresses till they know every pin by heart; talk of Parson Somebody's last sermon on the day of judgement, on Dr. T'otherbody's new pills for dyspepsia, till the 'tea' is announced, when they all console themselves together for whatever they may have suffered in keeping awake, by taking more tea, coffee, hot cake and custard, hoe cake, johnny cake, waffle cake, and dodger cake, pickled peaches, and preserved cucumbers, ham, turkey, hung beef, apple sauce and pickled oysters, than ever were prepared in any other country of the known world. After this massive meal is over, they return to the drawing room, and it always appeared to me that they remained together as long as they could bear it, and then they rise en masse, cloak, bonnet, shawl, and exit."

tennis: popular from 1875 on.

theater: shows were performed in churches, tents, saloons, showboats and concert halls throughout the century. The works of Shakespeare, then as now, were always playing somewhere, including on a floating barge, throughout the early portion of the century. Other notable works: *Brutus, or The Fall of Tarquin,* a play by John Howard Payne, which debuted in March 1819 in New York, enjoyed an unusually long run and was followed by another Payne play, *The Merry Monarch,* cowritten by Washington Irving in 1824. In 1852, the first stage version of *Uncle Tom's Cabin* appeared in Troy, New York. A smash, it played for the rest of the century in venues around the country. In 1857 debuted *Our American Cousin*, the play Lincoln was watching the night he was slain. From midcentury on, audiences thrilled to the swashbuckling melodrama of *The Count of Monte Christo*. In 1866, *The Black Crook*, a lavish extravaganza, ran up a hefty expense account, yet played profitably for sixteen months. *Davy Crockett*, by Frank Murdoch, appeared in 1872. The Civil War drama *Shenandoah* followed in the 1880s. From 1891-1893, *A Trip to Chinatown* held the stage at Madison Square Theater for 650 performances.

1800: The American seems well-disposed toward the theater; there is a very good playhouse in Philadelphia. Everywhere else marriage is the central concern of the drama; the plot develops up to that point and is generally resolved thereby. But such a content will be sought in vain in. . . . the stages of the United States. Liberty is the central theme of these. Everything turns about that. At the heart of the play is always some republican idea and the development is marked by the warmest patriotism.

Reise von Hamburg nach Philadelphia, excerpted in This Was America, *p.104*

1817: Yesterday I attended the opening performance of the Balitmore theater. . . . The main offering was an English drama, *She Stoops to Conquer*. . . . The play . . . was tedious. . . . Before the second item on the program a dancer performed a few steps that would have drawn peals of laughter in any French city, but it disturbed the gravity of the Americans not for a moment. . . . The second offering was a melodrama so annoying that I could hardly force myself to stay through to the end. It was a hash of robbers, caves, and kidnappings, stripped of any charm. *De Montlezun, excerpted in* This Was America, *p.127*

two-step: a lively dance in vogue from 1890 on.

waltz: adopted in the United States from Paris in the 1820s. It was originally called the valse.

1845: Cotillons, waltzes and polkas were danced in the house, on the lawn, and on the promenade deck of the steamer. *Hone,* Diary, *p.253*

SURRENDER OF GEN. LEE!

"The Year of Jubilee has come! Let all the People Rejoice!"

200 GUNS WILL BE FIRED

On the Campus Martius,
AT 3 O'CLOCK TO-DAY, APRIL 10,
To Celebrate the Victories of our Armies. 1865

Every Man, Woman and Child is hereby ordered to be on hand prepared to Sing and Rejoice. The crowd are expected to join in singing Patriotic Songs.
ALL PLACES OF BUSINESS MUST BE CLOSED AT 2 O'CLOCK.
Hurrah for Grant and his noble Army.

By Order of the People.

COURTSHIP AND MARRIAGE

The nineteenth-century term for dating, of course, was courting, known informally as sparking, keeping company, carrying on, coming to call or cavorting. Serious dating, with the intention of a future engagement, was more formally known as a courtship.

Regardless of the terminology, when a couple advanced to the engagement stage, a woman was likely to feel more ambivalent than joyful. Even though marriage was considered a woman's natural destiny—the unacceptable alternative being the shame of spinsterhood—the prevailing feminine viewpoint held that matrimony "brought some joys, but many crosses." It was a viewpoint based on harsh reality.

During the first half of the century, wives were largely confined to their homes, burdened with an average of five to seven children and saddled with endless sewing, mending, cooking and cleaning. They depended on their husbands for income and were therefore subjugated by them. If abuse was involved in the relationship, the woman often had no choice but to bear it. No wonder the nineteenth-century woman so frequently wrote in her diary that an impending marriage filled her with anxiety.

The men, on the other hand, saw marriage as a positive enterprise. Diary entries rarely reveal the dread many women felt. In fact, men often tried to rush the woman into matrimony. No surprise there since marriage meant sex. . . . at last. It also meant pampering and maid service. "The moment you taste the happiness of the marriage union, you will curse yourself a fool, that you lived so long without it," one young man wrote to another early in the century, thus summing up a widely held view of nineteenth-century males that marriage was a good thing.

Courting and Sex

chaperones: In the strictest years of the Victorian era, particularly the last thirty-five years of the century, girls from genteel families had little opportunity to go sparking with their beaus in private. At least in high or wealthy society, chaperones were de rigeur on most every type of date, including innocent parlor visits. The chaperone was usually the girl's mother or aunt or close family friend. The middle-class or lower-class couple was rarely if ever so encumbered, but the prudish attitudes of the upper classes did trickle down somewhat, so that parents throughout the period were quicker to dash passions than those earlier in the century. See also Premarital sex.

1884: She must accompany her young lady everywhere; she must sit in the parlor when she receives gentlemen, she must go with her to the skating rink, the ball, the party, the races, the dinner, and especially to theater parties.

Gilman Ostrander, quoted in American Civilization in the First Machine Age

coming to call: calling on or visiting one's lover. A variation was keeping company.

flirting and meeting: young men and women initially met and took a cotton to or a fancy to a member of the opposite sex at harvest celebrations and bees (in the fall farmers frequently invited local youths to participate in corn huskings and apple parings and put on barn dances in exchange for labor), at church and school (how could one remain shy year after year in the same one-room schoolhouse?), and at the ever-reliable ice cream parlor. Sometimes boy and girl boldy flirted on the streets or on a public beach. Accounts exist of young women strolling the sidewalks of New York in groups, openly flirting with men on Broadway and the Bowery and pairing off for a night of frolic.

Like their modern counterparts, however, most teens and young adults probably got to know a prospective date by simply hanging out together.

1830s: Elmina and I laid abed very late. We had hardly got the [house] work done before James Merril, Joel Slack and Thomas Fletcher came in. They staid and talked and sang an hour or two. Then we all walked down to the "Five Corners" where we met Solomon Carlisle, H. Willis, the two Briggs and Charlotte Duncan. Staid there and sang a few tunes and then walked up to Mr. Pinney's.

Diary entry of young girl living in Plymouth Notch, Vermont

give him the mitten: a common, euphemistic phrase meaning to dump or discard one's boyfriend, used throughout much of the century.

1840s: Young gentlemen that got the mitten, or young gentlemen who think they are going to get the mitten, always sigh. It makes them feel bad. *Joseph C. Neal,* Petter Ploddy, *p.14*

popular dates: in the North in winter, couples harnessed the family horse to a sleigh (sleighs were much cheaper than coaches or carriages, so many families owned one), snuggled up under a pile of buffalo robes, and went off alone or in groups for a moonlit excursion – an immensely popular date throughout the century.

Coaching was popular among upper-class couples. A hot date on wheels might include dinner and a night at the theater, followed by a few stolen kisses in the coach's darkened – and often plush – interior.

For the economically disadvantaged couple, an old swaybacked horse could provide a romantic escape by itself. Couples also took walks, went berrying, attended lectures, cuddled in haylofts, danced at neighborhood parties, communed at church socials, sang to one another and, most often perhaps, sequestered themselves in the girl's parlor, assuming her family was tactful enough to withdraw to other rooms.

1798: Wednesday, 4 July . . . In the course of the P.M. and evening had opportunity and danced several times with my little Ellen . . . between one and two set out to see my little partner home. We both being well mounted on one horse as I had purposely started before the others, that I might have the company of my little girl to myself. *Diary entry of a Massachusetts teen*

premarital sex: the late 1700s and early 1800s were marked by a notably higher incidence of premarital sex than in later years. Records show, in fact, that around the turn of the century one third of New England brides were already pregnant when they married, despite civil statutes against fornication. By the 1830s, premarital pregnancies dropped to 20 percent, and then to just 10 percent in the 1850s, suggesting better contraception and more widespread abstinence.

1798: The choice of a lover is unexceptional, it is public, and the parents hardly take notice because such are the customs of the country. The chosen man comes into the house whenever he pleases. He takes the object of his affections for a walk whenever he likes. He often comes for her on a Sunday in a cabriolet and brings her back in the evening without being questioned as to their doings. *Moreau de Saint-Mery, excerpted in* This Was America, *p.97*

set her cap for him: a popular phrase referring to a woman's endeavor to win a man's affections, used from early in the century on.

sexual attitudes of women: few Victorian women openly admitted to enjoying sex. Many "experts" of the day contended that it was impossible for women to have orgasms or derive much physical pleasure of any kind from sex; a woman who experienced such pleasure was probably abnormal. A rare survey of forty-five women who grew up in the second half of the century reveals the nature of female sexuality more accurately, however. In it, about 70 percent of the women acknowledged having sexual desire. When having sex, most said they experienced orgasms and one third said they "always did." Only 7 percent admitted to having premarital sex, while one fourth reported being repelled by their first sexual encounter. After marriage, most of the women said they had less desire for sex than their husbands, not unlike the results of modern surveys.

Although men were usually the aggressors when it came to sex, bold women were not unknown throughout the 1800s. A Quaker of the period reported that he was approached after meeting by "a real nice looking young lady [who] rode up . . . and said . . . 'Why won't you go out and take dinner with me?' " An Illinois school teacher warned her beau: "I mean to bite your neck if I have to get false [teeth] to do it." When a husband wrote to his wife after a long separation that he anticipated "unspeakable delight" in her embrace, she wrote back: "I'll drain your coffers dry next Saturday I assure you."

1830s: O! I really want to kiss you. How I should like to be in that old parlor with you. . . . I hope there will be a carpet on the floor for it seems you intend to act worse than you ever did before by your letter . . . but I shall humbly submit to my fate and willingly too, to speak candidly. *Mira Bigelow, letter to boyfriend*

1870s: Mabel will remember with pleasure the new sensation I caused her this evening. *David Todd, diary entry*

1870: Well, I couldn't help it. I woke up the next morning very happy though, and feeling not at all condemned.
Mabel, David Todd's fiancé, in her diary entry

1870s: In reference to passion in women, a vulgar opinion prevails that they are creatures of like passions with ourselves; that they experience desires as ardent, and often as ungovernable, as those which lead to so much evil in our sex. Vicious writers, brutal and ignorant men, and some shameless women combine to favor and extend this opinion. . . . Nothing is more utterly untrue. . . . The best mothers, wives, and managers of households know little or nothing of the sexual pleasure. Love of home, children and domestic duties are the only pleasures they feel. *Dr. George Napheys, The Transmission of Life*

sparking/spark it: courting; to court. Also used as a general euphemism for kissing, cuddling, etc., used primarily in the Northern states from at least the 1840s on.

1840s: You were a nation sight wiser than brother Jonathan, sister Keziah, poor little Aminadab, and all the rest; and above all, my owny, towny Lydia, the Deacon's darlin darter; with whom I've sparked it, pretty oftentimes, so late. *D. Humphreys,* The Yankee in England

1840s: Mr. Justice Crow was soon overtaken; Lieut. Col. Simcoe accosted him roughly, called him "Tory," nor seemed to believe his excuses; when, in the American idiom for courtship, he said, "he had only been sparking." *Simcoe,* Military Journal, *p.73*

1840s: He rolled his eyes horribly, and said that that was the way the young men cast sheep's eyes when they went a sparking. Mrs. Claver's Western Clearings, *p.16*

Weddings

age at marriage: from early in the century on, the typical man married in his middle or late twenties, usually to a bride a few years younger.

bridal attendants: bridal attendants were sometimes used in the 1700s but didn't become de rigueur until the second quarter of the nineteenth century. The typical wedding had one or two bridesmaids and groomsmen, although some bridal parties were as large as twelve.

1839: We have adopted the good Massachusetts faction of having bridesmaids and groomsmen. *Henry Poor, lawyer, Bangor, Maine*

bridal tour: see Honeymoon.

charivari: (pronounced shevaree) a custom of French Louisiana, Florida, Michigan and Canada in which a couple was serenaded on the night of their marriage by friends with horns, bells, whistles, pans, kettles and other noisemakers. The salute was kept up outside the couple's abode until the assembly was invited in for refreshments and entertainment.

home weddings: most couples were married by a minister at the bride's home, although church weddings grew in popularity from about the 1820s on and were the norm by the end of the century. Civil services by a justice of the peace were available throughout the period.

honeymoon: honeymoons were known from at least the 1820s, but they were most often called bridal tours, wedding tours, or nuptial journeys. Popular honeymoon locations included New York City, Niagara Falls, the Green Mountains and, in the Midwest, the new, thriving city of Cincinnati. In the first half of the century it was customary for couples to be accompanied by friends or close relatives on their nuptial journeys. The honeymoon didn't become a private affair until the 1860s.

housing after marriage: procuring living accommodations was almost always the man's obligation. Furnishing the home was almost always the woman's task. A large proportion of urban couples took up residence in boardinghouses until they got established financially.

invitations: fancy printed invitations were used by the middle class from the 1840s on, by the upper class from the 1830s on, and were usually sent out just a week before the big event. Because travel was so slow, and so many worked farms that could not be left untended, weddings in the first half of the century were usually made up of small gatherings of nearby friends and relatives. The more distant relatives were often visited by the married couple later.

jumping the broom: see Slavery and Black Plantation Culture, p.219.

levee: see Reception.

reception: the party or celebration following the wedding, sometimes referred to as a levee, or evening party. Liquor, wine, tea or lemonade was served at the reception, depending on local moral codes and the sensibilities of the host and hostess. White wedding cake was mentioned in print as early as the 1820s but was largely unique to upper-class weddings until later.

1840: At half past seven we repaired to Cousin Charles' [the groom's father] where we found quite a collection of relations. . . . These were all collected in the front parlour where they remained until eight o'clock when the folding doors were thrown open and the bridal party appeared all ready for the ceremony. They stood in the new-fashioned way each gentleman by his lady (there were two grooms-men and two bridesmaids). . . . At the close of the whole, [the minister] requested Arthur to present his bride with the wedding ring as a token of the sincerity of his intentions, etc. Soon after the levee commenced and the rooms were crowded with friends. After all had left, but those who were at the wedding, supper was announced which was got up in first rate style. *Account of a typical Boston wedding*

rings: Throughout most of the first half of the century, engagement rings were largely unknown. They became fashionable in the 1840s, but they were presented to the man as well as the woman. Wedding rings were mentioned in print as early as 1840, but historians are unsure when they became standard practice. An etiquette book from 1846 advised: "If a ring is to be used, the bridegroom procures a plain gold one previously."

spinsters: of women born between 1860 and 1880, 11 percent never married, the highest rate of unmarried women in American history. The high rate was thought due to the growing number of women attaining college educations and the male view that college grads made poor homemakers.

wedding day: possibly due to ministers' heavy weekend schedule, a large proportion of early nineteenth-century weddings were held on Tuesday, Wednesday or Thursday.

wedding dress: then as now, the bride wore white. Occasionally she wore brown or gray, but she risked being looked upon as queer by her peers. A wreath of white flowers—often orange blossoms—worn on the crown was popular. Veils were standard from the 1840s on.

wedding gifts: the giving of gifts was usually limited to immediate family members and very close friends in the first half of the century. The giving circle expanded to include acquaintances and co-workers during the second half of the century. Most gifts were of a decorative nature; sugar bowls, cake baskets, ice cream knives and napkin rings were typical.

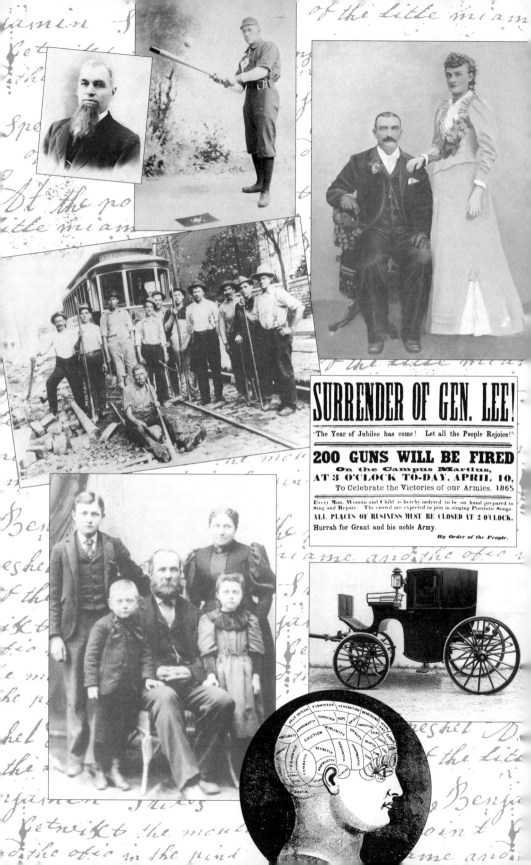

SURRENDER OF GEN. LEE!

"The Year of Jubilee has come! Let all the People Rejoice!"

200 GUNS WILL BE FIRED
On the Campus Martius,
AT 3 O'CLOCK TO-DAY, APRIL 10,
To Celebrate the Victories of our Armies. 1865

Every Man, Woman and Child is hereby ordered to be on hand prepared to
Sing and Rejoice. The crowd are expected to join in singing Patriotic Songs.
ALL PLACES OF BUSINESS MUST BE CLOSED AT 2 O'CLOCK.
Hurrah for Grant and his noble Army.

By Order of the People.

SLAVERY AND BLACK PLANTATION CULTURE

Slave trade between Africa and America was ended by federal law in 1808. However, sales continued illegally for many years after. Legal domestic trade, meanwhile, persisted until the eve of the Civil War. Domestic traders purchased slaves cheap at estate and execution sales and resold them at public auctions to plantation owners short of help, especially in the deep South.

The professional trader had a reputation for being unscrupulous and often went to great lengths to deceive prospective buyers, as a former slave working for a St. Louis trader recalled: "I was ordered to have the old men's whiskers shaved off, and the gray hairs plucked out, where they were not too numerous, in which case we had a preparation of blacking to color it, and with a blacking brush we would put it on. . . . These slaves were also taught how old they were . . . and after going through the blacking process, they looked ten or fifteen years younger.

After the Civil War, many slaves were beset by an odd ambivalence over their new-gained freedom. Millie Davis of North Carolina recalled that "Old Master didn't want to part with his niggers, and the niggers didn't want to part with Old Master. . . . We had such a good time, and everybody cried when the Yankees cried out: 'Free.' T'other niggers say they had a hard time 'fore they was free, but 'twas then like 'tis now. If you had a hard time, we done it ourselves."

But Jenny Proctor of Alabama recalled: "I's hear tell of them good slave days, but I ain't never seen no good times then."

Tines Kendrick of Georgia remembered that it was as difficult being free as it was to be in bondage: "You know there was some few free niggers in that time even 'fore the slaves taken out of bondage. . . . The slaveowners, they just despised them free niggers and make it just as hard on them as they can. They couldn't get no work from nobody. Wouldn't ary man hire 'em or give 'em work at all."

Indeed, statistics from 1855 reveal that the vast majority of free blacks worked as domestic servants and laborers, an occupational suppression that continued long after the Civil War ended.

abolitionist: one who favored the abolition of slavery.

auction: a public sale in which Negroes were put on display and sometimes stripped to facilitate the examination of their bodies. A robust male between eighteen and twenty-five could be sold for as high as eighteen hundred dollars at these auctions although the typical purchase price was far less. Babies, for example, were simply sold by the pound. Often for little more than the price of a cheap buggy, wives, husbands, sons and daughters were cruelly separated, never to see one another again. Such cold-hearted transactions continued up to the eve of the Civil War.

1846: We attended a sale of land and other property, near Petersburg, Virginia, and unexpectedly saw slaves sold at public auction. The slaves were told they would not be sold, and were collected in front of the quarters, gazing on the assembled multitude. The land being sold, the auctioneer's loud voice was heard, "Bring up the niggers!" A shade of astonishment and affright passed over their faces, as they stared first at each other, and then at the crowd of purchasers whose attention was now directed to them. When the horrible truth was revealed to their minds that they were to be sold, and nearest relations and friends parted forever, the effect was indescribably agonizing. Women snatched up their babes, and ran screaming into the huts. Children hid behind huts and trees, and the men stood in mute despair. . . . It was announced that no warranty of soundness was given, and purchasers must examine for themselves. A few old men were sold at prices from fifteen to twenty-five dollars, and it was painful to see old men, bowed with years of toil and suffering, stand up to be the jest of brutal tyrants, and to hear them tell their disease and worthlessness, fearing that they would be bought by traders for the Southern market. *Dr. Elwood Harvey,* A Key to Uncle Tom's Cabin

Aunty: white man's slang for an old Negro woman. See also Mammy and Uncle.

big house: slave's name for the master's house on a plantation.

body servant: a master's personal slave or servant. Body servants even served their masters while they fought in the Confederate Army during the Civil War. They gathered food, cooked, washed clothes, put up tents, shined boots, tended horses, and aided the wounded—all behind enemy lines. If the master was away, the body servant usually took orders from any officer.

1860s: Quite a large number had a boy along to do the cooking and washing. Think of it! a Confederate soldier with a body servant all his own, to bring him a drink of water, black his boots, dust his clothes, cook his cornbread and bacon, and put wood on the fire.

Never was there a fonder admiration than these darkies displayed for their masters. *Carlton McCarthy,* Detailed Minutiae of Soldier Life

bondman, bondsman, bondwoman: another name for a slave.

boy: a demeaning appellation used by some whites for a male slave.
1835: They always address . . . as "boy" or "girl" . . . all [slaves] under forty years of age. *Ingraham, South-West II, p.242*

brands: although not a general practice, branding of slaves was accepted in some quarters as a necessary means of owner identification. Newspaper advertisements describing fugitive slaves from the period attest to some of the methods used: "A few days before she ran away, I branded her with a red-hot iron on her cheek and tried to make an M"; "Molly, age 16, has an R branded on her left cheek and inside her legs; a piece of her ear has been cut off"; "Z, with several brands on his thighs . . . ," etc.

buck nigger: common slang for a male Negro.
1800s: Twenty-five buck-niggers, wid dey pants an' sleeves roll' up. Foller'n me wid de hoes. *Orland Armstrong, Old Massa's People, p.211*

buckra: a white man. The term was used by blacks of the African coast, the West Indies and the Southern states. Its literal meaning was a demon or a powerful and superior being, and it was frequently paired with "swanga." A swanga buckra was an elegantly dressed white man or dandy.

cabin: a one-room cabin or hut, sometimes whitewashed on the outside and plastered on the inside, and usually having glassless windows closed only by wooden shutters, the typical quarters of either one or two slave families on a plantation. Such huts were usually furnished with a crude hearth for cooking or for heating water for washing. A small garden plot was also provided for each family to raise vegetables and chickens.
1800s: Down in the quarters every black family had a one- or two-room log cabin. We didn't have no floors in them cabins. Nice dirt floors was the style then, and we used sage brooms. Took a string and tied the sage together and had a nice broom. . . . Our beds was stuffed with hay and straw and shucks, and, believe me, child, they sure slept good. *Millie Evans, North Carolina, in* Lay My Burden Down
1800s: My mammy lived in a hewn-oak log cabin in the quarters. There was a long row of cabins, some bigger than t'others, 'count of family size. My massa had over eighty head of slaves. Them little old cabins was cozy, 'cause we chinked 'em with mud and they had stick chimneys daubed with mud, mixed with hog-hair.
Cato, Alabama, in Lay My Burden Down

cake walk: a competition among blacks in which the person with the most stylized or fanciest walk or strut won a cake.

1889: In certain sections of the country, cake walks are in vogue among colored people. It is a walking contest, not in the matter of speed, but in style and elegance. *Farmer*, Americanisms: Old and New, *p.115*

cathaul: a form of slave punishment, in which a tomcat was used to claw at the back of the victim.

1816: What is the most ludicrous, but horrid, the cat-haul; that is, to fasten a slave down flatwise upon the ground, with stakes and cords, and then to take a huge, fierce tom-cat by the tail backward, and haul him down along the screeching wretch's bare back, with his claws clinging into the quick all the way. *Arthur Singleton*, Letters from the South and West, *p.79*

1840: The Anti-Slavery Almanac for 1840 is filled up with pictures, such as white people of the South branding slaves, — hunting slaves with dogs and guns, — cat-hauling, etc. *Mr. Benton, U.S. Senate*, Congressional Globe, *January 12*

chanteys: see Songs.

charm bag: a cloth filled with various charms (for example, a rabbit's foot, especially the left hind one, was considered good luck) and worn around the neck to bring good fortune, ward off illness, etc. Such bags were worn widely within the slave population due to a strong belief in the supernatural. One type of charm bag — a red flannel cloth containing the bones of a frog, a piece of snakeskin, a few horse hairs, and a spoonful of ashes — was used by a conjurer to cast spells or bring misfortune to someone by placing the bag under the steps of the home of an intended victim, sometimes a hated overseer.

chattel: euphemism for a slave, used by polite society.

children's house: on a plantation, a two- or three-room house where the slave children were looked after by the grandmothers as the parents worked in the fields. Known as the chilluns' house.

clothing: domestic slaves — butlers, maids, valets, coachmen — were almost always provided with excellent clothing to project an image of class and prestige to outsiders. However, the clothing provided to field hands was often inadequate. Some of it was homespun by the slaves themselves, while some items, such as shoes, were purchased ready-made. A typical clothing allotment, according to a plantation manual of the 1840s, was as follows: "Each man gets in the fall 2 shirts of cotton drilling, a pair of woolen pants and a woolen jacket. In the spring 2 shirts of cotton shirting and 2 pr. of cotton pants. . . . Each woman gets in the fall 6 yds. of woolen cloth, 6 yds. of cotton drilling and a needle, skein of thread and

½ dozen buttons. In the spring 6 yds. of cotton shirting and 6 yards of cotton cloth similar to that for men's pants, needle, thread and buttons. Each worker gets a stout pr. of shoes every fall, and a heavy blanket every third year." Children typically received two long shirts of sack cloth or tow-linen and no pants or shoes. The shirts, sometimes called banyans, were worn almost year-round. "[I] was kept almost in a state of nudity," said Frederick Douglass of his slave childhood in Maryland, "no shoes, no stockings, no jacket, no trousers; nothing but course sack-cloth or tow-linen, made into a sort of shirt, reaching down to my knees. This I wore night and day, changing it once a week."

concubines: many Southern masters kept slave concubines, a practice that resulted in the births of numerous mulatto children. "Any lady is ready to tell you who is the father of all the mulatto children in every-body's household but her own," a Southern white woman wrote. "These, she seems to think, drop from the clouds."

conjurer, conjur doctor: one thought to be blessed with the ability to cast spells, cure or prevent illnesses, bring good luck, etc., a highly respected man or woman on a plantation due to a widespread belief in the super-natural among slaves. The conjurer used a variety of charms (horse hairs, ashes, chicken feet, etc.) to attract good fortune. He or she also brewed potions and concoctions to cure a plethora of troubles. To relieve rheumatism, for example, a flannel strap wrapped about the affected limb would do the trick. For whooping cough, a drink of sheep-wool tea. For indigestion, a penny worn around the neck. For mumps, a charmed bacon rind, and so on.
1800s: He wore a snake's skin around his neck, carried a petrified frog in one pocket, and a dried lizard in the other. The Slave Community

contraband: see Civil War, p.228.

cooking on a plantation: cracklin' bread, collards, hominy, chitlins, chick peas, hog jowls, baked grits, sweet potato pone, corn pone and possum made up the typical fare of plantation slaves.

coon: pejorative slang for a Negro.

cuffy, cuffee: common appellation for the Negro or Negroes.
1836: At length a negro boy on a mule rode down and found me stand-ing rock still on the side of the road. . . . I could have embraced the little Cuffee. Journal of Southern History, *p.369*
1881: Amid all this transition from land-owner to tenant there is one . . . steadfast figure . . . this is Cuffee, the dusky farmer.
Harper's Magazine, *October*

darky: common pejorative slang for a Negro.

1882: This old darkey had lived in Richmond in her younger days. She spoke of grown men and women there as "children what I raised. Lord! boss, does you know Miss Sadie? Well, I nussed her and I nussed all uv them chillun; that I did suh!"
Carlton McCarthy, Detailed Minutiae of Soldier Life, p.166

doughface: a Northerner who favored slavery.

1847: If we permit this, we shall justly merit the insulting epithet so often applied by the Whigs to the Democracy of the North, of Northern Dough-faces.
Mr. Wilmot, Pennsylvania, House of Reps., Congressional Globe, February 8

1861: If there's anything on airth that I utterly despise, it ar a Northern doughface. Knickerbocker Magazine, *December*

driver: a slave driver; one that supervised the work of the slaves and doled out punishments. A driver often worked under an overseer or was an overseer himself.

1800s: We might-a done very well if the old driver hadn't been so mean, but the least little thing we do he beat us for it and put big chains round our ankles and make us work with them on till the blood be cut out all around our ankles. Some of the masters have what they call stockades and puts their heads and feet and arms through holes in a big board out in the hot sun, but our old driver he had a bull pen. That's only thing like a jail he had. When a slave do anything he didn't like, he takes 'em in that bull pen and chains 'em down, face up to the sun, and leaves 'em there till they nearly dies.
Jenny Proctor, Alabama, in Lay My Burden Down

free Negroes: before the Civil War, free Negroes included those who lived in the North, or mulattoes born of free colored mothers, or manumitted slaves. Statistics show that even free Negroes had few job opportunities other than that of servant or laborer. (See sidebar.)

free soiler: one who advocated excluding slavery from the Western Territories of the United States.

1849: We do not charge him with Abolitionism, or Free-Soilism, but with duplicity.
Mr. Kaufman, Texas, House of Reps., Congressional Globe, December 13

1884: One party claimed the right to exclude slavery entirely from the Territories. These were the Free-Soilers. Another was for extending the Missouri compromise to the Pacific Ocean. Another party claimed that the people of the Territory should settle this question for themselves. This was Stephan A. Douglass's theory, and was called Squatter Sovereignty. Still another party claimed that the people could only determine this question when they came to be a State.
Shields, Life of S.S. Prentiss, p.410

OCCUPATIONS OF FREE NEGROES

1,025	domestic servants	19	tailors
536	laborers	18	clerks
499	waiters	17	boatmen
366	laundresses	16	longshoremen
176	porters	15	chimney sweeps
151	cooks	15	musicians
129	whitewashers	14	hotel and boardinghouse
111	dressmakers, seam-		keepers
	stresses	13	boot and shoemakers
102	drivers, coachmen,	13	nurses
	hackmen	13	teachers
78	barbers	12	clergymen
56	stewards	12	carpenters
55	cartmen, draymen,	11	peddlers, traders
	teamsters	10	sawyers
19	butchers		

New York State Census of 1855

---

funeral rites: slave funerals on a plantation were usually held at night with the rites, rich in African custom, held weeks later.

1824: When a slave dies, the master gives the rest a day, of their [slaves] own choosing, to celebrate the funeral. This, perhaps a month after the corpse is interred, is a jovial day with them; they sing and dance and drink the dead to his new home, which some believe to be in old Guinea. *Arthur Singleton,* Letters from the South and West

1850s: Negro graves were always decorated with the last article used by the departed, and broken pitchers and broken bits of colored glass were considered even more appropriate than the white shells from the beach nearby. Sometimes they carved rude wooden figures like images of idols, and sometimes a patchwork quilt was laid upon the grave.

Sarah Torian, *"Ante-Bellum and War Memories of Mrs. Telfair Hodgson,"* Georgia Historical Quarterly, *December, p.43*

Jim Crow car: any railroad car in which Negroes were segregated from white passengers. The name was derived from a minstrel routine— "Jump Jim Crow"—performed in 1828 by Thomas Rice and others. The name grew quickly into a pejorative epithet for blacks. (See also Railroad, p.74.)

1841: [The Eastern Railroad] considers this Jim Crow car good enough for a "Nigger," if said "Nigger" be a free man or woman. Let a southern slaveholder, however, get into one of their first-class cars, accompanied by his "chattels personal," and no matter how black those "chattels" may be, not a word will be uttered against the arrangement. After all, then, it is not color alone which excludes a man from the best car. The colored person to be excluded must also be free! *Letter in the* Liberator, *November 5*

1841: Slaves can travel beside their masters in all our public vehicles without offending northern nerves; why, then, is such a fuss made about colored freemen? *Letter in the* National Anti-Slavery Standard

Jim Crow law: any one of the laws that enforced the segregation of blacks from whites, especially when using public transporation, in the South after 1877.

Jim Crow pew: a church bench reserved for Negroes only, generally after 1841. Previously known as a Negro pew.

jobs: not all slaves worked as field hands or as domestic servants. The job breakdown of sixty-seven slaves on a typical plantation in 1854 attests to the wide variety of jobs slaves held:

1 butler	4 drovers
2 parlor maids	2 stablehands
1 cook	1 cowman
4 housemaids	1 pigman
1 nursemaid	2 carpenters
1 washerwoman	5 masons
1 seamstress	1 miller
1 gardener	2 smiths
1 coachman	2 shoemakers
4 plowmen	5 spinning girls
22 hoe hands	1 weaving girl
2 wagon drivers	

In 1860, about half a million slaves were engaged in work completely unrelated to agriculture. They labored in cotton mills, iron foundries, machine shops, served as assistants to mechanics, carpenters, bakers and shop owners; they cut wood for steamboats; they produced shingles, barrel staves, pickets, posts and turpentine; they mined gold in North Carolina, iron in Kentucky and Tennessee, and coal and salt in Virginia; they constructed roads and bridges and built nearly all of the railroad beds (one thousand miles in Georgia alone) throughout the South. See also Slave-hiring.

Juba: a widely popular Negro dance characterized by patting the hands on the knees, then striking the hands together, then striking the right shoulder with one hand, the left with the other—all while keeping time with the feet and singing.

1841: [It was] really astonishing to witness the rapidity of their motions, their accurate time, and the precision of their music and dance.

I have never seen it equalled in my life.
Lewis Paine, Six Years in a Georgia Prison

jump the broom: a marriage ritual in which bride and groom leapt backwards over a broom handle to seal their vows, a practice of many black weddings on plantations.

1800s: All Old Master's niggers was married by the white preacher, but he had a neighbor who would marry his niggers hisself. He would say to the man: "Do you want this woman?" and to the girl, "Do you want this boy?" Then he would call the Old Mistress to fetch the broom and Old Master would hold one end and Old Mistress the other and tell the boy and girl to jump this broom, and he would say: "That's your wife." They called marrying like that jumping the broom.
Millie Evans, North Carolina, in Lay My Burden Down, *p.61*

1800s: When they got married on the places, mostly they just jumped over a broom and that made 'em married. Sometimes one the white folks read a little out of the Scriptures to 'em, and they felt more married. *Botkin, in* Lay My Burden Down, *p.86*

Ku Klux Klan: the secret antiblack organization, formed after the Civil War to keep Negroes from voting.

mammy: a black woman servant who served as a second mother to the children of a master. She sometimes cared for the children more than their natural mother and was often a source of great affection even after the children had grown into adults.

maroon: a fugitive slave in hiding. Camps of bands of maroons sometimes went undetected for years while hidden in Southern swamps.

massa/marse/master: a slaveholder. The appellation was frequently used by the more subservient slave in deference to any white man.

1860s: I stopped for a few minutes near a camp-fire, in a piece of woods, where our infantry halted, and I remember hearing the colored cook of one of the messes asking in piteous tones, over and over again, "Marse George, where's Marse Charles?"
Edward Moore, The Story of a Canoneer Under Stonewall Jackson, *p.33*

missus: slave's appellation of respect for the master's wife.

mulattoes: the offspring of a mixed black/white union. According to Southern law, the offspring of a free white mother and a Negro slave father was free, while the offspring of a free white father and a Negro or mulatto slave mother was a slave. Consequently, some mulatto slaves were actually white or nearly white in appearance.

names: slaves commonly took the surnames of their masters after being freed. Thus some blacks named Jefferson today are actually the descendants of the slaves owned by Thomas Jefferson. First names were often taken from someone in the master's family, for example, an uncle or aunt, or were chosen by the master himself. Most often, the slave parents chose a name themselves, but it was usually of Anglo-Saxon origin.

Negro dogs: dogs specifically raised and trained to track runaway slaves. They were either sold or hired out.

negroism: favoring the Negro.
1860: They have taken the negro to their bosoms, and lodged him into their hearts, till they know him from the sole of his splay foot to the top-knot of his woolly head, and they have imbued their minds and souls with the very quintessence of negroism.
   Mr. English, Indiana, House of Reps., Congressional Globe, *May 2*

negrophilism: fondness for Negroes.
1846: The gentleman from Ohio, the advocate of negrophilism.
   Mr. Chipman, Michigan, House of Reps., Congressional Globe, *May 18*

Negro slaveowners: In 1830, more than 3600 free Negroes and mulattoes owned slaves. Most of these slaves were purchased to serve as husbands, wives or children, a lesser number to work on plantations.

nigger heaven: a theater balcony or gallery reserved for or used by Negroes, especially in Boston from 1888-1891.

octoroon: one who is one-eighth Negro; one having one Negro great-grandparent. One descended from a white person and a quadroon.

overseer: a supervisor who managed the daily operations of a plantation, including planting, tillage and harvesting and the care, feeding and work output of slaves. Overseers used flogging and other punishments to discipline the slaves and were thus frequently hated by the slaves, sometimes even subjected to beatings. On large plantations, overseers often employed one or more slave drivers, who wielded whips to motivate gangs of workers.

pass: a pass written and signed by a master allowing one or more of his slaves to visit a neighboring plantation or town.

patois: a mixture of English and African words and speech patterns, used by many slaves up to the first quarter of the century and declining thereafter. Slaves in Georgia and South Carolina, for example, often used groups of words to form nouns, verbs, adjectives and adverbs; for example, "day clean" for dawn, "a-beat-on-iron" for mechanic, and "sweet mouth" for flatter.
1820s: [The language was] a mixture of Guinea and everything you

please. . . . "Oo you dem long to?" means "Whom do you belong to?" "Oo dem got any peachy?" means "Have you got any peaches?" I could scarcely understand them so broken was their speech.
Frederick Douglass, My Bondage and My Freedom, *pp.76-77*

pattyrollers: slaves' term for neighborhood patrollers who made sure that any slaves traveling off their plantations had passes from their masters. Patrollers were appointed by state counties from 1831 on to help prevent slave insurrections. The patrollers whipped slaves they found roaming about without passes.

1800s: If dey ketch you without a pass, dey goin' whip you. An' law — how I plagued 'em wid my goin's-on! I wuh all time runnin' off de place. . . . Marster wouldn't let 'em cross de fence onter his place. Tell de pattyrollers dey needn' pay no mind to de cullud folks on his side de road. *Orland Armstrong,* Old Massa's People, *p.151*

pickaninnies: Negro children.

punishments: the most well-known form of slave punishment was flogging or whipping, but slaveowners and overseers employed dozens of lesser-known penalties to keep their workers in line. These included: forcing a slave to eat all the worms he failed to pick off tobacco leaves; giving male slaves women's work, such as washing clothes; denying passes to social events off the plantation; forcing slaves to work on Sundays and holidays; confiscating crops from a slave's personal garden or truck patch; selling a family member to another plantation; locking a slave in a private jail built on the plantation; placing a slave in stocks with a ration of bread and water and no communication with anyone; placing slaves in chains and irons, etc.

quadroon: a person who is one-quarter Negro. One having one Negro grandparent.

recreation/leisure time: most slaves were given Saturday afternoon and all day Sunday off as well as some holidays (Christmas especially). Saturday afternoons were often spent washing clothes, cleaning one's cabin, and tending the family garden. Saturday nights might be spent at a dance or other social event, while Sundays were reserved for church-going, fishing, hunting, wrestling, socializing at neighboring plantations and so forth.

salting: washing a slave's whip-wounds with brine as further punishment; not a common practice.

Sambo: appellation given to a particularly subservient slave who grinned or trembled frequently, who typically shuffled or stuttered in front of whites, or who had a "down guilty" look. Although outwardly docile, the stereotypical Sambo was also known to be artful and clever and sometimes ran away.

slave-hiring: the hiring out of slaves, a profitable practice employed by a master whenever he had a surplus of laborers. Although slaves could be rented out for short periods, it was a common practice to hire them out for one-year periods. Such slaves were hired to work in factories and stores, on other plantations, and as domestics in private households.

songs: a wide variety of chanteys and spirituals sung in the fields, in church, and at social gatherings.

> William Rino sold Henry Silvers;
> Hilo! Hilo!
> Sold him to de Gorgy trader;
> Hilo! Hilo!
> His wife, she cried, and children bawled,
> Hilo! Hilo!
> Sold him to de Gorgy trader;
> Hilo! Hilo!
> — *Song sung by Maryland slaves, recounted by John Dixon Long,* Pictures of Slavery in Church and State, *1857*

> We raise de wheat,
> Dey gib us de corn;
> We bake de bread,
> Dey gib us de cruss;
> We sif de meal,
> Dey giv us de huss;
> We peal de meat,
> Dey gib us de skin
> And dat's de way
> Dey takes us in.
> — *Song recounted by Frederick Douglass,* My Bondage and My Freedom, *p.253*

> Old black bull come down de hollow,
> He shake hi' tail, you hear him bellow;
> When he bellow he jar de river,
> He paw de yearth, he make it quiver.
>   Who-zen-John, who-za.
> — *Virginia slave song performed while clapping Juba, recounted in* Farmer's Register, *1838, pp.59-61*

soul-driver: contemptuous nickname given to overseers by abolitionists. 1818: A few evenings since, two men, in the character of soul drivers, lodged in the jail for safe keeping, five Negroes.

Massachusetts Spy, *November 4*

1849: [She was grateful] for the prospect that she would soon cease to tremble at the thought that the soul-driver would tear from her the object of her tenderest affections.

Mr. Giddings, Ohio, House of Reps., Congressional Globe, *February 17*

squatter sovereignty: the doctrine or belief that the Western territories should settle the slavery issue for themselves.

this child: an expression referring to oneself, widely used by Negroes, sometimes by whites.

1843: You've got this child into a tarnation scrape this time.

Knickerbocker Magazine, *August*

1845: This child ain't to be beat, no how you can fix it.

W.T. Thompson, Chronicles of Pineville, *p.23*

1857: Dem common niggers is only good to hoe de corn an' fry de hoecake. De next thing, he'll say he knows more about cookin' dan dis chile does. Knickerbocker Magazine, *December*

Uncle: Southern nickname for an old Negro.

1835: Nor are planters indifferent to the comfort of their gray-headed slaves. They always address them in a mild and pleasant manner as Uncle or Aunty. The South West, *ii, p.241*

1850: Old Uncle Ned, — every family in Kentucky has some old family servant bearing this endearing title. *James Weir,* Lonz Powers, *i, p.32*

1861: We passed through the market [at Charleston] where the stalls are kept by fat negresses and old unkeys. *W.H. Russel,* Diary, *April 16*

underground railroad: a system of Northern sympathizers and free Negroes who sheltered fugitive slaves from the South and helped them on their way to freedom in Canada.

1857: This Greeley is one of their popular characters in the East, and one that supports the stealing of niggers and underground railroad.

John Taylor at the Bowery, Salt Lake City, Journal of Discourses, *August 9, v, p.119*

1859: When a man's slaves run away and comes to their houses, they will feed him and send him into Canada through the underground railroad. *Mr. Logan, Illinois,* Congressional Globe, *December 9*

wench: a Negro girl.

1823: A young sturdy Negro wench stood by doing nothing.

American Anecdotes, *p.107*

SURRENDER OF GEN. LEE!

"The Year of Jubilee has come! Let all the People Rejoice!"

200 GUNS WILL BE FIRED

On the Campus Martius,
AT 3 O'CLOCK TO-DAY, APRIL 10,
To Celebrate the Victories of our Armies. 1865

Every Man, Woman and Child is hereby ordered to be on hand prepared to Sing and Rejoice. The crowd are expected to join in singing Patriotic Songs.
ALL PLACES OF BUSINESS MUST BE CLOSED AT 2 O'CLOCK.
Hurrah for Grant and his noble Army.

By Order of the People.

SECTION TWELVE

THE CIVIL WAR

Ironically, the biggest killer in the Civil War wasn't a bullet or a cannonball; it was disease. While 110,000 Northern and 94,000 Confederate soldiers were mortally wounded in battle, a whopping 388,580 died from illnesses, most often from diarrhea, typhoid, typhus, malarial fevers and pneumonia. Indeed, the condition of one's bowels sometimes became a greater source of anxiety than enemy gunfire. "You got on sich a nice new-niform, you got sich nice boots on, you ridin' sich a nice hoss, an' you look like yer bowels wuz so regular," was an actual compliment paid by a worn-out, poorly cared for Confederate soldier to a well-fed, well-tended Union soldier at war's end.

Few would argue that the Civil War soldier faced more misery and more kinds of misery than did his counterparts in either World War I or II. In addition to receiving poor medical treatment, the Civil War soldier was frequently underfed, poorly clothed, and at times unshod. After battle, his wounded limbs were hacked off with little or no anesthesia by assembly-line surgeons; gaping bullet wounds were simultaneously dressed and infected by the dirty hands of these inadequately trained physicians. Blood transfusions would have saved many, but the technique was so poorly understood that it was attempted only twice during the entire war.

Unlike modern, calculated warfare, some Civil War battles were little more than free-for-all slaughters. At the battle of Cold Harbor in 1864, seven thousand Union soldiers and fifteen hundred Confederates were slain within eight minutes. A Confederate witnessing the scene said, "The dead covered more than five acres of ground about as thickly as they could be laid." The Battle of Gettysburg was even worse: fifty-one thousand men died of their wounds—more than all the American soldiers killed in the Vietnam War.

At the end of it all, a quote from a Confederate soldier, fraternizing with the enemy between the lines, stands out: "We talked the matter over and could have settled the war in thirty minutes had it been left to us.

Civil War Terms

avalanche: nickname for a two-wheeled, springless ambulance cart that severely jostled wounded passengers and sometimes compounded their injuries.

bawdy house: a house of prostitution, hundreds of which were spawned by the Civil War to serve its thousands of lonely troops. Washington, D.C., was home for an estimated 450 bordellos during the conflict. Among them: the Blue Goose, the Haystack, the Ironclad, Hooker's Headquarters and Mother Russel's Bake Oven.

bayonet: an 18-inch-long, triangular-shaped blade that was attached to the end of a rifle and meant for hand-to-hand combat. Bayonets typically made troops queasy, and many were reluctant to use them. Thus only 5 percent of war deaths were attributed to their use. More often, bayonets were used as candle-holders or spits for roasting meat.

belly band: a flannel band many soldiers wore in the mistaken belief that it would relieve dysentery.

Billy Yank: nickname for the Union soldier, actually not adopted until after the war. During the war, a Union soldier was simply referred to as a Yank or Yankee. See also Johnny Reb.

black soldiers: 178,975 blacks in some 166 regiments served in the war. Their pay was ten dollars per month, significantly less than their white counterparts.

1863: Facts are beginning to dispel prejudices. Enemies of the Negro race, who have persistently denied the capacity and doubted the courage of the Blacks, are unanswerably confuted by the good conduct and gallant deeds of the men whom they persecute and slander. From many quarters comes evidence of the swiftly approaching success which is to crown what is still by some persons deemed to be the experiment of arming whom the Proclamation of Freedom liberates. New York Tribune, *March 28, 1863*

bounty: an enlistment bonus. The Union paid new recruits three hundred dollars in 1863.

bounty jumper: one who joined the Union army to get the enlistment bonus, then deserted to sign on for another bonus elsewhere. Such deserters were shot when caught.

1889: Desertion was most prevalent in 1864, when the town and city governments hired so many foreigners who enlisted solely to get the large bounties paid, and then deserted, many of them before getting to the field, or immediately afterwards. . . . These men were called bounty jumpers. *J.D. Billings*, Hard Tack and Coffee, *pp.161-162*

boy: many Confederate units had a negro slave do their chores for them. (See also Slavery and Black Plantation Culture, p.213.)

1860s: Quite a large number had a boy along to do the cooking and washing. Think of it! a Confederate soldier with a body servant all his own, to bring him a drink of water, black his boots, dust his clothes, cook his cornbread and bacon, and put wood on his fire. Never was there fonder admiration than these darkies displayed for their masters. Their chief delight and glory was to praise the courage and good looks of "Mahse Tom."

Carlton McCarthy, Detailed Minutiae of Soldier Life

brigade: four regiments, or 4,184 men.

bucktails: nickname for the Union Thirteenth Pennsylvanian Reserves. New recruits had to display the tail of a buck as proof they could shoot with skill.

bull: slang for exaggeration or lies, first popularized by Civil War soldiers.

butternuts: Confederate uniforms dyed brown with walnut shells or bark. Such uniforms were used when the standard grey uniforms were in short supply. The soldiers who wore these uniforms were also called butternuts.

1865: From the extreme front you catch an occasional glimpse of the Rebels, Butternuts, as they are termed in camp, from their cinnamon-hued homespun, dyed with butternut extract.

A.D. Richardson, The Secret Service, *p.256*

canister: artillery ammunition comprised of tin cannisters filled with iron balls that produced a giant, shotgun-like effect when fired from a cannon.

chevaux-de-frise: spiked logs used to protect defensive positions.

colporteurs: employees of religious groups who assisted chaplains and distributed bibles and tracts to the troops. Some of their pamphlets included "How Do You Bear Your Trials?" "The Destitution and Wretchedness of a Drunkard," and "Why Do You Swear?"

Colt revolver: the 1860 model was standard U.S. issue.

Columbiad: An 8-, 10- or 12-inch cannon that could shoot a 128-pound shell five thousand yards, used by the Union.

company Q: another name for the Confederate sick list.

Confederate States: in the order of their secession: South Carolina, Mississippi, Florida, Alabama, Georgia, Louisiana, Texas, Virginia, Arkansas, North Carolina, Tennessee.

contraband: former slaves protected as soldiers by the Union government.

1862: The general commanding wishes you to employ the contrabands in and about your camp in cutting down all the trees. . . . I have ordered tents for the contrabands to be quartered in.
Order of General Butler, July 31

1864: A coal-black, brutal-looking negro soldier, an escaped contraband, as Beast Butler styles the stolen and refugee slaves.
Southern Historical Society Papers, *ii, p.233*

copperhead: a Northerner who sympathized with the Southern cause.

1863: The treason of Copperheads manifests itself in a pretended loyalty to the Government, while all their sympathy is transferred to the South, to aid and comfort the rebellion. Harper's Weekly, *September 19*

1864: The Tories in England, and the Copperheads in this country, talk of the war in exactly the same strain. Harper's Weekly, *April 9*

copperheads: small copper tokens the size of cents, used during the war to help alleviate the coin shortage. (See also Hard times tokens in Money and Coinage, p.146.)

corduroying: the construction by the Engineer Corps of log or plank roads to facilitate transport of troops and supplies over muddy terrain.

1860s: Corduroying called at times for a large amount of labor, for Virginia mud was such a foe to rapid transit that miles upon miles of this sort of road had to be laid to keep ready communication between different portions of the Army.
Philip Stern, Soldier Life in the Union and Confederate Armies, *p.269*

corps: three divisions, or nine brigades.

disease: 62 percent of deaths in the war were caused by disease. Leading such causes of death were, in order: diarrhea, typhoid, typhus, malaria, pneumonia and smallpox.

division: three brigades.

doughboy: a foot soldier, named after the globular buttons he wore.

1867: She was so accustomed to fast riding with our cavalry, she does not know how to treat a dough-boy. *Letter of Mrs. Custer, March*

1888: Early in the Civil War, the term was applied to the large globular brass buttons of the infantry uniform, from which it passed by natural transition to the infantry themselves.
Mrs. Elizabeth Custer, Tenting on the Plains, *p.516*

drumming out of camp: in the Union army, a coward's formal escort out of camp after he had been stripped of his uniform. Four soldiers wielding charge bayonets marched the coward out of camp as a drum and fife corps followed behind. The coward was usually met with humiliating jeers from his peers as he passed.

executions: a combined total of 267 soldiers were executed during the war, for desertion, murder, rape and mutiny.

fatigue duty: policing and cleaning the camp, building stables, collecting food and water, etc.

Federals: another name for the Union soldiers.
1860s: The front of the infantry regiment had now reached a point within twenty steps of us on our right, when the Federals turned their gun toward us and fired, killing the five men of the regiment at the front. *Edward Moore,* The Story of a Canoneer Under Stonewall Jackson

goober grabbers: nickname for Confederate soldiers from Georgia, describing their relationship with peanut farming.

graybacks: Confederate soldiers, named after their uniforms.
1864: The last thing he is likely to attempt is to send a solitary grayback or an army of graybacks beyond the mountains.
Daily Telegraph, *March 17*

havelock: a linen cover for a kepi (the Confederate cap) with a small cape for protecting the back of the neck from sunburn.

haversack: a one-strapped canvas bag carried over the shoulder.
1860s: The haversack held its own to the last, and was found practical and useful. It very seldom, however, contained rations, but was used to carry small articles generally carried in the knapsack. . . . Somehow or other, many men managed to do without the haversack, and carried absolutely nothing but what they wore and had in their pockets. *Carlton McCarthy,* Detailed Minutiae of Soldier Life, *p.23*

Henry: a 16-shot, breech-loading rifle used in 1864 by Union troops. Confederates said the Yanks "loaded it in the morning and fired it all day."

horses: these were deliberately shot at by the enemy on both sides and thus thousands were either killed or injured.
1860s: Just after we got to the top of the hill, and within fifty or one hundred yards of the position we were to take, a shell struck the off-wheel horse of my gun and burst. The horse was torn to pieces, and the pieces thrown in every direction. The saddle horse was also horribly mangled, the driver's leg was cut off, as was also the foot of

a man who was walking alongside. . . . A white horse working in the lead looked more like a bay after the catastrophe.

Edward Moore, The Story of a Canoneer Under Stonewall Jackson, pp.30-31

1860s: There being no room in the rear, their caisons and limbers stood off to their right on a flat piece of heavily wooded ground. This was almost covered with dead horses. I think there must have been eighty or ninety on less than an acre; one I noticed standing almost upright, perfectly lifeless, supported by a fallen tree.

Edward Moore, The Story of a Canoneer Under Stonewall Jackson, p.75

1860s: An artillery man—he must have been a driver—says: when the firing had ceased an old battery horse, his lower jaw carried away by shot, with blood streaming from his wound, staggered up to him, gazed beseechingly at him, and, groaning piteously, laid his bloody jaws on his shoulder, and so made his appeal for sympathy. He was beyond help. *Carlton McCarthy, Detailed Minutiae of Soldier Life, p.102*

housewife: a sewing kit carried by soldiers on both sides.

ironclad: an iron fighting ship, such as the *Monitor*.

Johnny, Johnny Reb: nickname for a Confederate soldier. See also Billy Yank.

1867: There lay one of the enemy, dead, with his gun cocked ready to fire at his Johnny; but another Johnny was too quick for him.

J.M. Crawford, Mosby and his Men, p.223

1876: He had his pistol out on any occasion while dealing with the majority of Johnnies. Southern Historical Society Papers, *i, p.264*

1885: By the Widow Perkins, if Johnny Reb hasn't taken their rudders away, and sent them adrift.

Admiral Porter, Incidents of the Civil War, p.170

kepi: a cap with a flat, circular top and visor, worn by the French military and Confederate soldiers.

Ketchum grenade: the most commonly used grenade in the war.

lampposts: Civil War soldiers described artillery shells in flight as flying lampposts because to the naked eye they looked like elongated blurs.

mess: a group of five to twenty men in the Confederate army who worked, ate and fought together.

1860s: There were some good voices in the company, two or three in our mess.

Edward Moore, The Story of a Canoneer Under Stonewall Jackson, p.36

On going about fifty yards to the rear, I came up with my friend and messmate, Gregory, who was being carried by several comrades.

Edward Moore, The Story of a Canoneer Under Stonewall Jackson, p.56

minié ball: a soft lead slug one-half inch in diameter and one inch long, with a conical nose and hollow base that expanded in the rifle barrel and was imparted with spin to increase accuracy. It also expanded on impact, producing a devastating wound.

1860s: He had scarcely struck three blows before he fell dead, pierced by Minié ball.

Edward Moore, The Story of a Canoneer Under Stonewall Jackson, *p.57*

monitor: an ironclad warship with a low deck and gun turrets. Similar ships that came after it were also called monitors.

mortar boat: a simple, low-decked boat designed specifically for carrying and firing mortars.

music: a popular diversion throughout both Confederate and Union camps, supplied by organized bands or by individual soldiers playing banjos, fiddles, harmonicas, etc. Songs were frequently sung on marches to boost morale and in camps to stir sweet memories of home. Two of the most popular songs on both sides were "Home, Sweet Home" and "When This Cruel War is Over." "Home, Sweet Home" (along with "Auld Lang Syne") stirred such a deep well of emotion in soldiers that the Union army actually banned its performance in the winter of 1862-1863. The bugle song "Taps" was another tearjerker but it served the useful purpose of quieting Union soldiers at the end of the day. Among more upbeat Union favorites were "Yankee Doodle Dandy," "Tramp, Tramp, Tramp," "The Star Spangled Banner" and, a favorite marching song, "John Brown's Body," which was later revised to become the "Battle Hymn of the Republic." Among Confederate favorites were "Dixie," "When Johnny Comes Marching Home Again," "The Bonnie Blue Flag" and "The Yellow Rose of Texas."

1860s: How the woods did ring with song! There were patriotic songs, romantic and love songs, sarcastic, comic and war songs, pirates' glees, plantation melodies, lullabies, good old hymn tunes, anthems, Sunday-school songs, and everything but vulgar and obscene songs; these were scarcely every heard, and were nowhere in the Army well received or encouraged.

Carlton McCarthy, Detailed Minutiae of Soldier Life, *p.200*

Napoleon: a 12-pound, smoothbore cannon; the standard artillery gun of both sides. It had a bronze barrel and could shoot grape and canister, literally shredding troops who were hit at close range.

nostalgia: Union physician's term for the disease of homesickness.

occupations: 47 percent of Union soldiers and 61 percent of Confederates were either farmers or had farm- or plantation-related jobs before the war.

pastimes: leisure activities included wrestling, horse racing, cockfights, boxing, baseball, dice games, cards (mostly draw poker), cribbage and checkers. See also Music.

pay: in the beginning of the war, privates on both sides earned eleven dollars per month. In 1864, the Union paid soldiers sixteen dollars a month, while the Confederates paid eighteen dollars. However, runaway inflation in the South made the Confederate's pay worth much less than that of the Federals.

picket: one or more soldiers placed outside an encampment to watch and warn of an enemy approach. Also, picket duty.

1860s: . . . I spent the greater part of the night drilling them in the town-hall, getting news from time to time from the pickets in the mountain pass.

Edward Moore, The Story of a Canoneer Under Stonewall Jackson, p.26

1860s: On our way down on another expedition, hearing the enemy were driving in our pickets, and that we would probably have some lively work and running, I left my blanket . . . .

Edward Moore, The Story of a Canoneer Under Stonewall Jackson, p.39

1860s: Two boys who had volunteered for service with the militia in the same neighborhood, were detailed for picket duty. It was the custom to put three men on each post—two militia boys and one veteran.

Carlton McCarthy, Detailed Minutiae of Soldier Life, p.112

pontoniers: engineers who specialized in building pontoon bridges.

quaker guns: phony cannons built of logs and painted black, used by the Confederates to fool the Federals.

1862: [They] found that they had been awed by a few quaker guns— logs of wood in position, and so painted as to resemble a cannon.

J.B. Jones, A Rebel War Clerk's Diary, i, p.113

1863: [It was said] that we had men at the head of the Army who were . . . too dilatory in attempting to advance, allowing the enemy to deter them from making attacks by the exhibition of quaker guns and other artful contrivances.

Mr. Allen, Ohio, House of Reps., Congressional Globe, February 2, p.85

rebel: another name for a Confederate soldier.

rebel yell: a war cry of the Confederate soldiers.

1860s: A little way ahead the regiment jumps a fence, and pop! bang! whiz! thud! is all that can be heard, until the rebel yell reverberates through the woods.

Carlton McCarthy, Detailed Minutiae of Soldier Life, p.96

regiment: 1,046 men. Four regiments made a brigade.

sawbones: soldier nickname for an army surgeon.

secession: the separation of the eleven Southern states from the Union in 1860-1861.
1860s: Buckhannon, twenty miles in advance of us, is said to be in the hands of the secession troops.
John Beatty, The Citizen Soldier, p.11

shoddies: shoddy uniforms made from wool scraps that fell apart in bad weather; supplied for a time to the Union Army.

Sibley tent: a teepee-like tent; one of several different types of shelters used by Federal troops.

skirmishers: a small group of troops used to draw out the enemy for a larger body of troops following close behind. Any soldiers involved in either a minor or preliminary confrontation.
1860s: Left alone to face the advance of the immense host eagerly pursuing the worn remnant of the invincible army, they waited until the enemy's skirmishers appeared in the field, when, with perfect deliberation, they commenced their fire.
Carlton McCarthy, Detailed Minutiae of Soldier Life, p.131

slang: slang phrases invented by or widely used by Civil War soldiers: "let her rip," "snug as a bug in a rug," "scarce as hen's teeth," "between shit and sweat" (meaning between a rock and a hard place).

Springfield rifle: the U.S. rifle musket, the principal rifle used by both sides, costing $14.93 each. It was accurate for long-distance shooting (up to three hundred yards) because its minié ball projectile was imparted with spin as it left the barrel. However, even veteran soldiers could fire off no more than two shots per minute due to a rather complicated loading procedure:

1. Infantryman tears open paper cartridge containing powder and ball with his teeth.
2. Pours powder down barrel.
3. Pushes in bullet with thumb.
4. Draws ramrod and pushes projectile down.
5. Pulls back hammer.
6. Places percussion cap on nib beneath hammer.
7. Aims and shoots.

submarine: an underwater boat used by the Confederate navy. Its propellors were turned by a hand crank; an air hose ran to the surface so its crew could breathe.

surgery: field surgery was conducted with ether or chloroform and, when neither was available, the patient was instructed to bite down on a bullet or piece of wood—while a limb was being amputated. More arms and legs were amputated during the Civil War than at any other time in U.S. history.

1860s: A large hole was dug in the yard, about the size of a small cellar, and into this the legs and arms were thrown as they were lopped off by the surgeons, with a coolness that would be a terror to persons unaccustomed to the sights of military surgery after battle. The day was hot and sultry, and the odor of the ether used in the operations and the effluvia from the receptacle of mangled limbs, was sickening in the extreme.

A private from the Twenty-second Massachusetts, as quoted in Soldiers Blue and Gray, *p.162*

three-inch U.S. rifle: a wrought iron artillery gun; it was more accurate and had a greater range than the Napoleon, but it was prone to malfunction at critical moments.

torpedoes: name for Confederate navy mines made of beer kegs, barrels or old boilers filled with powder and suspended just under the water.

Virginia quickstep: Union nickname for diarrhea, a common affliction during the war.

wagon dogs: nickname for Confederate malingerers who traveled in the rear of the wagon trains to avoid battle.

Yankees: nickname for Union soldiers. Also, Billy Yank.

Civil War Rations

alcohol: small amounts of whiskey were occasionally issued to soldiers in some units after a particularly difficult battle or during a spell of bad weather. Suspicions—probably correct—often arose that some officers got drunk before leading their troops into battle. Union nicknames for alcohol: tanglefoot, oil of gladness. Confederate nicknames: old red-eye, pop-skull.

beans: a staple on both sides.

Borden: a brand of condensed milk sold to troops by sutlers.

bread: soft bread issued on both sides.

bully soup: a hot cereal comprised of cornmeal and mashed hard tack boiled in water, wine and ginger, and served to Union troops. Also known as panada.

coffee: originally issued as raw green beans that the soldiers had to roast themselves in camp kettles. Union soldiers later were given a crude paste form of instant coffee mixed with cream and sugar. Confederates were also given coffee but suffered frequent shortages.

cookies: molasses cookies were among the favorite foods of Union soldiers. They were sold by sutlers, six for a quarter.

corn bread: a staple of the Confederate army. It was frequently of poor quality.

cush: a Confederate stew comprised of beef or bacon, corn bread and water, with most of the water boiled away. Also known as slosh.

desiccated vegetables: Union issue of dried, compressed, mixed vegetables in cakelike form. The vegetables were of highly questionable quality and nicknamed "desecrated vegetables" by the troops.

1860s: Occasionally, a ration of what was known as desiccated vegetables was dealt out. This consisted of a small piece per man, an ounce in weight and two or three inches cube of sheet or block of vegetables, which had been prepared, and apparently "kiln-dried," as sanitary fodder for the soldiers. . . . When put in soak for a time, so perfectly had it been dried and so firmly pressed that it swelled to an amazing extent. . . . In this pulpy state a favorable opportunity was afforded to analyze its composition. It seemed to show . . . layers of cabbage leaves and turnip tops stratified with layers of sliced carrots, turnips, parsnips, a bare suggestion of onions . . . and some other among known vegetable quantities.

John D. Billings, Hard Tack and Coffee, *pp.138-139*

embalmed beef: nickname given by Union troops to the tinned beef sold to the army by Chicago meat packers. See also Salt horse.

foraging: a necessary means of survival because both armies tended to be only sporadically supplied. Common forms of foraging included raiding and stealing from a sutler's cart; stealing vegetables and livestock from nearby farms; "borrowing" goods from a country store and telling the proprietor to "charge it" to Uncle Sam; and soliciting invitations to dinner at neighboring homes.

hard tack: a Union staple officially known as hard bread, consisting of flour and water and measuring about $3 \times 3 \times \frac{1}{2}$ inches, often stale or infested with weevils and worms. Nicknames for the crackers included teeth dullers, worm castles and sheet-iron crackers. They were frequently crumbled into coffee to help soften them up.

1861: Camp gossip says that the crackers have been in storage since the Mexican War. They are . . . almost as hard as a brick, and undoubtedly would keep for years and be as palatable as they now are.

From a Pennsylvania soldier's diary

lobcourse: Union soup made of salt pork, hard tack and anything else available.

salt horse: army-issued beef so saturated with salt it had to be soaked in water for several hours before it could be eaten. The salt reportedly preserved the meat for as long as two years.

1860s: It was . . . yellow-green with rust from having lain out of brine and, when boiled, was four times out of five . . . a stench in the nostrils, which no delicate palate cared to encounter at shorter range.
John D. Billings, Hard Tack and Coffee, *pp.134-135*

1860s: The boys call it salt horse because they say that iron horse shoes and mule shoes have been found in barrels, with the meat, but never an ox shoe. *Millett Thompson,* Thirteenth New Hampshire

salt pork: a principal meat ration on both sides.

skillygalee: hard tack soaked in water and fried in pork grease, a Union specialty.

slapjacks: pancakes of flour and water and salt fried in pork grease, on both sides.

sutler: a merchant/private contractor appointed by the government to supply the troops with such civilian goods as pastries, canned meats, books, tobacco, toiletries, and so on. Appointed one per regiment, the sutlers had a reputation for greediness, sometimes inflating their prices by as much as 300 percent. Butter, for example, was sold for $1.00 a pound; condensed milk, $.75 a can; navy tobacco, $1.25 per plug. Sutlers sold their goods on credit, and the bill was deducted directly from a soldier's payroll. Their products were much sought after by the troops, but the sutlers themselves were usually acutely despised.

OUT ON THE RANGE

By 1840, all of the principal Indian tribes east of the Mississippi, including the Kickapoo, Shawnee and Delaware from the Northeast, and the Cherokee, Creek, Chickasaw, Seminole and Choctaw from the Southeast, had been relocated to the territory of Oklahoma and Kansas by the U.S. government. In addition to natives already there and western bands brought in later, some forty major tribes were making the range area—known as Indian Territory—home by the end of the century.

Though outraged over the government's actions, the Indians were badly outmanned and outgunned, and after bloody skirmishes and battles between 1860-1890, resistance eventually died out. "Savages" is what some white men preferred to call the Indian, but the reverse was true in many nineteenth-century minds. The Indian, after all, was merely defending his homeland, while the white settler was stealing his.

The cowboy entered the scene in the second half of the century. His massive cattle drives helped to open and feed the West, but his heyday was relatively short: The cattle-driving era peaked from 1867-1885.

Cowboys and the Wild West

All of the following terms were gleaned from the second half of the century (the cattle-driving era having peaked from 1867 to 1885) unless otherwise noted.

afoot: said of a cowboy without his horse.

Arbuckle's: the most common brand of coffee used on the range.
1880s: Having secured the information we wanted, Flood gave to each Apache a package of Arbuckle coffee, a small sack of sugar, and both smoking and chewing tobacco. *Andy Adams, The Log of a Cowboy, p.141*

auger: a boss or a big talker.
1880s: It's the easiest thing in the world for some big auger to sit in a

239

hotel somewhere and direct the management of the herd.
Andy Adams, The Log of a Cowboy, *pp.135-136*
1880s: In spite of the fact that the cowman had a rep'tation on the outside for bein' 'bout as talkative as a Piegan Injun, there were men on the early range with such talkin' talents they got big rep'tations as augers. *Ramon Adams*, The Old-Time Cow-hand, *p.20*

bedroll: in its simplest form, a couple of blankets rolled out near a fire, where one would "roast on one side and freeze on the other." The better-equipped cowboy also used a canvas tarp to protect him from the elements.

bed-wagon: a wagon used by the larger cattle outfits to carry bedding, branding irons, hobbles, ropes and other range supplies. Smaller outfits simply carried these in the chuck wagon.

Bible: cowboy slang for a book of cigarette papers.

big fifty: nickname for the .50 caliber Sharps rifle, used for hunting buffalo and other big game.

blacksmithing: slang for pimping or hiring out a woman of ill-repute for profit.

blacksnake: a long, cruel whip.
1869: In the midst of it all, he would start up with a sudden yell of anguish, whirl his black-snake, and let fly at the mules.
J. Ross Browne, Adventures in the Apache Country, *p.40*
1878: The fearful black-snake curled and popped over the animals' backs, sometimes gashing their skin. *J.H. Beadle*, Western Wilds, *p.53*
1888: The Mexicans vied with one another as to who could snap the huge black-snake the loudest.
Mrs. Elizabeth Custer, Tenting on the Plains, *p.356*

bogged cattle: cattle stuck in mud. One of the cowboy's most difficult jobs was to extricate cattle from thick mud, especially around river crossings.

bowie knife: a single-edged hunting knife with a ten-inch blade, popularized by Colonel James Bowie. (See also Crime, p.268.)
1836: Col. Travis introduced Col. Crockett to Col. Bowie and, writes Crockett:—while we were conversing, he had occasion to draw his famous knife to cut a strap, and I wish I may be shot if the bare sight of it wasn't enough to give a man of a squeamish stomach the colic, especially before breakfast. Colonel Crockett in Texas, *pp.172-173*
1887: The name Dull Knife was selected on account of it once having been my nickname on the cattle ranges of Texas. It was given to me by cowboy companions who were in the habit of borrowing my pearl-

handled bowie knife and always finding it dull, from having killed so many rattle snakes. *Charles Siringo,* A Cowboy Detective, *p.45*

brand: the emblem or identifying letter of a ranch, literally burned onto the hides of cattle by a red hot iron.

bronc buster: one who broke or trained wild horses for riding. Some men made a career of bronc busting and traveled from ranch to ranch to offer their services.

brush roper: one adept at roping cattle by the feet in heavy brush, a difficult task even for a veteran.

buckaroo: Northwestern term for a cowboy.

buckboard: see Carriages, Coaches and Wagons, p.55.

buck out: to die.

buck out in smoke: to die in a gunfight.

buffalo skinner: one who skinned and sold buffalo hides for a living.

buffalo wallow: a depression in prairie ground, caused by rolling or wallowing buffalo.

bullwhacker: one who drove a team of oxen.
1861: Five yoke of oxen is the motive power for each wagon [going to Pike's Peak], and these are urged forward by a bull-whacker armed with a whip carrying a lash from six to twelve feet in length. Knickerbocker Magazine, *August*
1890: We employed a Pike county bull-whacker, who agreed to deliver us and our effects in Hangtown. *Haskins,* Argonauts of California, *p.52*

bunkhouse: sleeping quarters of all cowhands while at the ranch.

burro: widely used in the West as a kind of carryall. A donkey. Also a stand or holder for a saddle not in use.

butcher: during a branding, one who cuts earmarks, dewlaps, wattles and other permanent marks of owner identification in cattle.

buttermilk: nickname for a motherless calf.

calf wagon: a wagon used on a drive to pick up and carry any newborn calves, which could slow the herd. Smaller outfits did not have such a wagon and usually killed new calves.

calico: cowboy's slang for a woman, named after the popular dress material of the period. Also, a pinto horse.

California collar: a hangman's noose.

casa grande: a large ranch house in the Southwest.

cash in one's six-shooter: outlaw's term for holding up a bank.

chaps: short for chaparejos, the leather breeches worn over a cowboy's pants to help protect his legs from being scraped while riding through brush or maneuvering among cattle. Commonly referred to as leggins.
1883: I grabbed my hat and jumped for my horse, forgetting to put on my chaps, and I spent half the night chasing the cattle through that thorny brush. When daylight came . . . we hadn't lost a head. But I was a bloody sight . . . my knees was worst of all.
E.C. Abbott (Teddy Blue), We Pointed Them North, *p.61*

chip wagon: a two-wheeled cart used to haul cattle chips. Chips were used as fuel in areas where wood was scarce.

chuck: cowboy term for food; grub.

chuck-box: a table or shelf that folded out at the back of a chuck wagon, used by the cook.

chuck wagon: the food or mess wagon, used out on the range. It was the center of all social activities.

cinch up: to fasten a saddle on a horse's back.

cocklebur outfit: cowboy's pejorative term for a small ranch, especially one with a questionable reputation.

coffin varnish: slang for bad coffee.

collar and hames: a stiff collar and necktie.

Colt .45: the cowboy's favorite pistol, also known as the peacemaker. It was primarily used to help turn a stampede or to kill sick or injured cattle and to dispatch snakes.
1883: Cowboys and men who were much in the saddle usually contented themselves with the favorite navy revolver, Colt's .45, the peacemaker, serviceable, accurate, and powerful. This was loosely housed in a heavy, open-top leather scabbard, looped upon a cartridge belt. This was often supplemented by a Winchester model '73 carbine, slung in its leather holster under the right knee.
John Barrows, U-Bet, A Greenhorn in Old Montana, *p.162*

cook: nicknames for range cooks included Cookie, Coosie, Dough-Belly, Dough-puncher, Sallie and Sourdough.

corn freight: any freight carried by mule teams. This name was adopted because large quantities of corn had to be carried to feed the mules. Corn freight traveled faster than grass freight (see entry).

counterbrand: any incorrect brand crossed out by burning-in a bar over it and placing the correct brand above it or below it.

cowboy change: bullets or cartridges used as dimes and quarters during coin shortages in the West.

cow town: a town at the end of a cattle trail.

dead man's hand: a combination of aces and eights, which was considered bad luck throughout the West because Wild Bill Hickock was holding this hand when he was killed by Jack McCall during a poker game at Deadwood, South Dakota.

decorate a cottonwood: to be hung.

derringer: popular from the 1860s until the end of the century, a short, easily concealed one-shot pistol used for close-range assaults. Its ease of concealment made it a favorite among gamblers, dance hall girls and bunco men.

> 1875: The drivers were all armed, and spare rifles hung inside the ambulances. I wore a small derringer, with a narrow belt filled with cartridges. An incongruous sight, me thinks now, it must have been. A young mother, pale and thin, a child of scarce three months in her arms, and a pistol belt around her waist!
> *Martha Summerhayes,* Vanished Arizona

dogie: an emaciated calf that has suffered through a rough winter with little food; a motherless calf. Originally known as a dough-gut due to its protruding or pot belly.

drag: the rear of a column of cattle during a drive; the stragglers in a herd, usually young calves or weak or injured cattle.

drag rider: one who rode behind the herd on a drive. The drag position in a drive was one of the most difficult because the rider breathed kicked-up dust all day and had to contend with some of the most uncooperative or inexperienced animals in the herd.

drownings: frequent cause of death among cowboys, occurring when driving cattle across a river.

> 1880s: That she was merciless was evident, for although this crossing had been in use only a year or two when we forded, yet five graves, one of which was less than ten days made, attested her disregard for human life . . . at this and lower trail crossings on Red River, the lives of more trail men were lost by drowning than on all other rivers together. *Andy Adams,* The Log of a Cowboy, *p.121*

dry drive: a cattle drive through waterless expanses. On some dry drives, cattle survived for up to three days without water.

dutch oven: a large cast-iron skillet with a heavy lid, used to cook cowboy fare—and especially bread—out on the range.

earmark: a cut made in a cow's ear, used for identification.

farmer: nicknames for farmers: churn-twister, drylander, fodder forker, hay slayer, nester, plow chaser, sod-buster, squat, squatter.

fightin' wages: extra wages paid to hands who took part in fighting rustlers, Indians or others.

figure eight: lassoing a steer by the neck and both front feet at the same time with a twisted loop, a difficult task performed only by the most experienced ropers.

fireman: a hand in charge of the irons and branding fires.

firewater: Indian name for whiskey.

fish: slang for the yellow oilskin slicker worn to protect a cowboy from the rain.

flank rider: a cowhand who rode about two thirds of the way back behind the point riders along the length of a herd.

foreman: also known as the wagon boss, range boss, or trail boss—the manager of a ranch or outfit's range and hired hands.

forty-niner: anyone who took part in the California gold rush of 1849.

frijoles: dried beans, the range cowboy's basic staple.

gaboon: a sand-filled plug-tobacco box that served as a spitoon in some saloons.

get the drop: in a gunfight, to beat one's opponent to the draw.

gone over the range: said of one who has died.

grass freight: goods shipped by a team of bulls, who required grass to eat. This method of freight transport was cheaper but slower than corn freight.

greaser: pejorative for a Mexican.
1849: The Mexicans are called Spaniards or Greasers (from their greasy appearance) by the Western people. *Ruxton,* Life in the Far West, *p.4*
1861: Lastly comes a Greaser or New Mexico native, clad in the sombrero and serape of his region, with a pair of enormous spurs. He would not be seriously injured, if held under a pump for the space of half an hour. Knickerbocker Magazine, *August*
1890: His short, stocky figure, swarthy skin, and coarse features, made

him a typical Greaser, and quite the replica of many we had seen in Texas. *Mrs. Elizabeth Custer,* Following the Guidon, *p.25*

greenhorn: same as a tenderfoot.

grub-line rider: one who went from ranch to ranch in winter in search of work. Also known as a chuck-line rider.

hasta la vista: the Spanish equivalent of "see you later," used in the Southwest.

head-and-tail string: a single-file line of pack mules tied together by halters running from the head of one animal to the tail of the preceding animal, especially useful on narrow trails.

heel-fly time: the height of the fly season in cattle country, from February to mid-April.
1846: Arter I'd gone to bed I heern him thrashin round like a short-tailed bull in fli-time. Biglow Papers, *No.1*

hell on wheels: see entry in Railroad, p.73.

hemp committee: vigilantes conducting a hanging.

Henry: a sixteen-shot, breech-loading rifle popular until 1866, when it was replaced by the Winchester model.

hobble: a device used to prevent horses from running away. It consisted of two leather cuffs—joined with a chain—that were buckled about the forelegs of the horse. It allowed the horse to graze and roam a short distance out on the range without being tethered.

hog-leg: slang for any big frontier pistol.

homestead: land claimed by a squatter or settler. The Homestead Act of 1862 guaranteed ownership of a 160-acre tract of land to any head of household after he had improved the land and lived on it for five years.

honda: the knotted eyelet at the end of a rope for making a loop.

honkytonk: a cheap saloon or dance hall.

Indian haircut: slang for a scalping.

jerky: dried beef, sometimes eaten on the range.

John Law: frontier nickname for any officer of the law.

Justin's: high-quality, Texas-made cowboy boots, from 1879 on.

lady broke: said of a very gentle horse.

lariat: a rope.

lasso: a fifty-foot rope made of rawhide and having a running noose, the cowboy's standard rope. Rawhide ropes were usually not used in the rain, however, due to a susceptibility to moisture.

latigo: Spanish for the end of every strap which must be passed through a buckle. More specifically, the strap used to fasten a saddle on a horse.

lazy brand: one in which the emblem or letter is lying on its side.

leggins: commonly used term for chaps.

Levi's: widely popular brand of pants worn throughout the West, from 1850 on. (See also Clothing and Fashion, p.116.)

longhorns: the long-horned cattle of Texas.

long sweetenin': slang for molasses.

lynching: a hanging or other form of execution conducted by vigilantes without due process of law. From 1882 to 1903, more than thirty-three hundred people were executed in this fashion, according to the *Chicago Tribune*. In the vast majority of cases no arrests of the perpetrators were ever made. (See also Crime, p.274.)
1884: This was the old store that was used by Billy Downs and the gang of horse thieves, and that he was living in when Granville Stuart and his raiders came and got him and hanged him in the summer of '84, a few months before we got up there. They hanged or shot fourteen of them at different places along the Missouri River, including Billy Downs, who was more or less the bookkeeper and storekeeper for the bunch. *E.C. Abbott (Teddy Blue)*, We Pointed Them North, *p.114*

mail-order cowboy: a tenderfoot who knew nothing about being a cowboy but had all the proper clothes, or get-up, of one.

makin's: materials for making cigarettes; cigarette papers and Bull Durham tobacco.

maverick: an unbranded cow or calf of unknown ownership. Also, in human terms, a loner or independent type.
1887: Nowadays you don't dare to clap a brand on a maverick even.
F. Francis, Saddle and Moccasin, *p.172*

mavericker: one who rode the range in search of mavericks to claim and brand. A mavericker eventually became synonymous with cow thief.

messenger: a man hired to ride with a sawed-off shotgun beside a stagecoach driver to protect the shipper's property.

mess wagon: another name for a chuck wagon.

mill: to slow or stop a stampede by driving a column of cattle around in a circle. This action causes so much congestion that the cattle are gradually forced to stop running.

1882: Leaving Joe to turn the rear as they came up, I rode to the lead, unfastening my slicker as I went, and on reaching the turned leaders . . . flaunted my fish in their faces until they re-entered the rear guard of our string, and we soon had a mill going which kept them busy, and rested our horses. Once we had them milling, our trouble, as far as running was concerned, was over, for all two of us could hope to do was to let them exhaust themselves in this endless circle.
    Andy Adams, The Log of a Cowboy, *p.47*

mill rider: one who inspected and maintained all the windmills on a ranch.

Mormon brakes: a tree lashed to the back of a wagon to help slow the wagon's descent down a hill, originally used by the Mormons.

mount: a number or string of horses assigned to each rider in a ranch outfit. Typically, each cowhand was assigned from seven to ten horses, and this usually included two wild or unbroken horses that eventually had to be trained by the hand.

mule-earred boots: high-topped cowboy boots with pull-on straps on top.

muleskinner: a muledriver. In this case, skinning was synonymous with driving.

1870: I took to the plains . . . in the capacity of a mule-skinner.
    J.H. Beadle, Life in Utah, *p.224*

1888: The brawny teamsters, known either as bullwhackers or as muleskinners, stalking beside their slow-moving teams.
    Theodore Roosevelt, Century Magazine, *February*

muleys: hornless cattle. Because they tended to be abused by their horned peers, muleys usually bedded down outside of the herd at night.

mutton puncher: cowboy's contemptuous term for a sheepherder.

nester: Southwestern cattleman's contemptuous term for a squatter who claimed range land and farmed it.

night guard: one who rode circuits around the herd at night to guard against predators and to keep animals from wandering away.

night hawk: one who wrangled, or herded, saddle horses at night.

night herder: one who herded cattle at night.

1880s: . . . the sun not yet risen, we were in our saddles and on our way to relieve the two night herders who had held the herd during the night. *John Barrows, U-Bet, A Greenhorn in Old Montana, p.63*

outfit: a word having various meanings, from the employees of a ranch to a cowboy's rigging.

1869: In the Far West and on the Plains, everything is an outfit, from a railway train to a pocket knife. [The word] is applied indiscriminately—to a wife, a horse, a dog, a cat, a row of pins.
A.K. McClure, Rocky Mountains, p.211

1870: In company with a Mormon outfit of sixteen men, ten wagons, and sixty mules, I had made the wearisome journey from North Platte. *J.H. Beadle, Life in Utah, p.217*

1887: The American herder speaks of his companions collectively as the ranch or as the outfit. Scribners Magazine, *p.509*

outrider: a hand who rode far outside of a moving herd to watch for trouble and to redirect wandering steers.

parlor gun: another name for a derringer.

parlor house: a high-class bawdy house with a parlor.

pay: pay for cowboys was typically around forty dollars per month and his board, although wages could go much higher under special circumstances. See also Fightin' wages.

peacemaker: the most widely owned revolver throughout the West, the 1873 model Colt.

picket: to stake a horse.

1880s: He always kept a horse on picket for the night, and often took the herd as it left the bed ground at clear dawn.
Andy Adams, The Log of a Cowboy, p.25

pilgrim: a tenderfoot; a new arrival to the West.

pistol whip: to strike someone with the barrel of a pistol.

playin' cat's cradle with his neck: said of one who has been hung.

point rider: one of two men who rode at the head of a herd and worked to keep the animals moving in the proper direction. Riding point was the high status position of any outfit.

1880s: The two men in the lead were called point men, and then as the herd strung out there would be two men behind them on the swing, two on the flank, and the two drag drivers in the rear. With the cook and horse wrangler and boss, that made eleven.
E.C. Abbott (Teddy Blue), We Pointed Them North, p.62

posse: a group of men banded together to track down and apprehend criminals.

quirt: a whip comprised of three or four thongs and a foot-long stock usually filled with lead, used for striking a rearing horse.
1880s: Spurs were a matter of taste. If a rider carried a quirt, he usually dispensed with spurs. *Andy Adams,* The Log of a Cowboy, *p.15*

rawhide: the hide of a cow.

red-eye: slang for whiskey.

remuda: Spanish collective term for the strings of horses assigned to cowboys on the range or on the ranch. These horses were preferably geldings and numbered ninety to one hundred for an outfit of ten to twelve cowboys. One string was known as a mount. A remuda was called a cavvy or saddle band in the Northwest.

renegade rider: one who rode to neighboring ranches to collect any of his employer's cattle that had either wandered away or had been stolen.

rough string: a string of wild or unbroken horses.

roundup: conducted twice per year, in the spring to brand new calves and in the fall to drive the cattle to market. Because cattle were often allowed to wander over open range, a roundup sometimes encompassed hundreds of miles.

rustle: to steal cattle. Also, to wrangle horses.

rustler: Originally, a horse wrangler. Later, a cattle thief.

saddlebag doctor: one who rode the range and carried medicines in his saddlebags.

saloon drinks: plain whiskey was the most common drink served at the cheap saloons, but better establishments served a wide range of alcoholic concoctions. (See also Food, Drink and Tobacco, p.184.)
1878: We doubt if it would go around but for the innumerable saloons which furnish beer and whiskey at a bit [12½ cents] a drink, the two bit [25 cents] place being the exception.
J.H. Beadle, Western Wilds

scatter gun: another name for a shotgun.

shakin' a hoof: cowboy term for dancing.

Sharp's rifle: a single-shot, lever-action rifle of heavy caliber, used by frontiersmen to hunt big game, especially buffalo. It was popular throughout the 1850s but was eventually eclipsed by the Henry and Winchester repeaters of the 1860s.

shindig: a dance. Also called a stomp.

shooting iron: slang for a gun.

singing and whistling: a cowboy commonly sang or whistled to the herd at night, especially when approaching the animals, to prevent them from being startled by his presence. Cattle were particularly wary of predators at night and could be frightened into stampeding simply by the sudden appearance of a buffalo.

skinner: one who made his living skinning buffalo. Also, a mule-driver.

son-of-a-bitch stew: a stew of calf brains, tongue, liver, heart, kidneys and sweetbreads, mixed with various vegetables according to what was available — a favorite cowboy dish.

sourdough keg: a five-gallon wooden keg in which sourdough was kept by the range cook.

squatter: one who claimed and settled on government-owned land. See also Homestead.
1852: We will take up the land, and, as they used to say in the States, become Squatters, and we will become thicker on the mountains than the crickets ever were. *H.C. Kimball at the Mormon Tabernacle, October 7*

Stetson: the cowboy's favorite brand of cowboy hat.

string: a mount.

swing rider: one of two hands who ride about one third of the way back behind point riders.

tarantula juice: slang for whiskey.
1870s: Arriving at the camp, we pitched our tents and got our supper. . . . The station consists of one adobe house covered by a roof of brush. This ranch is occupied by a man who, even in this desert wilderness, can boast of a wife to share with him in his unenviable solitude. Their chief means of support is the sale of tarantula juice and other such scanty merchantable articles as can be obtained in this barren country. *Old West Magazine, Adventures in Arizona, p.28*

tenderfoot: a new arrival to the West; an inexperienced person.
1890: I would be too smart to run another ranche in this country. I would unload it on some tenderfoot . . . all that I have been buying was stuff fit only to sell to tenderfeet, who wanted it only to sell to other tenderfeet. *Vandyke, Millionaires of the Day, p.19*

tinhorn: a cheap, flashy or generally contemptible gambler.
1885: We have been greatly annoyed of late by a lot of tin horn gamblers and prostitutes. *Weekly New Mexican Review, February 26*

trail boss: the foreman of a ranch outfit.

underwears: cowboy's contemptuous term for sheep.

vaqueros: Spanish name for cowboys.

war-bag: a sack used by cowboys for carrying belongings, cigarette makins, playing cards, cartridges, old love letters, etc.
1880s: The cartridge belt containing my supply of ammunition was in my war-bag, and this I put under my head.
  Charles Siringo, A Cowboy Detective, *p.59*

water barrels: barrels full of water were often placed near buildings in Western towns to be used in case of fire. These were frequently shot up by cowboys "hurrahing" the town after a night of heavy drinking.

whiskey mill: another name for a saloon.

Winchester: the 1873 model was easily the most popular rifle in the West.

wohaw: Indian name for the white man's cattle.

wolfer: man hired by a ranch to trap or hunt wolves for a bounty.

woolies: cowboy's contemptuous name for sheep.

wrangle: to herd horses.

wrangler: one who herded horses.

Indians

Apache: an Indian tribe of the desert Southwest.

Arapaho: an Indian tribe of the middle Plains.

bedding: most of the Plains Indians slept on buffalo robes.

Blackfoot: an Indian tribe of the high Plains of the United States and Canada.

buck: white man's name for a male Indian.

bull boat: a small, bowl-shaped boat having a skin-covered frame, used by the Plains Indians to ferry people and supplies across rivers.
1880s: I saw my first bull boat, a basket framework covered with buffalo hide and much resembling a washtub, and I saw the ludicrous craft in use. *John Barrows,* U-bet, A Green Horn in Old Montana, *p.31*

burial customs: the Plains Indians employed various methods of putting their dead to rest. The Blackfoot placed the head of a household on a scaffold in the tent in which he died. By contrast, a young Blackfoot was

---

WESTERN SLANG PHRASES

all horns and rattles: referring to someone who is very angry.

as blind as a post hole: very blind.

barkin' at a knot: doing something useless; wasting your time.

colder'n a witch's tit: cold.

could draw quickern' you can spit and holler howdy: referring to a fast gunfighter.

could follow a woodtick on a solid rock: referring to one adept at tracking or following a trail.

couldn't hit a bull's ass with a handful of banjos: referring to one with poor aim.

dead as a can of corned beef: dead.

doesn't use up all his kindlin' to make a fire: doesn't waste words on small talk.

don't go wakin' snakes: don't make waves.

enough to peel the hide off a gila monster: referring to cussing or to extremely hot weather.

grinnin' like a possum eatin' a yellow jacket: happy or embarrassed.

hardern' tyin' down a bobcat with a piece of string: difficult.

hot enough to wither a fence post: very hot.

loosened his hinges: said of one thrown from a horse.

mad as a peeled rattler: very mad.

mad enough to swallow a horn-toad backwards: very mad.

more gurgle 'n guts: referring to someone whose bark is worse than his bite.

more wind than a bull in green corn time: referring to someone who is full of hot air.

only a fool argues with a skunk, a mule or a cook: self-explanatory.

poor as a hind-tit calf: poor.

short as a tail hold on a bear: very short.

yuh can't hitch a horse with a coyote: referring to opposites who marry.

---

usually buried in a ravine or placed up in the fork of a tree. The Chippewa buried their dead in a sitting position, sometimes with a rooflike structure constructed over the grave. The Cheyenne placed the body on a scaffold. Only after several years had passed and the flesh was gone were the bones gathered and ultimately buried. The Dakotas or Sioux also placed bodies on scaffolds or in the forks of trees. The Shawnee adopted the white man's coffin burial but added their own twist: They cut a hole at the head of the casket to allow the deceased's spirit to enter and revisit the body. The Sauk and Fox buried about half of their dead in sitting positions, facing West.

1862: The body was still upon the scaffold, although so far decayed that the leg bones were visible on raising the side of the covering. It was dressed, and covered with the remains of a buffalo robe and a blanket, and in its present condition it was difficult to see which was the outside covering. The head was to the north.The body was lashed to the scaffold with raw hide and also with a hemp rope.

Lewis Henry Morgan, The Indian Journals, *p.153*

cache: a pit in the ground, sometimes dug as deep as eight feet, in which Indians stored food.

1823: He observed a recent mound of earth, about eight feet in height, which he was induced to believe must be a cache, or place of deposit, for spoils taken from an enemy. He saw several caches, which had been broken open and robbed of their corn by the Omahawhaws.

E. James, Rocky Mountain Expedition, *p.90*

calumet: the Indian's ceremonial peace pipe.

Cherokee: an Eastern tribe ultimately relocated to Oklahoma.

Cheyenne: a tribe that migrated from Minnesota and North and South Dakota to Colorado and Kansas, ultimately relocated to Oklahoma.

Chippewa: tribe of the high Plains of the United States and Canada.

clothing: before contact with white traders, a typical Plains Indian wore a skin shirt, leggings, moccasins and buffalo robe. Women wore long, deerskin dresses, knee-high leggings and moccasins.

Comanche: a powerful tribe of the southern Plains, ultimately relocated to Oklahoma.

coup: a feat of bravery that bestowed special status upon an Indian warrior of the Plains. One "counted coup" by touching an enemy's body with the hand or with a special stick, after the enemy had been wounded or killed. Touching an enemy's body was sometimes considered an even greater accomplishment than killing.

Cree: Indian tribe of the high Plains, largely in Canada.

Dakota: also known as the Sioux; a large group, with several subtribes, of the high Plains of the United States and southern Canada.

dogs: kept as pets and eaten by many tribes, including the Dakotas. The Arapahos were so widely known for their eating habits that they were called Dog-eaters by neighboring tribes. Dogs were also employed as sentries. Indian dogs were known to savagely attack strangers.

Dog soldiers: a military society or warrior club of Plains Indians.

earthlodge: a domelike structure covered with earth, sometimes holding up to forty people, used by the Omaha, Hidatsa and Pawnee tribes.

eyebrows: it was a practice of the Comanche to pluck out their eyebrows as a decorative device.

firedrill: a stick of wood whirled between the hands and pressed into a small hole in another piece of wood on the ground. It was the standard tool for lighting a fire before the white man introduced flint and steel, largely before the nineteenth century.

hair combs: the Plains Indians brushed their hair with the rough side of a buffalo tongue, porcupine bristles attached to a stick bound with rawhide, or horsehair bound with rawhide.

hairstyles: men of the Pawnee, Osage and Iowa tribes wore their hair closely cropped with a central ridge called a roach. Women of several tribes commonly parted their hair from the forehead to the nape of the neck and then painted the part line red. Omaha women wore two braids tied together at the ends, which were allowed to fall behind the ears. Blackfoot women wore their hair loose or in braids. The Crow often added horse hair to their own for decorative effect.

half breed: common nineteenth-century term for one who is part white and part Indian.

horse-raiding: the Indian practice of stealing horses from rival tribes.

Indian Territory: the territory that is now Oklahoma and a portion of Kansas. By 1840, all of the principal tribes east of the Mississippi, including the Kickapoo, Shawnee and Delaware from the Northeast and the Cherokee, Creek, Chickasaw, Seminole and Choctaw from the Southeast, had been relocated to this area by the U.S. government. In addition to natives already there and Western bands brought in later, some forty major tribes were making this territory their home by the end of the century.

kinnikinnic: Indian smoking blend of tobacco, sumac leaves and dogwood bark. (See also Food, Drink and Tobacco, p.181.)

lacrosse: a sport originated by the Indians, played by the Cheyenne, Iowa and Oto tribes.

maize: Indian name for corn.

medicine dance: a ritual dance employed by North American Indians to drive away disease and sickness.

medicine man: a shaman. He performed magic and was thought to have supernatural powers of healing. Many medicine men used sleight-of-hand to perform tricks and impress their laity.

Navajo: Indian tribe of the desert Southwest.

Nez Perce: tribe of the Northwest, inhabiting the territories of Oregon, Washington and Idaho.

paleface: Indian name for the white man.

Pawnee: tribe of the Plains, originally dwelling around the territory of Nebraska, but ultimately relocated to Oklahoma.

pemmican: sun-dried buffalo meat or venison pounded with a maul and mixed with fat, marrow and a dried cherry paste; an Indian staple.

powwow: a ceremony with dancing and feasting, employed by North American Indians to conjure good fortune on a hunt or in a war. Also, council or conference.
1840s: A murder was recently committed upon a Sioux by two Chippewas. The body of the murdered Indian was taken to the fort, where a most terrific powwow was held over it by the friends of the deceased, 300 in number. *Western newspaper*

savages: the nineteenth-century white man commonly called the Indians savages, although many whites thought the reverse was closer to the truth.

Shawnee: an Eastern and Midwestern tribe, ultimately relocated to Oklahoma.

shinny: popular game of field hockey, played mostly by Indian women.

Shoshone: Western tribe inhabiting the territory of Idaho, Utah, Wyoming and California.

signaling: the Indians used various methods to convey long-distance signals, the most famous of which was the smoke signal, produced by throwing wet leaves or wood on a fire or fanning a fire with a blanket or buffalo robe. A long column of smoke was sometimes used to signal a war party's success. Several columns side by side sometimes indicated the number of scalps taken. Puffs of smoke were used for more elaborate signaling.
  Other signaling methods: a flaming arrow shot into the night sky; a horse and rider riding back and forth on the summit of a high hill; a mirror (obtained from white traders) used to reflect the sun's rays.

sign language: the Plains Indians spoke different languages and dialects but had a common sign language. The hand gestures used were comparable to those used by the deaf today. Often, signs were logical and readily understood by anyone. "Cold," for example, was indicated by crossing the arms and clenching the fists in front of the chest and shivering. "Chief" was signed by pointing the forefinger up, then down. Rain or snow was indicated by holding the hands out and letting the fingers

hang toward the ground while pushing down. The "white man" was signed by drawing the right hand across the forehead to suggest a hat.
1862: He counted the days on his fingers, and to indicate a day put his thumb and forefinger together to represent the sun, and then passed it over the sky from east to west and then with a throw of the hand he indicated its setting. He turned down one finger to indicate one day. This he repeated five times to indicate five days. . . . For the Sioux he drew his finger across his throat, for the number of horses taken he put two fingers across a finger of the other hand, which means a man on a horse.
Lewis Henry Morgan, The Indian Journals, *pp.155-156*

Sioux: another name for the Dakota Indians.

Sun Dance: a ritual dance of some twenty different tribes. It was most noted for its element of self-torture. The dancers had skewers plunged into their breasts and backs, with ropes attached from the ends of the skewers to a central pole. The dancers strained against the attachments until they were torn free. The Pawnee, Wichita, Omaha and some southern Dakotas were not known to perform the Sun Dance.

sweat bath: a ceremonial vapor bath taken under a skin-covered hut. Steam was produced by heating stones and pouring water over them. Thoroughly sweated out, or purified, the participants ended the ritual bath by diving into a nearby creek to cool down.

thunderbird: in the lore of some tribes, the giant bird thought to produce thunder, lightning and rain.

tipi: a conical tent made of skins and used by the nomadic tribes of the Plains.
1880s: The typical tepee was a conical lodge of specially tanned elk or buffalo skins stretched over a framework. . . . The bottom of the tepee was held down by stones. The door was a slit opening, covered in bad weather by a shield-shaped flap. Within this circular interior with its ever present smoldering fire and simmering kettle, the tent wall was ingeniously wainscotted to a height of three or four feet with tanned buckskin. *John Barrows,* U-bet, A Greenhorn in Old Montana, *p.72*

travois: a crude sledge or litter, sometimes constructed of tipi poles and covering, used to carry belongings and sometimes the Indians themselves to new living sites. The travois was dragged along by a horse (early versions were hauled by dogs), with the high pole ends resting on the animal's shoulders and the lower end dragging on the ground.

war bonnet: the ceremonial, feathered headdress, worn by Indian warriors.

war pipe: a tobacco pipe carried by a leader and smoked by members of a war or horse-raiding party to help conjure good fortune.

war whistle: a bone whistle decorated with feathers. Before a battle, it was blown to symbolize the cry of the eagle and to appeal to the thunder to come to the warriors' aid. Used by the Dakotas and others.

weir: a fish trap used by some Plains tribes, especially the Cree.

wickiup: a crude Indian shelter constructed of a loose thatch of tree branches.
> 1878: The rest of the winter they pass in a half comatose state, crouching over a little fire in brush wickiups, or lying on the sunny side of a rock. *J.H. Beadle,* Western Wilds, *p.173*

Cattle Trails

California Trail: begun in the 1850s, leading from central Texas between Belton and San Antonio and through the waterless desert stretches of southern New Mexico and Arizona to southern California, sweeping up to the center of the state—just beyond San Francisco—to the gold diggings.

Chisholm Trail: a north-south trail running from points around Houston to Abilene, Kansas, used from 1867-1885.

Cox Trail: from central Kansas to northeast Oklahoma and joining with the Chisholm Trail at Pond Creek and Cimarron River in Oklahoma.

Dodge-Goodnight Trail: from Palo Duro Canyon in north Texas to Dodge City in Kansas.

Goodnight-Loving Trail: originating in the mid-1800s, from between Belton and San Antonio, Texas, and following the Pecos River to New Mexico and on to Pueblo, Colorado.

Northern Trail: from 1869-1875, beginning at northeast Montana and following the Yellowstone River to Boseman, through central Idaho to nearby Baker City, Oregon, where it joined with the Oregon Cattle Trail.

Oregon Cattle Trail from just northeast of Kansas City, Missouri, through Ogalalla, Nebraska, through Casper, Wyoming, then following the Snake River in Idaho through Oregon to a point just east of Portland.

Western Trail: from Dodge City, Kansas, to points along the Brazos River in Texas, to Belton.

Horses

bangtail: a wild horse; a mustang.

barefoot: said of an unshod horse.

bottom: endurance.
1872: I had a nail-driver, very swift, and no end to his bottom.
Life of Bill Hickman, *p.54*

breaking age: between 3½ and 4 years.

bridle: a sudden whiplashing or raising of the head. Also, the harness fitted around the head.

bridle wise: used to describe a horse that can be prompted to change direction when the rider lays the reins on the side of the neck the rider wishes to go.

bronco: a wild or untrained horse.
1875: One day I saw Jacky wrestling with a wild bronco, but he was afraid to mount him. . . . Taking hold of the rope I volunteered to take the wire edge off the bronco for him. He was a wiry Texas four-year-old, and he gave me a ride, as he bucked pretty hard at times.
Charles Siringo, A Cowboy Detective, *p.76*

broomtail: a horse with a long, bushy tail.

calf horse: one trained to back up and take up the slack after a calf has been roped.

canter: a three-beat gait or slow gallop.

caste: a state in which a horse is lying down in its stall and is unable to get up.

churn-head: slang for a stupid, stubborn horse.

cob: a stocky, short-legged horse.

cold back: an unbroken or green horse.

cow-hocked: a deformity in which the hind legs nearly meet at the hocks, similar to those of a cow.

crockhead: a stupid horse.

croppy: a nasty, ill-tempered or outlaw horse who has had its ears cropped to warn any potential rider of its temperament.

curry: to groom a horse with a currycomb.

currycomb: metal-toothed comb for grooming horses.

cutting horse: an agile, highly intelligent horse trained to corner and cut cattle out of a herd with little or no assistance from its rider.

HORSES OF ANOTHER COLOR
Colors and Markings

albino: white with blue eyes.

appaloosa: a distinct breed noted for its spotted rump.

bald: a white streak on a horse's face and covering one of its eyes. See also blaze.

bay: a reddish brown with a black mane and tail.

blaze: a broad, white streak running from between the eyes to the muzzle.

blood bay: a deep-red bay.

buckskin: beige with black mane and tail; may or may not have an eel stripe.

buttermilk: another name for a palomino.

calico: spotted or piebald; a pinto.

California sorrel: reddish gold.

chestnut: chestnut, bronze or coppery. Also known as sorrel.

claybank: yellowish cross of a sorrel and a dun.

cremello: cream albino with pink skin and blue eyes.

dappled: spotted or mottled.

dun: beige with a beige or brown mane and tail.

eel stripe: a dark stripe extending from the withers to the tail.

grulla: bluish-gray or mouse-colored. Also known as smokey.

medicine hat: black speckles found on mustangs, considered good luck by the Indians.

moros: bluish.

paint: patterned irregular white with colored areas. A pinto.

palomilla: milk white with white mane and tail.

palomino: light tan or golden with ivory mane and tail.

piebald: black and white.

pinto: a piebald, spotted or irregularly marked horse. Also known as a paint or Indian pony.

race: a crooked blaze on the forehead.

roan: bay, chestnut or sorrel sprinkled with gray or white.

sabino: light red or roan with a white belly.

skewbald: patches of white over any color except black. Sometimes humorously referred to as a stewball.

snip: a white marking along the nostril.

sock: white on leg below the fetlock.

sorrel: chestnut or brown.

star: a patch of white on the forehead.

stocking: any white extending above the fetlock. See Sock.

zebra dun: dun-colored with a dorsal stripe and stripes on its legs.

dobbin: a gentle farm horse.

draft horse: any large or strong horse bred for pulling or plowing, as on a farm.

epizootic: the cowboy's term for distemper, a common disease of horses.

fiddle: slang for the horse's head.

filly: a young female horse.

foal: a newborn.

forging: a running disorder caused by overextension in which the rear hooves scrape against the front hooves, especially when trotting.

gallop: a full run; a three-beat gait, faster than a canter.

gee: traditional command to a horse to turn right or go forward. See also haw.

gelding: a castrated male horse.

hammerhead: nickname for a stupid horse.

hand: a unit of measurement in which one hand equals about four inches.

haw: traditional horse command to turn left.

hogback: a horse with a rounded back; opposite of a swayback.

Indian broke: a horse trained to receive a rider mounting from the right or offside, Indian style, instead of from the left, as a white man mounted.

jib: nervous, fidgety foot movements.

jughead: another cowboy name for a stupid horse.

killer: any vicious horse.

knothead: a stupid horse.

lather: a horse's sweat.

livery: boarding and care of horses for pay.

livery man: one who stables and cares for horses for pay.

livery stable: where horses are boarded and tended for a fee.

loco: a horse's crazy behavior after eating locoweed on the range.

manada: Spanish term for a herd of mares.

manger: horse's wooden feeding trough.

mockey: a wild mare.

mule-hipped: a horse with hips that slope too much.

mustang: a wild horse.

navvy: a Navajo Indian pony, considered to be the worst quality horse by cowboys.

neigh: the cry of a horse.

nigger-heeled: term used to describe a horse whose toes point out.

notch in his tail: referring to a horse who has killed someone.

offside: the right side of a horse when viewed from the rear; Indians mounted horses on this side.

Oregon bigfoot: a cross of a riding horse and a draft horse such as a Percheron or Clydesdale, bred for mountain work in Oregon. Also known as Oregon puddin' foot.

outlaw: a vicious, untrainable horse.

owlhead: a horse that cannot be trained or ridden.

peg pony: a particularly agile horse; a cutting horse.

pigeon-toed: a horse having toes pointed in.

plug: an old, worn-out horse.

pole team: the horses aligned closest to a coach or wagon when more than one team is used.

puddin' foot: a horse with big feet; a clumsy horse.

quarterhorse: a horse adept at running the quarter-mile race, originally known as a short horse.

rack: cowboy term meaning to ride.

range horse: a horse bred on the range.

raw one: an untrained bronc.

rear: to stand up on its hind legs.

remuda: Spanish word for the strings of horses assigned to cowboys on a ranch. These horses were preferably geldings, numbering ninety to a hundred for an outfit of ten to twelve cowboys. One string was known as a mount. A remuda was known as a cavvy or saddle band in the Northwest.

ridge runner: a wild horse that watches from high ground to protect the herd from predators.

shavetail: a horse whose tail has been shaved, weeded out and thinned, or cut off. Northern ranches cut or pulled tails so that broken horses let out to roam on the range in the Fall could be easily identified from wild horses in the Spring, when they were rounded up again. Southern ranches tended mostly to weed or thin out tails.

short horse: a quarterhorse.

smooth mouth: an old horse.

snake eyes: nickname for a nasty, ill-tempered horse.

snorter: a horse that is easily agitated or excited.

snortin' post: a hitching post or rack.

span: a pair of horses working in tandem.

spooky: said of a nervous horse.

squaw horse: cowboy term for a next-to-useless horse.

steer horse: one trained to back up and take up the slack of a roped steer.

swayback: horse with a concave back.

turned the cat: said of a horse who is tripped by a prairie dog hole.

volt: a sideways step.

walkdown: catching wild horses by wearing them down on a run with spaced relay teams.

walleyed: a blue-eyed horse.

wet stock: horses smuggled illegally from Mexico. Any stolen horse.

whey belly: a pot-bellied horse.

witch's bridle: tangles in a horse's mane.

SURRENDER OF GEN. LEE!

"The Year of Jubilee has come! Let all the People Rejoice!"

200 GUNS WILL BE FIRED

On the Campus Martius,
AT 3 O'CLOCK TO-DAY, APRIL 10,
To Celebrate the Victories of our Armies. 1865

Every Man, Woman and Child is hereby ordered to be on hand prepared to Sing and Rejoice. The crowd are expected to join in singing Patriotic Songs. ALL PLACES OF BUSINESS MUST BE CLOSED AT 2 O'CLOCK. Hurrah for Grant and his noble Army.

By Order of the People.

SECTION FOURTEEN

CRIME

When it comes to lawlessness, nothing much changes from century to century. In the nineteenth century, much as now, intoxication, disorderly conduct, assault and battery, and petty larceny were the most common reasons for arrest in any big city. In New York in 1865, 68,873 arrests were made. Of these, 48,754 were males, 20,119 females; 53,911 arrests were for offenses against the person; 14,962 for offenses against property.

The chart on the next page breaks down New York's crime that year. A few items stand out. Drug arrests, for example—there were none, although thousands at the time were hooked on opium, openly sold in drugstores in pill form or as laudanum. Note also the greater arrest numbers for "keeping a disorderly house" and "bastardy" than for "attempt at rape."

assignation house: a house or hotel where prostitutes met their customers. Also known as a house of assignation. See also Bagnio.

badger: a panel thief. See also Panel thieving.

bagged: imprisoned.

bagnio: a brothel.
1872: Greene Street, with its horrible bagnios claims her next. She becomes the companion of thieves—perhaps a thief herself—and passes her days in misery.
James McCabe, Lights and Shadows of New York Life, *p.583*

balram: money.

bar-key: a bar or shaft of an ordinary key having a slot in which bits of various shapes and sizes could be inserted to fit and open simple locks, such as those on hotel room doors.

CHARGE	MALES	FEMALES	TOTAL ARRESTS
Assault and battery	6,077	1,667	7,744
Assault with intent to kill	197	1	198
Attempt at rape	40	–	40
Abortion	2	2	4
Bastardy	141	–	141
Bigamy	14	5	19
Disorderly conduct	8,542	5,412	13,050
Intoxication	11,482	4,936	16,418
Juvenile delinquents	154	25	179
Kidnapping	20	5	25
Suspicious persons	1,617	440	2,057
Vagrancy	978	838	1,816
Arson	35	–	35
Attempts to steal	236	9	245
Burglary	978	838	1,816
Forgery	151	3	154
Fraud	104	17	121
Grand larceny	1,675	946	2,621
Gambling	249	3	252
Highway robbery	199	6	205
Keeping disorderly house	177	165	342
Picking pockets	225	20	275
Petit larceny	3,380	1,860	5,240
Passing counterfeit money	414	46	460
Receiving stolen goods	166	51	217
Swindling	5	3	8
Violations of the Sunday laws	183	20	203

New York's population, according to the 1860 census, was 805,651.

barking iron: a pistol; a gun.
1825: [He] seeing the barking iron shrunk back.
   J.K. Paulding, John Bull in America, *p.56*
1847: Put up your barking iron, and no more noise.
   Le Fanu, T. Obrien, *p.63*

bastardy: the begetting of a bastard child.

bedchamber sneak: a thief's assistant, chiefly employed to obtain wax impressions of keys of places to be robbed.
1872: Closely allied with the Safe-blowers and bursters is a class known as Bed-chamber Sneaks. These men are employed by the burglars to enter dwellings and obtain impressions in wax of keys of the places

to be robbed. They adopt an infinite number of ways of effecting such an entrance, often operating through the servant girls. They never disturb or carry off anything, but confine their efforts to obtaining impressions. . . . The keys of business houses are mainly kept by the porters, into whose humble dwellings it is easier to enter. When they wish to obtain the keys of a dwelling, they come as visitors to the servant girls, and while they stand chatting with them manage to slip the key from the lock, take its impression in wax, and return it to the lock, unobserved by the girl.

James McCabe, Lights and Shadows of New York Life, *p.527*

bene: slang for first-rate.

bilk: to cheat.

bingo: slang for liquor.

black gown, get the: to be sentenced for a crime.

blackleg: a swindler, sharper or professional gambler, a term used widely from 1835-1870.
1845: A slight suspicion had crossed my mind that some of our card party might possibly be blacklegs—in other words, gamblers.
S. Smith, Theatr. Apprent., *p.147*

black Maria: a closed box coach, usually painted black, used as a police or prisoner transport van.
1847: A new Black Maria . . . a new wagon for the conveyance of prisoners to and from courts of justice. Boston Evening Traveller, *September 25*

bloke buzzer: a pickpocket who specializes in picking the pockets of men only. See also Moll buzzer.

boarding school: slang for the penitentiary.

bogus: anything fake, sham or forged, especially counterfeit money.
1842: Cowdery, Whitman, and others were guilty of perjury, cheating, selling bogus money [base coin], and even stones and sand for bogus.
John Clark, Gleanings by the Way, *p.340*
1850: We employed that same Bill Hickman to ferret out a bogus press and a gang of counterfeiters that were going into operation in our frontier country. James H. Mulholland was one of the principal actors in the bogus business. . . . A part of the bogus machine has been found here in Mulholland's possession. Frontier Guardian, *January 23*

boodle: counterfeit money. Also, stolen money.
1858: Boodle is a flash term used by counterfeiters. . . . The leaders [of the gang] were the manufacturers and bankers of the boodle.
Harper's Weekly, *April 3*

1888: The office [of a City Councilman] is an unsalaried one, and any money that is made out of it is boodle. Philadelphia Bulletin, *February 24*

Bowery boys: notorious ruffians or toughs from the Bowery in New York.
1840: The Bowery boys of New York have, in our opinion, eclipsed the nice young men of Baltimore. New Orleans Picayune, *August 28*

bowie knife: a very large knife, worn concealed in the back of the coat by criminals in the Southwest. The bowie knife was intended as an outdoor or hunting knife but was often used to intimidate and, in some cases, to commit murder. (See also Cowboys and the Wild West, p.240.)
1838: The trial of John Wilson, who officiated as Speaker of the Arkansas House of Representatives, during the last legislative session of that State, and who walked down from his chair and slew Major T.T. Anthony with a Bowie knife on the floor of the House, took place a few days ago. The verdict of the jury was, not guilty of murder, but excusable homicide. Louisville Journal
1841: [A resident of Washington] who entertained a strong feeling of resentment towards Mr. Wise, one of the members for Virginia, went constantly armed with loaded pistols and a long bowie knife, watching his opportunity to assassinate him. *J.S. Buckingham,* America, *p.356*

bugger: slang for a pickpocket.

bunco/bunko: to swindle.

burner: a swindler.
1842: The burners make better plots than most of our dramatists. Moreover, burners, male and female, are mortal men and women, have their frailties, and miss their figures occasionally.
Philadelphia Spirit of the Times, *January 15*
1842: An old convict and notorious burner, just out of the Moyamensing tombs, was caught in the vicinity of St. Stephen's Church, trying to wheedle a countryman. A lot of bad money, a book for telling fortunes, a pack of playing cards, and other things belonging to the burner's calling, were found upon his person.
Philadelphia Spirit of the Times, *February 21*
1844: Two negro burners were arrested in the act of trying to burn two Pottsville boatmen with a plated chain worth about fifteen cents.
Philadelphia Spirit of the Times, *August 19*

calaboose: a prison.

century: thieves' slang for one hundred dollars.

cooler: jail.

cracksman: a burglar, housebreaker or safecracker.

1899: The cracksman especially dreads the electric light, which can be turned on with such instantaneous brilliancy to expose him and his nefarious proceedings.

Major Arthur Griffiths, Mysteries of Police and Crime, p.179

1899: The most up-to-date cracksman has been known to use dynamite and other explosives, but few care to play with such excessively dangerous tools. *Major Arthur Griffiths, Mysteries of Police and Crime, p.184*

1884: In the years that have passed, marked improvements have been made in the tools and implements of these cracksmen. They no longer burden themselves with the heavy, massive, and unwieldly tools and appliances of former times, or those which even now are in use by the English burglar, but substitute for them small and ingenious, but powerful implements of their own design, and frequently of their own manufacture. Not the least important among these are the simple lamp and blow-pipe for destroying the temper of the metals upon which they operate, and which science has taught these gentry to dexterously use, to soften the hardened metals which heretofore had occasioned so much trouble, and necessitated such a vast amount of labor. The small and highly tempered drills, which silently and surely, gnaw their way into the very heart of a safe—and that wonderful invention, the diamond drill, which has been proven on several occasions to be more than a match for the hardest metals of modern manufacture. Then, too, there are the air-pump; the copper sledge-hammers and mallets with their coatings of leather, whose tremendous blows are scarcely heard; and the all-powerful "Jack-screw," which is capable of a pressure of tons. These and many other like improved and finished tools . . . comprise the implements of the burglar of the present day, and in practiced hands render powerful assistance in their nefarious operations.

Allan Pinkerton, Thirty Years a Detective, pp.265-266

dueling: the custom of settling a dispute between two men by setting a time and place and combating each other with pistols or other deadly weapons. The winner regained his honor while the loser was either injured or killed. This bizarre custom was practiced by some of the most learned men of the day, including top-ranking politicians. (See sidebar.)

(dueling) Code of Honor: a sixteen-page pamphlet setting forth the rules of dueling, published by Governor John Lyde Wilson of South Carolina from 1838 to 1858 and eventually apologized for and retracted by same.

dupe: one taken in by a swindle or confidence game.

false keys: filed-down skeleton keys.

1899: False keys are still largely used, and every burglar carries a whole

FAMOUS DUELS OF THE NINETEENTH CENTURY

Philip Hamilton (son of Alexander) vs. George Eacker, lawyer, Died this morning, in the twentieth year of his age
1801: Philip Hamilton, eldest son of General Hamilton — murdered in a duel.

On Friday morning last, young Hamilton and young Price, sitting in the same box with Mr. George I. Eacker, began in levity a conversation respecting an oration delivered by the latter in July, and made use of some expressions respecting it, which were overheard by Eacker, who asked Hamilton to step into the lobby. Price followed. Here the expression, "damned rascal," was used by Eacker to one of them, and a little scuffle ensued, but they soon adjourned to a public house. An explanation was then demanded, which of them the offensive expression was meant for; after a little hesitation, it was declared to be meant for each. Eacker then said, as they parted, "I expect to hear from you;" they replied, "You shall;" and challenges followed. A meeting took place, between Eacker and Price, on Sunday morning; which, after their exchanging four shots each, was finished by the interference of the seconds. [Ed. note: Assistants to the duelists were called seconds.]

Yesterday afternoon, the fatal duel was fought between young Hamilton and Eacker. Hamilton received a shot through the body at the first discharge, and fell without firing. He was brought across the ferry to his father's house, where he languished of the wound till this morning, when he expired.

. . . Reflections on this horrid custom must occur to every man of humanity; but the voice of an individual or of the press must be ineffectual without additional, strong, and pointed legislative interference. Fashion has placed it upon a footing which nothing short of this can control.

New York Evening Post, *November 24*

Aaron Burr vs. Alexander Hamilton, 1804

My religious and moral principles are strongly opposed to the practice of dueling, and it would ever give me pain to be obliged to shed the blood of a fellow creature in a private combat forbidden by the laws. . . . I am conscious of no ill will to Colonel Burr, distinct from political opposition, which, as I trust, has proceeded from pure and upright motives . . . it is not to be denied, that my animadversions on the political principles, character, and views of Colonel Burr, have been extremely severe; and on different occasions I, in common with many others, have made very unfavorable criticisms on particular instances of the private conduct of this gentleman.

From a note written by Hamilton before his murder in a duel with Aaron Burr

William Crawford, U.S. Senator, vs. John Clark, General, 1806
Crawford's wrist shattered by gunshot wound.

Andrew Jackson vs. Charles Dickinson, lawyer, 1806
Dickinson succumbed, his last words being, "Why have you put out the lights?" Jackson was wounded but recovered. He was later involved in "free-fighting" duel with Benton brothers.

M. De Grandpre vs. M. Le Pique, 1808
Following a dispute over a female, the two agreed to a duel while floating in balloons high above Paris. Grandpre punctured Le Pique's balloon with a blunderbuss. Le Pique and his second plunged a half mile to their deaths.

Thomas Benton, lawyer, vs. Charles Lucas, lawyer, 1817
A first meeting between the combatants resulted in a cut artery in Lucas's neck, which bled copiously and prevented him from continuing. A second meeting resulted in Lucas again being hit, this time the bullet lodging near his heart and killing him. Lucas forgave Benton and shook his hand as he lay dying.

James Barron, Commodore of the U.S. Navy, vs. Stephen Decatur, Commodore, U.S. Navy, 1820
Decatur shot through the abdomen. Barron shot in the thigh. Decatur perished within twelve hours. Barron survived.

Henry Clay, Secretary of State, vs. John Randolph, Senator, 1826
The first volleys missed their marks. In the second, Randolph's coat was struck by a bullet. "You owe me a coat, Mr. Clay," Randolph said, after which the combatants shook hands and, with great relief, concluded unharmed.

William Graves, Congressman, Kentucky, vs. Jonathan Cilley, Congressman, Maine, 1838
Cilley was killed and a public outrage against duelling followed.

James Watson Webb, editor of New York Courier and Enquirer, vs. Thomas Marshall, Congressman, Kentucky, 1842
The duel between Thomas F. Marshall and James Watson Webb was fought this morning at four o'clock, at the old duelling ground, just this side of the State line, about seven miles north of this city. Mr. Marshall was attended by Dr. Carr of Baltimore, as second, and Dr. Gibson, of the same place, as surgeon. Mr. Morrel, of your city, acted as Webb's friend.

The parties exchanged one shot without injury. Marshall demanded immediately a second pistol, and wounded Webb upon that fire, in the fleshy part of the hip, sustaining no damage himself. Marshall, who came determined to fight it out, demanded a third shot, but Webb could not stand it and the matter was made up. . . .

New York Herald, *June 25*

bunch of them when doing business. Half a dozen must often be tried, and more especially when dealing with a lever lock, before the

---

Thomas Clingman, Congressman, North Carolina, vs. William Yancey, Congressman, Alabama, 1845

The rules of the duel were put in writing by the seconds:

1. Weapons to be used, smooth-bore pistols of the usual duelling length.
2. Distance ten paces (thirty feet).
3. Pistols to be held perpendicular, the muzzles up or down, at their selection.
4. The word to be given in a clear, distinct tone, as follows, "Gentlemen, are you ready? Fire—one-two-three-halt!" at intervals of one second each.
5. The wind and sun to be equally divided.
6. The giving of the word and the choice of positions to be decided by the toss of a dollar.
7. The pistols to be loaded by the seconds with powder and single ball, in the presence of all parties.
8. Each party to be permitted to have on the ground a surgeon and three friends, all of whom must be unarmed.
9. The seconds to be armed with pistols, loaded with powder and single ball.
10. The seconds to be permitted to examine the person and dress of each principal.
11. Neither principal to commence lowering or raising his pistol before the word "fire" nor after the word "halt." This confrontation was, after a first missed volley, stopped by the police.

---

right one is found. They are, of course, skeleton keys, the central parts being filed away so that when inserted in a lock the key may miss its wards and principal parts and throw up the lever or bolt. *Major Arthur Griffiths,* Mysteries of Police and Crime, *p.183*

fanning: a pickpocket's term for feeling a mark's clothing for a wallet or pocketbook.

fence: one who received and sold stolen goods.

forking a super: slang for stealing a watch. See also Super, Super twister.

fox: thief's synonym for a police officer.

hoister: slang for a thief.

hoodlum: a ruffian; crook; criminal.

1876: Three hoodlums in San Francisco were convicted on a charge of stealing beer. . . . The friends of the hoodlums came forward and liquidated the damage. New York Tribune, *November 7*

1888: They were met by three young hoodlums, who jostled against the young lady. Missouri Republican, *April 1*

hook: in a pickpocketing scheme with one or more accomplices, the one who does the actual stealing. Also known as the tool. See also Stall.

1884: The thieves follow him within easy distance, but will not make any attempt to accomplish their purpose unless they notice that he is about to enter a crowded thoroughfare, a car, a narrow street, or through a hallway into a building. If in a crowd or narrow street the thieves will, without any preliminary notice whatever, act as follows: Two of the stalls will immediately manage to get in front of the man — and these men are called front stalls — this is done for the purpose of stopping him or blocking his way for a moment when the time arrives. The tool or hook will also get slightly ahead of the man, and when the moment for action arrives a slight cough will bring the two front stalls to a standstill. This, of course, impedes the progress of the victim. Quick as a flash, and yet with an ease of motion that attracts no particular attention, the tool turns sideways, almost facing the man, but upon his right side. The tool usually carries a coat upon his arm for the purpose of covering his hand; with the concealed hand he will work under the man's coat, and taking the wallet or package by the top, will raise it straight up, until it's entirely clear of the pocket; then drawing it under his own coat, the robbery is complete. During this operation, which requires but a few seconds, the stall behind the man is pushing and shoving him repeatedly on the left side, as if with the intention of getting past him.
Allan Pinkerton, Thirty Years a Detective, *pp.39-40*

house of ill-fame: euphemism for a whorehouse.

iron worker: slang for a safe cracker.

jimmy: a bar or crowbar used to pry open doors, chests of drawers, boxes, etc.; the burglar's favorite tool.

1884: A great many fire proof safes throughout the country have been opened simply by the pick and jimmy. With safes that are manufactured of ordinary plate iron, all that is necessary is, first with several well directed blows with a pick to make an aperture just sufficient to receive the sharp end of the jimmy in one corner of the panel, then with the jimmy the iron is ripped and torn out the whole length of the panel, thus exposing the filling — the latter is picked out in a few moments — the bent end of the jimmy is then inserted behind the bolt, and the same pried back by main force, breaking the wards in the lock. This operation has frequently been performed in from 15 to 20 minutes. *Allan Pinkerton,* Thirty Years a Detective, *p.314*

kick: code word used by pickpockets to communicate which pocket a wallet or money is in, e.g., left kick.

kid: a child pickpocket.

1872: These are usually termed kids, and are very dangerous, as people are not inclined to suspect them. They work in gangs of three or four, and, pushing against their victim, seize what they can, and make off.
James McCabe, Lights and Shadows of New York Life, *p.532*

knuck: a thief.

1848: There is a house in Cherry St. . . . [that] has been known to the crossmen and knucks of the town as "Jack Circle's Watering Place" and "fence." *Judson*, Mysteries of New York, *p.33*

leather: slang for a pocketbook.

leatherhead: a policeman.

1888: The old police or leatherheads tried to restrain them.
New York Mercury, *July 21*

lynch: to execute someone (usually by hanging) without due process of law. Also called Judge Lynch or Judge Lynch's law.

1827: . . . a Mr. McNeily having lost some clothing or some other property of no great value, the slave of a neighboring planter was charged with the theft. McNeily in company with his brother found the negro driving his master's wagon; they seized him and either did or were about to chastize him, when the negro stabbed McNeily so that he died in an hour afterwards. The negro was taken before a justice of the peace, who after serious deliberation waived his authority — perhaps through fear, as the crowd of persons from the above counties [Bibb and Perry in Georgia] had collected to the number of seventy or eighty near Mr. Peoples' (the justice) house. He acted as president of the mob and put the vote, when it was decided he should be immediately executed by being burnt to death. The sable culprit was led to a tree and tied to it, and a large quantity of pine knots collected and placed around him, and the fatal torch was applied to the pile even against the remonstrances of several gentlemen who were present: and the miserable being was in a short time burnt to ashes. The sheriff of Perry County, with a company of about twenty men, repaired to the neighborhood where this barbarous act took place, to secure those concerned, with what success we have not heard: but we hope he will succeed in bringing the perpetrators of so high-handed a measure to account.
Washington National Intelligencer, *July 23*

mark: a thief's selected victim.

mob: a group of criminals working together.

moll buzzer: a pickpocket who specializes in stealing from women.

necktie sociable: a hanging; a lynching.
1878: [He presided] at a necktie sociable, where two of the men who
had robbed him were hanged. *J.H. Beadle*, Western Wilds, *p.46*

nerve tonic: whiskey.

off the crook: to abandon crime either temporarily or permanently.

out on hocus pocus: released from custody by the clever work of a lawyer.

overhaul: to frisk someone or to search one's premises.
1872: If they once get sight of them, the police rarely fail to overhaul
the thieves. *James McCabe*, Lights and Shadows of New York Life, *p.538*
1872: Their shops are overhauled almost every week by the detectives
in searching for stolen property, and the pawnbrokers . . . prefer to
turn this business entirely to the fences.
James McCabe, Lights and Shadows of New York Life, *p.547*

pad the hoof: to leave a crime scene as quietly as possible.

palm nippers: thief's small wire cutters, used to snip jewelry from a
mark's ear or neck.

panel crib: a prostitute's room, constructed with a secret compartment
or closet to be used by a panel thief.
1848: We will leave her to seek a victim for her panel crib, for she has
long been an active panel thief. *Judson*, Mysteries of New York, *p.14*

panel thieving: popular method of stealing money and watches from the
customers of prostitutes.
1872: . . . panel thieving . . . is closely connected with street walking. The
girl in this case acts in concert with a confederate, who is generally a
man. She takes her victim to her room, and directs him to deposit his
clothing on a chair, which is placed but a few inches from the wall at
the end of the room. This wall is false, and generally of wood . . . a
visitor cannot detect the fact that it is a sham. A panel, which slides
noiselessly and rapidly, is arranged in the false wall, and the chair
with the visitor's clothing upon it is placed just in front of it. While
the visitor's attention is engaged in another quarter, the girl's confederate, who is concealed. . . . slides back the panel, and rifles the pockets of the clothes. . . . The panel is then noiselessly closed.
James McCabe, Lights and Shadows of New York Life, *p.593*

pennyweighter: a jewel thief.

pettifogger: an unscrupulous lawyer.
1796: A little dirty attorney, ready to undertake any litigious or bad
case. *Captain Frances Grose*, Classical Dictionary of the Vulgar Tongue
1843: Ignorant blackguards, illiterate blockheads, besotted drunkards,

drivelling simpletons, ci devant mountebanks, vagabonds, swindlers and thieves make up, with but few exceptions, the disgraceful gang of pettifoggers who swarm about its [New York City Prison, the Tombs] halls. New York City Subterranean, *July 22*

pinched: to be caught by the police.

police: known as watchmen or constables early in the century, and patrolmen or roundsmen in the second half of the century. With the advent of gas street lighting, patrolmen sometimes doubled as lamplighters. Much like today, patrolmen walked a beat in a district. They were observed (often secretly) on their beats by roundsmen — men of lesser rank than sergeants, who in turn were below captains. Police uniforms were worn in Boston, New York and Philadelphia from about midcentury on.
1872: The uniform of the force is a frock coat and pants of dark blue navy cloth, and a glazed cap. In the summer the dress is a sack and pants of dark blue navy flannel. The officers are distinguished by appropriate badges. Each member of the force is provided with a shield of a peculiar pattern, on which is his number. This is his badge of office, and he is obliged to show it when required. The men are armed with batons or shot clubs of hard wood, and revolvers. The latter they are forbidden to use except in grave emergencies. *James McCabe,* Lights and Shadows of New York Life, *p.174*

prostitution: widespread throughout the century, with an especially booming business during the Civil War. A census taken in New York in the 1860s uncovered some 700 houses of prostitution and more than 2500 streetwalkers. At about the same time, Washington, D.C., boasted 450 of its own bawdy houses or bordellos. Among them: the Blue Goose, the Haystack, the Ironclad, Hooker's Headquarters, and Mother Russel's Bake Oven.
1868: A peculiarity of the Twenty-ninth Police Precinct . . . in which the majority of the better class of houses are located, is the large number of lady boarders, who do nothing, apparently, for a living. They live in furnished rooms, or they may board in respectable families. They leave their cards with the madame of the house, together with their photograph. They live within a few minutes call, and when a gentleman enters the parlor he has a few minutes' chat with the madame, who hands him the album. He runs his eye over the pictures, makes his choice, and a messenger is dispatched for No. 12 or 24. These are what may be termed the day ladies, or outside boarders. Some of them are married, living with their husbands, who know nothing of what is going on. . . . Those ladies who hire furnished rooms all dine at restaurants, but they are never found soliciting men in the street. *Edward Winslow Martin,* Secrets of the Great City, *pp.294-295*

prussic acid: also known as nux vomica or ox vomit, a poison used by burglars to put away any troublesome watchdog.

pulled: to get caught by the police.

punishments: usually jail time but also use of the pillory, early in the century, and hangings, throughout the century. Boston police records illustrate some of the crimes criminals were hung for:

1812: Samuel Tully, for piracy, hung on Nook's Hill at South Boston. John Dalton, an accomplice was reprieved on the gallows.

1822: Gilbert Close and Samuel Clisby hung on the Neck lands, near the burying grounds, for robbing Ezra Haynes in Cambridge Street, on the tenth of August last.

1822: Samuel Green hung on the Neck lands for killing Billy Williams in State Prison, in November last.

1831: Joseph Gadett, and Thomas Colinett, hung in the rear of Leverett Street jail, for piracy.

1835: Pedro Gilbert, Manuel Costello, Monelle Bogga, Jose Bassello De Costa, and Angeloa Garcia, five Spanish pirates, hung in the rear of Leverett Street Jail.

1836: Simeon Crockett and Stephen Russel, for setting fire to Mr. Hammond's house in South Street Place, were hung in the jail yard.

1850: Professor John Webster hung at the jail yard for the murder of Dr. George Parkman, the 23rd of November last, at the Medical College.

put up: a burglary assisted by a servant or other person with free access inside a home or business.

1899: In most cases the job is put up, as the saying is—in other words, assistance is obtained from inside, one or more of the servants are suborned, especially the female servants, one of the burglars being told off to ingratiate himself with some maid, whose "follower" he becomes if he can, and so gains all the information he requires.
Major Arthur Griffiths, Mysteries of Police and Crime, *p.181*

rascal: commonly used term for a corrupt or criminal character.

rat pit: a pit or crib constructed in the cellar of a bar where gamblers go to bet on how many rats a selected dog can kill in a specified amount of time. Sometimes dog fights were conducted in these arenas. At other times a dog was pitted against a woodchuck or raccoon (known as the chuck game).

1873: The pit consists of a board crib of octagon form in the centre of the cellar, about eight feet in diameter and three and one half feet high. . . . On three sides of the cellar are rows of board seats, rising one above the other, for the accommodation of spectators. On the other side stands the proprietor and his assistant and an empty flour barrel, only it is half full of live rats. . . . The ampitheatre is lighted with oil lamps or candles, with a potatoe, a turnip, or an empty bottle for a candlestick. Spectators are admitted at twenty five cents a head, and take their seats. . . . The proprietor . . . with an instrument looking much like a pair of curling tongs, begins fishing out his game, rat by rat, depositing each carefully inside the pit until the requisite number are pitted. The assistant has brought in the dog, Flora, a favorite ratter, which he is obliged to hold fast by the nape of the neck, so eager is she for the fray. Then commences the betting which runs high or low according to the amount of funds in the hands of the sports.

"A dollar. She kills twenty rats in twelve seconds!" "I take that!" "Half a dollar on the rats!" "Don't put in them small rats!" "Two dollars on Flora in fifteen seconds!" "Done, at fourteen!" "No, you don't!" "Don't put in all your big rats at once!"

Flora evidently understands that her credit is at stake; but the growling, and champing, and squealing, and scratching is soon over, and the twenty rats lie lifeless at the feet of the bloodthirsty Flora, when time is again called, and the bets decided, and all hands go up and liquor. The exhibition is repeated several times, with different dogs, and lasts as long as the live rats holdout. [Ratting was sometimes followed by the chuck game. See above.]
Edward Savage, Police Records and Recollections, *pp.161-162*

ratter: a dog trained to kill rats in a rat pit.

reefing: a pickpocketing technique in which a mark's pocket lining is pulled up with two fingers in order to get at a wallet.

road agent: a highway robber. A criminal who specializes in robbing stagecoaches.

1869: This organization became known as Road Agents, from the fact that they committed most of their depredations on the routes of travel; and to this day no other term is applied to highway robbery in the Far West. They numbered over fifty desperate men, all well armed and skilled in the use of weapons, and had besides probably a hundred or more outside allies and dependents.
A.K. McClure, Rocky Mountains, *p.230*

1881: The great distances between the settlements enable the road agents to have a fine time of it.
MacMillan's Magazine, *xlv, p.124*

1890: It could hardly be expected that a well-traveled road like this, over which so much treasure was being transported, should be free from the inquisitive eye of the road agent.

Haskins, Argonauts of California, *p.208*

rogue: commonly used term for a criminal or ruffian; a bad man; a scoundrel.

1872: Strange as it may seem, the city is constantly suffering from similar robberies, and the rogues almost invariably escape.

James McCabe, Lights and Shadows of New York Life, *p.529*

rogues' gallery: a picture gallery of wanted criminals, displayed in police headquarters.

1861: A rogue's picture-gallery was also commenced, and about one hundred valuable likenesses collected.

Edward Savage, Police Records and Recollections, *p.101*

rook: to rip someone off; to swindle or cheat someone.

rough: a ruffian; a tough-looking or tough-acting character.

rounder: a habitual offender.

1881: A rounder from Baltimore, who claimed to have "influence" with the Maryland delegation, was paid five thousand dollars.

Boston Globe, *August 30*

1891: The regular rounders . . . are beginning to receive long sentences.

Boston Journal, *July 7*

rowdy: a ruffian; a punk; a troublemaker.

1819: Mr. B said the Rowdies had threatened him with assassination.

W. Faux, Memorable Days, *p.284*

1824: The riotous roisters, or, as they are here called, rowdies, will fight for the mere love of fighting.

Arthur Singleton, Letters from the South and West, *p.93*

1864: A mass of swearing, gaming, drinking rowdies.

J.G. Holland, Letters to the Joneses, *p.19*

safe blower/burster/breaker: burglars adept at breaking into safes by various means.

1872: The safeblowers are accounted the most skillful. They rarely force an entrance into a building, but admit themselves by means of false keys made from wax impressions of the genuine keys. Once inside they lower the windows from the top about an inch. This is usually sufficient to prevent the breaking of the glass by the concussion of the air in the room, and not enough to attract attention from without. The safe is then wrapped in wet blankets, to smother the noise of the explosion. Holes are then drilled in the door of the safe near the lock, these are filled with powder, which is fired by a fuse, and the safe is blown open. . . .

The safe-bursters are the silent workers of the profession. . . . They first make the safe so fast to the floor, by means of clamps, that it will resist any degree of pressure. Then they drill holes in the door, and into these fit jack-screws worked by means of levers. The tremendous force thus exerted soon cuts the safe literally to pieces. . . .

The safe-breakers . . . are looked upon with contempt . . . by their more scientific associates in crime. They enter buildings by force, and trust to the same method to get into the safes. Their favorite instrument is a jimmy. . . . With this they pry open the safe, and then knock it to pieces with a hammer. They are not as successful as the others in their operations, and are most frequently arrested. *James McCabe*, Lights and Shadows of New York Life, *pp.526-527*

1884: Several modes of blowing a safe with powder have been used, but the easiest and more general one is to drill a hole into the lock, and then force powder through this hole and explode it, which would result in the destruction of the lock and the removal of all obstacles. . . . In this process very frequently gun-cotton and nitro-glycerine have been used as the explosives, and an ingenious sort of syringe is used for this purpose. *Allan Pinkerton*, Thirty Years a Detective, *p.311*

sandbagger: a robber who uses a sandbag to knock out or stun his victim.

1888: Kansas City is the only town in the world where women are sandbagged. Missouri Republican, *January 25*

scoundrel: a rogue; a criminal; a villain.

scratcher: a forger.

shadow: to follow someone secretly, as a detective. Also, a detective.

1877: The detectives followed two men whom they had been shadowing, from Prince Street to the office of the American Express Company. New York Tribune, *January 4*

sharper: a swindler; a crook.

1884: Meredith was what is known as an Oil Sharper, who had been identified with several fraudulent oil companies. *Allan Pinkerton*, Thirty Years a Detective, *p.579*

shooting iron: a gun or a pistol.

1834: In spite of your silver-mounted shooting iron. Novellettes of a Traveler, *ii, p.175*

1853: Drop yer shootin' iron, or ye'll get more'n ye send. Paxton, A Stray Yankee in Texas, *p.51*

shyster: an unscrupulous lawyer. See also Pettifogger.

1857: The shysters, or Tombs lawyers, were on hand, and sought to intercede for their clients. New York Tribune, *March 13*

six-shooter: a revolver with six chambers.

1855: I regard Col. Colt's six-shooter as the most formidable fire-arm that can be placed in the hands of men engaged in close quarters. *Mr. Lane, Oregon, House of Reps.,* Congressional Globe, *February 3*

skin game: any fraudulent card game or other game of gambling; a swindle.

slang: thieves' slang for a watch chain.

spot: thieves' slang for a policeman.

stall: in a pickpocketing team, one who watches where a wallet or cash is placed (which pocket) after a mark's bank transaction and communicates this to the hook or tool. A stall may also work to block a mark's path suddenly so the tool can get at him. Any accomplice used to distract a mark in some way while another accomplice frisks the mark for money or jewelry.

sugar: thieves' slang for stolen money.

Sunday Blue Laws: laws prohibiting business, travel and sporting events on the Sabbath. Some jurisdictions, particularly those in New England, maintained these laws throughout the century. (Maine enforced its Sunday closing law as late as 1991.) Some cities went as far as to rope off their streets to restrict buggy travel. Other communities were even stricter. In 1893, the New York Court of Appeals upheld a conviction against a man who was caught on a Sunday fishing on a private lake.

super: thieves' slang for a watch.

super twister: a pickpocket specializing in stealing watches.

swag: thieves' slang for stolen money.

swartwout: to swindle someone and flee.

1839: Considerable excitement prevailed at Cincinnati, in consequence of the real or supposed swartwouting [of a bank cashier]. New Bedford Daily Mercury, *September 18*

1841: [Mr. Howard] talked to us about the land officers Swartwouting, and all that. *Mr. Kennedy, Indiana, House of Reps.,* Congressional Globe, *June 30*

swartwouter: one who swindles and flees.

sweat-box: another name for the forced confessions solicited from criminals by the police through the third degree.

1902: The prisoner has become almost a physical wreck, under the sweat-box ordeal. New York Nation, *August 28, p.169*

tool: see Hook.

touching a jug: thieves' parlance for robbing a bank.

tumbled: to get caught by the police.

turn trick: distracting a mark from his money so that it can be stolen. This was commonly done at a bank's counting table. The thief would purposely drop a ten-dollar bill on the floor, then tap some innocent dupe on the back and ask, "Is that your ten on the floor?" While the dupe bent over to pick up the ten the thief or his accomplice would make off with part of any money left on the counting table. By the time the dupe discovered some of his money was missing, the crooks would be long gone.

wax impressions: obtaining an impression of a safe, vault or building key in a glob of wax in order to produce an exact duplicate for criminal purposes.

weeding: pickpocket's slang for removing bills from a wallet while the wallet remained intact in a mark's pocket. Also known as weeding a leather.

whisk: pickpocket's slang for frisking or searching a mark's person for money.

widdy: a device used by thieves to unlock a lock.
1884: The widdy is a small piece of bent wire with a string attached, forming a sort of bow. With this simple instrument running through a keyhole, if the bolt is below the lock, or a gimlet hole made for the purpose, if above the lock, a burglar can throwback any mortise, spring or sliding bolt now in use.
Allan Pinkerton, Thirty Years a Detective

Chronology of Events

1800: Capital moved from Philadelphia to Washington.
Land Act passed; allows frontier land of 320 acres to be purchased for as little as $160.

1801: Thomas Jefferson, President; Aaron Burr, Vice President.
District of Columbia established.
Tripoli declares war against the United States.
John Chapman (Johnny Appleseed) spreads his seeds throughout Ohio, Indiana and Illinois.

1802: West Point Military Academy established.

1803: Louisiana purchased for fifteen million dollars.
Ohio becomes seventeenth state.

1804: Vice President Burr kills Alexander Hamilton in duel at Weehawken, New Jersey.

1805: Jefferson begins second term; George Clinton, Vice President.

1806: Zebulon Pike travels west, names Pike's Peak.

1807: Robert Fulton tests steamboat *Clermont* on Hudson River, ushering in steamboat era.

1808: Slave trade with Africa banned.

1809: James Madison becomes fourth president: George Clinton, Vice President.

1810: Rebels in west Florida take over Spanish fort at Baton Rouge; west Florida annexed from Baton Rouge.

1811: Trading posts among Indians established.
Battle of Tippecanoe with Indians.
First steamboat on the Ohio River.
Construction of Cumberland Road (National Road), from Cumberland, Maryland, to Wheeling, West Virginia, begins; completed 1818.

1812: Louisiana admitted as state.
United States declares war on Great Britain. British vessels captured.
Canada invaded.

1813: Perry captures English fleet on Lake Erie.
Madison reelected; Elbridge Gerry, Vice President.
Toronto, Canada, captured.

1814: British burn buildings in Washington, D.C., bomb Fort McHenry at Baltimore.
Frances Scott Key writes "Star Spangled Banner."
Americans defeat English fleet in the battle of Lake Champlain.

1815: Battle of New Orleans, Jackson defeats British.

Peace Treaty ratified with Great Britain.

Algerian war.

1816: U.S. bank chartered by Congress.

First steamboat on Great Lakes.

Indiana admitted.

1817: James Monroe, President; Daniel Tompkins, Vice President.

Mississippi admitted.

Construction of Erie Canal begins.

Seminole Wars.

1818: Illinois admitted.

Andrew Jackson captures Spanish forts in Florida.

1819: The *Savannah*, first transatlantic steamship.

Alabama admitted.

Spain sells Florida to United States for five million dollars.

Economic depression begins.

1820: New York is America's largest city with a population of 124,000; Philadelphia is second with 113,000; Baltimore third with 63,000.

Maine, formerly a part of Massachusetts, admitted.

Missions begun in Hawaii.

1821: Monroe elected to second term: Daniel Tompkins, Vice President.

Missouri Compromise Bill passed.

Missouri admitted.

1823: Monroe Doctrine.

1825: John Quincy Adams, President; John Calhoun, Vice President.

Erie Canal completed.

1827: First railway in United States constructed in Massachusetts.

1828: Protective Tariff Bill passed, setting high rates on imports.

1829: Andrew Jackson, President; John Calhoun, Vice President.

Welland Canal from Port Dalhousie to Port Robinson (Canada) completed.

1830: Indian Removal Bill signed, authorizing Indians in the Southeast to be moved to lands west of the Mississippi.

First steam locomotive, *Tom Thumb*, built in Baltimore, loses race against horse-drawn train after mechanical failure.

Nat Turner slave rebellion in Virginia.

1832: Black Hawk War.

1833: Jackson reelected; Martin Van Buren, Vice President.

1834: Whig Party first takes its name.

1835: First assassination attempt against a U.S. president; guns misfire and Jackson is unharmed.

Second Seminole War begins.

1836: Massacre at Alamo, Texas.

First railway in Canada.

1837: Martin Van Buren, President; Richard Johnson, Vice President.
Economic panic and depression.

1840: First regular steamship service betwen Boston and Liverpool;
a crossing takes fifteen days.
Wilkes discovers Antarctic continent.

1841: William Harrison, President; John Tyler, Vice President.
Harrison dies on April 4, Tyler takes over as President.
New York Tribune founded by Horace Greeley.

1842: Ashburton Treaty settles boundary between United States and
Canada.

1843: First substantial wagon to Oregon leaves Independence, Missouri, on May 22, ushers in "Oregon Fever."

1844: Samuel Morse's famous first telegraph message, "What hath
god wrought," sent from Baltimore to Washington, D.C.,
ushering in telegraph era.

1845: Texas annexed to the United States.
James Polk, President; George Dallas, Vice President.
Florida admitted.
Texas admitted.
Oil discovered near Pittsburgh.

1846: Mexican War begins.
Smithsonian Institution established in Washington.
Iowa admitted.
Mormons follow Brigham Young from Illinois to Utah.

1847: Mormons found Salt Lake City.
Mexican War ends after Mexico City surrenders.

1848: Gold discovered in Sacramento, California.
Wisconsin admitted.
Mexican Peace Treaty signed, United States acquires California, New Mexico.
First Women's Rights Convention, Seneca Falls, New York.

1849: Zachary Taylor, President; Millard Fillmore, Vice President.
Gold rush to California begins.

1850: Taylor dies, Millard Fillmore takes over as President.
California admitted.
Slave trading banned in Washington, D.C.

1851: *New York Times* founded.

1852: *Uncle Tom's Cabin* published, sells three hundred thousand copies first year, over a million in the second.

1853: Franklin Pierce, President; Rufus King, Vice President.
United States buys southern Arizona and New Mexico from
Mexico for ten million dollars.

1854: Republican Party formed.

1856: Grand Trunk Railroad (Canada) opened.
1857: James Buchanan, President; J.C. Breckenridge, Vice President.
Dred Scott decision.
Haugwout's five-story department store opens in New York City, R.H. Macy's follows in 1858.
1858: Minnesota admitted.
First message over transatlantic cable sent.
1859: Oregon admitted.
John Brown's raid.
Gold rush to Colorado and Nevada.
First oil well drilled, Titusville, Pennsylvania.
1860: Pony Express mail service begins between St. Joseph, Missouri, and Sacramento, California.
South Carolina secedes from Union.
1861: Abraham Lincoln, President; Hannibal Hamlin, Vice President.
Secession of Mississippi, Florida, Alabama, Georgia, Louisiana and Texas; Virginia, Tennessee, Arkansas and North Carolina eventually follow and form Confederacy.
Kansas admitted as thirty-fourth state.
First income tax (3 percent of income over eight hundred dollars) implemented.
Transcontinental telegraph becomes operational; Lincoln receives message from California.
Jefferson Davis, President of Confederate States; A.H. Stephens, Vice President.
1862: Battle between *Merrimac* and *Monitor*.
Slavery abolished in District of Columbia.
Capture of Fort Henry.
Grant takes Ft. Donelson.
Battle of Shiloh.
Battle of Antietam.
Greenbacks issued for the first time.
Homestead Act signed; a 160-acre tract of Plains land is granted free to any settler who lives on it for five years.
1863: Emancipation Proclamation.
West Virginia admitted.
Battle of Gettysburg.
Fall of Vicksburg.
Gettysburg Address, November 19.
1864: Nevada admitted.
Battles of Wilderness, Spotsylvania, Cold Harbor and Petersburg cost Grant 68,000 soldiers, either wounded or killed.
Sherman's march to the sea.

1865: Lincoln reelected; Andrew Johnson, Vice President.
Lee surrenders at Appomattox.
Lincoln assassinated at Ford's Theater.
Andrew Johnson becomes President.
Reconstruction begins.

1866: Western Union monopolizes telegraph services after absorbing U.S. Telegraph Co.
Civil Rights Bill passed after Johnson's veto is overridden.

1867: Nebraska admitted.
Black males given right to vote in Washington, D.C.
"Seward's Folly"; Senate agrees to buy Alaska from Russia for $7.2 million.
Ku Klux Klan organized in Tennessee.
Cattle-driving era begins in earnest after first rail shipment of cattle from Abilene, Kansas, to Chicago stockyards.

1868: President Johnson impeached, tried and acquitted.
Seven Southern states readmitted to Union.

1869: Fifteenth Amendment passed.
U.S. Grant, President; Schuyler Colfax, Vice President.
Union-Pacific Railroad opened.
National Woman Suffrage Association founded.

1870: Northern Pacific Railroad begun.
Four more Southern states readmitted to Union.

1871: Victoria Woodhull advocates women's suffrage and "free love" rights outside marriage before House Judicial Committee.
P.T. Barnum opens circus in Brooklyn.
Great Chicago fire.

1872: Yellowstone National Park established.
Three million buffalo killed annually for hides; only two hundred survive on Plains by 1883.
Grant reelected; Henry Wilson, Vice President.

1873: Financial panic in New York.
First School of Nursing established at Bellevue Hospital.
First cable cars in San Francisco.

1874: One of the worst grasshopper plagues in U.S. history wipes out Great Plains wheat crop.
First electric streetcar in New York.

1875: Civil Rights Act guarantees blacks equal access in all public places, including public transportation.

1876: Telephone demonstrated by Bell.
Centennial Exposition in Philadelphia.
Custer's massacre by Crazy Horse and Sitting Bull.

1877: Rutherford B. Hayes, President; William Wheeler, Vice President.

First telephone lines established from Salem to Boston, and from Chicago to Milwaukee.

1879: First Woolworth store opens in Lancaster, Pennsylvania.

French Atlantic cable laid.

1880: Cattle business booms in the West.

1881: James Garfield, President; Chester Arthur, Vice President.

President Garfield shot, July 2; Chester Arthur becomes President on September 20 after Garfield succumbs to blood poisoning.

Clara Barton establishes American Red Cross.

1882: War with Apache Indians.

1883: Northern Pacific Railroad completed.

Brooklyn Bridge opened.

United States adopts standard time zones to facilitate railroad scheduling; Canada adopts same time zones.

1884: Ohio Valley floods.

Financial crisis in New York.

1885: Grover Cleveland, President; Thomas Hendricks, Vice President.

1886: Unveiling of Statue of Liberty.

Drought begins in Plains.

1888: Chinese immigration prohibited.

1889: Benjamin Harrison, President; Levi Morton, Vice President.

Johnstown flood.

North Dakota, South Dakota, Washington and Montana admitted.

1890: Idaho and Wyoming admitted.

Massacre at Wounded Knee.

1891: Edison seeks patent for motion picture camera.

Canadian Pacific Railway completed.

1893: Grover Cleveland, President; Adlai Stevenson, Vice President.

Great economic depression.

Ford tests his gasoline-powered buggy in Detroit.

1894: Great railroad strike.

1895: Sears, Roebuck begins mail-order business.

1896: Utah admitted as forty-fifth state.

Segregation in public places ruled constitutional.

1897: William McKinley, President; Garret Hobart, Vice President.

Yukon gold rush.

First subway completed, in Boston.

1898: Destruction of USS *Maine* in Havana Harbor.

War with Spain.

Spanish fleet destroyed at Manila.

Santiago, Cuba, surrenders to United States.

Treaty of Paris: United States acquires sovereignty over Cuba, Puerto Rico, and the Philippines.

1899:   Peace treaty with Spain signed by McKinley.

Congress authorizes use of voting machines for federal elections.

Chronology of Noted Books and Novels

(Selected books and novels, some classic, some simply popular in their time.)

1796: *American Cookery*, Amelia Simmons. America's first cookbook, with several editions published from 1800-1900.

1800-1900: Almanacs. Almanacs were read by all classes of people throughout the century, with literally hundreds of different "farmers' almanacs" being published as early as 1820. Some had been around since the 1700s. (*The Farmer's Almanac* was founded in 1792.) In many families, the annual almanac was the only "literature" read all year.

1800: *Aristotle's Masterpiece*, anonymous. A "sex" book masquerading as the work of the Greek philosopher. It featured woodcuts and descriptions of bodies, the mechanics of intercourse, etc. Originally written in the 1600s, sixteen editions were printed from 1800-1831. This was the book fathers hid and young men read behind the barn.

1800: *The Life and Memorable Actions of George Washington*, Mason Weems. A fictionalized biography that went through eighty-six printings from 1800-1927.

1801: *The Wild Irish Girl*, Lady Morgan. Written in the form of letters, the adventures of the son of an English nobleman.

1802: *New American Practical Navigator*, Nathaniel Bowditch.

1805: *Shewing the Evil Tendency of the Use of Tobacco*, Benjamin Waterhouse.

1807-1808: *Salmagundi: Or the Whim-Whams and Opinions of Launcelot Langstaff, Esq. and Others*, Washington Irving.

1809: *History of New York from the Beginning of the World to the End of the Dutch Dynasty*, Washington Irving.

1814: *Undine*, De La Motte Fouque. A German fantasy featuring water spirits, romance and an enchanted forest.

1815: The indiscriminate reading of Novels and Romances is to young females of the most dangerous tendency . . . it agitates their fancy to delerium of pleasure never to be realized . . . and opens to their view the Elysium fields which exist only in the imagination . . . fields which will involve them in wretchedness and inconsolable sorrow. . . . The most profligate villain, bent on the infernal purpose of seducing a woman, could not wish a symptom more favorable to his purpose than a strong imagination inflamed with the rhapsodies of artful and corrupting novels. The Clergyman's Almanack

1818: *Frankenstein*, Mary Shelley.

1819-1820: *The Sketch Book of Henry Crayon, Gent.*, including "Rip Van Winkle," Washington Irving.

1821: *The Spy*, James Fenimore Cooper.

1823: *Leatherstocking Tales*, James Fenimore Cooper.

1826: *The Last of the Mohicans*, James Fenimore Cooper.

1827-1838: *The Birds of America*, 4 vols., John James Audubon.

1828: *American Dictionary of the English Language*, Noah Webster.

1830: *The Book of Mormon*, Joseph Smith.

1832: *Indiana*, George Sand (Madame Dudevant). A romance that takes place alternately in a castle and in Paris.

1834: *The Last Days of Pompeii*, Edward Bulwer-Lytton. Novelized version of the ancient volcanic disaster.

1836: *Pickwick Papers*, Charles Dickens.

1836: *Eclectic Readers*, Volumes 1 and 2, William McGuffey. Volumes 3 and 4 appeared the following year; 122 million copies sold.

1836: *Nature*, Ralph Waldo Emerson.

1837: *Essays*, Ralph Waldo Emerson.

1837: *The Bible Against Slavery*, Theodore Weld.

1837: *Twice Told Tales*, Nathaniel Hawthorne.

1838: *Letters on the Equality of the Sexes and the Condition of Woman*, Sarah Moore Grimke.

1839: *American Slavery As It Is*, Theodore Weld.

1840: *Two Years Before the Mast*, Richard Henry Dana.

1841: *Tales of the Grotesque and Arabesque*, Edgar Allan Poe.

1841: *Letters and Notes on the Manners, Customs and Condition of the North American Indians*, George Catlin.

1845: *Narrative of the Life of Frederick Douglass, an American Slave*, Frederick Douglass.

1847: *Vanity Fair*, W.M. Thackeray.

1847: *Jane Eyre*, Charlotte Bronte.

1849: *On the Duty of Civil Disobedience*, Henry David Thoreau.

1849: *The Gold Seeker's Manual, a Practical and Instructive Guide to All Persons Emigrating to the Gold Diggings in California*, David Ansted.

1849: *Kaloolah*, W.S. Mayo. African adventure novel.

1850: *The Scarlet Letter*, Nathaniel Hawthorne.

1851: *The Wide, Wide World*, Elizabeth Wetherell. Popular woman's novel following the heroine Ellen Montgomery from childhood to marriage. It sold three hundred thousand copies, impressive for its day.

1851: *Meteorology*, Charles Wilkes.

1851: *The House of the Seven Gables*, Nathaniel Hawthorne.

1851: *Moby Dick*, Herman Melville.

1851: *Sixteen Months at the Gold Diggings*, Daniel Woods. Nonfiction account of gold fever in California.

1852: *Uncle Tom's Cabin*, Harriet Beecher Stowe.

1856: *Madame Bovary*, Gustave Flaubert.

1859: *Tale of Two Cities*, Charles Dickens.

1860: *The Mill on the Floss*, George Eliot.

1861: *Silas Marner*, George Eliot.

1864: *Journey to the Center of the Earth*, Jules Verne.

1865: *From the Earth to the Moon*, Jules Verne.

1867: *Ragged Dick*, Horatio Alger. The original "Great American Dream" novel.

1867: *File No. 113*, Emile Gaboriau. French detective mystery.

1868: *The Friendship of Women*, W.R. Alger. A popular nonfiction exploration of women's friendships.

1868: *Little Women*, Louisa May Alcott.

1869: *Twenty Thousand Leagues Under the Sea*, Jules Verne.

1870: *The Story of a Bad Boy*, Thomas Bailey Aldrich. The humorous story of an ill-mannered boy, popular with children in the United States and Europe.

1873: *The Fair God*, Lew Wallace. Historical romance revolving around the conquest of Mexico by Spaniards.

1876: *The Adventures of Tom Sawyer*, Mark Twain.

1877: *The American*, Henry James.

1878: *The Return of the Native*, Thomas Hardy.

1879: *Travels with a Donkey in the Cevennes*, Robert Louis Stevenson. An account of Stevenson's travels through the mountains of southern France.

1881: *The Portrait of a Lady*, Henry James.

1882: *Anne*, Constance Fenimore Woolson. Popular novel following the life of a young orphan.

1882: *The Prince and the Pauper*, Mark Twain.

1883: *Life on the Mississippi*, Mark Twain.

1884: *The Adventures of Huckleberry Finn*, Mark Twain.

1886: *Little Lord Fauntleroy*, Frances Hodgson Burnett.

1888: *Looking Backward, 2000-1887*, Edward Bellamy. A Utopian fantasy that sold one million copies.

1889: *A Connecticut Yankee in King Arthur's Court*, Mark Twain.

1890: *The Influence of Sea Power upon History*, Alfred Mahan.

1890: *Black Beauty*, Anna Sewell.

1892: *The Adventures of Sherlock Holmes*, Arthur Conan Doyle. Collection of short stories.

1893: *The Strange Case of Dr. Jekyll and Mr. Hyde*, Robert Louis Stevenson. Published previously in England.

1894: *Ships That Pass in the Night*, Beatrice Harraden. A tragic love story.

1895: *The Red Badge of Courage*, Stephen Crane.

1895: *The Time Machine*, H.G. Wells.

1898: *War of the Worlds*, H.G. Wells.

1899: *The Man Who Corrupted Hadleyburg*, Mark Twain.

Chronology of Selected Magazines

1800-1806: *Philadelphia Repository and Weekly Register*

1801-1827: *Port Folio*. Eight-page weekly featuring literature, poetry, politics, music, art, fashion, etc.

1802-1806: *Boston Weekly Magazine*

1804-1811: *Philadelphia Medical Museum*

1805-1808: *Lady's Weekly Miscellany*

1806-1811: *Christian's Magazine*

1808-1817: *American Law Journal*

1811-1849: *Niles' Weekly Register*. Political, historical, geographical, scientific, economic, biographical news and facts; essays.

1812-1826: *New England Journal of Medicine and Surgery*

1816-1824: *Christian Herald*

1818-1829: *American Medical Recorder*

1818-throughout: *American Journal of Science*

1819-1897: *American Farmer*

1819-throughout: *Christian Watchman*

1821-throughout: *Saturday Evening Post*

1823-1857: *New York Mirror*

1826-1866: *National Preacher*

1827-throughout: *American Journal of the Medical Sciences*

1828-1836: *Ladies' Magazine*

1830-1898: *Lady's Book*, later *Godey's Lady's Book*. One of the most popular women's magazines of the period; it featured fashion plates and was an advocate of proper etiquette.

1831-1865: *Liberator*. Anti-slavery magazine published in Boston.

1831-1861: *Spirit of the Times*, New York. General sporting journal.

1833-1865: *Knickerbocker Magazine*. Literature, travel, humor.

1833-1842: *Emancipator*

1833: *Anti-Slavery Reporter*

1834-1844: *Ladies' Companion*

1836-throughout: *Yale Literary Magazine*

1837-1849: *Ladies' Garland*

1838-1911: *Phrenological Journal*

1840-1858: *Graham's Magazine*. Sensational fiction, poetry, travel, book reviews.

1841-1876: *Ladies' Repository*. Moral and religious magazine, written largely by ministers.

1842-1898: *Peterson's Ladies' National Magazine*. Modeled after *Godey's Lady's Book*.

1845-throughout: *Scientific American*

1845-throughout: *National Police Gazette.* Accounts of crimes, lurid and otherwise.

1846-1901: *Home Journal.* Society, manners, literature.

1848-1857: *Boys' and Girls' Magazine and Fireside Companion*

1850-1854: *American Vegetarian and Health Journal*

1850-throughout: *Harper's Monthly Magazine.* Fiction, essays, biographical sketches, popular science, travel, etc.

1853-1857: *Putnam's Monthly*

1855-1922: *Frank Leslie's Illustrated Newspaper,* later *Leslie's Weekly.* Weekly miscellany of news, music, drama, fine arts, sports, serial fiction, book reviews, etc., with large illustrations. It cost ten cents per issue, or four dollars per year.

1859-1876: *Phunny Fellow*

1860-1908: *Home Monthly*

1860-1904: *Illustrated Police News.* Crime reporting, with a growing interest in sex crimes and sex scandals after the Civil War.

1863-1878: *Frank Leslie's Boys of America,* later *Frank Leslie's Boys' and Girls' Weekly*

1864-1883: *Freedman's Friend*

1865-1930: *Carriage Monthly,* later *Motor Vehicle Monthly*

1866-throughout: *Good Health*

1867-throughout: *Farmer's Home Journal*

1867-throughout: *Harper's Bazaar.* A "Repository of Fashion, Pleasure and Instruction." A popular woman's magazine featuring fashion patterns, large woodcuts of current styles, serial fiction and miscellany.

1867-1888: *Sporting Times*

1868-1916: *Lippincott's Magazine,* later *McBride's.* Serial novels, short stories, literary criticism, book reviews, travel, manners.

1870-1930: *Scribner's Monthly,* later *Century Magazine.* General interest magazine featuring politics, current events, religion, manners, science and nature, serial fiction, short stories, etc.

1870-1893: *World Magazine*

1871-1881: *Frank Leslie's Ladies' Journal*

1872-throughout: *Popular Science*

1872-throughout: *Publishers Weekly*

1876-throughout: *Frank Leslie's Popular Monthly,* later *American Magazine.* General interest magazine featuring serials, short stories, essays, travel articles, science, art, recipes, jokes, etc.

1876-throughout: *Harvard Lampoon*

1877-1887: *Ladies Home Journal*

1877-throughout: *Puck.* Politics, political cartoons, social topics, wit, humor, verse, etc.

1878-throughout: *Woman's Home Journal*

1879-throughout: *Bicycling World*

1880-1907: *Golden Days for Boys and Girls*
1881-1890: *Boys' Library of Sport, Story and Adventure*
1883-throughout: *Journal of the American Medical Association (JAMA)*
1883-throughout: *Ladies Home Journal*
1883-throughout: *Life*. A satirical weekly picture magazine.
1885-throughout: *Good Housekeeping*. Women's miscellany, helpful hints, etc.
1886-throughout: *Cosmopolitan*. General literary magazine featuring essays, articles and fiction.
1888-throughout: *Once a Week*, later *Collier's*. General interest and news.
1888-throughout: *National Geographic*
1889-throughout: *Munsey's Magazine*. General illustrated magazine.
1892-throughout: *Vogue*
1893-throughout: *McClure's Magazine*. Serials, short stories, science, train travel, nature, exploration, personalities.

Chronology of Innovations

1779: Screw and screwdriver
1783: Balloon
1792: Cotton gin
1798: Lithography
       Steamship
1800: Battery
1801: Gaslighting
       London had gas streetlighting by 1807. Boston had 71 gaslights
           on its streets by 1835 and 180 by 1839. Most large towns had
           gaslighting by the 1870s.
1802: Planing machine
1803: Application of steam to the loom
1803: Steel pen
1805: First life preserver
1808: Band saw
1810: Ultraviolet lamp
1811: Breech-loading shotgun
1812: Storage battery
       Hydraulic jack
1814: Steam-powered rotary printing press, London
       First locomotive in United States
       First circular saw
       Kaleidoscope
1816: Camera
       Knitting machine
1818: Blood transfusion. Poorly understood and rarely attempted.
           Only two Civil War soldiers received transfusions, and one
           died. Generally not in use until the twentieth century.
1819: Stethoscope. The first was a simple wooden tube. This was im-
           proved with the introduction of a flexible tube in 1839.
1820: Elastic
1821: Electric motor
1822: Multicolor printing
       Calculating machine
       Gaslight introduced in Boston
1825: Portland cement
       First passenger railway in England, between Stockton and Dar-
           lington
1826: First railroad in United States, near Quincy, Massachusetts
1827: Friction matches. These had to be drawn swiftly through sand-

paper to ignite. They worked poorly and were replaced by phosphorous matches in 1836. These were often referred to as "loco-focos," after a popular brand name. "Our loco-foco matches would not ignite" *C.F. Hoffman,* Wild Scenes, *1839*

1829: First bus in New York

1830: Food canning
Portable steam fire engine
First steam locomotive, *Tom Thumb*, races against horse-drawn railcar in Baltimore
Chain-stitch sewing machine

1831: Chloroform discovered
Dynamo
Transformer

1832: Tram and trolleybus

1833: First steam whistle for locomotives
Water turbine

1834: McCormick reaper
Refrigeration

1836: Revolver

1837: Screw propellor
Driving apparatus
Telegraph demonstrated by Morse. "What hath God wrought?"—first message sent by telegraph between Washington and Baltimore in 1844. Hundreds of miles of telegraph lines had been established by 1846, reaching from Boston to Washington; by 1847 they had reached Pittsburgh. Florida was the only state east of the Mississippi not serviced by telegraph in 1848.

1839: Vulcanization of rubber
Daguerreotype (photograph)
Envelopes manufactured in New York. Previously, letters were simply folded over and mailed.
Velocipede, the forerunner of the bicycle. Due to a number of design shortcomings (the velocipede had no pedals, for example), the bicycle was not widely popular until 1877, when improvements were made.

1840: Postage stamp
Celestial photography
Artesian well

1842: Player piano

1843: Typewriting machine

1844: Nitrous oxide used as anesthetic

1845: Pneumatic tire

1846: Lock-stitch sewing machine

Printing telegraph
Suez Canal begun
Ether used as anesthetic
Artificial limbs
1847: Chloroform in surgery
Ophthalmoscope
Nitroglycerin
1849: Magazine gun
1850: American machine-made watches
Paraffin
1853: Electrolysis
Safety lift
1854: Photographic roll films
Diamond rock drill
1855: Cocaine
1856: Sleeping car
Bessemer steel
1858: Cable car
First Atlantic cable
1860: Can opener
Internal combustion engine
Linoleum
1861: Barbed wire fence
1862: Gatling gun
1864: Rubber dental plate
1865: First antiseptic surgery
1866: Torpedo
Dynamite
1868: First practical typewriter
Oleomargarine
Railroad air brake
Plastics
1874: First practical use of barbed wire
1875: Submarine
1876: Telephone. There were only 3,000 telephones nationwide by
the end of 1876; by 1900, there were 1.4 million.
Automatic cigarette-making machine
1877: Phonograph
Gas engine
Carbon microphone
1878: Electric light introduced
1879: Filament lamp
1880: Innoculation
1881: Stereophony

1884:   Public electric cars on streets of Cleveland
          Safety bicycle, with equal-sized tires, allowed women and children to ride with ease.
          Motor car
          Airship
          Fountain pen
          Steam turbine
1885:   Motorcycle
1886:   Aluminum
1887:   Combine harvester
1888:   Kodak "snapshot" camera
1889:   One-armed bandit
1890:   Rubber tires used on bicycles
1893:   Carburetor
          Diesel engine
1895:   X ray
          Cinematograph
1896:   Radio
1897:   Teleprinter
          Cold cereals
1899:   Aspirin
          Magnetic tape recorder

Chronology of Popular Songs

1798: "Hail, Columbia"

1799: "Old Colony Times"

1800 and earlier: "Barbara Allen," traditional Scottish-English ballad.

1812: "Hey, Betty Martin," favorite marching song in the War of 1812.

1823: "Home Sweet Home," the timeless classic.

1824: "From Greenland's Icy Mountains"

1831: "New York," or "Oh, What a Charming City"

1832: "America"

1834: "Old Zip Coon," hugely popular minstrel song that eventually evolved into "Turkey in the Straw."

1835: "Amazing Grace," originally penned in 1789 but not published for forty-six years.

1837: "Woodman, Spare That Tree," a song of childhood nostalgia and an old tree due for the woodman's axe.

1838: "Old Rosin the Beau," so popular it served as a theme song for four different presidential campaigns.

1843: "Old Dan Tucker," favorite minstrel song.

1844: "Buffalo Gals," variously known as "Pittsburgh Gals," "Bowery Gals," "Louisiana Gals" (depending on where the minstrel performers were playing) and "Lubly Fan, Will You Cum Out Tonight?" The words and music were by Cool White.

1845: "Oh! Susanna," a Stephen Foster classic that became a pet song of the 49ers during the gold rush.

1846: "Jim Crack Corn," also known as "The Blue Tail Fly."

1850: "Camptown Races," Stephen Foster classic.

1852: "My Old Kentucky Home," a favorite plantation melody by Stephen Foster.

1853: "Pop Goes the Weasel," actually sung by children as early as the 1600s.

1854: "Jeanie With the Light Brown Hair," Stephen Foster.

1855: "Listen to the Mockingbird"

1859: "Dixie's Land," the most popular song among Southern soldiers in the Civil War.

1861: "All Quiet Along the Potomac"

1861: "The Bonnie Blue Flag," the second most popular song among Southern Civil War soldiers.

1861-1862: "The Battle Hymn of the Republic"

1862: "Lorena," haunting love song that made Confederate soldiers so homesick they actually deserted after hearing it. Confederate Gen. John Hunt Morgan called it "that cursed ballad" and ordered his officers to actually kill its author. Thousands of girls all over America were christened Lorena due to the song's powerful influence.

1863: "When Johnny Comes Marching Home," a favorite of the Union soldiers, and mocked by the Confederates. It was also popular during the Spanish-American War at the end of the century.

1864: "Tramp! Tramp! Tramp!" Also known as "The Prisoner's Hope," a Civil War marching song about a soldier writing to his mother from a prison cell.

1866: "Goober Peas!" a lighthearted ditty sung by the Southern soldiers during the war but not published until the war was over.

Sitting by the road-side on a summer day,
Chatting with my messmates, passing time away,
Lying in the Shadow underneath the trees,
Goodness, how delicious, eating goober peas!
Peas! Peas! Peas! Peas! Eating goober peas!
Goodness, how delicious, eating goober peas!

1866: "You Naughty, Naughty Men," from the play *The Black Crook,* which featured perioxide blondes in tights and extravagant stage effects.

1867: "Nobody Knows the Trouble I've Seen," Negro slave song.

1868: "The Flying Trapeze"

1869: "Little Brown Jug"

1873: "Silver Threads Among the Gold"

1876: "Grandfather's Clock"

1876: "I'll Take You Home Again, Kathleen," best-loved Irish tune.

1877: "Out of Work"

1879: "Oh, Dem Golden Slippers," hugely popular minstrel song, widely played on pianos in saloons throughout the West.

1884: "Oh My Darling Clementine"

1886: "Johnny Get Your Gun"

1891: "There is a Tavern in the Town"

1894: "The Sidewalks of New York"

1895: "Streets of Cairo," based on the bump-and-grind dance — the "hootchy-kootchy — performed by Little Egypt at the Chicago World's Fair in 1893.

1896: "A Hot Time in the Old Town," one of the first songs to be recorded on wax cylinders for play on the new phonograph machine.

1899: "On the Banks of the Wabash, Far Away"

References

SLANG AND EVERYDAY SPEECH

General References

Adams, Henry, *The United States in 1800*, Cornell University Press, 1955, reprinted from an 1889 edition.

Bartlett, John, *The Dictionary of Americanisms*, Crescent Books, 1989, reprinted from an 1849 edition.

Bettmann, Otto, *The Good Old Days — They Were Terrible!*, Random House, 1974.

Bode, Carl, *American Life in the 1840s*, Anchor Books, 1967.

Cable, Mary, *American Manners and Morals*, American Heritage Publishing, 1969.

Craigie, Sir William, and Hulbert, James, *A Dictionary of American English*, 4 vols., University of Chicago Press, 1936.

Emerson, Edwin, *A History of the Nineteenth Century, Year by Year*, Collier and Son, 1900.

Gayet, Robert, *Everyday Life in the United States Before the Civil War, 1830-1860*, Frederick Ungar Publishing, 1969.

Handlin, Oscar, *This Was America, As Recorded by European Travelers in the Eighteenth, Nineteenth and Twentieth Centuries*, Harper & Row, 1949.

Kouwenhoven, John, *Adventures of America, 1857-1900, a Pictorial Record from Harper's Weekly*, Harper & Brothers, 1938.

Landon, William, *Everyday Things in American Life, 1776-1876*, Charles Scribner's Sons, 1941.

Larkin, Jack, *The Reshaping of Everyday Life, 1790-1840*, Harper & Row, 1988.

Martin, Edward, *The Secrets of the Great City*, Jones, Brothers and Co., 1868.

Martineau, Harriet, *Society in America*, 1837.

McCabe, James, *Lights and Shadows of New York Life*, National Publishing, 1872.

McGinnis, R.J., *The Good Old Days*, Harper & Brothers, 1960.

Ross, Ishbel, *Taste in America*, Thomas Crowell Co., 1967.

Schartle, Patricia, and Rapport, Samual, *America Remembers, Our Best-Loved Customs and Traditions*, Hanover House, 1956.

Thornton, Richard, *American Glossary*, J.B. Lippincott, 1912.

Trollope, Frances, *Domestic Manners of the Americans*, Dodd, Mead, 1832.

Weymouth, Lally, *America in 1876, the Way We Were*, Vintage, 1976.

Wilson, Everett, *Early America at Work*, A.S. Barnes and Co., 1963.

Woodward, William, *The Way Our People Lived, An Intimate American History*, Liveright Publishing, 1944.

Swear Words, Taboo Words, Euphemisms
Rawson, Hugh, *Wicked Words, a Treasury of Curses, Insults, Put-Downs, and Other Formerly Unprintable Terms from Anglo-Saxon Times to the Present*, Crown Publishers, 1989.

CARRIAGES, COACHES AND WAGONS

Banning, William and George, *Six Horses*, Century Co., New York and London, 1930.
Berkebile, Don, *American Carriages, Sleighs, Sulkies and Carts*, Dover Publications, 1977.
Forbes, Allan, *Taverns and Stagecoaches of New England*, State Street Trust Co., 1953.
Harris, Stanley, *The Coaching Age*, R. Bentley and Son, 1885.
Moody, Ralph, *Stagecoach West*, T.Y. Crowell Co., 1967.
Tristam, William, *Coaching Days and Coaching Ways*, MacMillan and Co., 1888.
Tunis, Edwin, *Wheels, a Pictorial History*, World Publishing Co., 1955.
Wheeling, Kenneth, *Horse-drawn Vehicles at the Shelburne Museum*, Shelburne Museum, 1974.
Winther, Oscar, *Express and Stagecoach Days in California*, Stanford University Press, 1936.

STAGE LINES

Barnes, Demas, *The Far Western Frontier, from the Atlantic to the Pacific Overland, a Series of Letters by Demas Barnes*, 1865, reprinted by Arno Press, 1973.
Forbes, Allan, *Taverns and Stagecoaches of New England*, State Street Trust Co., 1953.
Moody, Ralph, *Stagecoach West*, Thomas Crowell Co., 1967.
Nevin, David, *The Expressmen*, Time-Life Books, 1974.

RAILROAD

Brown, Dee, *Hear That Lonesome Whistle Blow*, Holt, Rinehart & Winston, 1977.
Holbrook, Stewart, *Story of American Railroads*, Crown, 1947.
Mencken, August, *The Railroad Passenger Car*, Johns Hopkins Press, 1957.

Throm, Edward, *Popular Mechanics Picture History of American Transportation*. Simon & Schuster, 1952.

Wheeler, Keith, *The Railroaders*, Time-Life Books, 1973.

SHIPS, BOATS AND CANALS

Blacburn, Graham, *Ships, Boats, Vessels*, Overlook Press, 1978.

Donovan, Frank, *River Boats of America*, Thomas Crowell Co., 1966.

Drago, Henry Sinclair, *Canal Days in America*, Clarkson Potter, 1972.

Merrick, George, *Old Times on the Upper Mississippi*, Arthur Clark Co., 1909.

Shay, Frank, *Sailor's Treasury*, W.W. Norton and Co., 1951.

AROUND THE HOUSE

Hebard, Helen, *Early American Lighting in New England*, Charles Tuttle Co., 1974.

Langdon, William, *Everyday Things in American Life, 1776-1876*, Charles Scribner's Sons, 1941.

Maas, John, *The Victorian Home in America*, Hawthorne Books, 1972.

Ormsbee, Thomas, *Field Guide to Early American Furniture*, Little, Brown & Co., 1951.

Ormsbee, Thomas, *Field Guide to Victorian Furniture*, Little, Brown & Co., 1951.

Sloane, Eric, *ABC Book of Early Americana*, Doubleday, 1963.

Sloane, Eric, *American Yesterday*, Funk and Wagnalls, 1956.

CLOTHING AND FASHION

Cunnington, Phillis, *Costumes of the Nineteenth Century*, Plays, Inc., 1970.

Davenport, Millia, *The Book of Costume*, Crown Publishers, 1948.

Earle, Alice, *Two Centuries of Costume in America*, Vol. 2, MacMillan Co., 1903.

Evelyn, Hugh, *History of Costume, the Nineteenth Century*, Plays, Inc., 1968.

McClellan, Elisabeth, *Historic Dress in America, 1800-70*, George Jacobs and Co., 1910.

Waugh, Nora, *The Cut of Women's Clothes, 1600-1930*, Theatre Arts Books, 1968.

Worrel, Estelle, *Children's Costume in America, 1607-1910*, Charles Scribner's Sons, 1980.

OCCUPATIONS

Larkin, Jack, *The Reshaping of Everyday Life, 1790 to 1840*, Harper & Row, 1988.

Wilson, Everett, *Ealry America At Work*, A.S. Barnes and Co., 1963.
Wright, Richardson, *Hawkers and Walkers in Early America*, J.B. Lippincott Co., 1927.

MONEY AND COINAGE

Coffin, Joseph, *Our American Money*, Coward-McCann, 1940.
Columbia University Press, *A History of the Dollar*, 1957.
Davis, Norman, *The Complete Book of United States Coin Collecting*, MacMillan Publishing, 1976.
Massey, Earl J., *America's Money*, Thomas Crowell Co., 1968.
Schwarz, Ted, *A History of United States Coinage*, A.S. Barnes and Co., 1980.
Thornton, Richard, *American Glossary*, J.B. Lippincott, 1912.
Yeoman, R.S., *A Guide Book of United States Coins*, Western Publishing, 1988.

HEALTH, MEDICINE AND HYGIENE

Bettmann, Otto, *A Pictorial History of Medicine*, Charles Thomas, Publisher, 1956.
Bordley, James, and McGehee, Harvey, *Two Centuries of American Medicine, 1776-1976*, W.B. Saunders Co., 1976.
Carson, Gerald, *One for a Man, Two for a Horse, a Pictorial History, Grave and Comic, of Patent Medicines*, Doubleday, 1961.
Cerf, Christopher, and Navasky, Victor, *The Experts Speak, the Definitive Compendium of Authoritative Misinformation*, Pantheon, 1984.
Flexner, James, *Doctors on Horseback*, Viking Press, 1937.
Gayet, Robert, *Everyday Life in the United States Before the Civil War*, Frederick Ungar Publishing, 1969.
Marks, Geoffrey, and Beatty, William, *The Story of Medicine in America*, Scribner's Publishing.
Peale, R.S., *The Home Library of Useful Knowledge*, Home Library Association, 1883.
Shryock, Richard, *Medicine in America, Historical Essays*, Johns Hopkins Press, 1966.

FOOD, DRINK AND TOBACCO

American Heritage Magazine, Editors, *The American Heritage Cookbook*, American Heritage Press, 1964.
Bartlett, John, *Dictionary of Americanisms*, 1849, reprinted by Crown Publishers, 1989.

Better Homes and Gardens, *Heritage Cookbook*, Better Homes and Gardens, 1975.

Campbell, Hannah, *Why Did They Name It . . . ?*, Fleet Publishing, 1964.

Child, Mrs., *The American Frugal Housewife*, 1836, reprinted by Harper & Row, 1972.

Simmons, Amelia, *American Cookery*, (America's first cookbook), 1796, reprinted by Silverleaf Press, 1984.

AMUSEMENTS

Durant, John, and Bettmann, Otto, *Pictorial History of American Sports from Colonial Times to the Present*, A.S. Barnes and Co., 1952.

Kouwenhoven, John, *Adventures of America, 1857-1900, a Pictorial Record from Harper's Weekly*, Harper & Brothers, 1938.

Martin, Edward, *The Secrets of the Great City*, Jones, Brothers and Co., 1868.

McCabe, James, *Lights and Shadows of New York Life*, National Publishing, 1872.

Time-Life Books, *This Fabulous Century*, 1970.

Woodward, William, *The Way Our People Lived*, Liveright Publishing, 1944.

Wright, Richardson, *Hawkers and Walkers in Early America*, J.B. Lippincott Co., 1927.

COURTSHIP AND MARRIAGE

Bartlett, John, *Dictionary of Americanisms*, Bartlett and Welford, 1849.

D'Emilio, John, and Freedman, Estelle, *Intimate Matters, a History of Sexuality in America*, Harper & Row, 1988.

Rothman, Ellen, *Hands and Hearts, a History of Courtship in America*, Basic Books, 1984.

SLAVERY AND BLACK PLANTATION CULTURE

Armstrong, Orland, *Old Massa's People*, Bobbs-Merrill Co., 1931.

Blassingame, John, *The Slave Community, Plantation Life in the Ante-Bellum South*, Oxford University Press, 1972.

Botkin, B.A., *Lay My Burden Down*, University of Chicago Press, 1945.

Douglass, Frederick, *My Bondage and My Freedom*, New York, 1855.

Meier, August, and Rudwick, Elliott, *Making of Black America*, Atheneum, 1969.

Stampp, Kenneth, *The Peculiar Institution, Slavery in the Ante-Bellum South*, Alfred Knopf, 1965.

Weyl, Nathaniel, *Negro in American Civilization*, Public Affairs Press, 1960.

THE CIVIL WAR

Beatty, John, *The Citizen Soldier*, Wilstach, Baldwin and Co., 1879.

Billings, John, *Hard Tack and Coffee*, George M. Smith and Co., 1887.

Gragg, Rod, *Civil War Quiz and Fact Book*, Harper & Row, 1985.

McCarthy, Carlton, *Detailed Minutiae of Soldier Life*, Carlton McCarthy and Co., 1882.

McKim, Randolph, *A Soldier's Recollections*, Longmans, Green and Co., 1910.

Moore, Edward, *The Story of a Canoneer Under Stonewall Jackson*, Neal Publishing Co., 1907.

Robertson, James, *Soldiers, Blue and Gray*, Warner Books, 1988.

Wiley, Bell, *The Life of Billy Yank*, Bobbs-Merrill Co., 1943.

Wiley, Bell, *The Life of Johnny Reb*, Bobbs-Merrill Co., 1951.

COWBOYS AND THE WILD WEST

Abbott, E.C. (Teddy Blue), *We Pointed Them North, Recollections of a Cowpuncher*, Farrar and Rinehart, 1939; University of Oklahoma Press, 1989.

Adams, Andy, *The Log of a Cowboy*, Houghton Mifflin, 1903.

Adams, Ramon, *The Old Time Cowhand*, University of Nebraska Press, 1948.

Barrows, John, *U-bet, A Greenhorn in Old Montana*, University of Nebraska Press, 1990.

Old West Magazine, Western Publications.

Potter, Edgar, *Cowboy Slang*, Golden West Publishers, 1986.

Siringo, Charles, *A Cowboy Detective*, W.B. Conkey, 1912; reprinted by University of Nebraska Press, 1988.

Trimble, Marshall, *In Old Arizona, True Tales of the Wild Frontier*, Golden West Publishers, 1986.

Wild West Magazine, Empire Press.

INDIANS

Barrows, John, *U-bet, A Greenhorn in Old Montana*, University of Nebraska Press, 1990.

Edwards, Ruth, *American Indians of Yesterday*, Naylor Co., 1948.

Lowie, Robert, *Indians of the Plains*, McGraw-Hill, 1954.

Morgan, Lewis Henry, *The Indian Journals, 1859-62*, University of Michigan Press, 1959.

Taylor, Colin, *The Warriors of the Plains*, Arco Publishing, 1975.

CRIME

Griffiths, Major Arthur, *Mysteries of Police and Crime*, G.P. Putnam's Sons, 1899.

McCabe, James, *Lights and Shadows of New York Life*, National Publishing Co., 1872.

Partridge, Eric, *A Dictionary of the Underworld, Being the Vocabularies of Crooks, Criminals, Racketeers, Beggars and Tramps*, MacMillan Co., 1950.

Pinkerton, Allan, *Thirty Years a Detective*, G.W. Carleton and Co., Publishers, 1884.

Savage, Edward, *Police Records and Recollections*, or *Boston by Daylight and Gaslight for Two Hundred and Forty Years*, Patterson Smith, 1873.

Siringo, Charles, *A Cowboy Detective*, W.B. Conkey Company, 1912; reprinted by University of Nebraska Press, 1988.

CHRONOLOGIES

Emerson, Edwin, *A History of the Nineteenth Century Year by Year*, P.F. Collier and Son, 1900.

Jackson, Richard, *Popular Songs of the Nineteenth Century*, Dover Publications, 1976.

Jensen, Malcolm, *America in Time*, Houghton Mifflin Co., 1977.

Lloyd, Norman and Ruth, *The American Heritage Songbook*, American Heritage Publishing, 1969.

Mott, Frank, *A History of American Magazines*, 4 vols., Belknap Press, Harvard University, 1957.

Peale, R.S., *Library of the World's Best Literature, Synopses of Noted Books*, J.A. Hill Co., 1896.

Ruoff, Henry, *The Standard Dictionary of Facts*, The Frontier Press Co., 1914.

More Great Books for Writers!

The Writer's Guide to Everyday Life in the Middle Ages—This time-travel companion will guide you through the medieval world of Northwestern Europe. Discover the facts on dining habits, clothing, armor, festivals, religious orders and much more—everything you need to paint an authentic picture. *#10423/$17.99/256 pages*

The Writer's Guide to Everyday Life from Prohibition through World War II—Uncover all the details you need to add color, depth and a ring-of-truth to your work. You'll find an intimate look at what life was like back then, including popular slang, the Prohibition, the Depression, World War II, crime, transportation, fashion, radio, music and much more! *#10450/$18.99/272 pages*

Writer's Market—This edition brings you over 4,000 listings of buyers of freelance work—their names, addresses, submission requirements, contact persons and more! Plus, helpful articles and interviews with top professionals make this your most essential writing resource. *#10432/$27.99/1008 pages*

The Writer's Ultimate Research Guide—Save research time and frustration with the help of this guide. Three hundred fifty-two information-packed pages will point you straight to the information you need to create better, more accurate fiction and nonfiction. *#10447/$19.99/352 pages*

How to Write Like an Expert About Anything—Find out how to use new technology and traditional research methods to get the information you need, envision new markets, write proposals that sell, find and interview experts on any topic and much more! *#10449/$17.99/224 pages*

The Writer's Digest Guide to Good Writing—In one book, you'll find the best in writing instruction gleaned from the past 75 years of *Writer's Digest* magazine! Successful authors like Vonnegut, Steinbeck, Oates, Michener and over a dozen others share their secrets on writing technique, idea generation, inspiration and getting published. *#10391/$18.99/352 pages*

Thesaurus of Alternatives to Worn-Out Words and Phrases—Rid your work of trite cliches and hollow phrases for good! Alphabetical entries shed light on the incorrect, the bland and the overused words that plague so many writers. Then you'll learn how to vivify your work with alternative, lively and original words! *#10408/$17.99/304 pages*

Writing for Money—Discover where to look for writing opportunities—and how to make them pay off. You'll learn how to write for magazines, newspapers, radio and TV, newsletters, greeting cards and a dozen other hungry markets! *#10425/$17.99/256 pages*

The Writer's Digest Character Naming Sourcebook—Forget the guesswork! Twenty thousand first and last names (and their meanings!) from around the world will help you pick the perfect name to reflect your character's role, place in history and ethnicity. *#10390/$18.99/352 pages*

Write Tight—Discover how to say exactly what you want with grace and power, using the right word and the right number of words. Specific instruction and helpful exercises will help you make your writing compact, concise and precise. *#10360/$16.99/192 pages*

National Writer's Union Guide to Freelance Rates & Standard Practice—A must-have for all freelancers! Tables and charts compiled from surveys of freelance writers, editors and agents give you the going rates for six major freelance markets. Plus, information on rights, the electronic future and more! *#10440/$19.95/200 pages/paperback*

Get That Novel Started! (And Keep It Going 'Til You Finish)—If you're ready for a no excuses approach to starting and completing your novel, then you're ready for this get-it-going game plan. You'll discover wisdom, experience and advice that helps you latch on to an idea and see it through, while avoiding common writing pitfalls. *#10332/$17.95/176 pages*

How to Write & Sell Your First Novel—Improve your chances for getting your first (or any) novel published by learning the successful strategies of other first time writers. You also get do's and don'ts on editorial submission, marketing advice and news on the latest, best-selling genres. *#10168/$13.99/230 pages/paperback*

How to Write Fast (While Writing Well)—Learn step-by-step how to cut wasted time and effort by planning interviews for maximum results, beating writer's block with effective plotting, getting the most information from traditional library research and on-line computer bases and much more! *#10473/$15.99/208 pages/paperback*

The 29 Most Common Writing Mistakes And How to Avoid Them—Weak comparisons, too many adjectives, excessive self-expression—with clarity and good humor, Delton shows how to correct these and 26 other common writing mistakes to help you get published! *#10221/$9.95/96 pages/paperback*

The Writer's Digest Guide to Manuscript Formats—Don't take chances with your hard work! Learn how to prepare and submit books, poems, scripts, stories and more with the professional look editors expect from a good writer. *#10025/$19.99/200 pages*

30 Steps to Becoming a Writer—This informational, inspirational guide helps you get started as a writer, develop your skills and style and get your work ready for submission. *#10367/$16.99/176 pages*

Make Your Words Work—Loaded with samples and laced with exercises, this guide will help you clean up your prose, refine your style strengthen your descriptive powers, bring music to your words and much more! *#10399/$14.95/304 pages/paperback*

How to Write a Book Proposal—Don't sabotage your great ideas with a so-so proposal. This guide includes a complete sample proposal, a nine-point Idea Test to check the salability of your book ideas, plus hot tips to make your proposal a success! *#10173/$11.99/136 pages/paperback*

Writing the Short Story: A Hands-On Program—With Bickham's unique "workshop on paper" you'll plan, organize, write, revise and polish a short story. Clear instruction, helpful charts and practical exercises will lead you every step of the way! *#10421/$16.99/224 pages*

Roget's Superthesaurus—For whenever you need just the right word! You'll find "vocabulary builder" words with pronunciation keys and sample sentences, quotations that double as synonyms, plus the only word-find reverse dictionary in any thesaurus—all in alphabetical format! *#10424/$22.99/624 pages*

Freeing Your Creativity—Discover how to escape the traps that stifle your creativity. You'll tackle techniques for banishing fears and nourishing ideas so you can get your juices flowing again. *#10430/$14.99/176 pages/paperback*

Creating Characters: How to Build Story People—Learn how to build characters that jump off the page. In-depth instruction shows you how to infuse characters with emotion so powerful they will touch every reader. *#10417/$14.99/192 pages/paperback*

Writing the Blockbuster Novel—Let a top-flight agent show you how to weave the essential elements of a blockbuster into your own novels with memorable characters, exotic settings, clashing conflicts and more! *#10393/$17.99/224 pages*

20 Master Plots (And How to Build Them)—Write great contemporary fiction from timeless plots. This guide outlines 20 plots from various genres and illustrates how to adapt them into your own fiction. *#10366/$17.99/240 pages*

Handbook of Short Story Writing, Volume II—Orson Scott Card, Dwight V. Swain, Kit Reed and other noted authors bring you sound advice and timeless techniques for every aspect of the writing process. *#10239/$12.99/252 pages/paperback*

Beginning Writer's Answer Book—This book answers 900 of the most often asked questions about every stage of the writing process. You'll find business advice, tax tips,

plus new information about on-line networks, data bases and more.
#10394/$16.99/336 pages

A Beginner's Guide to Getting Published—This comprehensive collection of articles will calm your worries, energize your work and help you get published! You'll find in-depth, expertly written articles on idea generation, breaking into the business, moving up the ladder and much more! *#10418/$16.99/208 pages*

The Writer's Book of Checklists—In this easy-to-use resource, Edelstein covers the gamut of subjects you'll face in your writing and publishing career. Organized checklists will help you keep track of your thoughts as you tackle tough decisions! *#10222/$16.95/224 pages*

Getting the Words Right: How to Rewrite, Edit, & Revise—Reduction, rearrangement, rewording and rechecking—the 4 Rs of powerful writing. This book provides concrete instruction with dozens of exercises and pages of samples to help you improve your writing through effective revision. *#10172/$12.99/218 pages/paperback*

The Complete Guide to Writing Fiction—This concise guide will help you develop the skills you need to write and sell long and short fiction. You'll get a complete rundown on outlining, narrative writing details, description, pacing and action. *#10158/$18.95/312 pages*

28 Biggest Writing Blunders (And How to Avoid Them)—Must you sacrifice style on the altar of grammar? Are you chained to canon and convention? William Noble says "No!" In this book you'll see one of the worst mistakes you can make is sticking too closely to the rules. *#10282/$12.95/120 pages*

The Wordwatcher's Guide to Good Writing & Grammar—Discover quick answers to pesky grammar and writing problems with this useful guide! You'll get explanations and examples to help clarify usage, meaning, spelling and pronunciation. *#10197/$16.99/320 pages/paperback*

How to Write Irresistible Query Letters—Don't shortchange your idea with a luke-warm query! Cool shows how to select a strong slant, hook an editor with a tantalizing lead, sell yourself as the expert for the job and more. *#10146/10.95/136 pages/paperback*
